Marketing Decision Making:

Analytic framework and cases

William F. O'Dell
Chairman, Executive Committee
Market Facts, Inc.

Andrew C. Ruppel
Robert H. Trent
McIntire School of Commerce
University of Virginia

Published by

S51   **SOUTH-WESTERN PUBLISHING CO.**

CINCINNATI   WEST CHICAGO, ILL.   DALLAS   PELHAM MANOR, N.Y.   PALO ALTO, CALIF.

Preface

Marketing Decision Making: Analytic Framework and Cases, 2d ed., is designed for courses in which decision making in marketing is to be scrutinized and sound procedures mastered. The book is in response to the oft-leveled criticism made by marketing practitioners that the classroom teaching of marketing is unrealistic and overly theoretical, leaving students inadequately prepared for the business world.

Marketing Decision Making is not intended as an introductory text in marketing or marketing management, although it could be used as a companion to a marketing management or marketing research text because of its stress on the information needs of marketing decision makers. Emphasis is given to the *role of information* in marketing decision making; thus, much marketing research data are provided in many of the cases. The book is appropriate for use in capstone marketing courses as well.

For the reader *Marketing Decision Making* provides these features:

1. A readily grasped, commonsense, five-step framework for analyzing classroom cases and real-world marketing decision-problems.
2. A pragmatic development of each step and its application.
3. An extensively explicated five-part marketing management case that illustrates the basic analytical framework.
4. Twenty-nine cases, all drawn from real-world marketing episodes, for honing decision-problem analysis skills.
5. Repetitive use, throughout the book, of a simple flowchart of the analytical framework to aid the memory in keeping discussion and analysis "on track."
6. Guidance on preparing business reports, especially the distillation and presentation of data.
7. Helpful hints on written and oral presentation of study findings to management groups.

Students using this book are presumed to have a basic background in marketing, accounting, finance, and the managerial process. No supersophisticated quantitative techniques are treated, but a knowledge of elementary statistics is presumed.

Our work is based on the ideas and philosophy of William F. O'Dell, as expressed earlier in his book, *The Marketing Decision,* published in 1968 by the American Management Association. These ideas and procedures for marketing decision-problem analysis have been tested in the real world, in the classroom, and in management development seminars.

Our principal premise is that decision making in marketing (and in other endeavors) can be improved dramatically when decision makers have a comprehensive understanding of the decision-making process. The necessity to be explicit thus allows creative insight to be focused, underlying disagreements to be made visible, true information needs to be identified, and decision resolution to be completed.

In this second edition the introductory chapter and Chapter 1 have been extensively revised and new material added. Chapters 2 through 5 were also revised to bring them more in line with our five-step analytical approach to decision making. A major revamping was made of the five-part illustrative case. The development and subsequent analysis of its parts have been mated closely with the five-step decision-making framework (and major substeps) advocated in this book. Two appendices dealing with business report preparation and oral presentations have been added. Four new cases have been added to the initial set. In addition, all cases now have discussion questions in the text to aid students in focusing on the case and to assist instructors in making proper use of the cases. A comprehensive instructor's manual is available.

In preparing this book we have been fortunate in having the willing cooperation of both Market Facts, Inc., and Market Facts of Canada, Ltd. Access to data in several of their reports to clients has made possible the development of a number of cases presented in *Marketing Decision Making*. We are especially grateful to David K. Hardin, who made textual criticisms as well as providing access to Market Facts' reports. We also wish to thank Verne K. Churchill and Thomas Payne of Market Facts, Inc., and John Robertson of Market Facts of Canada, Ltd. They were most helpful in reviewing cases and supplying highly constructive criticisms.

William Leighton and Byron W. Goulding of Oak State Products and Barton Ladd of N W Ayer ABH International all contributed by providing both industry and specific survey data used in selected cases.

We wish to thank marketing professors M. Wayne DeLozier (University of South Carolina), Donald W. Eckrich (Illinois State University), John F. Grashof (Temple University), Douglas V. Leister (University of Nevada-Reno), and Michael J. Ryan (Columbia University) for their comments on the previous edition. While we did not heed all of their suggestions, their thoughts were helpful to us in shaping this revision.

At the McIntire School of Commerce of the University of Virginia, two colleagues in particular deserve mention and thanks. Associate Professor William J. Kehoe provided several insightful comments and suggestions on the first edition. Associate Dean Bernard A. Morin made enthusiastic use of the decision-making framework in management development seminars and provided us with feedback on those experiences.

William G. Shenkir, Dean of the McIntire School, like his predecessor, Frank S. Kaulback, Jr., has been consistently encouraging of our efforts. We are also most appreciative of the typing support we received at the University, particularly that from Mrs. Lynda Birckhead.

William F. O'Dell
Andrew C. Ruppel
Robert H. Trent

Contents

INTRODUCTION

The Marketing Decision Situation and This Book

THE NATURE OF MARKETING DECISIONS

Marketing decisions are often more complex than those required of managers in other functional business areas. There are essentially four major reasons for the high degree of complexity.

1. *There are a large number of variables involved.* For example, when a company plans to introduce a new product, the number of variables affecting its success (or failure) are many. Competitive reaction, changing economic conditions, reaction of dealers to the product, consumers' willingness to change to the new product, and material cost increases requiring a boost in the selling price are all variables that influence the product's profitability.

2. *Many of these variables are external and thus uncontrollable.* In the example above, certainly the decision makers cannot control how competition will attempt to counter the new product's introduction. National or international economic conditions will increase or decrease the product's sales. If the retail trade, for some reason, fails to endorse the product, this of course will have a profound effect on the new item's profits. And finally, a national strike or other factors could increase material and labor costs, resulting in higher selling prices—something that could not be controlled by the decision makers.

3. *The variables lack stability.* In the preceding illustrations, the variables change through time, sometimes rapidly. An unexpected government tax on a given product class can have a devastating effect on sales. Or, a declining trend in consumer spending can discourage a product's sales.

1

4. *The market response is nonlinear.* Doubling an advertising appropriation rarely doubles sales, as usually only a modest increase results. While the underlying forces that make for nonlinear responses to marketing variables are several, the end result for the marketer is one of diminishing returns to marketing efforts.

In addition to having high complexity, marketing decisions frequently involve high levels of financial risk. Marketing costs typically account for a significant percentage of the final cost of most goods and services. In some instances, one marketing decision alone can require funding that exceeds the total after-tax profits of the company. One meat packer was considering increasing its advertising appropriation by nine million dollars; its after-tax profits during the entire prior fiscal period were less than that figure.

Another reason marketing decisions have great financial risk is that they initiate many of the decisions of other functional areas. For example, in a large firm the finance group cannot complete budgets and the manufacturing staff cannot complete production schedules until the marketing department provides sales estimates. Moreover, while all business functions are responsible for holding down costs, only the marketing function has the dual role of holding down costs *and* generating revenue.

Additionally, marketing decision results are more exposed to public scrutiny than are other functional area decision outcomes. Not only do consumers assess marketing decisions, but so do competitors, governmental agencies, financial analysts, stockholders, and other interested publics. This scrutiny is increasing as greater concern with the societal role of marketing is expressed.

Because of this complexity and cruciality, marketing decision makers generally strive to acquire and utilize available data to the fullest extent possible. In particular, they make heavy use of external data and information—primarily that concerning consumer response. But marketing decision makers often find that it is not always possible to obtain the desired data; cost, time, and measurability constraints are usually present. Selecting appropriate substitute data and knowing when to apply judgment are therefore important considerations.

Because of the complex nature of marketing decisions, problem solving and decision making in actual practice tend to be more an art than a science. Understandably, then, there is considerable interest in improving decision making and problem solving in marketing. This book is one expression of that interest.

WHO MAKES MARKETING DECISIONS?

Every organization that provides goods or services to others, for profit or not, makes marketing decisions in providing those goods and services. They may not be good decisions, but they are marketing decisions nonetheless. The organization may not be aware that it is making marketing decisions, i.e., the organization is not aware of the marketing concept. Nonprofit enterprises typically fall into this category. On the other hand, today few profit-oriented enterprises fail to recognize the significance of marketing to their success and that marketing decisions are important decisions.

The echelon or hierarchy concept is one way to broadly classify marketing decision makers in the typical business enterprise—a packaged consumer goods producer, for example. From the bottom up the general labels for managerial levels are: supervisory management, middle management, and top management. The progression upward reflects a shift in focus from day-to-day operational considerations toward greater concern with long-run strategic issues. The marketing counterparts of these three managerial levels may be labelled roughly as: marketing instrument managers, marketing executives, and marketing committees.

Marketing Instrument Managers

Job titles commonly used in this category include: brand manager, product manager, advertising manager, and sales manager. These individuals on the front line deal with the day-to-day pressures of carrying out fundamental marketing tasks. Their job is to supervise the application of basic marketing efforts or factors, e.g., advertising, price. Some writers refer to these controllable factors as marketing instruments; they must be "tuned" and "played" properly to get good results. The time horizon of these managers is, perforce, short and their focus is generally on marketing communication—developing and executing advertising campaigns, administering promotional efforts including trade and consumer price deals, and guiding the selling efforts. In some instances product or brand managers have a wider jurisdiction that includes new product development and obtaining intraorganizational coordination for marketing programs. In almost every instance, however, marketing instrument managers must operate within the context of guidance provided by higher levels in the organization—guidance that is typically articulated in the form of a marketing plan.

Marketing Executives

Typical job titles used in some industrial companies at this level are: marketing manager, vice-president of marketing, or general sales manager. Central concern in these roles is directed toward product and market development; e.g., what products to add or to drop, what pricing policy to adopt, and what channels to use in reaching target markets. Such questions demand that the decision maker adopt a longer time horizon. They are strategic questions; they involve the enterprise in significant commitments of financial and organizational resources and often involve contractual relationships extending over a long period of time. Obtaining the answer to these questions compels the firm to formulate a marketing plan. The basis for the marketing plan is the corporate plan and its oversight is provided typically by some sort of executive committee. Chief executive officers, corporate presidents, and other top management executives participate in major marketing decisions, often making key strategy choices. In some instances they may fulfill their marketing role through a committee mechanism.

Marketing Committees

Membership in marketing committees consists not only of an organization's several marketing executives and managers (who may be linked to product groups, key market segments, geographic regions, or some other meaningful subdivision) but also of marketing staff support managers, e.g., the manager of market research. Occasionally nonmarketing executives may be members, with the vice-presidents for production, research and development, and finance as the most likely participants. Top management officials are typically members of corporate-level marketing committees. Strategic marketing questions dominate the agenda of these committees. The integration of marketing plans with overall corporate plans is a central concern.

Other Marketing Decision Makers

In many large consumer goods corporations in which marketing plays a vital role, the firm's top executives assume the decision-making responsibilities of lower level marketing managers. For example, the chief executive officers of several large national beer producers actively participate in advertising decisions. In a proprietary drug firm, the board chairperson, among other activities, works closely with the company's advertising agency. Such involvements typically stem from the executive's personal marketing interests.

The small enterprise lacks the human resources that major corporations can assign to the marketing task. The small business proprietor is often the product manager, the advertising manager, the distribution manager, the sales manager, and the director of planning all rolled into one. The small entrepreneur must make strategic and tactical decisions alike.

Once major, long-run decisions are agreed upon (for example, selecting a store location), the framework for the daily operating decisions is established. Poor choices on major questions, such as an inadequate store site, can seldom be compensated for by advertising and other tactical marketing factors alone. Again, all the more reason to be concerned with improving marketing decision making.

THE MARKETING PLAN

The concepts and philosophies underlying a given marketing plan are typically shaped in the marketing or executive committee process. The details of a plan, however, are generally developed by a product or market manager and approved by higher ranked marketing executives. These details usually include analysis and evaluation of the following:

1. The market situation.
2. Corporate capabilities.
3. Problems and opportunities.
4. Approaches for meeting problems and capitalizing on opportunities.
5. Pro forma statement display of consequences.

One version of a marketing plan outline is presented in Figure 1. An illustration of what details might appear initially in a marketing plan is shown in Figure 2 on page 6. The section headings and details of a marketing plan will vary, of course, from company to company.

- **WHERE ARE WE NOW?**

  What is the situation regarding:
  1. Our marketing performance?
  2. Our financial health?
  3. Our production capability?
  4. Industry performance?
  5. The competitive climate?
  6. Customer characteristics and needs?
  7. Environmental factors and developments?

- **WHERE DO WE WANT TO BE?**

  What are our objectives regarding:
  1. Sales levels?
  2. Market penetration?
  3. Profitability?
  4. Corporate stature?

- **HOW SHALL WE GET THERE?**

  What are our options regarding:
  1. Product development?
  2. Pricing?
  3. Promotion?
  4. Distribution?

Figure 1   Typical Questions Addressed by a Marketing Plan

MARKETING DECISION AREAS

In designating categories of marketing decisions one must recognize what it is that can be decided about. What are the controllable factors? What are the uncontrollable factors or environmental forces? The decision clusters associated with the major factors or instruments open to manipulation by marketers are:

1. Product/brand development and deletion decisions.
2. Pricing decisions.
3. Physical distribution and "pipeline" or channel decisions.
4. Promotion/communication program decisions.

It is important, of course, that these various decisions be made in concert and consonance with one another. Stated marketing plans attempt to assure this coordination.

- **WHERE ARE WE NOW?**
  1. Annual sales at $12 million; growing at 11% per year; yielding 15% return on sales; market share at 20% in quality portion of market, 0.6% in economy portion.
  2. $60,000 in cash on hand; $900,000 bank loan.
  3. No excess capacity. Aluminum extrusions in ample supply, but prices are rising. Manufacturing and design skills regarded as superior by the trade.
  4. Current industry sales at $60 million; 50% growth expected over next three years.
  5. Many firms, especially at local level. Price competition intense, especially in areas with several local producers. Easy entry.
  6. Contractors constitute the principal customer category. Brand names not generally important; bid price by supplier is primary consideration. Economy portion of market is approximately 70%. Tract housing contractors especially sensitive to price and desire no after-installation service requirements.
  7. Greater federal government involvement in safety standards (safety glass in sliding doors may become mandatory). Energy conservation concerns (argument for double panes).

- **WHERE DO WE WANT TO BE?**
  1. 20% increase in sales over next 3 years.
  2. Increase share in economy market to 5% over next 3 years. Maintain share in quality portion of market.
  3. Boost ROI to 20% on net worth.
  4. Maintain reputation for quality and design superiority.

- **HOW SHALL WE GET THERE?**
  1. Exploit aerospace plastics and sealant technologies in developing a low-maintenance, safe, energy-saving sliding door/window wall panel.
  2. Price in upper range of economy market.
  3. Enable contractors/developers to integrate door's features into their advertising efforts—stress savings to homeowner.
  4. Concentrate on major building supply dealers in areas of significant tract home construction.

Source: Adapted from Figure 1–4 in D. J. Dalrymple and L. J. Parsons, *Marketing Management: Text and Cases* (New York: John Wiley and Sons, Inc., 1976), p. 11.

Figure 2   How a Hypothetical Sliding Glass Door Manufacturer Might Begin Addressing Marketing Plan Questions (Keyed to Figure 1)

There is the temptation on the part of many (a temptation worth resisting) to classify marketing research as a prime marketing decision area. It will be argued at several points in this book that, while marketing research does indeed raise a host of decision issues and is a key decision area itself, it should not be classified as a *marketing* decision area. Rather, marketing research reflects the need for relevant data and information to complete and carry out marketing decisions. In looking at decision making in a generic way, research is an important, separate activity running parallel to the main decision effort and whose intensity is proportional to the main decision's need for data and information. Further discussion of the role of marketing research is included in Chapter 2.

TYPES OF MARKETING DECISIONS

In looking at real-world decisions, marketing or otherwise, one is aware that some decisions are expected or anticipated whereas others are forced as a result of unexpected or unplanned circumstances.

Unanticipated vs. Anticipated Decisions

Unanticipated decisions often give the decision maker little time to contemplate fully the proper course of action. An example of an unanticipated, forced decision situation was created by a Food and Drug Administration ruling that saccharine contains a potential cancer-inducing agent and should be removed from the market. Other examples of such situations include unexpected competitor price reductions, distribution foul-ups in major markets, or a work stoppage in a key supplier's plant. Managers attempting to cope with such situations often speak of "putting out brush fires." In the worst of situations there is a continual parade of crisis decisions and such conditions create much of the pressure associated with the managerial role.

Anticipated decisions, on the other hand, stem directly from the planning process and from the conversion of plans into operational programs. The pressure content of these decisions is considerably lower than those associated with "putting out fires." These two broad decision categories imply different conditions under which data and information may be acquired and brought to bear on the main questions. In one instance there may be little or no time available for gathering information (the fire must be put out); in the other—the planning/programming effort—there may be considerable time available.

"Bright-Idea" Decisions

There is yet another category of marketing decisions—those that emanate from someone's *bright idea* (not meant here in the derogatory sense of "Whose bright idea was that?"). Marketers typically take great pride in being creative, in having innovative, profit-making ideas. Translating those ideas, especially when they involve efforts outside the organization's regular stream of affairs, can raise decisions that demand considerable additional data before resolution is complete. The bright idea often occurs during the decision process when the factors involved are viewed from a totally different perspective by one of the decision makers. Sometimes this phenomenon is the result of experience or it may be simply a better insight into the particular situation at hand. Sometimes the marketing outcome of a bright idea will be a new product, other times it will be a modification of the existing program.

Bright-idea decisions are akin to brush-fire decisions in that both are unanticipated, at least in their particulars. The former have a pleasant opportunity, sense-of-excitement character to them while the latter tend to be irritating and problematical, and induce furrowed brows and considerable concern. Brush-fire decisions can seldom be deferred; bright-idea decisions often may be delayed—though in certain instances if the firm does not decide quickly enough, a bright idea can become an "if only we had . . ." lament.

To recap, the source of a marketing decision episode can be:

1. Based on plans and the planning process (anticipated decisions).
2. Brush-fire fighting efforts (unanticipated decisions).
3. Bright-idea capitalization attempts.

Each category has its own general time pace and its own demands for data and information. The decision-making procedures advocated in this book apply to all three categories.

MARKETING DECISION MAKING: THE BASIC FLOWCHART APPROACH

There are a number of ways to look at decisions—marketing decisions or other types. The authors have chosen a five-step process framework that is familiar to many and readily grasped and retained by those to whom it is not. The five steps are portrayed in the accompanying flowchart (Figure 3), which shall be referred to as the *basic flowchart*. The next five chapters in this book will treat each of the steps of the flowchart in detail. At the beginning of each chapter is a duplicate of the basic flowchart that highlights in bold outline the particular step under discussion in that chapter. As a summary of each chapter, the basic flowchart, augmented with key points, is repeated at the end of the chapter. This repetitive use is intended not only to aid the reader but also to emphasize the belief that explicit, conscious recognition and systematic application of the five-step process pays enormous dividends toward improved decisions.

Each chapter contains concepts, techniques, and procedures for completing a single step in the basic flowchart. To illustrate the application of each chapter's contents, a marketing case (Grandin Laboratories) is analyzed. Details of the case are presented in stages and the analysis of each stage is provided separately. The reader may wish, at this point, to review the table of contents and to skim through the book so as to become acquainted with its format.

THE FRAMEWORK OF MARKETING DECISIONS

Throughout this book the basic flowchart serves as the frame of reference. It is essential that one fully understand this model. Grasping the fundamental ideas of the framework enables one to proceed in a more logical fashion. The role of creativity is recognized. The function of data is comprehended. The significance of analysis is seen. But perhaps of even greater value is the contribution the flowchart makes to participation in group efforts. Understanding this

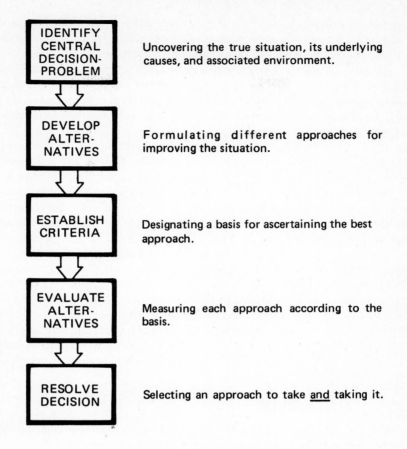

IDENTIFY
CENTRAL
DECISION-
PROBLEM

Uncovering the true situation, its underlying causes, and associated environment.

DEVELOP
ALTER-
NATIVES

Formulating different approaches for improving the situation.

ESTABLISH
CRITERIA

Designating a basis for ascertaining the best approach.

EVALUATE
ALTER-
NATIVES

Measuring each approach according to the basis.

RESOLVE
DECISION

Selecting an approach to take and taking it.

Figure 3   Basic Flowchart of Decision-Making Process

model enables one to become involved in a meaningful way when the discussion moves from one phase of the decision process to another. Of benefit to the person fully grasping the decision model is the aid it gives in focusing group discussion—to see where the group is in the process versus where the group should be. Keeping the discussion on a logical and coherent plane is one of the chief gains of applying the model to group decision efforts.

Whether confronting a classroom case or a real-world decision situation, one should, at the very outset, ask the questions:

1. Where do the decision makers *appear* to be with regard to the decision process as schematically portrayed in the basic flowchart?
2. Where *should* the decision makers be?

For example, an episode may open with a meeting of decision makers and staff members. Their interest may be focused on choosing one of three new advertising themes to correct lagging sales. Ostensibly they are at Step 5: Resolving the Decision. But is this where they should be? Do the facts indicate that the current advertising approach is the cause of poor sales? Indeed, have the data and information been assembled to indicate clearly what the central issue is and why it has come about? Assuming that advertising is the culprit, one could (and should) ask the question: Are these three alternatives the only ones possible? And assuming that they are, what criteria are being used to choose one from among the set of alternatives? Have the criteria been definitely expressed? Is additional information needed by the participants? How precise should the data be?

Use of the basic flowchart as a framework does not mean that the decision process must occur in lock-step fashion. It is entirely possible, and appropriate, to return to a prior step, to recirculate or recycle, in effect. New insights, fresh ideas, and additional relevant information all may warrant returning to some previous step to reshape what was done there, e.g., to add new possible actions to the list of alternatives. In some instances it may be difficult to separate clearly one stage from the next. This is especially true in the identification stage; pinpointing the central question may seem to suggest some obvious alternatives. Interplay between the steps is to be expected and, indeed, encouraged. The key is to recognize it.

Unless the elements represented in the flowchart are clearly articulated—out on the table in full view of the decision makers so to speak—the analysis will often be fuzzy and the ensuing decision will likely be unsatisfactory. Many decision situations are incorrectly handled simply because of the failure to discern how the problem to be solved is being tackled versus how it should be tackled—namely, systematically and explicitly.

SUGGESTED READINGS

Boyd, H. W., Jr., and W. F. Massy. *Marketing Management.* New York: Harcourt Brace Jovanovich, Inc., 1972. Chapters 1 and 2.

Christopher, William F. "Marketing Planning That Gets Things Done." *Harvard Business Review,* Vol. 48, No. 5 (Sept.-Oct., 1970), pp. 56–64.

Cravens, D. W., G. E. Hills, and R. B. Woodruff. *Marketing Decision Making: Concepts and Strategy.* Homewood, Ill.: Richard D. Irwin, Inc., 1976. Chapters 1 and 13.

Howard, John A. *Marketing Management—Operating, Strategic, and Administrative,* 3d ed. Homewood, Ill.: Richard D. Irwin, Inc., 1973. Chapters 5 and 12, pp. 137–139, 305–308, and 399.

Kotler, Philip. *Marketing Management—Analysis, Planning, and Control,* 2d ed. Englewood Cliffs, N.J.: Prentice-Hall, Inc., 1972. Chapters 9 and 11.

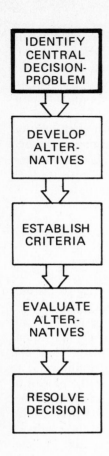

1

Identifying the Central Decision-Problem

"We are either progressing or retrograding all the while; there is no such thing as remaining stationary in this life."

—J. F. Clarke

"Facts are stubborn things."

—René LeSage

In undertaking an examination of marketing decision making one should recognize that problem solving and decision making are not quite the same thing. *Problem solving* focuses on finding problem causes and companion solution alternatives. It is largely an investigative, analytic, creative process. *Decision making* focuses on choosing among action alternatives and then taking action. It is an evaluative, judicial, action process. Decision making tends to presume the alternatives already exist. Problem solving on the other hand, presumes that the key is to get some alternative solutions from which to choose in the first place. Identifying the underlying cause(s) is a necessary and substantial preliminary to the development of alternative solutions. After a list of viable solutions is compiled, then choice (i.e., decision making) becomes the concern.

WHAT IS A DECISION-PROBLEM?

The disconcerting aspect about most marketing, and management, situations is that they require both tasks—problem solving and decision making.

11

Marketing activity seldom produces situations where only one solution is possible. The vast majority of situations require first the identification of causes, then the specification of alternative solution paths, and finally a subsequent resolution of which path to use, i.e., the choice. Because of this compound nature of most marketing situations, *decision-problem* seems an appropriate term to describe what emerges from them.

Much of the art associated with marketing lies in the creative interpretation of marketing problems and identification of their possible solutions. And much of the science associated with marketing lies in the logical evaluation of alternative solutions. The successful marketing manager must have both types of skills to tackle decision-problems.

Finding Decision-Problems

One management educator[1] has pointed out that schools of business lead students to spend too much time analyzing the solutions to known problems but far too little time learning to find problems that warrant solving. That this should be the case is not entirely surprising. It is relatively easy to instruct managers-to-be in rational, quantitative procedures for evaluating preidentified alternatives—procedures such as discounted cash flow, linear programming, and expected monetary value. It is considerably more difficult to teach individuals to recognize the decision-problems that are present in the first place. This book offers no magical techniques, no cure-all procedures for problem finding. The authors recognize that there is a substantial creative element in the process of ferreting out the "true" decision-problem and linking it to a set of causal factors. The authors do, however, advocate a procedure they believe will speed the process of problem finding, and, equally important, will enable the results of the process to be communicated readily to others. The procedure recommended is to be *explicit* in the articulation of the decision-problem supposedly uncovered. By actually writing down the problem and its causes, the writer is forced to be more precise and thoughtful about what is being said. Others may thus more easily inspect and criticize constructively the problem's specification. Getting the problem *individuated* (i.e., clearly set out in relation to its context and clearly linked to presumed causes) will pay enormous dividends in the subsequent steps of the problem-solving, decision-making process. It is far better to resolve the right decision-problem partially than to resolve the wrong problem fully. (Individuating the decision-problem is discussed further on page 29.)

Given that ferreting out decision-problems is no easy task, where does one begin? One begins by recognizing that the fundamental cause of decision-problems is change—problems are rooted in change.

Change as the Source of Decision-Problems

The Latin base of the word profit is *profectus,* a noun meaning progress or improvement. Progress is obviously one kind of change. Thus, to say that

---

[1] J. Sterling Livingston, "Myth of the Well-Educated Manager," *Harvard Business Review,* Vol. 49, No. 1 (Jan.–Feb., 1971), pp. 79–89.

business people pursue profit is to say that they pursue change. But it is a kind of change they strive consciously to produce, a kind of change for which they plan.

There are various ways to measure the success of planned change (or profit). In a straightforward way profit is the residual from revenues after costs are accounted for. In a more sophisticated way profit is measured as return on investment (ROI). This measure shows how efficiently resources (i.e., investments) have been used in garnering the return. Increases in profits (changes) over some norm or benchmark (e.g., last year's ROI, last quarter's profit) are produced by increases in revenues relative to costs. Note that a substantial reduction in costs can mean increases in profits even though revenues are declining.

Since business people have, or at least hope they have, control over costs, they are especially sensitive to revenue performance. Sales goals or quotas and market share targets are expressions of planned or desired change in revenues. When actual performance (concerning costs as well as revenues) fails to match expectations or plans, undesired, unplanned change comes about. Adjustment, that is, a new round of planned change, is called for.

Planned change is oriented toward the future; it is a change that should be brought about. The question is how? Here is a decision-problem in the bud.

Unplanned change is linked to the past, usually the most recent past. Unplanned change can be satisfactory (such as higher than anticipated sales increases) or unsatisfactory (such as lower than anticipated advertising response or unanticipated price cuts by a competitor). Each case calls for action (sustaining the sales growth in the first case, modifying promotion in the second, and responding competitively in the third). In each case planned change is required, creating more decision-problems in the bud.

RECOGNIZING THE ENVIRONMENT: HOME OF CHANGE

Changed and unchanged conditions comprise an environment in which the central decision-problem is embedded. It is in that environment where the causes of change will be found and where corrective changes should be instituted. Each decision-problem has its own particular setting, its own particular environment.

The term *environment* has wide usage in the literature of marketing and management. Typically it is used to refer to the total setting in which the organization finds itself. Thus, the environment of a firm includes the other firms, clients, organizations, etc., with which it must compete, cooperate, confer, and so on. The environment in this sense also includes less tangible elements such as general economic conditions, the world political situation, the regulatory climate, public opinion, and the like. Figure 1–1 summarizes these various aspects of the environment of an enterprise. Figure 1–2 lists some major environmental factors affecting marketing in the years ahead. One important consideration to note here is that most environmental elements are not under the direct control of the individual firm. True, the firm makes efforts to improve economic conditions, to influence regulation, to intensify competition,

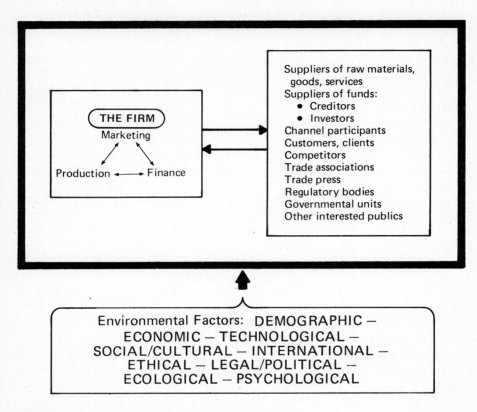

Figure 1-1 *Aspects of the Total Environment*

and to shape public opinion. But similar efforts, often with cancelling effects, are conducted by all the organizations in the environment.

Why is this usage of the term "environment" helpful? Because it encourages managers to recognize that the success of their enterprise depends on its ability to adapt and survive in a larger setting. Further, recognition of environmental forces, and successful response thereto, demands that managers have adequate and timely data and information about the environment, which is constantly turbulent to say the least.

In this book an additional but entirely compatible usage of the term environment is made. In addition to employing it to denote the milieu of the organization, "environment" will also denote the context of a decision-problem. Any data and information that shed light on that context and, therefore, on the decision-problem itself, will thus be labelled *environmental data and information.* It is environmental data that permit the initial discovery of decision-problems, facilitate the identification of their causes, and suggest possible remedies.

SPECIFIC FACTOR	DISCUSSION
SLOWED POPULATION GROWTH	Without the umbrella of population growth rates of the 1950s and 1960s, the 1970s and beyond seem destined to experience compensating competitive intensification. Competitive intensification implies accelerating dependency on marketing. As population growth slows, it accelerates the marketing importance of understanding and responding to the distribution and desires of that changing population. One note of caution is to keep ever-alert for signs of reversion to previous high population growth rates.
SUNBELT MOVEMENT	Beyond people and business, southern and western states are *attracting support institutions* such as expanded and upgraded university instruction and research. Recurring energy stresses seem likely to reinforce this movement. Already it's permeated a consequential segment of marketing strategy and practice.
INSTITUTIONALIZED INFLATION	Egalitarian predispositions, government fiat, cost-of-living escalator clauses, energy imports-induced balance of payments deficits, and the like provide powerful and mounting inflationary pressures. Perhaps institutionalized inflation may subsequently entail institutionalized unemployment above traditionally acceptable levels. Of tandem concern is the apparent built-in public expectation (if not acceptance) of continued inflation as reflected in longitudinal surveys such as by the Harris organization.
LAGGING R&D INVESTMENT	When will postponed R&D investment . . . particularly on *basic* research . . . seriously threaten the U.S. competitive position in world commerce? Of note is the increase of United States awarded patents to foreign residents from 19% (1966) to an estimated 34% (1975, the latest available year.) [1] Has the U.S. been slipping in its dominance of world innovation?

[1] These estimates were made from computations of data contained in *Commissioner of Patents and Trademarks Annual Report Fiscal Year 1976*, U.S. Department of Commerce/Patent and Trademark Office, February, 1977.

Figure 1–2   Factors Influencing the Marketing Environment of the 1980s

SPECIFIC FACTOR	DISCUSSION
COMMODITY SUPPLY—DEMAND-PRICE UNCERTAINTIES	Interacting impacts of geopolitical forces and apparently changing weather patterns in key agricultural areas of the world have recently produced destabilizing conditions in the availability and prices of such commodities as sugar, vegetable oil and coffee. Are such price gyrations past or future?
EGALITARIANISM	This movement is virtually global cutting across countries, political systems and cultures in the pursuit of economic, legal, political and social equality. The so-called "psychology of entitlement" is widespread and ever-widening in its spread.
SOCIAL RESPONSIBILITY RISE	Social responsibility is increasingly intersecting business financial planning and the difficult and sensitive realities of economic-societal tradeoffs. Still largely ignored by the majority in marketing strategy formulation is the *strategic marketing opportunity* afforded by blending marketing strategy with social responsibility.
SHIFTING CONSUMER VALUES AND DEMOGRAPHICS	Almost a new lexicon encompassing such phrases as "single parent families," "zero population growth," and "voluntary simplicity" seems to be emerging. These phrases reflect the fundamental changes in how a significant proportion of the population views and practices living. Marketing implications (and sometimes complications) can be enormous.
WOMEN: MOUNTING MARKETING FORCE	We can anticipate the increasing influence of women on marketing to continue unabated. That influence comes through direct and indirect channels. It comes directly through more and more women (1) entering and remaining in the labor force with the attendant lifestyle and buying pattern shifts this induces and (2) taking positions in marketing management where they can influence marketing policies, strategies, and tactics. Indirectly—but no less significantly—activist groups, EEOC, and women's self-actualization expression continue to influence women's marketing careers, their compensation, and their buying patterns.

Figure 1–2   Factors Influencing the Marketing Environment of the 1980s (Continued)

SPECIFIC FACTOR	DISCUSSION
SENIOR CITIZEN POWER	Always an economic force, senior citizens are emerging as a *political force.* Their growing power stems from numbers expanding at a faster rate than for the population as a whole, steadily improving health, a growing disenchantment with retirement among many, and political activism through such groups as the Gray Panthers which has already succeeded in convincing the National Association of Broadcasters to insert into its television code prohibitions against age discrimination in program portrayals. We'll likely see substantial modification of current mandatory retirement regulations within the next few years. Just think of the marketing impact.
TELECOMMUNI- CATIONS EXPLOSION	Whether computer-based or satellite-based, telecommunications technology is advancing swiftly. Banking wrestles with EFTS while retail food chains do likewise with universal product code scanners. These and other industries seeking to implement these efficiencies are already learning the *critical importance of effective marketing* in overcoming consumerist resistance and in restructuring consumer habits and predispositions.
HEALTH CARE CONSIDERATIONS	The health care is an outstanding example of a U.S. industry likely to undergo drastic changes during the 1980s. Soaring costs, technological breakthroughs, enhanced public concern, growing knowledge and an emphasis on nutrition, plus government pressures on professional societies to relax traditional competitive barriers are indicative of the pervasive change-agents at work. Look for health care and health care marketing to be sharply different ten years from now.
ENERGY	No commentary on the future marketing environment could be realistic were it to exclude energy in *all* its forms. This most disruptive influence of the 1970s may prove more so during the 1980s. Therefore, it bears continuous and close monitoring and attendant translation into corporate threats, opportunities, options and contingencies through strategic corporate planning down in to marketing planning.

*Figure 1–2   Factors Influencing the Marketing Environment of the 1980s
(Continued)*

SPECIFIC FACTOR	DISCUSSION
GOVERNMENT REGULATION	This ongoing influence is still in its ascendancy and broadening in scope. In significant ways, government regulation reflects egalitarianism and health care considerations (both earlier cited). Of note is the fairly recent sentiment for *de*regulation (in airlines, trucking, natural gas, etc.). This apparent backlash movement could develop and deserves attention.
ENVIRONMENTALISM	The impact of environmental legislation Congress passed in 1972 alone will probably surpass that of all previous laws passed. Environmentalism is here to stay. Recent and anticipated economic stresses place economic and environmental aims in conflict on everexpanding fronts. The auto, strip mining, steel, beverage container, and paper industries are visible harbingers of future faceoffs and, ultimately, the tradeoffs involved. Marketing cannot help but be significantly impacted.

Source: John G. Keane, "Telescoping Future Marketing," *The New Role of the Marketing Professional,* 1977 Business Proceedings of the American Marketing Association, edited by P. J. LaPlaca (Chicago: AMA, 1977), pp. 9–16.

Figure 1–2   Factors Influencing the Marketing Environment of the 1980s (Concluded)

Because of the considerable importance of obtaining and using environmental data and information, a major portion of this chapter is devoted to those activities. However, first some comments on tracing change and its causes are offered.

LINKING CHANGE TO CAUSES

We have emphasized that at the root of all decision-problems is change: change that has occurred, change that should occur. Change of any kind is always perceived relative to some standard, some reference point or conditions, or some model of the way things should work. These reference measures and models reside in the memories of managers and in the "memories" of their organizations, i.e., internal planning, budgeting, and reporting systems. Differences, which are the quantification of change and which can be expressed in absolute as well as percentage terms, are regular features of such systems. Sales results, for example, are often expressed as a percentage change relative to the same period of the prior year.

Whenever differences are not what the managers feel they should be, either as compared to historical performance deemed satisfactory or as compared to budgeted/planned target results deemed desirable, the inevitable question is

"Why?" No more important question can be asked (and it should be persistently asked) than "Why?" The junior manager quickly learns that inability to answer "why's" means a retarded, perhaps even shortened, business career.

Developing Reasons for Change

How does one develop answers to why differences, i.e., changes, have occurred? A starting point is to note whether measurements of similar activity elsewhere have correspondingly changed. At the same time, make note of what has not changed. The isolation of the central decision-problem is obviously expedited if one can be confident about what the problem is *not*.

For example, sales in City X are discovered to be down from last year's level. Are sales for the region similarly down or is it just City X? Another example: reader responses using write-in cards are found to be less than anticipated. Is readership and circulation also down for the periodicals employed? Is television viewing up instead? Are these indications that the media habits of potential customers are shifting?

The scrutiny of detected change should extend from the initial finding of a marketing performance variation all the way to the ultimate consumer level. What has gone up? What has gone down? What has remained essentially unchanged? Are they related? Is there a connection? What data lend support to causal explanations? Are there refuting data? Such is the dialogue of marketing detective work.

It would be naive to assume that simply by asking questions the true causes of the decision-problem in question will be immediately located. Additional data and information will very likely be needed to provide adequate answers to the problem-defining, cause-detecting questions asked. Such data and information (i.e., environmental data and information), should shed light on the decision-problem at hand.

Bringing About Change

Marketing decision situations arise from unanticipated changes in consumer response, competitive reaction, or other facets of the marketplace. Marketing people desire, of course, to institute change as well as respond to it. They want to plan change. As will be discussed in Chapter 3, planned change can be expressed in the form of criterion statements; that is, a specific action will be chosen from a set of alternatives if data and information indicate it will bring about the planned change.

Linking desired ultimate changes in market response to actions (causes) that the marketer can initiate is clearly a challenging task. The central question to pose under these conditions is not so much "Why?" but rather "How?" How is a desired change in consumer purchasing behavior brought about? What other factors must be altered? How should they be altered? When? In advance? Concurrently? What are the relevant intervening variables that must be operated on? How do they interrelate? What is the appropriate model? Answers to these kinds of questions are constantly being sought by marketing practitioners, academicians, theorists, and researchers. Their accumulated writings constitute externally available environmental data and information. It is a body of knowledge that is being updated continually and so it behooves the marketer to stay abreast of developments in the literature. Naturally, additional environmental data are often needed to augment or to particularize marketing models and concepts for a specific firm's use.

In short, whether one is responding to a change in the marketing environment or trying to bring about change, the key is having relevant environmental data and information.

OBTAINING ENVIRONMENTAL DATA AND INFORMATION

Generally speaking, data refer to numerical compilations of statistics, results, observations, etc. Interpretation of data yields information. Different meanings can be attached to the same data depending upon the orientation of the interpreter. A decline in the birth rate bodes ill for the baby-food producer, but may augur well for contraceptive makers. Because the distinction between data and information is not always clear (what is information to one person could serve as data to another), the two terms are used interchangeably here.

Environmental vs. Actionable Data

To understand the role of information in the decision-making/problem-solving process, one must fully recognize the difference between environmental and actionable data and information. Environmental data indicate *what is*; actionable data and information are pertinent to *what should be done*—the action that should be taken.

Environmental data are communicated to the marketer before any possible courses of marketing action have been formulated. The salesperson who reports the introduction of a competing product in the marketplace is providing environmental data. Out of this report eventually may emerge some possible marketing alternatives, one of which may be "to do nothing." But even doing nothing is a decision in the real sense.

If a new environment is significant in that some adjustment is deemed necessary, the decision makers will pose several marketing alternatives. Finally, one of these decision choices will be designated as the action to be taken. It should be clear that *any information which comes to light, in any form whatsoever, prior to the final formation of the alternative courses of action is labelled environmental data or information.*

The other type of information, actionable data, is sought after the alternatives have been formulated and is sought for the specific purpose of evaluating those alternatives. In regard to the illustration of the salesperson who discovered a newly introduced competitive product and who reported it to company management, the report itself was environmental in nature. Certainly no action was being considered when the report was received. Assume that the marketing manager had a survey conducted to determine how well this new competitor's product was selling—a study to compile data thought to be necessary to evaluate the competing product's impact on the company's sales and market share. Such data would be environmental in nature because any countermoves (alternative courses of action) still had not been formulated. The marketing manager was still in the process of determining the significance of the competitive introduction, i.e., how serious a decision-problem it was.

The data, let us suppose, revealed marked inroads into the marketing manager's product sales. Thus, some adjustment is needed. The alternatives subsequently developed include such possible actions as a price reduction, increased advertising, and a change in the existing product. With these options in mind, the issue is: Which of these choices should be selected? On what basis should the decision be made? It is decided to gather additional data directed specifically at determining which of the various alternatives under consideration would be "best" for the company. The data obtained to resolve the issue as to which of the alternatives should be the final choice are actionable data. The data were sought solely to aid the decision makers in the selection of one alternative over others under consideration. Figure 1–3 summarizes the proper roles of environmental and actionable data.

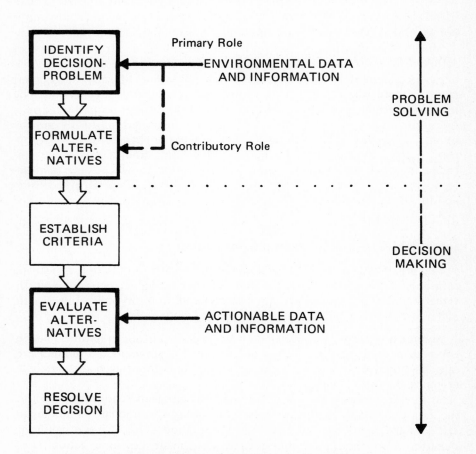

**Figure 1–3   Role of Data and Information in Problem-Solving/
Decision-Making Process**

Often environmental data and actionable data are obtained jointly during a single information-gathering effort. Some studies may seek chiefly actionable data, but environmental data will also be uncovered as a by-product. Combining the efforts is an efficient use of research funds. However, for discussion purposes it is well to view them separately. This chapter, then, restricts itself to environmental information. Chapter 4 covers the development of actionable data and information.

In the collection of additional environmental information experience has shown that environmental data need not be as precise, relatively, as actionable data. In other words, environmental evidence can have a low precision level (such as in exploratory studies) but actionable data generally should be of high precision. Much environmental data collected are highly precise (e.g., Bureau of Census documents, Nielsen reports), but actionable data should be as precise as possible so as to facilitate adequate discrimination of the alternatives. The high/low distinction with regard to the precision of actionable versus environmental data is a useful one to remember; it cautions decision makers not to spend too much time and money for a precise environmental data study that is not warranted. More will be said about data collection in Chapter 4.

Much environmental information is conveyed informally. It is not sought or gathered in a systematic fashion. The information is often unsolicited. The salesperson's report of the competitor's new product is informal. Subsequent study of those sales would involve formal environmental data collection. The informal method is difficult to categorize because there is no patterned relationship between the nature of the information uncovered informally and the method employed in uncovering it. However, many changes in the environment surface via the informal method. One letter from a dissatisfied customer—informal information—may reveal a situation to which some valid adjustment should be made. Conversations at trade shows, competitive literature, and luncheon discussions with company peers are other examples of informal information exchange.

Internally Available Data and Information

The firm itself is a source of environmental data and information, generating substantial amounts of material pertinent to marketing decision-problems. Internally generated data are perhaps best discussed in terms of accounting data and nonaccounting data.

Accounting Data. Accounting data are basically historic in nature. They record the past, chronicling the performance of the company, its products, its sales territories. Corporate activities, of course, are not portrayed adequately by accounting records alone.

At its broadest level the corporate financial statement is a form of accounting data that relates the historical performance of the company. These financial data are environmental. They reveal a situation which, if it is a significant departure from the norm, requires some adjustment, i.e., some action. However, like most environmental data, they do not in themselves suggest possible corrective action. If the monthly profit-and-loss statement shows an unexpected loss, this observed condition deviates from the goal. Thus, some action, not yet designed, not yet agreed upon, must be taken.

The broad financial statement describing the corporate picture does not aid the marketer greatly because the data are too general. It can, however, signal the presence of a problem. Some additional data may then be sought to pinpoint the specific problem areas. The marketer seeks data more specific than the financial statement typically provides.

Some accounting data are prepared specifically for marketing management; these often cover product performance and are contained in various profitability reports. Such reports on product profitability reveal the extent to which the performance is a deviation from the expected norm. They become more revealing when broken down by geographic area, class of trade, type of product, sales division, and any other subclassification in keeping with the accounting department's practices and the marketing department's information needs. The more specific the data, the more likely is the chance of locating a cause of a problem. For example, national aggregates obscure territorial weaknesses. One sales territory may be performing so poorly that it drags the national company average to a point below the total corporate objective for that product. Examination of performance by territory narrows the problem, although by no means is the solution immediately apparent. The cause of the profitability decline in one territory may be due to a wide variety of factors, some exogenous and beyond the control of the sales division manager. But having area data enables the decision makers to restrict the additional environmental data search to that one geographic division.

Profit contribution figures are also commonly provided through accounting data, but in most situations they are not the most pertinent data available for fruitful evaluation of the marketing environment. Since contributions to profit are made up of sales and expenses, they must be broken down to determine which of the components may be causing a problem. Data must be examined to determine whether contribution deficiencies are caused by a revenue or a cost problem. The data may be further analyzed to determine the product, region, market territory, etc., that may be causing a problem.

Also of considerable aid to the marketing decision maker are ratios developed by the accounting department and/or the marketing administrative staff which can reveal highly specific and often significant deviations from the marketing objectives. These ratios enable the marketer to review continually the marketing plans in operation and to detect when meaningful deviations are taking place. Data used to construct the ratios may come from marketing operations reports in addition to accounting reports.

For example, data for a quarter may show expense account totals, as a percentage of that quarter's sales, to be ten percentage points above the figure for the corresponding quarter of the prior year. In the context of past operations of the firm this deviation is judged to be unusual and warrants further investigation. Breakdowns of the source data by sales district reveal two districts having unusually high expense-account-to-sales ratios. Further breakdowns identify the "offending" salespersons. Discussions with them reveal new customers settling into their territories with resultant intensified competition, hence the extra travel and meal expenses by the salespersons. Sales management may not only accept these explanations but may provide the "active" territories with additional sales and advertising support.

Accounting data provide the marketer with a type of environmental information available from no other source. Failure to employ accounting information to the fullest extent possible is often the fault of both the marketer and the accounting people. They do not speak the same language. The marketer, cognizant of the vagaries of the environment, is more willing to accept data that are not completely accurate, a position frequently misunderstood by financial and accounting people alike. Accounting records are not generally set up to serve marketing departments. Moreover, marketing people sometimes are insecure when working with financial accounting departments. Some accounting people may even see marketing as a marginal company activity, questioning its worth. These are not healthy attitudes for organizational members to hold.

It is essential that the marketing and accounting departments work in close harmony so that the needs of marketing can be efficiently met. Accounting data represent a wealth of environmental information, and the astute marketer will take full advantage of their availability.

Nonaccounting Data. The accounting department is not the sole information-gathering arm of an organization. Each operating department has its own data collecting, processing, and evaluating efforts. These nonaccounting data concern mainly nondollar measures of performance and activity. For example, the number of sales calls made is developed in the marketing group. Quality control data are produced in manufacturing.

Of great help to the marketer is current information on competitive moves and on the activities of various channels of distribution. What is the estimated share of market garnered by selected competitors? What are their pricing policies? How large are their sales organizations? What moves have been made recently by dealers and other middlemen? Are they altering their positions on certain types of promotion? Are their servicing policies being revised? Are they deviating from past pricing practices?

Such information can be gathered by company representatives and recorded systematically at designated time intervals. This backdrop information is essential as environmental data for marketing planning and decision making. Out of such information emerge new thoughts for planning, strategy formulation, and tactical actions. Small companies, with a limited number of customers, are usually in close touch with all aspects of their markets. The need for formalized efforts to gather marketing information is often not great. As companies increase in size, however, and their customers become more widely dispersed, the need for some systematic effort to collect meaningful information becomes more demanding. The large firm should eschew relying solely on secondhand data and informal methods of environmental data collections. It should employ a formal marketing intelligence and information system.

The sales department can be an auxiliary arm of the marketing intelligence activity. Salespeople are in touch with customers and middlemen daily, and their sales call reports can serve as a fruitful source of environmental data. Salespeople, however, tend to be biased in their reporting. Reasons for a lost sale, for example, cannot be objectively viewed by the salesperson who lost the order. Competition "had a lower price" or "had better design support from the factory" could typify comments from salespeople, not recognizing that they had failed to follow through by communicating with prospective customers' design engineers as well as with their purchasing agents. Customer attitudes are rarely reported accurately by salespeople. Moreover, special opinion surveys conducted by salespeople are often a poor use of a sales department's time. Such environmental data can usually be obtained more reliably and at less cost by using marketing research personnel. Their talents and skills properly used, sales personnel are valuable adjuncts to a marketing intelligence staff.

Externally Available Data and Information

An often-used categorization of data is that of primary and secondary. *Primary data* are those gathered by an organization or by designated agents (such as marketing research firms) for their own use, to resolve decision-problems, to control operations, etc. *Secondary data* have been compiled not by the using organization but by some external body, e.g., the Bureau of the Census. Secondary information is already available—someplace. Primary data, on the other hand, are usually thought of as problem-specific—data collected for some specific need, whether a recurring or a one-time need. Primary data result from a first-time collection effort.

Secondary data may have the word "published" added to it, which refers to existing data in some published form available to interested parties. This definition does not include marketing research studies which, even though published, were the result of primary data collection for the benefit of a relatively small number of possible users, usually the sponsors.

Published secondary information is almost without exception environmental in nature. Rare indeed are published secondary data employed in an actionable sense. Secondary information usually aids in describing a situation. For example, when the Social and Economic Statistics Administration of the Bureau of the Census issues a report on the composition of the urban population, it contributes to delineating urbanized areas. The characteristics of all persons living in urbanized areas, even though they live in places of differing population sizes, are presented. Such data describe a part of an environment. To some marketers this information is important. It may suggest altering an existing marketing plan. But there is little in the data that suggests what action to take.

State and federal government agencies are not the only sources of published secondary information. Professional and trade associations also compile and publish data related to their areas of interest. Not all trade association data are made available to the general public, of course. University research bureaus and commercial publishers, e.g., Rand-McNally, also are important sources of secondary information and data. In many instances the data they provide are specialized tabulations and interpretations of governmental data.

Secondary data, then, are a vital source of environmental information. Moreover, such data are low in cost to users and much of the secondary material, such as that gathered by the Bureau of the Census, is highly accurate. Therefore, it behooves the organization to make as effective and efficient use of this class of environmental information as possible, especially since it is relatively inexpensive to obtain.

Role of Marketing Research in Obtaining Environmental Data and Information

Marketing research is to the marketer what accounting is to the financial person. Both are information arms of the decision makers in these two areas. Decision makers utilize marketing research to provide both environmental and actionable data. Much of the marketing research employed for gathering environmental data is sponsored by the company itself since they will make use of the information. Such studies range from simple and inexpensive exploratory surveys to highly precise, national studies. In either case, the purpose of the data collection is to provide the decision makers with information that will lead to the uncovering of change and its causes.

Such data are also an aid to creativity. They suggest possible courses of action, revealing situations that may have gone unnoticed prior to the study. One metal producer, for example, conducted a study to determine whether consumption of kitchen aluminum wrap varied by age of the homemaker. This was one of a broad spectrum of data sought regarding the consumption of kitchen wrap products. The data are shown in Table 1-1.

Table 1-1 Aluminum Wrap Preferences Among Homemakers, By Age

	Homemakers by Age Brackets					
	18–25	26–35	36–45	46–55	55 +	Total
Prefer Wrap A	30%	32%	40%	51%	55%	39%
Prefer Wrap B	70%	68%	60%	49%	45%	61%
Number of Interviews	390	480	700	330	160	2060

Source: Reprinted, by permission of the publisher, from William F. O'Dell, *The Marketing Decision,* © 1968 by American Management Association, Inc., p. 101. All rights reserved.

Having this information does not lead to obvious action by the marketers. All the data do is establish that for some reason Wrap A has a greater following among older homemakers while the contrary is true of Wrap B. As Wrap A followers mature, if younger users are not attracted the long-run prospects for Wrap A would not be good. Revised goals for this product should therefore be set. It would be highly desirable to garner a larger share of the market among the younger homemakers. How this is to be accomplished has yet to be agreed upon. In fact, at the time these data were gathered, the alternative marketing actions had not yet been phrased. All the metal producer had at that moment were the environmental data uncovered by the survey.

Environmental marketing research data are sometimes gathered by manufacturers who supply such data to customers or prospective customers as a service. It is thought that such a gesture enhances the relationship between the supplier and the user. It is a subtle way of establishing sales contacts. A leading processor of malt, a major beer ingredient, conducted a study of beer consumption, the object being to determine the most efficient advertising appeals to be employed by brewers. The marketing or sales objective behind the study was to open the doors of top brewery management for the malt processor. Malt is purchased by the upper echelons of brewery managements, and the malting firm envisioned a survey of this type as an opportunity to meet with major malt buyers even though the subject of malt purchases was never mentioned during the presentation of the survey data to the brewers.

U.S. Steel Corporation conducted a study as a service to manufacturers of automatic washers and dryers which described the extent of servicing problems in the eyes of owners. One result of the study is shown in Table 1–2.

Table 1–2 Degree of Owner Satisfaction With Repair or Maintenance Service Required for Automatic Washers and Dryers

Service has been:

Much less than expected	47%
Somewhat less than expected	34
About as expected	2
Somewhat more than expected	12
Much more than expected	5
Number of owners interviewed:	2006

Source: "Consumer Attitudes Toward Automatic Washers and Dryers: A Summary Report," a study conducted for the U.S. Steel Corporation (Chicago, Ill.: Market Facts, Inc., 1965).

Such data do not lead directly to action by manufacturers; instead, the information portrays a situation which may lead to the posing of possible courses of action by the appliance companies.

Trade and industry associations also provide a variety of environmental marketing research data to their members. Indeed it is one of the principal reasons for their existence.

Virtually all of the mass marketers maintain elaborate marketing research departments, with some of them spending upward of several million dollars annually on data collection and analysis. Industrial firms, with less emphasis on marketing than consumer goods companies, tend to lag behind them in terms of marketing research expenditures and sophistication.

Most firms utilize a combination of in-house and outside marketing research to amass data and information concerning environmental change and its significance. Outside marketing researchers are also called upon to undertake studies yielding actionable data.

Commercial Research Firms. The users of research data—the decision makers—often conduct their own marketing research studies because they have a closer knowledge of the need for the data and because they feel it is unwise to assign the research to outside companies. However, no manufacturer maintains the kinds of specialized research facilities available through some outside professional commercial research organizations. The A. C. Nielsen Company, for example, maintains national store auditing services which measure the movement of merchandise through retail establishments. Such a facility is costly to maintain, and manufacturers share the cost of the Nielsen services by subscribing to the various indices (food, drug, TV, etc.). Most of the Nielsen data can be classified as environmental in that the marketing alternatives have not yet been formed when the data are presented to subscribers. Such decision options are posed after the data have been received and interpreted.

Another type of outside data collection facility is the national consumer mail panel, such as those maintained by Market Research Corporation of America (MRCA), National Family Opinion (NFO), and Market Facts, Inc. These panels are comprised of many thousands of families or households that have agreed to participate in certain types of studies. MRCA gathers food, drug, and other information at the household level, reporting sales to subscribing firms with a variety of cross tabulations (by age of homemaker, economic level of family, brand loyalty, etc.). Market Facts, Inc., through its Consumer Mail Panels Division, corresponds with some 70,000 families who participate in special studies, such as attitudinal research and product testing. Because of constant participant screening, high response rates are obtained with these panels. Market Facts, Inc., typifies the so-called "full-service house" because in addition to mail panels, it conducts studies by telephone, personal interview, and store auditing.

Some commercial research firms specialize in highly quantitative radio and television ratings. American Research Bureau conducts nationwide telephone and diary surveys to establish viewership and listenership in many cities. National data are also issued. The Nielsen ratings are widely known and used by the broadcast media, in some cases as actionable data—i.e., a TV series may be dropped due to its ratings having fallen below some pre-set level.

Other research firms specialize in one particular phase of marketing research. Motivation research is often conducted by firms employing sociologists and psychologists, such as Social Research, Inc. *Motivation research* is a broad term, but is defined here as that information collection method employing the completely unstructured interview and embracing the small, nonprobability sample. Almost without exception, motivational research data are environmental. The information is not conclusive in the sense that it leads to immediate action. Based on small, unrepresentative samples, the data are difficult to analyze and are usually not adequate for projecting to larger segments of the population. However, this type of research is an excellent source of ideas for developing marketing alternatives, such as new product types.

Advertising Research. Advertising agencies naturally conduct large volumes of advertising research. Such research is directed largely toward developing and testing ideas for new approaches to copy themes and obtaining demographic data for media decisions. The scope of the agency research work varies greatly from one firm to another, depending on relationships with clients and understanding of the areas in which the advertising agencies are expected to restrict themselves. Some types of advertising studies are normally not appropriate tasks for advertising agencies. For example, gathering data to aid in determining the size of the advertising budget is best left to the advertisers themselves in view of possible bias on the part of the advertising agencies.

Advertising media are excellent sources of environmental data. Publishers and broadcast media often conduct sophisticated and worthwhile research on audience characteristics and habits as a service to their advertisers. Some of these studies have sales overtones in that the media are desirous of influencing advertisers and prospective advertisers in their media selection. However, even with this obvious intent many such studies are useful as a source of environmental information.

INDIVIDUATING THE DECISION-PROBLEM

The word "individuate" does not enjoy widespread usage and so it strikes the reader's eye (and ear) as different. This is precisely the effect being sought in completing this chapter on identification of the central decision-problem. The reader has been urged to articulate the decision-problem explicitly and to describe it clearly in relation to the environment, to set it apart, to differentiate it from other, less correct expressions of the problem at hand; in other words, to *individuate* the decision-problem.

Here are some additional considerations in carrying out that effort.

At some point this question must be raised: Is the problem at hand a marketing decision-problem? Or at least is it a decision-problem in which marketing has an interest? Clearly, if the situation requires strong attention by some other functional area within the firm, then the marketing group should concentrate on making that fact known. The marketing manager should certainly not presume to make decisions outside the marketing department's domain. This, of course, does not rule out contributory participation in such decisions. For example, the inability of the production department to meet scheduled customer delivery dates is not a problem within marketing's jurisdiction, although the marketing department will have considerable interest in its proper resolution. By the same token, when decisions arise in other areas of the firm that impinge upon marketing, then marketing management should participate. Likewise, it is sometimes the case, and unfortunately so, that the budget amount for advertising is set by financial management alone at some percentage of sales (expected or historical). Marketing must provide input to this resource allocation decision. Nothing can hinder the execution of decisions more than the failure to involve those who will participate in their implementation and be held responsible for success.

Another question that should be asked is: Who should make the final choice of the action to be taken? Having identified the decision-problem, what levels of the organization should be involved in its subsequent handling and ultimate resolution? A decision involving whether or not to hold a "cents-off" sale to trim inventories might be made, for example, by a brand manager. A decision to expand plant facilities so as to permit the manufacture of a new product would clearly involve an executive committee. It is usually obvious as to whether the choice situation deals with day-to-day, operational decision-problems or rather with long-run strategic issues. As noted in the introductory chapter, as the decision-problem becomes less of the former and more of the latter then resolution moves more into the domain of top management.

Continuing the reference to the introductory chapter: Is the identified decision-problem plan-related or pressure-related, i.e., is it a brush fire that needs dousing? How much of a threat is it? Or, as a Chinese proverb would suggest, is the apparent obstacle really an opportunity in disguise?

The reader has been prodded in this chapter to ask questions for which answers may not be immediate or complete. But striving to obtain them keeps the process rolling. It may well turn out that in subsequent steps of the problem-solving, decision-making effort revisions of the initial definitions will come about. But at least there will be something of substance with which to work.

APPRECIATING THE SUBTLETIES OF THE DECISION SITUATION

A recognized fact of organizational life is that there will be some managers and executives who vie for personal prestige and power. This striving can be dysfunctional for the organization. It can produce intraorganizational conflict. As a result, decision-problem resolution can be affected at each step of the process. Problems may be "manufactured" to make one manager look bad or to create an opportunity for another to look good or simply more visible. The formulation of alternatives could favor one area unnecessarily over another. Data and information could be presented in a biased manner in order to favor a particular choice. Marketing research personnel, both those in house and the outside contractor, can get caught in the middle of these situations. Accordingly, they should be wary of research requests based on political motives.

By the same token, sincere attempts to be objective in the decision-making/problem-solving process can produce ill will. One individual may feel that the decision-problem has been adequately identified when, in fact, a closer examination by another person reveals it to be something else. Improperly handled, such situations could produce misunderstanding and "ruffled feathers."

All of the above reinforce the concern for gathering relevant data and information. At the same time, the warning message is: Whatever the approach to a decision-problem, do not neglect the importance of behavioral factors—individual, interpersonal, and group.

SUMMARY

This chapter opened with a display of the basic flowchart. It closes with a repeat of that diagram, embellished with the subsidiary steps involved in identifying the central decision-problem. Each subsequent chapter will open and close with similar flowcharts.

The basic messages of this chapter are that change is the key to identifying decision-problems, that environmental data should be utilized, and that explicitness and individuation in expressing the decision-problem will speed its proper resolution.

QUESTIONS FOR DISCUSSION

1. Distinguish between planned and unplanned change. Give an example of each within the context of a current business situation.
2. What is the conceptual relationship between unplanned change and the external environment?
3. What are the characteristics of environmental data? Actionable data? How can one readily differentiate between the two types? Discuss the sources of such data.
4. Why, in general, can environmental data be less precise than actionable data? Why does the Census Bureau strive to develop highly precise data, even though virtually all of the data can be considered environmental in nature?
5. Why is it desirable to be able to differentiate between environmental and actionable data?
6. What steps can be taken by a company's marketing management to increase the use of accounting data in the marketing decision-making and problem-solving areas?
7. Explain the role of marketing research in the decision-making/problem-solving process.

SUGGESTED READINGS

Dewey, John. *How We Think.* Boston: D. C. Heath, 1910.

Eilon, S. "What Is a Decision?" *Management Science,* Vol. 16, No. 4 (December, 1969), pp. B-172—B-189.

Emory, C. William, and Powell Niland. *Making Management Decisions.* Boston: Houghton Mifflin Co., 1968. Chapters 1–4.

Ewing, David W. "Discovering Your Problem-Solving Style." *Psychology Today* (December, 1977), pp. 69–70ff.

Kepner, Charles H., and B. B. Tregoe. *The Rational Manager.* New York: McGraw-Hill Book Company, 1965.

Larson, Richard L. "How to Define Administrative Problems." *Harvard Business Review,* Vol. 40, No. 1 (Jan.-Feb., 1962), pp. 68–80.

Livingston, J. Sterling. "Myth of the Well-Educated Manager." *Harvard Business Review,* Vol. 49, No. 1 (Jan.-Feb., 1971), pp. 79–89.

MacCrimmon, K. R., and D. W. Taylor. "Decision Making and Problem Solving." Chapter 32 in *Handbook of Industrial and Organizational Psychology,* edited by M. D. Dunnette. Chicago: Rand-McNally and Company, 1976.

Pounds, William F. "The Process of Problem Finding." *Industrial Management Review,* Vol. 11, No. 1 (Fall, 1969), pp. 1–19.

Smith, J. S. "Problem Analysis." *The Statistician,* Vol. 13, No. 1 (1963), pp. 17–32.

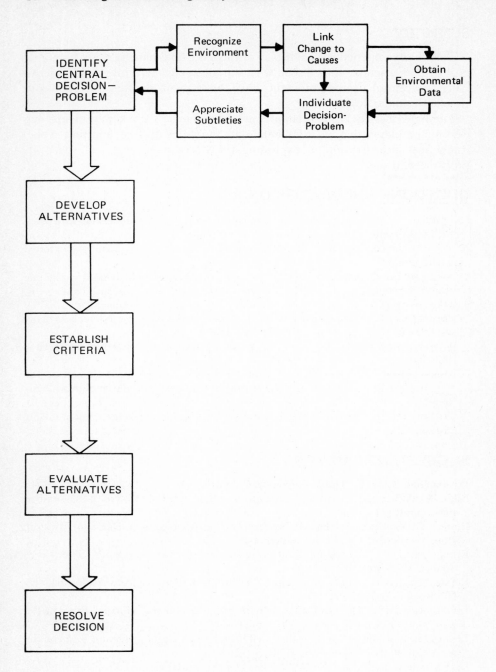

Summary Flowchart, Chapter 1

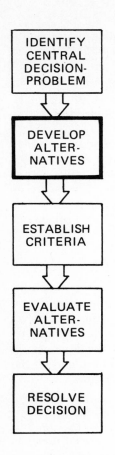

2

Developing Alternatives

> "Alternatives do not usually have the courtesy to parade themselves in rank order on the drill ground of the imagination."
>
> —Kenneth E. Boulding

In Chapter 1 it was pointed out that the term "decision-problem" was chosen because it reflected the dual requirements present in most business situations—a need first to specify alternative solutions and then to choose one for implementation. As the quotation above suggests, the specification of alternatives is not usually an easy task. But it is a task of paramount importance, for if the "best" option does not get listed as a possibility in the first place, it can never become the chosen course of action.

PREPARING THE INITIAL LIST OF ALTERNATIVES

Starting an initial list of alternatives is generally not too difficult; the process of decision-problem identification seems to readily induce thought about possible solutions. For example, sluggish sales of a company's electric lawn trimmer, amidst a generally strong market, may lead to comparisons with competitive trimmers. The comparison may reveal lack of or deficiency in several product features (cord length, handle placement, etc.). These findings lead naturally to candidate alternatives related to additions and improvements of specific product features. Or the decision-problem may be one for which a "response repertoire" has been prepared under strategic planning efforts. An example here might be a "cents-off" deal by competition on a product they had not used deals on before, causing the company to respond in kind.

While starting the initial compilation is not difficult, completing the list is. Producing a complete set of alternative actions is vital to successful decisions. Failure to include all possible, pertinent actions is a common error and a serious one.

Just as there is a backdrop, an environment, for the changes and causes that give rise to decision-problems, so too is there a context in which alternative solutions are generated. Whether the decision-problem is one originating within the marketing planning process, or whether it originates from a brush-fire or bright-idea context, overall organizational objectives and philosophy constitute the basic setting in which candidate solutions will appear. It is from these objectives and goals that strategies, tactics, and actions flow.

The Framework of Objectives

The marketing executive pursues the goal of gaining maximum profits within a framework of basic objectives established by the top management of the organization. This framework of basic objectives shapes the alternatives available to the marketing decision maker. These basic objectives typically relate to: (1) the position in the industry sought by the firm, (2) the degree of operational stability desired, (3) the image the firm desires to project, and (4) the firm's management philosophy. These factors are described as follows:

1. *Industry Position.* Industry position refers to: (1) the function the organization wishes to perform—whether retail, wholesale, manufacturing, or service; (2) the extent of diversification—whether to handle few or many products; (3) the quality level of its product—whether it will be a Tiffany's or a Woolworth's; and (4) the size of operation desired—whether to be a small or a large company.
2. *Operational Stability.* The degree of operational stability a firm may enjoy relates to the level of progressiveness, aggressiveness, and willingness to take technological and entrepreneurial risks and to share ownership control.
3. *Image.* The image of a firm as a "good citizen" is suggested by its sense of social responsibility as reflected in its community relations, its acceptance of social and economic responsibilities, its customer service, its supplier contact, and its regard for employees. For example, the Xerox Corporation explicitly strives for a "good citizen" image.
4. *Management Philosophy.* Finally, management philosophy has to do with such things as centralization versus decentralization, quality of key personnel, extent of research and development activities, and the strictness of supervisory control.

The composite of these factors has been referred to as the "character" of the firm.[1] Choices concerning the preceding objectives are determined in many

---

[1] William H. Newman, "Basic Objectives Which Shape the Character of a Company," *Journal of Business*, XXVI (1953), pp. 211–23.

ways, often involving the personal preferences of top management. However, "character" component choices are also constrained by their effect on profit. The important point to emphasize is that there is an existing framework of previously made decisions within which the marketing manager must make choices.

Basic or superordinate objectives reflected in the firm's character are too often taken for gospel ("We've always done things this way."). Environmental change can leave the firm behind if it refuses to change. The planning process is designed to bring scrutiny to organizational objectives and capabilities with the aim of enabling the firm to adapt to change.

The initial stages of planning take place within situations so varied that it is difficult at best to generalize as to their nature. No two companies face identical situations. Even though they may be in the same industry, encounter the same competition from outside the industry, and are virtually identical in size, they live in total environments so different that their forward planning could well result in completely dissimilar corporate objectives. To illustrate, Companies A and B both produce and market a nonferrous metal sold largely to manufacturers of items made of that metal. Somewhat suddenly, a plastic is developed that results in many of their customers switching to this nonmetallic material. Neither Company A nor B is initially prepared to produce the plastic within the near future. Thus, both firms appear to be living in the same external environment and seem to be facing similar problems. This may be true, but how each adjusts depends on their respective characters. Company A, let us assume, has a highly talented research and development department with an ample budget. Company B is not so fortunate, lacking the R&D skills and the funds. The firms have different capabilities and different resources which could therefore result in completely dissimilar planning and objectives. Company A, engaging in the planning effort of "thinking ahead," sets an objective of entering into plastics production and meeting its new, "outside" competitors head on. Company B, reviewing the situation, feels that it is more prudent to expand its marketing effort and compete more aggressively with the plastics producers as well as with Company A. The objectives of the two hypothetical companies are quite different. One company sets the objective of diversifying into plastics; the other company's objective is that of meeting the plastics competition with its current product—two different strategic responses to one environmental change.

A company that states an objective is really saying, "This is where we want to be three years from now. This is our goal." Company A could be saying that its objective or goal is to enter plastics production and at the end of three years to garner a dollar sales volume in plastics that will more than offset their newly acquired costs and losses in metal orders. Company B's aim might be to add distribution facilities, thereby reducing delivery time, to gain a competitive edge.

Much corporate marketing planning emerges, however, from regular reviews and formalized efforts, rather than resulting from new and unpredicted situations as in the case of Companies A and B.

Developing Strategy

Setting objectives pertains to agreeing on the company's destination at a given point in time; i.e., where the company wants to be two, four, or ten years hence. Developing strategy locates the broad road down which the company will travel in order to arrive at its destination. In other words, a company's strategy specifies those principles that will guide it toward the desired goal.

Structuring objectives in a hierarchical fashion helps in tying objectives to strategy. Figure 2-1 illustrates how marketing objectives and strategy can flow from corporate aims.

Strategy vs. Tactics

As with determining objectives or goals, decisions involving strategy are not mechanistic in nature. They do not involve the actual spending of marketing funds. Instead, they lay out the broad plan for achieving the goal or goals and allocate the necessary funds. In contrast, the tactical decision is where action is taken and the funds being made available are spent. In one sense, this is the chief differentiation between strategic and tactical decisions. The former allocate resources; the latter expend them. *Strategy* is a part of planning, setting of broad principles, obtaining agreement on an approach—all the while recognizing corporate objectives and the resources available. *Tactics* spell out the actions to be taken to achieve the goals via the strategic route set forth by the planners. With the objective of survival in an energy-constrained environment, automotive manufacturers opt strategically to reduce car size. Tactically this decision requires spending money on new designs, on plant and equipment conversions, and on advertising efforts.

Suppose that Company A in the metal-producing business decides that it will seek a 20 percent growth in both sales and profits during the forthcoming four years. That is the objective, the goal. What strategy will be employed to achieve this goal? Management agrees that the company will diversify into the production and marketing of plastics. More specifically, management states that half of this growth will come from their entry into plastics. Company management has now recognized a new environment, set its goals, and agreed on diversification as its strategy. The funds needed were allocated, but at this point were not expended. The spending would be reserved for the tactical decision to follow: acquiring plastics production capacity, training workers and salespeople, advertising, etc. Some writers prefer to label these tactical decisions as *operating* or *administrative* decisions.

Strategic planning establishes the broad direction in which the firm wishes to go. Tactics may be viewed as the specific steps needed to proceed along the route and to get back on it when diverted by outside forces. To illustrate, if established strategy says that the firm will be price competitive and a competitor of consequence runs a special sale using a lower price, then the firm will have to consider a response in kind. Ideally strategic marketing planning should be comprehensive enough to provide the marketing manager with a clear array of responses. In actuality, given the diversity of possible environmental changes,

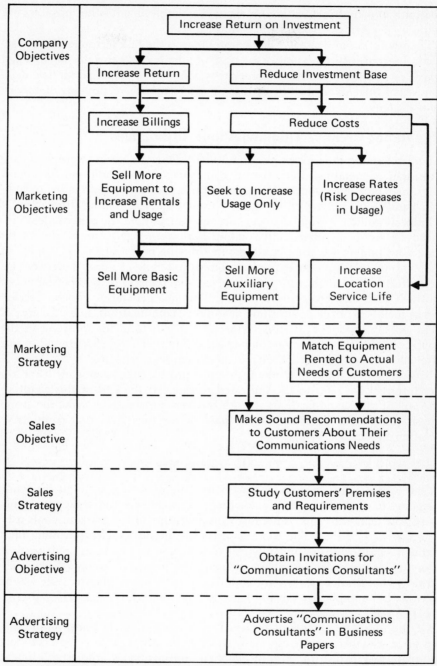

Figure 2–1   *Hierarchy of Objectives for the Interstate Telephone Company*

anticipation of and preparation for every new development is not possible; nor would it be a rational expenditure of effort.

The resolution of strategic decision-problems is the task of top-level management. In contrast, operating or tactical problems can generally be handled lower down in the organizational hierarchy. *The key in making a tactical decision is that the choice must be consistent with established company or department strategy.*

Stimulating Creative Thinking About Alternatives

Understanding the environment and identifying the decision-problem calls for insight. Generating alternatives demands creativity in addition to insight. Thus, marketers have sought ideas, techniques, etc., that would enhance individual and group creative efforts in the formulation of marketing alternatives.

Properly guided, a group can generate more ideas than the sum of ideas produced by group members acting alone. *Brainstorming* is one of the better known techniques for stimulating group thinking on problems. The spirit of brainstorming is to produce an uninhibited, free flow of ideas. To encourage such efforts, all criticism is suppressed. Negative remarks by one person about another's idea discourage contributions. The idea generation process accelerates as members of the group think of variants, combinations, spin-offs, etc., of ideas already produced. In this connection it is helpful for someone in the group to record the suggestions on a blackboard or on a flip chart for all to see. After all ideas are expressed, then critical evaluation can begin.

Several modifications of the brainstorming process have been made. (For further information, refer to the suggested readings at the end of this chapter.) The aim of these modifications, as with the basic process, is to make the group a positive force for creativity, rather than the negative force that committees are often criticized as being.

Marketing Alternatives: The Marketing Mix

One of the major mnemonic devices used by marketers to recall the many categories in which alternative marketing actions may be undertaken is the notion of the marketing mix. A popular capsule version of the marketing mix is E. J. McCarthy's "4 Ps."[2] The four elements are: product, place (meaning both channels of distribution and physical distribution), promotion, and price. A more detailed specification of the elements of the marketing mix is that provided by Neil Borden (shown in Figure 2–2). (Later in this chapter issue will be taken with the implication in Borden's list that research is a *marketing* alternative. It is not.)

Of the four components of the marketing mix—product, place, promotion, and price—the first two are especially strategic in nature. That is, both product and place will involve the firm in major commitments; e.g., the establishment and operation of a new production facility or the negotiation and running of a

---

[2] E. Jerome McCarthy, *Basic Marketing: A Managerial Approach* (6th ed.; Homewood, Ill.: Richard D. Irwin, 1978), pp. 39–43.

Product planning. Policies and procedures relating to:
Product lines to be offered—qualities, design, etc.
The markets to sell—to whom, where, when, and in what quantity
New product policy—research and development program

Pricing. Policies and procedures relating to:
The level of prices to adopt
The specific prices to adopt (odd-even, etc.)
Price policy—one price or varying price, price maintenance, use of list prices, etc.
The margins to adopt—for company, for the trade

Branding. Policies and procedures relating to:
Selection of trademarks
Brand policy—individualized or family brand
Sale under private brand or unbranded

Channels of Distribution. Policies and procedures relating to:
The channels to use between plant and consumer
The degree of selectivity among wholesalers and retailers
Efforts to gain cooperation of the trade

Personal Selling. Policies and procedures relating to:
The burden to be placed on personal selling and the methods to be employed in (1) the manufacturer's organization, (2) the wholesale segment of the trade, (3) the retail segment of the trade

Advertising. Policies and procedures relating to:
The amount to spend—i.e., the burden to be placed on advertising
The copy platform to adopt, (1) product image desired, (2) corporate image desired
The mix of advertising—to the trade, through the trade, to consumers

Promotions. Policies and procedures relating to:
The burden to place on special selling plans or devices directed at or through the trade
The form of these devices for consumer promotions, for trade promotions

Packaging. Policies and procedures relating to:
Formulation of package and label

Display. Policies and procedures relating to:
The burden to be put on display to help effect sales
The methods to adopt to secure display

Servicing. Policies and procedures relating to:
Providing service needed

Physical Handling. Policies and procedures relating to:
Warehousing
Transportation
Inventories

Fact Finding and Analysis. Policies and procedures relating to:
The securing, analysis, and use of facts in market operations

Source: Neil H. Borden, "The Concept of the Marketing Mix," reprinted from the *Journal of Advertising Research,* Vol. 4, No. 2 (June, 1964). Copyright © 1964 by the Advertising Research Foundation.

Figure 2–2   Elements of the Marketing Mix of Manufacturers

new channel of distribution. Note that the commitments are internal and external, pecuniary and psychological. Another way of saying this is that decisions concerning products and/or distribution tend to require long planning horizons.

The other two marketing mix elements—promotion and price—generally do not call for the magnitude of resource commitment nor the duration of commitment that product and place call for. In other words, they have short planning horizons. Note that price and promotion can be varied at the trade or intermediate level and/or at the final, consumer level.

The product life-cycle notion cited in Figure 2–3 has also been used by some as a conceptual device to trigger thinking about marketing actions. The cycle portrays the sales trajectory of a particular product or product class. A new brand of toothpaste may be at the introductory stage in *its* life cycle; toothpaste as a product *class* lies in the mature stage. Difficulties in precisely specifying and measuring life cycles have tended to make them conceptual rather than analytic notions. But they do force the marketer to recognize that the marketing mix has to change adaptively over time.

Agreed-upon strategy need not stifle creativity of the line managers. If the strategy dictates product innovation with emphasis on long-run consumer benefit rather than short-run consumer desires, the opportunities for innovativeness are many. When the brand manager is working within the constraints of a fixed marketing budget, coupled with planning statements on goals and strategy, creativity can be exhibited by developing an optimal marketing mix. What is the best approach to optimize price and advertising? Should the quality level of the product be lowered, the price reduced, and the advertising expenditures increased? The number of alternatives is virtually without limit. If the strategy is to enhance the "quality image" of the brand, the lowering of the product quality would be eliminated from consideration. If the marketing strategy calls for the overcoming of a known communications gap between the company and the consumer, greater reliance on selected types of advertising (e.g., direct mail) would be given serious consideration at the tactical level. Whatever the choice, the marketing mix must always be in keeping with corporate policy and marketing strategy.

REFINING THE INITIAL LIST OF ALTERNATIVES

If a creative approach has indeed been followed in producing the initial list of alternatives, then that list is likely to contain some very diverse items. A structure or order should therefore be imposed on the creatively generated alternatives. Refinement of the list is necessary so that the decision makers have a finite, internally consistent set of candidate choices for the decision-problem at hand. Without such a refined list it would be difficult to resolve the problem satisfactorily. Preparing the initial list required free-form thinking; refining it calls for systematic thinking. The following are some points to consider in the distillation process.

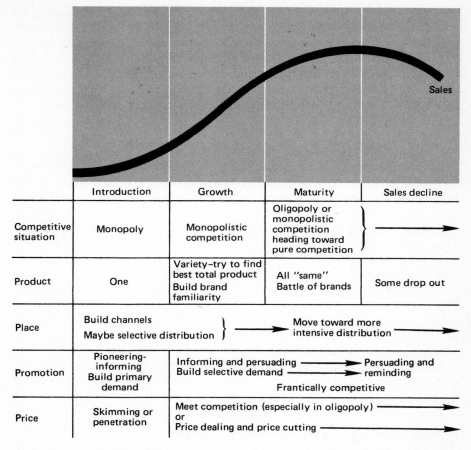

	Introduction	Growth	Maturity	Sales decline
Competitive situation	Monopoly	Monopolistic competition	Oligopoly or monopolistic competition heading toward pure competition } ——————▶	
Product	One	Variety–try to find best total product Build brand familiarity	All "same" Battle of brands	Some drop out
Place	Build channels Maybe selective distribution } ————▶		Move toward more intensive distribution ——————▶	
Promotion	Pioneering-informing Build primary demand	Informing and persuading ————▶ Persuading and Build selective demand ————▶ reminding Frantically competitive		
Price	Skimming or penetration	Meet competition (especially in oligopoly) ——————▶ or Price dealing and price cutting ——————▶		

Source: E. Jerome McCarthy, *Basic Marketing* (6th ed.; Homewood, Ill.: Richard D. Irwin, Inc., © 1978), p. 572.

Figure 2–3   Typical Changes in Marketing Variables Over the Course of the Product Life Cycle

1. Are the alternatives collectively exhaustive?
2. Are the alternatives independent of one another?
3. Are the alternatives mutually exclusive?

Alternatives Should Be Collectively Exhaustive

As has been pointed out, a common yet serious error made by decision makers is to produce an incomplete list of alternatives. The use of a matrix format can aid decision makers in avoiding that error.

Matrix tabulation is one way of assuring that possible alternatives are exhaustively considered in compiling an initial list of marketing actions. Figure 2–4 illustrates this approach using a basic example in which major avenues of growth are being studied. The major themes of the initial list here deal with markets (or market segments) and with products (or services). A successful initial list generation will yield entries for *each* and *every* cell in the matrix. The "standard" approaches that match up with the cells illustrated are listed below the example matrix. (Clearly, more elaboration is possible.) Matrix formats should be tailored to the type of marketing problem under consideration.

Alternatives Should Be Independent

Alternatives should be examined for interrelationships. Does the performance of one require the prior performance of another; i.e., is one alternative predicated upon another? (Company A in the earlier example has first to acquire plastics production capability before it can market plastics.) In addition to the necessity of sequencing some alternatives, it may be desirable to sequence others; i.e., to hold off action until some other essentially independent tasks are accomplished (for example, deferring the choice of a new product's name until after its price range has been determined).

Decision trees and network diagrams are useful devices for displaying the time sequence of decisions, actions, and events. Indeed, one of the prime values of these graphical tools is the demand they place on the user to be explicit about the sequence of actions and outcomes.

Figure 2–5 displays some of the decision situations and sequences created by a strategic decision to introduce a new food product. The diagram is based on the reported actual experience of one company. Decision situations spawned by the new product decision involve areas within as well as outside marketing.

Alternatives Should Be Mutually Exclusive

In addition to being collectively exhaustive, the refined set of alternative market actions must be mutually exclusive. If not, then the decision maker cannot logically make a single choice from the action set. The list of alternatives must be such that selecting one alternative automatically precludes selecting others. To increase price by ten cents or not to increase price are mutually exclusive alternatives; to increase price or reduce costs are not mutually exclusive alternatives, for increasing price does not prevent one from also reducing costs.

Alternatives must be mutually exclusive so that each can be evaluated properly on the criterion or criteria that will be used in making the choice. Mutual exclusiveness may be a difficult "rule" to follow in refining a list of complex alternatives. Subdividing the list into logical subgroups should be considered under these circumstances.

RECOGNIZING THE TRUE ROLE OF RESEARCH

A common mistake made in the formulation of a list of alternative marketing actions is to include "engage in some research" as an alternative. Research

	Present Products	New Products
Present Markets	1	2
New Markets	3	4

1. Increase use of present products in present markets.
   A. Increase current clientele's usage of the product.
      (1) Sell more units to existing customers.
      (2) Shorten the time it takes for a product to become obsolete.
      (3) Create and advertise new uses for the product.
      (4) Give price incentives for increased use.
   B. Attract buyers away from rival firms.
      (1) Increase promotional and sales efforts.
      (2) Establish sharper product (brand) differentiation.
      (3) Initiate price cuts.
   C. Attract nonusers to buy the product.
      (1) Induce trial use through free samples, cents-off coupons, and low introductory price offers to first-time buyers.
      (2) Create and advertise new uses.

2. Develop new products for present markets.
   A. Develop new features for existing products.
   B. Develop quality variations.
   C. Add new models and sizes.

3. Move to open up new markets for present products.
   A. Expand regionally, nationally, or internationally into new geographic areas.
   B. Broaden the product's appeal to new market segments.
      (1) Introduce new versions of the product to appeal to new classes of buyers.
      (2) Advertise in other types of media.
      (3) Distribute the product through other channels.

4. Develop/acquire new products for new markets.
   A. Enter into new businesses that are related to the firm's present business in terms of customer base, technology, or channels of distribution.
   B. Enter into businesses unrelated to present markets, technology, customer clientele, or channels of distribution.

Source: Extracted, with modifications, from Table 8–1 in Philip Kotler, *Marketing Management—Analysis, Planning, and Control* (2d ed.; Englewood Cliffs, N.J.: Prentice-Hall, Inc., © 1967), p. 237. Adapted by permission of Prentice-Hall, Inc., Englewood Cliffs, New Jersey.

Figure 2–4   Matrix Approach to Facilitate Exhaustive Listing of Alternatives— An Example

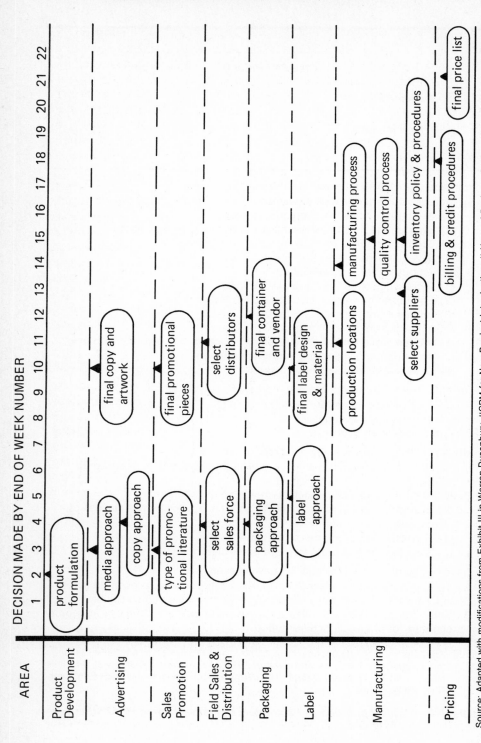

DECISION MADE BY END OF WEEK NUMBER

1 2 3 4 5 6 7 8 9 10 11 12 13 14 15 16 17 18 19 20 21 22

AREA

Product Development — product formulation

Advertising — media approach / copy approach / final copy and artwork

Sales Promotion — type of promotional literature / final promotional pieces

Field Sales & Distribution — select sales force / select distributors

Packaging — packaging approach / final container and vendor

Label — label approach / final label design & material

Manufacturing — production locations / manufacturing process / quality control process / select suppliers

Pricing — inventory policy & procedures / billing & credit procedures / final price list

Figure 2–5 **Some Decisions in a New Product Introduction**

activity is *not* a course of marketing action. Marketing research effort is, however, a course of action with regard to the decision-making/problem-solving process in general. To engage or not to engage in marketing research can be regarded as a *metadecision*, i.e., above and beyond the specific decision-problem under focus. Such metadecisions constantly crop up as one proceeds through the basic flowchart. They are concerned with progress through the chart itself. A separate decision-problem faces the decision maker if it is felt that there is inadequate relevant data and information at any stage of the process. Failure to recognize that "to do research" is not a marketing alternative is a failure to understand the basic flowchart.

In a very real sense, decisions concerning the gathering and analysis of marketing research data represent a "wheel within a wheel." That is, the director of the research effort faces a distinct decision-problem within the broader marketing decision-problem framework that dictated the need for the data. The researcher must pose the research alternatives (e.g., using a mail survey versus conducting personal interviews), set up the criteria, and then evaluate and act. The research options are related to the nature of the broader decision being made, but they pertain primarily to the data collection method that would be employed, the composition and size of the sample, whether or not to use the computer, which analytical technique to utilize, and a host of lesser options. The goal is to optimize the allocation of the research dollar. For the researcher to make the "wrong" decisions on the various research options could result in data that would, in turn, lead to marketing management taking a wrong course of action. The cost of this incorrect information would be difficult to calculate.

The role of marketing research with regard to the development of alternatives is to provide environmental data and information. For example, marketing research may be called upon to uncover the market response to action taken by a competitor in the hopes of spotting some weakness (e.g., an instant drink powder dissolves poorly in cold water) or triggering some entirely new idea on what to do. Just as marketing research may be called upon to provide additional information to clarify the nature of the decision-problem, marketing research can also serve as a catalyst in the formulation of alternatives.

Whatever role marketing research plays in the formulation of marketing alternatives, it must be remembered that "to conduct some research" is *not* one of those alternatives.

COMPILING THE FINAL LIST OF ALTERNATIVES

The overall aim in alternative-list preparation is to obtain a set of candidate courses of marketing action of the same "order"—be it strategic or tactical. Tactical alternatives will tend to be "variations of a theme," such as a spectrum of pricing possibilities. Strategic alternatives embrace a host of variables and so tend to be fewer in number—perhaps to the extent of being dichotomous; e.g., to introduce new product A or not to introduce it.

The generation of the initial list of alternatives is largely a creative task, with prejudging the relative worth of each alternative discouraged to stimulate a free flow of ideas. The refinement of alternatives, on the other hand, is largely an analytical task with the need for stringent applications of logic. This refinement of alternatives is designed to produce a final acceptable list that has been checked for exhaustiveness, independence, and mutual exclusivity. Admittedly this refinement requires a mental shifting of gears, but the transition must be made if the remainder of the decision-making/problem-solving process is to proceed in an effective, efficient fashion.

The importance of attentive completion of the procedures advocated in this chapter cannot be overemphasized. Failure to do so will raise innumerable difficulties in the measurement and evaluation of the final list according to the criteria established.

QUESTIONS FOR DISCUSSION

1. How can one determine the "character" of a firm?
2. How does setting objectives differ from developing strategy? How does the development of marketing alternatives relate to objectives and strategy?
3. Discuss the statement that in any organization tactical decisions must be consistent with strategic decisions.
4. What is the role of creativity in establishing marketing alternatives?
5. Explain why product and place—two components of the marketing mix—are strategic in nature.
6. Discuss procedures for refining a list of alternatives.
7. Why is marketing research activity not a course of marketing action?
8. Why must the alternatives be truly mutually exclusive? What complications arise in the decision-making process if they are not?
9. Assume you are a marketing manager. What recent government action has resulted in a new marketing environment? What alternatives would you suggest as an adjustment to the newly created environment?
10. The recognition of a new marketing environment can result in several decisions. Illustrate this schematically.

SUGGESTED READINGS

"B-School Buzzword: Creativity." *Business Week* (August 8, 1977), p. 66.

"Corporate Strategy." A regularly appearing section in *Business Week* beginning with the January 9, 1978, issue.

Gilmore, Frank F. "Formulating Strategy in Smaller Companies." *Harvard Business Review*, Vol. 49, No. 3 (May-June, 1971), pp. 71–81.

Gregory, Carl E. *The Management of Intelligence: Scientific Problem Solving and Creativity*. New York: McGraw-Hill Book Company, 1967.

Osborn, Alex. *Applied Imagination*, 3d ed. New York: Charles Scribner's Sons, 1963. (Source of the "brainstorming" approach to formulation of alternatives.)

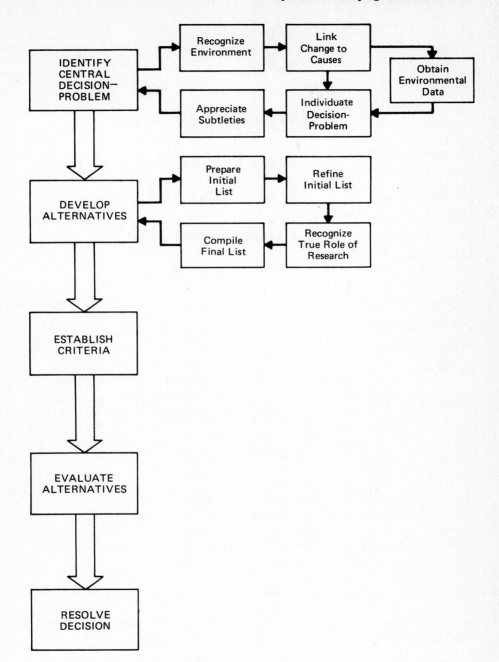

Summary Flowchart, Chapters 1–2

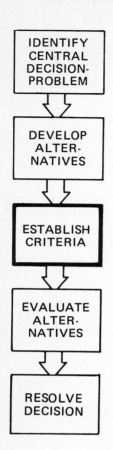

IDENTIFY
CENTRAL
DECISION-
PROBLEM

DEVELOP
ALTER-
NATIVES

ESTABLISH
CRITERIA

EVALUATE
ALTER-
NATIVES

RESOLVE
DECISION

3

Establishing the Criteria for Evaluating Alternatives

". . . it is not the attainment of the goal that matters, it is the things that are met along the way."
—Havelock Ellis

Given an agreed-upon, refined list of alternatives the next question to ask is: Which one is the best? "Best" according to what standard? How is "best" to be measured? How is each alternative to be judged? Should there not be an agreed-upon, predetermined definition of "best" for use in evaluating the expected outcome of each alternative? Yes, of course; and the basis for defining "best" constitutes the criterion for choice.

The role of criteria is to enable decision makers to discriminate among alternatives, singling out a preferred one. A given criterion establishes a standard against which each alternative is measured or scored. Such standards or criteria flow from the objectives and goals of the firm.

FOCUSING ON PROFIT AS THE CORE MARKETING CRITERION

Selecting the appropriate criterion for a given decision-problem is a mini-decision-problem in itself. It can be said that, at the core, there is but one criterion for marketing decisions in commercial enterprises—profit.

The profit motive is the most pervasive and persistent force underlying business behavior. It lies at the very core of corporate goals and objectives, despite occasional euphemistic re-expressions of corporate aims. Ideally, therefore, every marketing alternative should be evaluated as to its production of profit. However, there are several influences that make it difficult to employ profit directly as a criterion.

Influence of Environmental Uncertainty on the Profit Criterion

One principal difficulty is the uncertainty created by an unknown future environment. What the true state of affairs will be one year, five years, ten years, etc., from now is not perfectly known. The marketing decision maker must therefore try to anticipate what the future environment will be. Consideration should be given to the future legal environment, ecological environment, consumer environment (e.g., effect of consumer lobbies and consumer protection laws that may be passed), and any other areas that could have an effect upon future operations. (Review Figure 1–2 in this regard.)

One means of alleviating some of the uncertainty associated with the future environment is to use *expected profits* as a decision criterion. To arrive at expected profits, probabilities are assigned to the various states that might comprise the future environment. The profit payoff affiliated with each state is then multiplied by its respective probability and the results summed to yield an expected profit. (The reader may recognize this as an application of Bayes's rule. Additional discussion appears in Chapter 4.) Sketching out the various possible states of the future environment and attaching probabilities thereto is a very difficult task, requiring considerable subjective judgment. It is, nevertheless, one way to convert a decision setting under uncertainty to one with quantified risks.[1] The risks may be significant enough to cause retreat from an expected profit measure. Even if elaborate probability assessments are not made, managers are likely to talk of outcomes in terms of expected profits in recognition of the uncertainty involved.

Influence of Social Responsibility on the Profit Criterion

Corporate managements may sometimes appear to deviate from a profit maximization goal, such as when they support and assist community clean-up or employment programs. While there may be a short-term negative profit impact of such actions the firm is really taking the longer view. It recognizes that such efforts are important to the long-run social, physical, and economic order upon which the long-run survival of the firm and its customers depends. Hence the firm is not deviating from the pursuit of long-run profit maximization.

Obviously there may be occasions when a nonprofit consideration is the overriding factor for a particular decision, but in many cases, for the firm as a whole, such a factor will take the form of a *restraint* rather than a basic decision criterion. In other words, the particular decision may be made using the criterion of

---

[1] For a related approach see R. E. Linneman and J. D. Kennell, "Shirt-Sleeve Approach to Long-Range Plans," *Harvard Business Review*, Vol. 55, No. 2 (March-April, 1977), pp. 141–150.

maximization of expected long-run profits but subject to existing wage-price regulations or ecological impact restrictions.

In those situations where social responsibility criteria are utilized explicitly in the decision-making process, they are generally rationalized as being in the best long-run interests of the firm.

Full vs. Partial Optimization

Still another difficulty in using maximum long-run expected profit as a criterion concerns the ability of the firm and its managers to maximize (optimize) profit in the first place.

Full optimization requires the simultaneous consideration of all possible allocations of the firm's resources, that is, all possible alternatives and all possible allocations of the firm's resources among those alternatives. It requires the consideration of the possible impacts of all events (including those outside the firm and not under the decision maker's control and, perhaps, not yet known) and expectations about their occurrence. Obviously, full optimization is beyond the reach of ordinary mortals. The information processing capability of the human mind constrains decision makers' abilities to fully optimize. They can conceive only part of the possible array of alternatives and allocations and can carry their analyses only part way. Hence the realities of the situation dictate that only *partial optimization* can be achieved.

One illustration of the fact that decision makers recognize their inability to fully optimize is reflected in alternatives aimed at minimizing costs. For example, in considering alternative delivery systems analysts may have difficulty quantifying the revenue consequences (and, hence, the profit consequences). The competitive climate, however, may virtually dictate a logistics system that provides 48-hour delivery service. The decision analysis will, therefore, proceed with evaluating systems meeting the 48-hour specification in terms of lowest cost. Presumably the 48-hour capability assures satisfactory revenues, so by minimizing delivery-system costs profit contribution is "maximized."

Suboptimization

The previous example presents an opportunity to raise another issue—suboptimization. If, in establishing the minimum-cost, 48-hour delivery system, the production department has to employ higher amounts of overtime to meet new schedules then the added production costs may offset cost reductions achieved with the delivery scheme. Optimality in one area may, inadvertently, be gained at introduction of nonoptimality elsewhere; i.e., suboptimization may occur.

Suboptimization results from the process of choosing among a relatively narrow list of operations or resource allocations by a decision-making level other than the highest. Careful selection of criteria in suboptimization is both difficult and crucial. Unless the criteria are selected with great skill, a department may increase its efficiency in terms of its own test, yet decrease the firm's efficiency in terms of its total ability to make profits. Since decision making always succumbs to suboptimization, this negative complication is always present.

One reason that suboptimization presents these difficulties is that it may be computationally impossible for department heads to compare the alternatives facing them in terms of the criterion that would be appropriate for the entire firm. As the firm grows, the difficulties of coordination increase and genuine confusion can develop about objectives at departmental and lower levels. The chances of adopting inferior criteria multiply. If the sales department fights to maximize the ratio of sales per dollar of selling expense, or the production department tries to minimize cost per unit of output, or the production supervisor tries to minimize the number of defective units per month, it may cause the firm as a whole to sacrifice profits. Because suboptimization typically does not yield the best company-wide results, the term has come to be associated with ineffective management. *Suboptimization is a deficiency, however, only when the decision makers have the opportunity to optimize and do not take advantage of it.*

In general, the best criterion for the firm seems to be the maximization of gains minus costs. Suboptimization arises from and also creates difficulties in identifying costs of alternative programs or courses of action. The fact that lower administrative levels may allocate resources more or less independently increases the tendency to ignore the indirect effect of one operation on the costs (and profits) of the other operations. Assume the delivery department of a firm wanted to choose the cheapest way of achieving a given objective (e.g., 48-hour delivery service to all customers). They might consider costs only to that department, yet the delivery systems might have various impacts on the costs of other departments or operations. For example, the use of trucks for some deliveries might necessitate more expensive methods of shipping other items. To the individual department in charge of the operations, the impact on its costs are felt directly and are more likely to be considered than costs felt by other departments. To the firm as a whole, of course, the criteria for choosing among operations would involve the net impact of each operation on total revenue costs, and resultant profitability. Clearly it is important for suboptimizing decision makers to make the revenue-cost aspect of their criteria consistent with the revenue-cost aspect of higher level criteria.

It is not a simple matter to perceive a measure of gains for lower organizational levels that will harmonize nicely with objectives at higher levels. The reality of suboptimization fills this phase of criteria selection with problems. Additionally, suboptimization compounds the difficulties of measuring the gains from alternative operations. In measuring gains as well as costs, we need to take into account the indirect impact on operations other than the ones explicitly being compared. The operations under consideration may provide benefits to other departments. If a firm delivered its products with its own fleet of trucks rather than via air freight, it could presumably use the sides of trucks for advertising. These gains would occur in a different department and they might be substantial.

The fact that decision makers are forced to suboptimize helps lure them toward erroneous criteria. Therefore they must always keep a weather eye out for (1) the value of resources if they were used in other departments, (2) the impact of any one operation on the costs and gains from other operations, and (3) the consistency of the criteria employed with the aim of the firm as a whole. A constant awareness of higher level criteria is essential.

Partial optimization and suboptimization are terms that describe the actual nature of decision making in the real world. The inherent cognitive limitations of humans preclude global optimization. Humans cannot envision all alternatives, all criteria, all outcomes, and perform a mental calculus yielding the best choice. In an organizational context, this inability to take everything into account results in partial optimization and suboptimization.

The committee format is often used by organizations, admittedly not always effectively, as a vehicle for moving toward global, full optimization. Committee discussion can produce a wider list of possible alternatives as well as reveal the interplay among the goals and objectives of units in the organizational hierarchy. Mere use of committees and groups does not, in and of itself, guarantee that better decision making and problem solving will result. All one can hope for is that the decision-making effort will be directed toward fuller optimization rather than away from it. Sometimes the compromise choice reflects *satisficing* rather than optimizing. This means that the expected outcome of the chosen alternative, while not optimal, is at least satisfactory and, therefore, acceptable.

Partial optimization and suboptimization are facts of life regarding decision making, but they should not prevent one from trying to proceed in a more optimal fashion.

RELATING CRITERIA TYPE TO DECISION COST

Given the difficulty of bringing expected long-run profit to bear as a workable criterion in many decision-problems, some means for workable criteria selection need to be considered. A useful starting point is to recognize that criteria can be classified very broadly (and very quickly) into monetary or nonmonetary categories.

Monetary Criteria

Monetary criteria are obviously those expressable in dollar terms. According to Alderson and Green, monetary criteria should reflect:

a. *Future revenue and costs.* Since the market planner is dealing with future streams of revenues and costs, a method should be used in which the earnings of each alternative represent *added* earnings (or savings). If the alternatives consist of making a new investment and not making it, the estimates should reflect how revenues and costs would be expected to *change* as a result of making the investment or not making it.

b. *The time pattern of future earnings.* Because the market planner is usually considering alternative courses of action, the implementation of which can lead to different configurations of revenue and cost streams, a procedure should be capable of dealing with different time patterns of earnings and capable of converting these different time patterns to some common basis.

c. *The opportunity-cost principle.* Associated with the second characteristic is the fact that evaluation of alternative marketing plans usually assumes the availability of alternative uses for the firm's resources. A method should reflect both the opportunity cost of capital and the time value of money.

d. *The effect of taxes.* An investment method should reflect the net impact of tax laws on earnings.

e. *The effect of uncertainty.* In the actual world of decision making, all future revenue and cost streams represent outcomes dependent upon which alternative state of nature occurs. The method should reflect the probabilistic environment which the market planner faces.[2]

Financial, i.e., monetary, criteria that have been formulated and reflect some of the properties listed by Alderson and Green are displayed in Figure 3–1. Note that these criteria have particular data requirements, giving rise to the assumption that an information system exists within the organization that can produce reasonably accurate cost estimates and revenue predictions. This assumption is not to be accepted lightly. Accurate predictions of revenue stemming from alternative marketing actions are seldom available. When such predictions are available they are usually the result of considerable expenditure of time and money on research and market response model building. Usually there are considerable information gaps in the revenue-prediction effort—gaps that are often plugged by judgmental estimates. Those discomforted by such data needs and reliance on judgment in the use of monetary criteria will find some comfort in the fact that not all marketing decision-problems require the use of monetary criteria—nonmonetary criteria may be employed instead. (Just what the conditions are for such use will be discussed shortly.)

Nonmonetary Criteria

Many types of marketing decisions under certain circumstances can utilize nonmonetary criteria rather than financial or monetary ones. It is impossible to list completely such marketing criteria because they vary greatly from one set of marketing alternatives to another. A few of the most important nonmonetary marketing criteria are discussed in the following paragraphs. A discussion of when it is appropriate to use them follows.

Unit Sales. Sales as a nonmonetary criterion involves quantification of the volume of goods and services provided, e.g., number of cases sold, number of clients assisted. As is well known, some firms can become obsessed with maximizing sales volume, which can be expressed in dollar terms as well as in physical units. It does not follow, however, that pursuit of maximum sales automatically yields maximum profits.

Market Share. Share of market (also termed market position or market penetration) is generally defined as a firm's percentage of total industry sales. It is one obvious measure of the firm's relative success and, like sales volume, is often heavily employed in marketing decision making. Share maintenance is

---

[2] From Wroe Alderson and Paul E. Green, *Planning and Problem Solving in Marketing* (Homewood, Ill.: Richard D. Irwin, Inc., 1964), pp. 159–160.

METHOD	DEFINITION	COMMENTS
"NAIVE" METHODS		
Pay-back, Pay-out, Payoff Period	Time required for cumulative inflows to match investment.	1. Neglects benefits beyond pay-back point. 2. Neglects time value of money. (See Discounted Pay-back Period.)
Return on Original Investment	$\dfrac{\text{Average Net Annual Income}}{\text{Original Investment}}$	1. Ignores time value of money. 2. Distorted by extremes. 3. In effect, assumes perpetual benefits.
Return on Average Investment	$\dfrac{\text{Average Net Annual Income}}{\text{Average Investment}}$	1. Neglects time value of money. 2. Distorted by extremes. 3. Better as a performance measure after investment is made than as an investment decision criterion.
Rate of Return (Discounted ROI) (Investor's Method)	That annual interest rate which equates the present value of the net benefit stream to the investment required.	1. Implicitly assumes proceeds can be invested at the same rate of return as whole project. (See Modified DCF.) 2. Result is compared to a "standard" for Go/No Go.

BASED ON TIME VALUE OF MONEY CONCEPT		
Net Present Value	Benefit stream is discounted to reference time at preselected interest rate. Result is compared to investment. If net is positive, invest.	1. Problem is to get a valid discount rate, e.g., cost of capital, return on all investments. 2. When comparing projects, fails to distinguish the different scales of investment involved.
Profitability Index (Benefit-Cost Ratio)	$\dfrac{\text{Discounted Benefit Stream}}{\text{Discounted Investment}}$	1. Permits discrimination of alternatives (i.e., remedies #2 under Net Present Value above).
Modified Discounted Cash Flow	a. Compute PV of investment stream at "standard" rate. b. Compute Future Value of proceeds at the rates they can actually earn. c. Find the rate which equates a and b.	1. Avoids the implicit assumption concerning reinvestment of proceeds at project rate that occurs in the Investor's Method.
Discounted Pay-back Period	That time length of the benefit stream, when compounded at the chosen rate, yields the original investment.	1. An auxiliary criterion. 2. Discounted pay-back period is less than conventional pay-back period.

Figure 3-1 Types of Financial Analysis Criteria

often an expressed goal. Share maximization may be a disguised form of volume maximization.

Consumer Attitude. Consumer attitude is frequently employed as a decision criterion on the assumption that a relationship exists between favorable consumer attitude toward a specific brand and its sales. The supposition is that if a particular marketing alternative, such as an advertising theme, increases the favorable attitude of consumers toward a particular brand, then this alternative is better than another one that did not cause as great a shift. While the precise relationship between attitude change and sales remains nebulous, most marketers feel that effecting a measurable improvement in consumer attitude is a real achievement. Hence attitude change often is deemed an adequate marketing criterion.

Consumer Awareness. The extent to which consumers, dealers, or other channel participants recall a particular product, service, brand, or marketing effort is often employed as a marketing criterion, for much the same rationale as in using attitudes. It is measured by the degree to which those comprising the market can remember the item in question. Decision makers in advertising, especially those involved with media and copy, frequently employ this criterion.

Other Examples. The ability of one advertising campaign as opposed to another to produce written inquiries is frequently a highly precise measure of the relative productivity of alternative efforts. Coupon-redemption percentages are often employed as a measure of the worth of alternatives under consideration.

In other marketing decision areas, such as action aimed at increasing dealer business, the criterion might be the percentage increase in pedestrian traffic at a particular point, such as the dealer's showroom. Finally, consumer-stated intention to buy is sometimes employed as a criterion in determining which products to market. The marketer makes the assumption that the consumers' expression of purchase likelihood adequately foretells a product's chance of sales and profits success, i.e., that there is a direct connection between consumers' intention-to-buy statements and their actual purchase behavior.

Selecting Criteria Type

It is essential that criteria be specified in such a manner that, when the necessary relevant data are obtained, the alternative to be chosen will be indicated unequivocally to the decision maker. The specific criterion selected may be stated in monetary or nonmonetary terms, depending upon the ability to predict the outcomes associated with each specific alternative. The selection of criteria is thus directly related to the nature or type of decision being made as reflected by the agreed-upon set of marketing alternatives. A useful two-way classification scheme for decisions, relative to their cost nature, is according to whether they are identical-cost decisions or diverse-cost decisions.[3]

---

[3] Further discussion of cost character may be found in William F. O'Dell, *The Marketing Decision* (New York: American Management Association, Inc., 1968), Chapter 7. The discussion of identical-cost and diverse-cost decisions is adapted for inclusion here with permission of the American Management Association.

Identical-Cost Decisions. *Identical-cost decisions* are those in which the agreed-upon set of alternatives have identical costs. Media selection decisions, for example, would involve alternatives of varying cost. But a decision concerning which copy theme to employ would involve alternatives of equal cost, since advertisement production costs are not related to what is said therein.

To continue with this example, suppose an advertising manager is considering two basic copy themes. In selecting the criterion for this decision, the decision maker need not be concerned with a precise measurement of how much more profitable one alternative is than another. True, profits are the core criterion. However, in identical-cost decisions a measurement of the relative profitability of alternatives is not necessary (and may be hard to obtain). If the alternatives have been narrowed to specific advertising themes, and these are the only alternatives now under discussion, the advertising manager need not consider profits as the criterion at all. Instead, some other criterion, such as consumer "preference," could be introduced, the standard assumption being that the theme that pulls the greater number of "preferences" will generate greater sales and profits than the other. It would be interesting, of course, to know the relative profitability of each of the themes under consideration, but the funds spent to determine relative profitability would likely be an economic waste.

Even the preference criterion can be refined, and probably should be since "preference" is an ambiguous term. If the advertised product is, for example, a building material such as flooring or ceiling tile usually purchased jointly by husband and wife, attitude measurement of both the male and female market would be relevant. On the other hand, if the advertised product is almost always purchased by the female family head only, the relevant information as implied by the criterion would undoubtedly relate to the female market. Again, the controlling thought is that profit is not the necessary criterion when the marketing alternatives have identical costs. One must know only which alternative is better *in terms of the stated criterion.* It is not even necessary to know how much better one alternative is than another, although this type of information is usually available as a result of the research providing the data for selecting the best alternative. Additionally, such information is desirable to insure that the differences between alternatives are more than the estimated measurement errors.

Diverse-Cost Decisions. *Diverse-cost decisions* are those in which the execution of one marketing alternative will cost more than that of another alternative. In the diverse-cost decision the principal concern becomes how much better one marketing alternative is than another. And it is obviously preferable to know this in dollar terms. When alternatives have dissimilar costs, the marketing manager must be able to develop a decision criterion that will provide information as to how much better one alternative is than another, taking costs into account.

Diverse costs can take many forms. Most often they constitute what are termed *controllable marketing costs.* In many instances profits can be increased by boosting these controllable marketing costs. Increased selling effort, additional advertising, wider geographic distribution, and a more expensive package are examples of controllable costs which can enhance profits—without increases in selling price. The simple rationale supporting an increase in controllable costs is that the additional revenue from greater sales will more than compensate for the higher costs.

When marketing alternatives embrace diverse, controllable marketing or product costs, it is desirable to use profit (monetary) criteria. The marketer is thus required to predict the sales resulting from varying levels of the particular variable under consideration—two or three or four levels of advertising effort, a package which is more expensive than another, or an increase in the number of salespeople. While profit is the ultimate criterion, the key unknown here is revenue. Because revenue is a function of unit sales and price, the relevant data sought are unit sales. At this point it is important to make certain that the criteria and the associated relevant information are set in meaningful and feasible ways so that the ultimate decision can be truly made on the basis of the data— with minimum executive judgment necessary at the final stage of the decision-making process.

Table 3–1 illustrates two alternative advertising levels: $100,000 and $200,000. Before deciding between the two, sales for each advertising level must be predicted. The estimated number of units to be sold under one advertising cost versus another is the relevant information needed to compute profits.

Table 3–1   Profit as the Criterion and Sales as the Relevant Data When Diverse Costs Are Controllable Advertising Levels

	Advertising Level	
	$100,000	$200,000
Unit selling price	50¢	50¢
Unit sales predicted	1,000,000	1,500,000
Gross revenue	$500,000	$750,000
Unit product cost	20¢	15¢
Less variable unit product cost	$200,000	$225,000
Total	$300,000	$525,000
Less:		
Fixed costs	150,000	150,000
Diverse advertising costs	100,000	200,000
Profits	$ 50,000	$175,000

Source: Reprinted, by permission of the publisher, from William F. O'Dell, *The Marketing Decision,* © 1968 by American Management Association, Inc., p. 179. All rights reserved.

If only these two advertising level alternatives are to be considered by the marketing manager, then the choice is clear as indicated above. However, the decision maker will most likely wish to consider a number of advertising level alternatives and observe the effect of the change in costs on profits. Figure 3-2 illustrates the relationship between total incremental profits and advertising costs for ten levels of advertising. If the data required to indicate the values of the alternatives on the criterion can be feasibly obtained, then the approach illustrated in Figure 3-2 will not only produce the proper choice for the decision maker, but the effect of departures from the optimum decision will also be revealed.

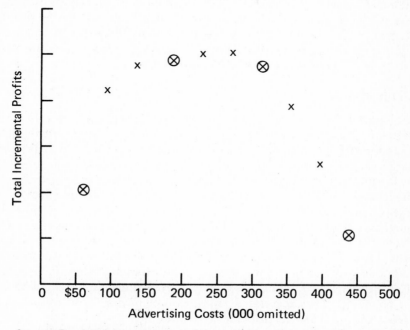

Source: Reprinted, by permission of the publisher, from William F. O'Dell, *The Marketing Decision,* © 1968 by American Management Association, Inc., p. 181. All rights reserved.

Note: For practical reasons it is likely that only about four levels (⊗) would be measured. In most instances it is difficult, if not impossible, to design a study to measure ten levels realistically.

Figure 3-2   *Profits Produced by Ten Different Advertising Levels*

For a variety of reasons, it is sometimes necessary for a firm to adopt a strategy different from that indicated by the analysis as described above. A highly desirable capability of any analytical framework for decision making is to be able to observe the effect of departures from the indicated optimum choice in terms of the specific criterion. Such an analysis is termed *sensitivity analysis;* i.e., determination of how the final choice varies with changes in the alternatives and in the environment. Fortunately, in many instances the criterion values exhibit a relatively flat profile, somewhat like an inverted saucer, in the vicinity of the best value. Figure 3–2 appears to have this property. The fortunate feature is that a range of alternatives will yield values close to the optimal, thereby giving the decision maker flexibility in making a choice.

RECOGNIZING LIMITATIONS ON CRITERIA UTILIZATION

The ability of marketing decision makers to actually use the appropriate criteria is governed by three primary considerations: (1) time limitations, (2) cost of data, and (3) research feasibility. These, in turn, have an impact upon final criteria selection. Each must be thoroughly understood both by the decision maker and by those who may be responsible for designing the research effort and gathering and analyzing the resultant data. Additionally, they all play a part in bringing about partial and suboptimization.[4]

Time Limitations

During the discussion of criteria by the decision makers, there must be a consideration of the amount of time available for gathering data that will satisfy the criterion statement. In other words, how long can the decision makers wait for data to be collected and processed? This time element issue is an outgrowth of the broader cost of decision delay, which will be discussed in Chapter 4.

The immediacy of the final marketing decision has a profound effect on criteria selection. In theory at least, it would be desirable to employ profit (sales, revenue) as the criterion on all decisions. But the conduct of studies aimed at producing sales predictions through market tests and the like require weeks or months. There are occasions, however, when management insists on making a decision quickly; it cannot wait weeks or months for data. Thus, some criteria short of "sales, revenue, profit" must be employed. Such criteria could be consumer preference, consumer-stated "likelihood of buying," and others where the data are secured directly from the consumer.

Time limitations placed on the marketing researcher by management may sometimes be unreasonable and even unnecessary due to a tendency of management to overstate the cost of delaying the final marketing decision. The researcher can point out, however, that the information resulting from an "overnight" or "weekend" survey could result in gross error and that the data would be scarcely better than the combined judgment of the marketing group. In any event, the time span between the agreement on the marketing alternatives and the date set for making the final decision affects the selection of the decision criteria.

Cost Limitations

In a general sense, profit-oriented criteria requiring monetary measures (sales, revenue, and so on) are usually more costly for which to compile data than criteria several steps removed from profit, such as traffic counts, consumer-stated

---

[4] Adapted from William F. O'Dell, *The Marketing Decision* (New York: American Management Association, Inc., 1968), Chapter 7, by permission of the American Management Association.

preferences, consumer attitudes, or brand awareness. Studies of this type, necessitating prediction of revenues, are usually quite costly, but they can be entirely justified if the profit consequences are high and coincide with a high level of managerial disagreement about what choice to make. In actual business situations, however, while insisting on employing the profit criterion for the making of a highly consequential decision, management is often unwilling to allocate the funds necessary for the gathering of the required data that would permit adequate utilization of monetary criteria.

In many instances the amount of money to be spent on a marketing research study is specifically stated before the marketing researcher is consulted. The marketing researcher is then in the equivocal and embarrassing position of attempting to design a study to develop necessary information for an agreed-upon criterion—information that might have a high level of error because of monetary restrictions. If at all possible, criteria requirements should be softened to the point where reliable information can be obtained within the approved budget. Of course, the researcher can take the unwavering stand that additional funds must be made available, but the outcome of this request depends to a large extent upon the organizational status of marketing research within the firm.

Feasibility of Gathering the Information

Both time limitations and cost of data contribute to feasibility. If insufficient time is available or if inadequate funds are allocated to the research effort, it is not feasible to gather information to satisfy properly the criteria demands.

Another dimension of feasibility centers on whether the issue can be practically researched regardless of time or cost. Some subjects appear to defy the researcher because of the lack of an appropriate marketing research technique or because of the unwillingness of individuals to provide data. In these cases it is necessary to adjust the criteria requirements. The decision makers must be made to see the necessity of making the decision on the basis of some other type of information.

The feasibility of developing and using research techniques or facilities must not be confused with the feasibility of operating within specific cost or time limitations. In cases of cost or time limitations criteria adjustments are made. In contrast, there are cases that may require criteria to be changed for the simple reason that it is almost impossible, at any price, to obtain adequate information for the established criteria.

DEVELOPING PROXY CRITERIA WHEN NEEDED

Whenever limitations force a change in the criterion originally desired, a proxy, or substitute criterion must be found. In a real sense, every criterion other than expected long-run profits is a proxy criterion. One has to retreat, however reluctantly, from this best of possible measures along a path that is marked with such possible, successive stopping points as: expected short-run profits, expected revenue, expected volume, market share, inquiries received, showroom traffic, stated intentions to buy, attitude and judgment measures, awareness indicators, media usage descriptions, etc. The path leads figuratively away from the pockets of the firm and into the minds of prospective customers.

The farther down this path one must retreat the less confident one is that there is a direct correlation between the proxy criterion and the premier criterion, i.e., profits.

Consider this example: a manufacturer of laundry detergents is contemplating a new soap product with a reduced polluting effect. The basic formula has been developed and agreed upon. However, such issues as cleansing power, sudsiness, and cost to the consumer have yet to be resolved. On what basis will the company make decisions on these issues? What will be the criteria? Test market sales of several likely variations of the soap would be most helpful data, but too costly to obtain. Instead measures of consumers' perceptions and assessments of the three attributes may be used as proxy criteria in the soap product formulation decision. Of course, the decision makers should ascertain the relative importance of the various attributes of the proposed product so as to determine how the company can maximize product acceptance by consumers. Even though the alternatives here may be of diverse cost (due to different costs of ingredients) nonmonetary criteria may have to be employed as proxies for more desirable monetary criteria because of cost and time limitations.

Figure 3–3 summarizes the general situation with regard to criteria utilization. Predictiveness as used in this figure is the ability to correctly assess the worth of alternatives. The cells in bold outline reflect the recommendations made earlier in the chapter; namely, that diverse-cost decisions warrant the use of monetary criteria, whereas identical-cost decisions may be dealt with satisfactorily using nonmonetary criteria. The point of this particular section is to alert

		DECISION ALTERNATIVES HAVE:	
		Identical Cost	Diverse Cost
CRITERIA ARE:	Monetary	Likely to provide more predictiveness than needed, and at a higher cost than necessary.	Can provide the requisite predictiveness, but may be costly and time-consuming.
	Nonmonetary	Can provide the requisite predictiveness, usually at acceptable cost.	Likely to provide less predictiveness than desired, but at a cost more likely to be acceptable.

Figure 3–3   Relationship of Criteria to Cost Nature of Decision

the reader that the limitations of cost, time, and research feasibility may require decision makers to abandon their first-choice criteria (monetary or nonmonetary) in favor of proxies (monetary or nonmonetary) whose limitations are less severe and which, therefore, permit the decision process to proceed.

In summary, it is not practical to say that the criterion to be employed should be true profit, although ideally profit would be the proper criterion. The most accurate way to use the term is simply the way the dictionary uses it: *criterion* is a rule or test for selecting the preferred situation or optimum course of action. To repeat, a criterion is not usually, in practice, a profit measure. It is generally some usable compromise, a proxy indicator, that is presumed to be clearly related to profit.

FORMULATING CRITERIA STATEMENTS

Criteria statements are rules or standards by which preferred alternatives are selected. As already indicated, the criterion selected for a particular decision is necessarily an imperfect substitute for the basic decision criterion of expected long-run profits. It is also clear that, depending upon the type of decision, the precise statement of an agreed-upon criterion may be expressed in either monetary or nonmonetary terms.

The Ultimate Goal: An If-Then Criterion Statement

As stated above, criteria are simply rules or standards by means of which preferred alternatives are selected. It is, therefore, essential that all agreed-upon criteria be stated in language that indicates clearly to the decision maker what the appropriate choice should be.

One way to accomplish such a goal is to use an "if-then" formulation. This syllogistic approach sets forth the antecedent condition or conditions that must occur or be observed before consequent specified action or actions will be taken. The *antecedent* is the first part of the total statement, between the "if" and the "then." The part of the statement following the "then" is the *consequent*. Such a statement in its simplest abstract form reads: If A, then B.

This type of conditional statement is especially helpful in developing meaningful criteria for marketing decisions. For illustration, assume a television network has narrowed its choices for a new situation comedy series to be introduced next season to two alternatives:

A: Introduce a new situation comedy series wherein the central character is a married psychologist, starring an established comedian.
B: Introduce a new situation comedy series wherein the central character is an unmarried career woman, starring an established comedienne.

If it is assumed that the two alternatives are essentially identical in terms of cost, then the criterion (nonmonetary) may be the size of viewing audience among adults 35 years old and younger. The decision will depend upon which of the two programs a stated population segment is more likely to view (possibly based on a few pilot episodes run during the summer). Simply stated, the decision criterion is:

If alternative A is viewed by more adults in the 35 and under age group than B, then alternative A will be selected.

In this example the criterion has been formulated as a conditional statement containing the if-then phrase. Such a formulation has aided in determining the basis on which the decision will be made in the following respects:

1. It has established that if one series is preferred (i.e., viewed more) to the other, the preferred one will be selected.
2. It has told the researcher the nature of the population from which the data will be gathered and thus influenced the design of the marketing research study—if such data are ultimately gathered.

Marketing decisions generally involve a degree of irresoluteness or uncertainty among the decision makers which cannot be completely eliminated. Decision makers do require, however, an indication of the uncertainty associated with a particular decision in order that consideration may be given to whether or not information which may reduce such uncertainty should be obtained through the marketing research effort. The if-then criterion statement formulation provides significant assistance to the decision maker in dealing with this uncertainty. In particular, consider the first part of the following hypothetical criterion statement—the "if" phrase:

If the psychologist series is viewed by more adults in the 35 and under age group than is the career woman series, then we will telecast the psychologist series.

The uncertainty associated with this decision is revealed in the antecedent or "if" phrase of the conditional criterion statement. In the event that subsequent research actually produces an observed rating for the psychologist series greater than that for the career woman series, then the uncertainty among the decision makers is either removed or reduced. There is no further need for executive judgmental consideration since it was agreed, as reflected in the consequent or "then" phrase of the conditional statement, that the psychologist series would be produced.

The principal advantage of employing the conditional criterion statement as a part of the decision-making process is that it forces both the decision makers and the data gatherers to agree on a statement of the alternatives and what would cause the decision makers to choose one course of action in preference to other choices. Every hypothetical conditional criterion statement must contain a course of action (a marketing alternative) as its consequent. The decision criterion is the antecedent in the if-then statement. Agreement is reached *in advance* of the research study regarding what would cause the selection of one particular alternative over the others.

Remember the Focus

While maximum expected long-run profits is the most desired articulation of the core criterion, it is not the most easily utilized or "operationalized." It should, nevertheless, serve as the reference point, the true base, for selecting criteria for actual use and for completing the decision-making process. Focusing on profit helps reduce the likelihood of selecting an inappropriate proxy criterion such as revenue maximization. Additionally, by thinking in terms of the profit criterion the marketing manager is better able to formulate satisfactory rules for guiding subordinates in their decisions and thus helping to overcome the problem of suboptimization.

QUESTIONS FOR DISCUSSION

1. What is the essential purpose of criteria in decision making?
2. How is the "expected long-run profit" criterion affected by the social responsibility of the firm making the decision?
3. Why is either partial optimization or suboptimization so often present in decision making?
4. What determines whether the criterion will be monetary or nonmonetary in nature?
5. Why could each of the following be inadequate as a decision criterion: unit sales, market share, consumer attitude?
6. When expected long-run profit is the criterion for a given decision, what information is missing and must be predicted before the final decision can be made?
7. What is meant by "proxy criteria"?
8. Who should take the lead in setting the criteria: the marketing management member of the decision-making group or the marketing research person who will be in charge of gathering the necessary data?
9. If the decision-making group cannot agree on a criterion, what is the next move?
10. In terms of the decision flow, what is essential before a criteria statement can be developed?
11. Why is it desirable to insist that the decision group reduce the criteria statement to writing?

SUGGESTED READINGS

Easton, Allan. *Complex Managerial Decisions Involving Multiple Objectives.* New York: John Wiley & Sons, Inc., 1973. (Presents a more elaborate approach to criteria selection and utilization.)

Green, P., and Y. Wind. *Multiattribute Decisions in Marketing.* New York: Dryden Press, 1973.

Helfert, Erich A. *Techniques of Financial Analysis*, 4th ed. Homewood, Ill.: Richard D. Irwin, Inc., 1977. Chapter 4.

Jones, M. H. *Executive Decision Making.* Homewood, Ill.: Richard D. Irwin, Inc., 1957. Chapter 3. (Use of if-then statements in tracing changes and causes.)

Miller, III, James R. *Professional Decision Making.* New York: Praeger Publishers, Inc., 1970. pp. 28–29.

O'Dell, W. F. *The Marketing Decision.* New York: American Management Association, Inc., 1968. Chapter 7.

Simon, H. *Administrative Behavior*, 3d ed. New York: The Free Press, 1976.

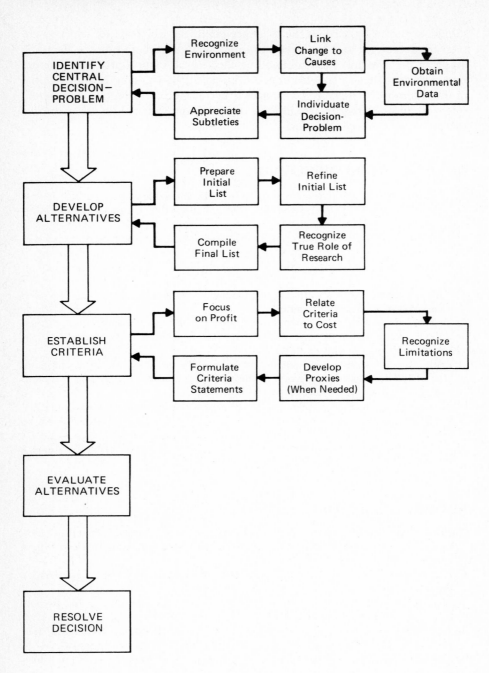

Summary Flowchart, Chapters 1–3

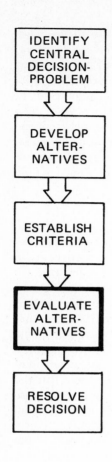

```
┌─────────────┐
│ IDENTIFY    │
│ CENTRAL     │
│ DECISION-   │
│ PROBLEM     │
└─────────────┘
      ⇓
┌─────────────┐
│ DEVELOP     │
│ ALTER-      │
│ NATIVES     │
└─────────────┘
      ⇓
┌─────────────┐
│ ESTABLISH   │
│ CRITERIA    │
└─────────────┘
      ⇓
┌─────────────┐
│ EVALUATE    │
│ ALTER-      │
│ NATIVES     │
└─────────────┘
      ⇓
┌─────────────┐
│ RESOLVE     │
│ DECISION    │
└─────────────┘
```

4

Evaluating the Alternatives

"Delay is preferable to error."

—Thomas Jefferson

"You have to make judgments; you can't wait until all the evidence is in."

—Hubert Humphrey

Evaluating the final list of marketing alternatives involves measuring or "scoring" them in terms of the specified criterion. For example, three mutually exclusive distribution strategies could be evaluated according to a criterion of return on marketing investment. The one ascertained to yield the highest return presumably would then be chosen.

BEGINNING WITH THE INITIAL EVALUATIONS

It is often the case that upon specifying the criterion for a particular marketing decision-problem, the decision makers will have some preliminary feel for how each of the alternatives measures or scores. This initial evaluation may be reached after some discussion by the decision makers and may or may not have been the subject of some staff study. Each decision maker may have impressions as to the relative worth of each alternative. The question thus arises: Is this initial evaluation sufficient to make a choice? If it is not, what refinement is required? How is a final evaluation achieved?

At this point it might be worthwhile for the reader to recall the discussion associated with the development of alternatives (Chapter 2). The development-of-alternatives process involved the creation of an initial list and its refinement to a final list. An analogous situation exists in the evaluation process—an initial assessment plus some possible refinement. Note, however, that refinement of the initial evaluation will entail a delay in resolving the decision.

Whether or not to delay clearly is a decision separate and distinct from the marketing decision-problem at hand. Such a decision might be termed a *meta-decision*, as described in Chapter 2. Whether or not to delay invariably is a crucial juncture in the decision process. It is important that decision makers fully understand this point.

RECOGNIZING WHEN TO DELAY A DECISION

It is well to remember that the primary function of executives is to make decisions. Since all business decisions are, in essence, predictions, executives are in effect saying that "If such and such a condition or situation occurs or is true, we predict this particular result." Marketing executives are therefore saying that under stated circumstances, which may or may not be known to them at that time, they can predict the business outcome of those given circumstances: that profits will show an improvement, that sales will increase, that a more favorable consumer attitude will result, etc.

These predictions—business decisions—take place in an uncertain environment. Like all foretelling, no one can be certain as to the outcome. But the fact is that these predictions must be made regardless of the number of variables that surround the decision. The variables are numerous. They range from fickle consumer attitude and loyalty to broad government regulations. They include such imponderables as competitive action and the changing level of the nation's economy. It is within this uncertain environment that marketing decision makers must predict an outcome—an outcome that is sometimes several years in the future.

The level of uncertainty varies greatly from one decision to another. What will happen tomorrow after a long period of constant performance is not too difficult to forecast with a high degree of accuracy. For example, predicting sunshine for Phoenix, where it rarely rains, is relatively easy. But predicting a minimum sales figure for a new product being considered for introduction into Russia is a formidable assignment. The uncertainties are without bounds. Yet, as stated earlier, someone must make these decisions. Simply because the outcome is often difficult to predict does not permit marketing executives to abdicate their roles as decision makers. Decision making is their prime responsibility.

On the other hand, most executives are typically involved with an array of decision-problems requiring resolution. Thus, it is not unusual for such individuals to press hard for rapid disposition of a particular decision situation. Also there is probably a natural tendency on the part of executives to want to see if their choice is correct in the sense that the predicted outcome actually occurs; i.e., profits improve, demand for a product increases, etc.

It does not follow, of course, that marketing managers must blindly barge forward merely because they are faced with the making of a decision, regardless of the uncertainty enveloping the outcome. They can step back and assess the situation, contending that for one reason or another they are not yet prepared to act. They can maintain that more information is needed before they can opt for one alternative over others under consideration. Marketing managers must understand that there are instances when a decision should be delayed. Moreover, it is their responsibility to recognize the *symptoms* that suggest a decision delay. There are times when these warning signs demand a delay in the choice of alternatives until it is clear that relevant data and information have been brought to bear on the decision-problem to the appropriate extent.

Warning Signs

Three major factors provide warning signals to decision makers. They are: (1) level of management disagreement, (2) profit consequences of a wrong decision, and (3) pressure to act. Each of these factors must be gauged by the decision makers and then considered altogether. Forced decisions, inadequate consideration of the effect of decision error on profits, and yielding to expediency can reduce the probability that the desired objective will be attained.

Two of the warning signals can be regarded as the criteria in the metadecision concerning whether to delay for additional data or not to delay in making a choice from the agreed-upon set of marketing alternatives. These two are the level of management disagreement and the perceived profit consequences of selecting the wrong alternative. As shall be discussed later in this chapter, these two criteria may each be measured on a five-step scale and the results added to yield a composite criterion to be used in deciding whether or not to delay the decision.

Management Disagreement. Management disagreement reflects the different perceived levels of uncertainty regarding the predicted or desired outcome associated with a particular alternative. Each individual involved may have a different opinion about the likelihood that a desired outcome will occur following a particular course of action. For some individuals this may be stated as "just a gut feeling." Others may articulate at length their depth of feeling concerning any alternative and the associated outcome.

Some explicit indication of the level of disagreement among decision makers is needed in order to determine what can be done to reduce uncertainty, which, of course, may delay the decision. Gauging such a disagreement level is often largely judgmental, but it can be accomplished through the use of quantifying techniques including, among others, ranking procedures and probability statements. Simply having each participant rank the alternatives in order of preference can reveal where serious disagreement (and agreement) exists.

Probability of likelihood statements can be expressed in two ways. They may either be empirical, based on the relative frequencies of observed past events, or they may be subjective, based on "best knowledge and experience." The range of degrees of specificity is illustrated in Figure 4–1. The more specific the

Expression Form	Degree of Specificity
1. Revenue from Product A sales will amount to $15.23M.	Implied certainty.
2. Revenue from Product A sales is estimated to be $15M.	Implied uncertainty.
3. Revenue from Product A sales is estimated to be $15M; however, this is an estimate and the decision makers are not sure (uncertain about the figure).	Acknowledged uncertainty. A vague qualitative expression of uncertainty is given.
4. Revenue from Product A sales are estimated to range between $11M and $19M.	A range is given to express the magnitude of uncertainty. However, no probability information is given; it is not stated whether the analyst believes there is a 1%, 10%, or 100% chance that revenue will fall between $11M and $19M, nor is it indicated whether revenue is likely to be closer to $11M or $19M.
5. There is a "strong probability" that the revenue from Product A sales will amount to $11M–$15M–$19M. The $15M is some measure of central tendency (mean, mode, or median). The $11M and $19M are the estimated lower and upper revenue limits.	An adjective descriptor is added to convey a rough indication of probability.
6. The chances are 95 out of 100 that the revenue from Product A sales will amount to $11M–$15M–$19M. The numerical expressions have the same meaning as in 5 above.	Adjective descriptor is replaced by more definitive numerical values.
7. 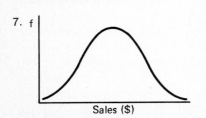	A complete probability distribution is given, and this is depicted by a curve.

(INCREASING SPECIFICITY)

Figure 4–1   Alternative Methods for Expressing Uncertainty

statement, the more clearly the level of disagreement will be subsequently revealed.

Too much agreement can be as harmful as too little. Managerial decision-making groups may develop a condition known as *groupthink*.[1] Blinded by internal peer pressures and overconfidence in their collective abilities, the group members fail to see omitted alternatives, weaknesses in those favored, and the unreal aspects of their deliberations.

Of course, marketing executives should be sensitive to the behavioral factors contributing to disagreement among the decision makers. These factors include personality conflicts, company politics, vested interests, the desire to be on the "right" side of an issue, and a variety of other matters that make it difficult to separate objectivity from bias. An executive must be able to obtain and assign appropriate weights to the opinions of all members of the decision-making group, including the least articulate member (who could happen to be the most knowledgeable).

Profit Consequences of a Wrong Decision. The profit consequences of a wrong decision is another criterion that can be used to determine whether there should be a decision delay. Certainly situations in which the wrong decision could result in large operating losses or even seriously threaten the existence of the firm obviously require the decision makers to proceed with care.

It should be noted that the number of marketing dollars involved is not always the way to view the profit consequences of a wrong decision. A decision involving the allocation of a $3 million advertising budget between two national news magazines that are similar in nature should not be influenced by the profit consequences if the returns from advertising in either of them are not expected to be significantly different.

It does not follow that the greater the profit consequences of a wrong decision, the higher the disagreement level. In many situations there is unanimity of opinion concerning which alternative to select, but the profit consequences of that alternative are potentially disastrous. However, when both the profit consequences and management disagreement are high, delay becomes highly essential. In the if-then criterion statement format, the situation is expressed: If the profit consequences and management disagreement are high, then the decision will be delayed until additional data can be obtained and analyzed.

Pressure to Act. Pressure to act is a pervasive factor in every decision-making/problem-solving situation. It has origins both external and internal to the organization. Environmental changes resulting from such things as competitor's actions, technological developments, and customer demand shifts create external pressure to act. The allocation of the executive's time among current problems, a concern about the opportunity costs associated with an executive's activity, and the fact that lower levels of the organization are waiting to implement a decision create internal pressure. The marketing manager, indeed any manager, must possess sufficient judgment and internal strength to

[1] Irving L. Janis, *Victims of Groupthink* (Boston: Houghton-Mifflin Company, 1973), pp. 8–10.

withstand these pressures and at the same time avoid creating a decision-making bottleneck.

Need for Additional Information

In the process of evaluating alternatives, how does the decision maker actually conclude when to delay the decision and seek more advice and information? The decision maker determines, or at least should determine, the extent of the delay and the amount of effort to be expended on obtaining more accurate information by examining the combination of profit consequences and managerial disagreement. These are the criteria in the metadecision problem described.

A useful technique that can indicate to the decision makers whether or not decision delay is called for involves quantifying the level of management disagreement (as evidenced by a consensus scaling by the decision participants) from high to low on a five-point scale. Profit consequences are similarly scaled, and a consensus ranking obtained. Figure 4–2 provides a two-dimensional array for these results which can be used to analyze the combined effect of management disagreement and profit consequences.

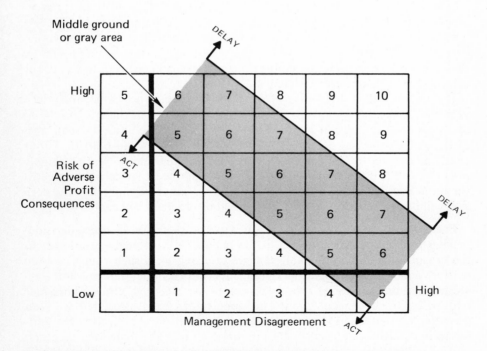

Figure 4–2   Combined Disagreement and Profit Consequences Scales

When the sum of the two scaled factors in a cell is eight or above, indicating a high disagreement/high profit consequences combination, the decision makers should obviously proceed slowly until the uncertainty surrounding the situation can be reduced. Such situations call for in-depth studies requiring highly accurate data so that the decision makers' chances of selecting the wrong alternative are reduced considerably. Of course, no study reduces the chances of making a wrong decision to zero; but when high levels of disagreement and profit consequences both occur, every effort should be made to reduce the area where executive judgment is required to as narrow a band as possible.

In cases where the sum of the two scaled factors in a cell is four or less, there is little reason to delay the decision or incur the expense of obtaining additional information. Many middle-ground situations, however, call for maximum business acumen. A situation in which the disagreement level is rated at 4 and the profit consequences is given a rating of 2, yielding a sum of 6, will undoubtedly call for some delay, largely because of the level of disagreement. The adverse profit consequences are quite low; but, as the decision makers are unable to approach unanimity on an alternative, they decide to delay the decision and seek some counsel or data that may aid in determining the correct alternative. The reverse situation, a $2 + 4 = 6$ scaling, means that almost but not quite complete agreement exists on a decision that has substantial profit consequences. In this case, perhaps one or two important and experienced members of a decision-making group are assuming a stand contrary to the others. Because of the knowledge and judgment of the two dissenters, plus the high level of the profit consequences, the decision-making body should seek a decision delay in this case.

Whenever the 1 position on the scale is combined with another scale position, no study or additional counsel is necessary. If the level of disagreement is so low, as reflected by the assignment of 1, that it is in essence one of complete agreement, the decision should be to move ahead with the preferred marketing alternative regardless of the profit consequences. In the reverse situation, if the profit level is so insignificant that a wrong decision would have almost no effect on profits, then regardless of the level of disagreement any one of the alternatives could be selected virtually at random (though, in reality, the choice is likely not to be made this way). If the profit consequences are zero or near zero, it makes no difference which alternative is selected.

The procedure for "scaling" the need for a decision delay is a workable one in actual practice. The resulting score enables decision makers to visualize clearly the need for additional data or expert counsel.

ACQUIRING ADDITIONAL DATA: COST AND VALUE ISSUES

When the disagreement level/profit consequences scores point to delaying the decision to obtain additional information to increase the likelihood of selecting the correct alternative, increased costs become a factor to consider. Decision delay is not without some cost; the reduction of uncertainty is not free of charge. This cost must be compared to the expected gain resulting from increasing the probability of selecting the best course of action; that is to say, the cost of such added information should not exceed its value.

If additional information is deemed necessary, how can the decision makers determine the amount of money to allocate to the marketing research unit that will gather it? If marketing research is the only cost associated with decision delay, the marketing manager could, in theory, allocate any amount that does not exceed the estimated profit consequences of a wrong decision. In other words, if additional research data improve the chances for a more profitable decision, then the maximum amount that should be expended for such data is the difference between the expected profit consequences of the decision taken without additional data and the expected profit consequences of the decision taken with additional data. This difference is sometimes referred to as the expected value of added information.

Table 4–1 is a payoff table for a marketing decision on the introduction of a proposed new product.

Table 4–1 Payoff Table for Decision on Introduction of New Product

| Sales | Probability of Outcome | Marketing Alternative Payoffs (Millions of Dollars) | |
		Introduce Product	Do Not Introduce Product
$40 million	.3	$4.0	$0
$20 million	.7	-$2.0	$0
Expected profit:	(.3) ($4) + (.7) (-$2) =	-$0.2	$0

In the context of the decision analysis framework developed in this book, the following should be noted regarding the marketing decision situation shown in Table 4–1:

1. The agreed-upon marketing alternatives are (a) to introduce the product and (b) not to introduce the product.
2. The criterion may be stated: If the expected profit is greater than some specified amount, say $0.1 million, then the new product will be introduced.
3. Profit consequences are high for a decision to introduce the product (a $2 million loss on sales of $20 million), and high for a decision not to introduce the product ($4 million foregone).
4. The estimate of .7 for low sales and .3 for high sales is decidedly stronger for low sales, but the high-sales estimate may come from the most experienced members of the decision group.
5. The expected monetary result (-$0.2 million) indicates that the appropriate action is to abandon the project (i.e., not to introduce the product).

The marketing alternatives in Table 4–1 have been evaluated in terms of the established monetary criterion, namely, expected dollar profit. The expected profit for each alternative was obtained by multiplying the *probabilities* of the outcomes by the *payoffs* for each alternative and summing as follows:

Alternative	Expected Profit in Millions of Dollars
Introduce Product	$(.3) \times (\$4.0) + (.7) \times (-\$2.0) = -\$0.2$
Do Not Introduce Product	$(.3) \times (\$0) + (.7) \times (\$0) = \$0$

Since the above values of the expected profit criterion are zero and negative for the two alternatives, the proper decision is clearly not to introduce the new product.

At this point the principal decision maker may be reluctant to pass up a chance to make $4 million, and may wonder if more information should be gathered before taking action, thus incurring delay. In terms of the combined disagreement (say, level 3) and profit consequences (say, level 5) scales shown in Figure 4–2, this situation might "score" 8 or 9. It would thus meet the criterion for deciding to delay the marketing decision and gather more information.

If the marketing manager authorized an expenditure of $0.5 million for a market survey and the results of this survey convinced the decision makers to revise their original estimates of the probabilities of the outcomes given in Table 4–1 to .6 for high sales and .4 for low sales, then the expected profit for the product introduction alternative would be $1.6 million as illustrated in Table 4–2.[2]

**Table 4–2 Payoff Table for Decision on Introduction of New Product
After Market Survey**

Sales	Revised Probability of Outcome	Marketing Alternative Payoffs (Millions of Dollars)	
		Introduce Product	Do Not Introduce Product
$40 million	.6	$4.0	$0
$20 million	.4	-$2.0	$0
Expected profit:	$(.6) (\$4) + (.4) (-\$2) =$	$1.6	$0

Based upon the evaluation of the alternatives in this case, the decision is plainly indicated to introduce the new product, since the expected profit is $1.6 million. When the cost of the survey, which was stated to be $0.5 million, is included, the net expected profit is $1.1 million. Since this is preferable to

---

[2] This procedure is actually an "informal Bayesian revision." Formal Bayesian procedures are fully described in Robert Schlaifer, *Probability and Statistics for Business Decisions* (New York: McGraw-Hill Book Company, 1959).

the zero profit from not introducing the product, the decision is to introduce the new product. Of course, one does not know in advance which direction the probability revisions will take, but conducting the research produces a known out-of-pocket cost.

The cost of marketing research is only one cost element in decision delay. Opportunity cost is another. Delaying the introduction of a new product pending the results of extensive consumer research may improve the chances of making the right decision. However, the expected benefits from such a decision should be compared to the amount of predicted sales revenue that would be lost during the testing period.

A third cost in decision delay stems from the reduction of lead time over competitive counteraction. Less and less frequently do companies enjoy long periods of competitive product advantage. A new product, even when a competitor is caught by surprise, can often be quickly duplicated, or a highly similar product soon introduced. To test a contemplated product line addition in the marketplace over a long period of time will make competitors aware of it. Competitors can purchase test products, analyze them, and produce similar ones in quantity while the originator is still seeking additional data for the reduction of uncertainty. Many grocery and drug manufacturers are bypassing large portions of the market-testing operation in order to increase their lead time over competitive responses. Less reliable data are being judged sufficiently adequate when contrasted with the financial losses that might follow early countermoves by competitors.

ACQUIRING ACTIONABLE DATA: RESEARCH DESIGNS

The evaluation of alternatives frequently depends upon information obtained for the specific purpose of indicating to the decision makers the best alternative among those available. As pointed out in Chapter 1, *actionable data* are required at this stage in the decision-making process—data pertinent to what should be done, the action to be taken.

Subject to time, cost, and feasibility limitations, the marketing researcher is often assigned the crucial role by the decision makers of developing an appropriate study for obtaining the required actionable data. It will be recalled that the time, cost, and feasibility constraints are often affected by the availability and understanding of marketing techniques. It is, of course, not vital that marketing management understand the finer points of research technology, but it is essential that they comprehend the contribution of marketing research and how it works. It is well for the marketing management people to have a working knowledge of research techniques because marketing research influences their selection of the criteria for decision.

It should be pointed out that the decision of whether to obtain marketing research data is not a *marketing* alternative. The marketing alternatives for a particular decision have, at this stage of the decision process, already been specified and agreed upon. The decision makers are simply deferring their decision on those alternatives until the necessary actionable data can be obtained. It is also important to note that the decision itself has not been transferred to the marketing researcher. *The selection of the proper course of marketing action remains with the decision makers.*

Once brought into the picture, however, the marketing researcher may be faced with similar choice situations that are amenable to the same kind of analysis as the overall marketing decision. Among these decisions is the choice of the type of research design or study to be employed in developing the actionable data required by the decision makers for evaluating alternatives.

Descriptive Studies

Descriptive studies clarify a situation through data collection and analysis. Such studies involve marketing research and employ statistical procedures in obtaining data from systematically designed population samples. The resulting data are usually presented in terms of averages or percentages. Some examples of descriptive research are: (1) determining demographic and attitudinal characteristics of heavy purchasers, occasional purchasers, and nonbuyers of a defined product class; (2) determining the brand-awareness levels and preferences for certain brands among certain kinds of consumers; and (3) determining the buying process and the role of buying influentials in a manufacturer's choice of sources of supply for a given technical product. A major type of descriptive study is sometimes referred to as *survey research* and is the most frequently used marketing research approach.

At the point in the decision process when alternatives and criteria are agreed upon, the required precision level is generally higher than that required for descriptive studies designed to identify environmental change. At this point a well-planned descriptive study can then be used to obtain prescriptive rather than diagnostic data.

Descriptive studies are too often regarded as merely fact-finding efforts. But if the study is carefully planned by the marketing researcher, it is possible to obtain evidence of certain critical relationships and thus provide decision makers with the actionable data required for evaluating alternatives.

Experimental Studies

As indicated earlier in this chapter, since all business decisions are, in essence, predictions, the decision makers need to have the best information obtainable that will help them determine the cause and effect relationships among the variables involved in the decision under consideration. In marketing, this is an enormously complicated problem because marketing data stem from actions of human beings. Many of the variables are behavioral in nature.

To clarify cause and effect relationships, marketing researchers must frequently provide information to the decision makers based on experimental studies. An *experimental study* is one in which one or several variables (advertising, a price change, a new package, etc.) are manipulated in an effort to measure the influence of any such variables (perhaps the effect on sales, on attitudes, etc.), through which a cause and effect relationship may be revealed.

The underlying key to experimentation is the realization that the primary interest of the marketing decision makers and the researcher is often in providing a comparison of marketing alternatives to reveal their relative worth rather than establishing absolute values. In other words, the designer of the experiment must recognize that a limited number of alternatives are being subjected to measurement. Examples of such alternatives are: two advertising levels, three price levels, two container designs.

The blending of the decision process with experimental design becomes apparent when the criterion statement is being formulated. The types of variables become clearer when the criterion statement is dissected with the parts of the experiment in mind. To illustrate, assume that the marketing issue is which of three advertising themes to employ. The three themes, then, are the marketing (advertising) alternatives. The criterion statement could be phrased as follows:

> *If* one of the copy themes will increase the favorable attitudes of consumers toward our brand more than the other two themes, *then* we will employ that theme.

In that simple criterion are several "variables":

1. The *marketing variable* is the advertising theme, in contrast, say, to the advertising medium. In essence the marketing variable delineates the specific decision-problem area.
2. The *experimental variable* is the advertising theme. A *treatment* is a particular "value" of the experimental variable. The three themes depict different treatments of the marketing variable. In another sense, each treatment is a marketing alternative (in this illustration, an advertising alternative).
3. The *dependent variable* is the consumer attitude change. Information about the change is required to reduce the uncertainty on the part of the decision makers. This is the information being sought by the marketing researcher.
4. *Independent or uncontrollable variables* are those in which there is no direct interest, except for attempting to assure their uniform effect among the experiment's subjects. In the advertising theme decision, for example, independent variables that could affect the data would be attitudes held by consumers prior to the experiment, or ages and incomes of consumers. These are the variables the experimenter attempts to hold constant or randomize during the conduct of the experiment.

The chief benefit of the experimental procedure is that it enables variables not being measured to be held constant or at least to have their effects randomized. This benefit, however, cannot be achieved in marketing easily. But since experimentation is highly effective in measuring cause and effect relationships in marketing, its use—when necessary—will usually justify its cost.

Even the most enthusiastic advocates of experimentation in marketing must admit its weaknesses. It is not a cure-all. Its inadequacies, however, do not preclude the employment of the experimental method. Perfect information is not required, even when predicting sales. A knowledge of the procedure's weaknesses will aid in an evaluation of its overall approach. Its limitations are summarized by Green and Frank:

1. Experiments typically must be limited to measuring short-term response, but long-term response is often relevant in marketing problems.
2. It is usually "expensive" to measure accurately actual sales in individual experimental units.
3. The variability of sales—whether between families, dealers, geographical areas, or time periods—is often large by comparison with hoped-for responses to marketing actions.
4. It is difficult to prevent "contamination" of control units by test units.
5. It is often difficult except for very short periods to execute experimental designs properly when they require people in a marketing organization to behave differently than they would otherwise have done.
6. It is often difficult to make marketing experiments sufficiently realistic to be useful.
7. Experiments raise "security" problems of a more serious nature than those associated with surveys.
8. The mortality of experimental units is relatively high in marketing experiments.[3]

These limitations, of course, are not restricted to experimental studies. Problems of security, cost, variability of sales, and depth of realism are common in many types of nonexperimental research efforts. The elimination of mortality, the prevention of contamination, and the proper execution of experimental designs are the responsibilities of the designer of the experiment. A high degree of creativity and a sound knowledge of the availability of research facilities go a long way toward overcoming many of these weaknesses.

If the marketing manager keeps firmly in mind that perfect information is not required, it will be apparent that even experimental work with some known contamination can make an important contribution to the decision makers. The goal of data is to *reduce* uncertainty. Rarely can data be expected to *eliminate* it, nor is it necessary to do so.

ACQUIRING ACTIONABLE DATA: RESEARCH DECISIONS

It is most desirable that the marketing research manager be called in early in the discussion of a marketing decision-problem. Knowledge of the background of the marketing alternatives, contribution to the selection of the decision criteria, and awareness of the profit consequences and managerial disagreement will combine to enhance the marketing research manager's capability of designing a study that will maximize the usefulness of the data at minimum cost.

Whether the research manager is in fact consulted during the initial stages of the decision is often a function of the status of the researcher within the firm.

---

[3] Paul E. Green and Ronald E. Frank, *A Manager's Guide to Marketing Research* (New York: John Wiley & Sons, Inc., 1967), pp. 91–94.

In too many firms marketing research is not held in high esteem; the research department is seen by top management as a compiler of statistical information and nothing more. In these companies the marketing research director does not participate in decision making, but is consulted *after* the need for data has been established—following the selection of the criteria. In such a situation the researcher cannot realistically be expected to design an efficient study, and in many instances the survey data actually obtained will not resolve the marketing issues that prompted the need for the study in the first place.

In other firms, however, marketing research is highly regarded, especially among the mass marketers. In these organizations the marketing research departments perform far more than data collection roles. They become an integral part of the decision-making group. They participate during the early stages of the decision process, and often make marketing recommendations when presenting the results of their studies.

Marketing managers need not be research specialists or skilled technicians. However, as marketing becomes more scientific, it behooves marketing managers to be trained in the social sciences, in quantitative methods, and in research methodology. Although it is not necessary to be skilled in all these fields, marketing managers must be prepared for their roles as generalists. The marketing manager's responsibility as it relates to marketing research centers on understanding the role of information in a professional sense. The manager must know "how to employ a variety of specialists; weigh different kinds of considerations; and . . . view the making of a given decision in the context of the whole situation. . . . The practitioner, though a generalist, tends to become more scientific as a field develops. Tomorrow's marketing managers will be more scientific than their predecessors. They will be better trained technically than most of today's marketing researchers. . . ." [4]

Even though it is not necessary to be a skilled, highly trained research technician, it is essential that the marketing manager understand the basics of the sample survey (Figure 4-3) through which so much primary data are gathered. The marketing manager must be informed on the various firms that maintain research facilities not normally available within one's own firm: A. C. Nielsen Company (retail index services and others), Market Facts, Inc. (test market auditing, consumer mail panels, plus others), Market Research Corporation of America (consumer purchase reporting panels), and hundreds of smaller firms engaging in a wide range of research activities.

The marketing manager must also be versed in ways to best allocate the research dollar and should be able to pass judgment on alternative research techniques and procedures. The marketing manager must be able to resolve differences of opinion regarding how the research funds can be most efficiently spent. In such situations, the design of a marketing research study is a "wheel

---

[4] Joseph W. Newman, "The Operational Relevance of an Emerging Science of Marketing to Education and the Discipline of Marketing," *The Conceptual Framework for a Science of Marketing* (Urbana, Ill.: University of Illinois Marketing Symposium, October, 1963).

Target Population	The primary body about which information is sought.
Sampling Unit	The specific element (e.g., homemakers) of the target population which is to comprise the sample and to whom the research instrument is to be directed.
Sample Frame	The "master list" or "directory" of target population from which the sample will actually be drawn.
Sample Size	That subset of the target population from whom information will be sought using the research instrument; reflects statistical and cost considerations.
Sample Selection Procedure	The scheme by which the sample is drawn from the sample frame; reflects statistical and cost consideration.
Sampling Plan or Design	The composite of activities associated with specifying the sampling unit, sample frame, size, and selection mechanism.
Research Instrument	The "device" (e.g., questionnaire) employed to elicit/record information yielded by the sampling units in the sample.
Survey Method	Generally the mode of communication between the surveyor and the sample: face-to-face as in personal interviews; telephone interviews; mail.
Survey Setting	Location where research instrument is administered to sample unit (e.g., at home, in store, street corner).

Figure 4–3   Basic Elements in a Survey Effort

within a wheel"; a decision within a decision. The marketing manager and the researcher must agree on how the resources available for a study can be most efficiently spent to maximize the utility of the gathered data. This requires a series of decisions on alternative uses of the research dollar. The major research decision areas are:

> Sample specification
>> Nature of basic sample units
>> Size of sample
>> Dispersion of sample units
>> Selection procedures

Research design
  Descriptive vs. experimental
  Timing

Data collection method
  Observation (e.g., store audit)
  Interviews (face-to-face, telephone)
  Mail

Sampling Procedures

In a most general sense, the accuracy of data resulting from a sample survey is closely related to the sample size, dispersion of the sampling units, and whether it is probabilistic or nonprobabilistic in nature. Figure 4–4 provides an inventory of different sample types and the terminology associated with each type.

In allocating the research dollar, obviously the larger the sample, the greater the expenditure of funds—all other conditions remaining the same. However, "all other conditions" can be varied to maximize the utility of the funds expended. For example, a sample of 750 may produce greater accuracy than a sample of 1,000. In addition, the sample can be rigorous in its probability characteristics. Thus, a smaller sample may yield more accurate data than a larger sample when the coverage of the former is great and the probability aspects are demanding.

Therefore, in allocating the sampling funds it may be more efficient to reduce the sample size, disperse the sample more, and, say, develop some modification of a probability sample so that funds can be saved without reducing the accuracy level of the resultant data.

How can one make such sampling decisions in advance of the actual study? How does one know whether to reduce the sample size or disperse the sample more, or to do both? In real life, time and cost constraints rarely allow for adequate testing prior to the final sample design; i.e., for commercial studies. (The Bureau of the Census, with its great financial resources, would usually have the time and money to conduct test studies in order to aid in making sampling decisions.) When time and money are limited, the researcher must frequently rely on experience and judgment to relate sampling details to the need for a desired level of accuracy.

It is possible, of course, to estimate in advance the accuracy level of sample data results by referring to tables of probabilities and by determining the expected error *due to sample size*. While such tables are helpful, they do not take into consideration the many *nonsampling* sources of error. These include errors resulting from failure to adhere to sampling instructions, poor question phrasing, response inadequacies, and improper coding and data processing—all of which at one time or in combination contribute to total error. These types of errors cannot be readily measured, and this inability in turn contributes to the weakness in relying blindly on measures of sampling error that are obviously

Probability	Designs based on some form of random choice of either individuals or blocks or clusters; every item in the universe of the particular study has a known chance of being chosen for the sample; sampling error is measurable.
• Simple random	Every item or person in the predetermined universe has an equal chance of being selected and included in the sample.
• Stratified	Division of the population into meaningful segments or strata and selection of sample members from each strata.
• Cluster	Division of population into groupings or clusters and sampling from only some of the clusters chosen at random.
• Area	A special type of cluster sampling with geographical restriction of sampling units.
• Systematic	A type of cluster sampling in which after a random start every nth member of a list or population is subsequently selected.
Nonprobability	Methods of sampling in which selection of items is arbitrary rather than random; consequently every item in the universe does not have a known chance of being chosen for the sample and sampling error is not measurable.
• Convenience	Items chosen for sample purely on basis of convenience—they are accessible, or articulate, or otherwise easy to measure.
• Judgment	"Expert" judgment is used to select those items which might be regarded as "representative" in some sense.
• Quota	Similar to stratified random sampling in that the universe is subdivided; however, the selection of respondents is done arbitrarily by the field representatives up to the number designated for each stratum (the quota).

Source: Table 11–1 from page 271 in *Marketing: Management and Social Change* by Robert F. Hartley. Copyright © 1972 by International Textbook Company. Reprinted by permission of Harper & Row, Publishers, Inc.

Figure 4–4   Summary of Sampling Methods

prevalent in interview-based studies and exist in varying degrees in other types of sample surveys.

The extent of sampling error due to sample size is shown in Table 4–3.

Table 4–3 ***Expected Accuracy of Percentages Observed From an***
               Individual Sample *(95% Level of Confidence)*

Size of Sample	Expected or Observed Percentage				
	10 90	20 80	30 70	40 60	50 50
100	6.00	8.00	9.16	9.80	10.00
200	4.24	5.66	6.48	6.92	7.08
300	3.46	4.62	5.30	5.66	5.78
400	3.00	4.00	4.58	4.90	5.00
500	2.68	3.58	4.10	4.38	4.48
750	2.20	2.92	3.34	3.58	3.66
1000	1.90	2.52	2.90	3.10	3.16
1500	1.54	2.06	2.36	2.52	2.58
2000	1.34	1.78	2.04	2.20	2.24
2500	1.20	1.60	1.84	1.96	2.00

The numbers in the body of Table 4–3 indicate the expected percentage error in either direction for the observed sample result due to sample size. For example, the observed sample result of an 80%–20% dichotomy shown at the top of the second column for a sample size of 100 could in fact be between 88% and 72% and 12% and 28%, an error of ±8.0 percentage points, due to sample size. The expected error is reduced to 4.0 percentage points if a sample size of 400 is used. Increasing the sample size to 750 produces an expected error of 2.92 percentage points.

The columns in Table 4–3 provide additional insight into the value of added information that can be attributed to increasing the sample size. Increasing the sample size beyond 1500 produces very little improvement in expected error at the 95% confidence level.

Data Collection Methods

There are four generally recognized methods for collecting marketing research data:

1. The *face-to-face interview,* wherein an interviewer directly queries a respondent.
2. The *telephone interview.*
3. *Data collection by mail.* There are two types. The *special list method* is usually a one-time, special study using a sample drawn from some appropriate source representing the universe or market being studied. The *controlled mail survey* employs a sample of households or families drawn from some existing panel, usually maintained by some professional marketing research firm.

4. *Observation studies.* These assume many forms, but the most common is the store audit where the purchasing behavior of the population is observed by measuring the sales movement of all or selected product categories. An example of another type of observation is the traffic count, recording the number of persons or cars passing a given geographic point or points.

In optimizing the allocation of the research dollar it is possible to conserve funds, for example, by employing the telephone method instead of the face-to-face personal interview. However, in some instances the telephone may not be appropriate, such as when illustrations are used in the questionnaire. Thus, in order to meet a fixed budget, if that is the case, the face-to-face interview could be employed with a reduction in the sample size. Or the controlled mail panel could be utilized at perhaps even less cost, but with some sacrificing of sampling efficiency.

An ironic aspect of making research decisions is that to maximize the efficiency of the expenditure completely, it would be desirable to conduct first an elaborate study, analyze the data, and then determine where and how the money could have been better spent. This utopian procedure is hardly feasible. The researcher is forced to fall back on judgment and experience, which should include the after-the-fact evaluation of actual studies.

Research Instruments

Except for observational studies, all primary marketing research data are obtained through some type of questioning process: face-to-face, telephone, or mail. It is incumbent on the researcher, then, to devise a questionnaire that elicits the correct information. This is a difficult task at best.

In a broad sense, there are two types of questionnaires: the *open ended* and the *highly structured,* or *closed ended.* The former relies largely on the interviewer for question phrasing and often the reporting includes response interpretation by the interviewer. This type of questioning is often used in "motivational research" where "reasons why" are being sought on a clinical basis and where precise samples are rarely employed. Environmental data are often obtained by this open-ended questioning. Closed-ended questioning is better at producing actionable data.

The structured questionnaire has several advantages: (1) the phrasing of the questions is developed by persons experienced in the field; (2) the interviewer is less likely to interject personal wording, resulting in less bias; (3) the sequence of the questions is assured; and (4) the data can be processed without being subjected to content analysis which in itself introduces another source of bias contributing to total error.

Many questionnaires incorporate "scaling" devices. This approach enables the respondent to reveal feelings or actions in degrees, rather than in dichotomous terms such as "yes" or "no." Scaled data lend themselves superbly to sophisticated statistical analyses.

RETURNING TO THE MAINSTREAM OF THE DECISION PROCESS

As discussed previously, consideration of whether to delay resolving a marketing decision for additional data creates a separate metadecision that is structurally identical to the marketing decision. There are alternatives to generate, criteria to establish, evaluations to perform, and choices to make.

If the decision is made to gather additional data through marketing research, then the marketing researcher is in turn faced with decision-problems concerning the optimizing of the allocation of marketing research funds, which also may be analyzed in the same way described. Choices concerning the sample, data collection method, etc., are required.

Such research decisions can divert the attention of participating marketing managers from other decisions—decisions in progress and decisions in the bud. Improving total marketing performance and corporate profitability is an on-going effort that should not be deferred for arrival of research results pertinent to one decision. The marketing manager has to stay in touch with the mainstream of marketing events—it is a stream of constant change.

After data obtained through marketing research have been gathered and analyzed, the marketing decision alternatives must be evaluated again in the light of the new information and the decision at hand resolved. Chapter 5 describes the matters to consider at this stage of the decision process. The flowchart that follows summarizes matters thus far.

QUESTIONS FOR DISCUSSION

1. Whether or not to delay a decision has been termed a metadecision. Discuss.
2. Describe the warning signals which may indicate that decision delay is the proper thing to do in a particular situation.
3. Why is it that the dollar amount of marketing effort involved may not be the correct view of the profit consequences of a wrong decision?
4. What are the weaknesses in attempting to quantify managerial disagreement?
5. Explain the concept of cost and value of additional information. Why is this concept sometimes of minimum worth to decision makers?
6. Outline the procedures in experimental market research studies. Contrast them with descriptive market research studies. Why are experimental studies, when feasible, favored?
7. If the accuracy of data resulting from a sample survey is closely related to sample size, how can one make a sampling decision in advance of the actual study?
8. Describe the four generally recognized methods for collecting marketing research data. What considerations influence their selection?
9. Many publishers and broadcasters conduct exhaustive studies regarding their subscribers, readers, listeners, or viewers. How do data of this type fit into the decision-making process?
10. What is the prime benefit to a company that optimizes the research dollar? Give an example of how a marketing research manager can optimize a company's research expenditures.

SUGGESTED READINGS

Cochrane, James L., and Milan Zeleny (eds.). *Multiple Criteria Decision Making*. Columbia, S.C.: University of South Carolina Press, 1973.

Easton, Allan. *Complex Managerial Decisions Involving Multiple Objectives*. New York: John Wiley and Sons, Inc., 1973.

Harrison, E. Frank. *The Managerial Decision-Making Process*. Boston: Houghton-Mifflin Company, 1975.

Janis, Irving L., and Leon Mann. *Decision Making: A Psychological Analysis of Conflict, Choice, and Commitment*. New York: The Free Press, 1977.

Keeney, Ralph L., and Howard Raiffa. *Decisions With Multiple Objectives: Preferences and Value Tradeoffs*. New York: John Wiley and Sons, Inc., 1976.

Miller, David W., and Martin K. Starr. *The Structure of Human Decisions*. Englewood Cliffs, N.J.: Prentice-Hall, Inc., 1967.

Schlaifer, Robert. *Analysis of Decisions Under Uncertainty*. New York: McGraw-Hill Book Company, 1969.

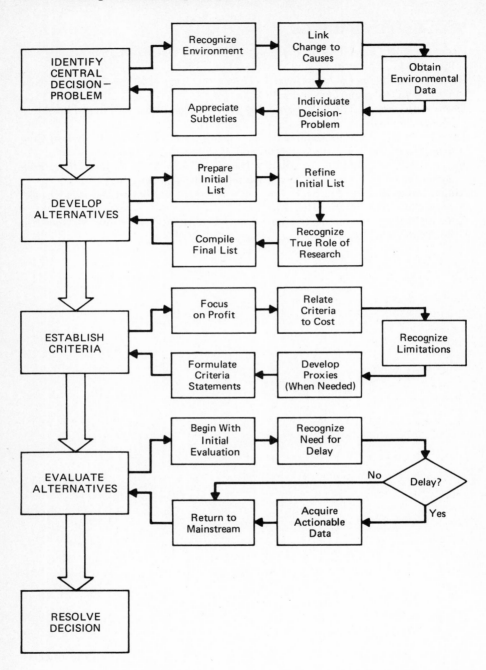

Summary Flowchart, Chapters 1–4

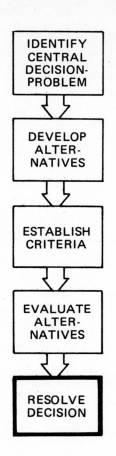

IDENTIFY
CENTRAL
DECISION-
PROBLEM

DEVELOP
ALTER-
NATIVES

ESTABLISH
CRITERIA

EVALUATE
ALTER-
NATIVES

RESOLVE
DECISION

5

Resolving
the Decision

"Nothing relieves and ventilates the mind like a resolution."

—John Burroughs

It was pointed out in Chapter 4 that when management elects to delay choosing a course of marketing action and instead calls upon marketing research assistance, a separate decision-problem situation is created. This separate situation revolves around the best course of marketing research action—the best way, consistent with available resources, to gather and analyze the needed data. Once obtained, these data and information must be injected into the mainstream of the marketing decision-problem activity, which, despite the delay, must progress toward resolution.

COMMUNICATING DATA AND INFORMATION
TO THE DECISION MAKERS

There are several considerations worth noting with regard to the injection process. Each of these several considerations relates to communicating the gathered and interpreted information to the decision makers so they can complete, effectively and efficiently, their resolution of the delayed decision-problem.

The Two Cultures Problem: Researchers vs. Managers

The reader has been cautioned previously not to neglect the behavioral factors embedded in decision situations. This caution is repeated here, as it definitely applies to the relationships between researchers and managers.

Researchers tend to be more cautious than managers, more given to reflection and skepticism. Managers, on the other hand, are typically more action-oriented and generally not concerned with the details and niceties of scholarship. Researchers usually like to impress other researchers; managers like to impress other managers.

These two different outlooks and two different sets of shared experiences often generate a communication gap.[1] This gap is most visible in the language each group uses. Figure 5–1 illustrates how such a gap may manifest itself.

Management demands:

- Simplicity
  (Can't you just ask "yes" or "no"?)

- Certainty
  (It is or it isn't.)

- Immediacy
  (Now.)

- Concreteness
  (Aren't we number one yet?)

Research offers:

- Complexity
  (The variability of response indicates . . .)

- Probability
  (Maybe.)

- Futurity
  (It appears that by the end of the year . . .)

- Abstraction
  (Our exponential gain indeed appears favorable.)

Source: Leslie Beldo, "Introduction to Attitude Research and Management Decisions," *Effective Marketing Coordination,* edited by George L. Baker (Chicago: American Marketing Association, 1961), p. 584.

Figure 5–1   Communication Gap Between Management and Research

While managers should strive to have some knowledge of research techniques and procedures (as pointed out in Chapter 4), the burden for clear communication of study results falls squarely on the marketing researcher, who should take pains to avoid couching findings in esoteric terms. Precise language does not mean arcane language.

The writer of a marketing research report must always remember that a communication is being addressed to a given group of persons. This group has a certain level of understanding of the subject being presented. If the readers are

---

[1] C. P. Snow has commented on the differences between scientists and humanists, seeing the problem as one of "two cultures." See *Science and Government* (New York: New American Library, 1961).

top management, they are not likely to be familiar with the highly technical aspects of statistics, psychology, sampling, analysis of variance, or the logic behind factor analysis. While the report writer may impress some people with heavy emphasis on narrow technicalities, the reader of the report will probably fail to grasp the essential points, and so the communication will fail.

The business report writer should employ a vocabulary that communicates with the intended readers—not one that subconsciously aims at impressing colleagues.

Precision and Significance of Data

The question of precision is pertinent to the numerical data and information compiled through marketing research. Two major categories of errors in sample surveys were identified in the prior chapter: (1) errors due to the probabilistic nature of sampling, and (2) nonsampling errors due to a host of causes. The marketing researcher must be sure to specify the estimated total error in the measures being developed. This is particularly important where the researcher is presenting data indicating how each of the alternatives in a delayed decision-problem "scores" on the criteria (monetary or nonmonetary) employed. Why? Simply because the data error may eliminate most of the differences that may seem to exist among the alternatives' scores. Choice obviously becomes difficult in such instances. For example, two alternatives may score 50 and 54 respectively on some scale. With a ± 1 percent total error level, the two would appear to be different; with a ± 10 percent total error level, they would not.

The question of the presence of a significant difference is a fundamental one in statistics. Researchers often take it for granted that others are cognizant of this issue. They should not take such an awareness for granted, particularly where nonsampling errors are substantial relative to sampling errors, as is so often the case. They should take pains to point out the relationship of potential total errors in the data to the apparent differences uncovered.

Related to the significant difference question is the question of the number of significant digits in numerical values. For example, seldom would an annual dollar sales estimate be given as $525,966; instead, $526,000 or $525,000 is more realistic, i.e., the leftmost three digits are "significant." While researchers and managers alike would recognize that sales estimates usually do not have more than three to four significant digits, both groups are occasionally mesmerized by computer output and accounting records. Simply because the computer prints out six or nine digits for some computational result or some accounting record shows costs to the penny does not mean that these values are indeed known to that level of precision. Most "canned" or standard statistical programs for the computer are geared to generalized input conditions. Rounded-off subroutines are seldom included. Because computer printouts are often incorporated directly into research reports, or used as reports themselves, researchers should be sure to caution report users against reading more significant digits in the output data than the caliber of the input data warrants.

Avoiding Misinformation

Unintentional as it may be, the writer of business reports should be alert to inadvertently misinforming the reader through misguided efforts of chart makers. It is obvious to all that in many instances quantitative data can be more readily grasped by report readers when the data are graphically portrayed in the form of bar charts, line graphs, pie charts, and other forms of "statistical pictures." It is for this reason that many business reports devote a substantial portion of their communication effort to graphic presentations—whether in the usual 8½ x 11 inch page report or an elaborate slide presentation. In either event, let the communicators beware of the many unsuspecting charting pitfalls that can mislead the audience. (Guidelines for report writing and oral presentations are found in Appendices A and B.)

Sequence of the Research Report Contents

Proper report content sequence is another factor directly related to reducing the communication gap between report writers and report readers.

Consider once again the two major categories of studies: the descriptive study and the experimental or actionable study. The descriptive study is generally undertaken in the early phases of the decision process: assessing changes in the environment, developing alternatives. Actionable studies are conducted to assist decision makers in the later decision process stages such as in choosing from an agreed-upon set of alternatives using specified criteria. In particular, actionable studies are requested in cases of uncertainty and disagreement. Accordingly, the report of an actionable study strives to dispel the doubt and resolve the disagreement. This is best accomplished by logical development of the background and status of the decision-problem up to the point of the request for research assistance. Then study methods and findings are discussed, followed by the summary, conclusions, and recommendations. By pursuing an orderly and logical sequence the conclusions emerge in an evolutionary rather than revolutionary fashion. Where the decision makers have taken care to develop an explicit, if-then criterion statement, this is given emphasis in presenting the findings and conclusions. Each alternative and its evaluation on the criterion is expressed in the if-then format to indicate clearly where that alternative stands. *The stronger the disagreement among the decision makers concerning the alternatives, the greater the need for building a clear, logical case.*

Many executives, especially those at the top level, prefer all reports to be prefaced by a one-page summary or condensation. This is fine for a descriptive study; it is not recommended for the actionable study. The single-page recap of any actionable study would have to highlight the recommended course of action. The underlying logic would not likely be displayed convincingly in a summary. Attention to other positions would have to be minimized. Executives favoring other courses of action could harden their stand if they read the one-page condensation first. Instead of reducing disagreement the summary could only heighten disagreement. Clearly, then, the recommendation here is not to include a summary of an actionable study at the beginning of the report.

Descriptive reports, in contrast to prescriptive reports, may lead off with a summary of conclusions and findings. The details of the investigation may then follow. No one course of action is urged. If, however, there was some initial management controversy about the topic or subject treated by the study, then the report sequence should assist in smoothly resolving the controversy.

Most marketing research reports are supplemented by some form of oral presentation to decision makers. Tact, of course, must be exercised in these meetings. Those decision makers whom the report reveals to be wrong are more likely to accept the report's conclusion and recommendations when their original positions are carefully and respectfully analyzed. The disagreement level may change for the worse if prescriptive conclusions are forced on individual decision makers. Thus, it is essential that the presentation unfold in a highly logical manner and with maximum use of reasoning. Questions by the "losing" side must be anticipated and answered in both the written and oral reports. Figure 5–2 lists some typical questions concerning research reports.

It may be the case that the audience for the oral presentation will be different in background and knowledge than the audience for the written report. Adjustments in the presentation should be made so that the presentation is consistent with the level of the audience. Attention to such considerations will enable the marketing researcher to reduce the communication gap and to be in a better position to assist management.

REVIEWING THE NEED FOR FURTHER DELAY

Evidence concerning the decision-problem amassed in the report of the marketing research group, along with other evidence that emerges and the simple passage of time, will all serve to modify the original disagreement level. The question is: In what direction?

Additional Disagreement About the Acquired Data and Information Itself

Just as decision makers can disagree over the alternative courses of action, so can they argue over the relevance and accuracy of the very data and information that are intended to resolve their disagreement. Clearly the marketing research people bear the burden of explaining why the particular evidence they have compiled is appropriate to the decision-problem at hand.

Often, however, there is disagreement among researchers as to what the best measures or procedures might be in a given study situation. Thus, there will be instances when resolution of the central decision-problem is hampered by controversy concerning the research methodology employed, the true level of error in the data, the interpretations given to the findings, and so on. Decision makers who see their positions weakened by the gathered data may attack,

Was the main purpose of the study to obtain environmental or actionable data?

If Environmental:
 1. Is a one- or two-page summary at the beginning of the report appropriate?
 2. What is the most logical classification and sequence in presenting the data? (By geographic area, alphabetical, by question number on questionnaire, by subject matter, by product class, by sales volume or profitability?)
 3. Is there a brief description of the research method appearing early in the report?
 4. Does a detailed description of the research procedure appear in the appendix of the report? (This is essential not only to satisfy the readers on the reliability level of the data but to provide a basis for duplicating the study at a later date should it become desirable to measure changes through time.)
 5. Is the report writer to make recommendations based on the data in the report? (Even though it is not an "actionable" study, it is entirely possible that some courses of action can emerge, e.g., the formation of an initial list of alternatives.)

If Actionable:
 1. Does the basic issue to be resolved receive the emphasis in the report?
 2. Does the sequence follow the decision model?
 3. Does the report attempt to stress those subject areas in which there has been strong managerial disagreement?
 4. Is the criterion clearly stated?
 5. Are the recommendations for action consistent with the findings?
 6. Is the report persuasive?
 7. Is the logical structure of the report clearly apparent?
 8. Does the report close with one or more recommended courses of action for the decision makers?
 9. Does the report include a complete description of the research methodology in the appendix?

Figure 5–2   Key Questions to Ask in Preparing and Evaluating Report Contents

justly or unjustly, the data and research procedures. In essence they are claiming that the data are inadequate and therefore do not reduce the uncertainty and resolve the issue being studied. It should be recognized that this kind of disagreement is additional to and separate from the original disagreement over the marketing alternative to be selected.

Residual Disagreement Concerning the Alternatives

Where the decision makers accept the data and information acquired, the findings nevertheless may be such that clear distinctions among the alternatives are still not possible to discern. For example, consumer panel results may reveal an ambivalence concerning three proposed package designs. Or sales estimates for a proposed new product may show an unusually wide range. The decision makers do not question the research findings; they may, however, disagree about what the findings tell them to do. A residue of disagreement, which may be considerable, remains.

The decision makers must deal with any disagreement, additional or residual, that exists after research results are in. They are thus confronted with another metadecision, i.e., one involving the decision process itself and not involving the various alternatives agreed upon. That decision concerns the need to recycle in the decision process. To illustrate, let us assume that research data revealed a sales prediction for a contemplated product that fell somewhat short of the criterion level stated by the decision makers. Management felt, however, that the sales prediction was not seriously below the necessary requirement. Thus, the decision makers had to decide on their next move. They could proceed with the introduction of the product. This action in essence would be a softening of the criterion. Or they could ask the research group to gather more data to further refine the evaluations. Or they could review the basic marketing alternatives, adjusting them sufficiently to yield a better market response, i.e., so that their sales predictions would be more favorable given another evaluation. In each of these examples, a recycling is taking place within the decision process.

DECIDING WHETHER TO RECYCLE

The nature of the return to some prior stage in the decision-making process (e.g., to modify criteria or to construct new alternatives) is likely to be shaped by two major considerations: increased urgency to act now rather than to delay further, and the confidence of the decision makers in expert judgment—either their own or that of outside counsel.

Increased Urgency to Act

Just because the decision makers opt to delay for additional data does not mean that competition will delay also. The competitive environment is seldom a courteous one. If the information-gathering effort has involved some test marketing, then competitors are most likely aware of what the decision makers are considering. Those competitors may be in the process of implementing responses to the marketing action they perceive. For the decision makers to delay further could give other firms the opportunity to preempt any true market opportunity that might exist.

Even if competitive reaction is not imminent, there still may be time pressures to act immediately instead of to recycle. The marketing decision may be linked to some seasonal pattern (bathing suit sales) or calendar event (World Series advertising deadline). Failure to act at once may mean a lost opportunity.

Or the decision-problem may be a highly strategic one with a host of subsequent decision-problems stemming from it. Subordinate decision groups and profit centers may be poised for action. To delay still longer could reduce morale and otherwise degrade organizational performance.

Sensing the urgency to act, whatever its source, is obviously a central consideration in deciding whether to recycle to some earlier point in the decision process.

Applying Expert Judgment

Expert judgment is called for when (1) there is no urgency to act but the available data do not resolve the decision-problem; (2) there is urgency to act and disagreement is still substantial. The expertise on a particular decision-problem may reside in one of the decision makers and so the group may defer to that person's judgment. Of course, that deference may be based on political considerations in addition to, or instead of, knowledge considerations. Such realities of real-world decision making must be recognized.

If expertise resides with several people, a question arises on how to combine their judgments. Kotler offers some advice on this question.[2] According to Kotler, the methods for treating the estimates of "experts" (e.g., sales managers, brand managers) must accomplish two things: (1) induce the experts to provide individual judgments, and (2) reduce the estimates to a single, usable value. (Review Figure 4-1 in this regard.) The most straightforward way to do this is simply to assemble the experts and ask them to produce a group consensus on, say, the expected sales for new product X over the next year. However, there often are situations wherein the politics and personalities of a group might suppress the contributions of the true expert or give more attention to the opinion of the nonexpert. In some organizational settings these behavioral forces are reduced by having one person (the analyst—a marketing researcher) poll the experts separately. The polling would include feedback to the participants as to the values being suggested without identifying who in particular suggested them. The feedback would also include justification of any extreme values. A new round of polling occurs and polling with feedback is continued until a consensus is apparent. This repetitive, anonymous polling is termed the *Delphi Approach*.[3] In most organizations the conventional group discussion method for developing a consensus is more likely to be the practice.

Should the analyst choose to weight the expertness of the participants and so weight the individual estimates in computing the consensus measure (e.g., median), then a basis for assigning the weights must be established. The "track record" of the experts could be such a basis, as could be the analyst's subjective assessment. Or the experts could rate themselves.

---

[2] Adapted from *Marketing Decision Making: A Model Building Approach* by Philip Kotler, pp. 594–595. Copyright © 1971 by Holt, Rinehart and Winston, Inc. Reprinted by permission of Holt, Rinehart and Winston.

[3] For a more detailed summary, see "The Basic Delphi Method," *Harvard Business Review*, Vol. 47, No. 3 (May–June, 1969), pp. 80–82.

Expert counsel can come from outside the organization as well as from inside. Consultants, ex-company executives, bankers, etc., may be called upon to render advice in resolving a decision-problem. Note also that experts may be called upon in lieu of conducting a study to gather additional data. The study required, even in its bare-bones form, may cost too much and/or require too much time. Getting the advice of someone knowledgeable in the problem area could be accomplished quickly and with an acceptable cost.

IMPLEMENTING THE CHOSEN COURSE OF ACTION

Many aspiring managers in today's organizations have been accused of succumbing to "analysis paralysis." [4] That is, they tend to get overly involved in the analysis effort and never proceed to convert a choice made into an operating reality. Paper decisions are not a substitute for real-world action. The decision makers must insure that the choice they have made is indeed implemented. Needless to say, the decision makers must account for difficulties in implementation (i.e., the psychological as well as dollar costs) when they develop alternatives and specify the basis for selecting one course of action.

It was noted earlier that there are often some observable differences between marketing managers and marketing researchers. At the risk of making too sweeping a generalization, it might be said that marketing researchers tend to be "people of thought" while marketing managers tend to be "people of action." The successful resolution of marketing decision-problems requires both types.

MONITORING THE ENVIRONMENT: A CONTINUAL TASK

Implemented decisions alter the environment—both the internal and the external environment. Change is produced. The decision makers hope that the changes are in favorable directions. But, of course, there is no guarantee that they will be. Figure 5–3 illustrates a case in which the initial consequences of a marketing decision were unfavorable, creating a new environment and raising new decision-problems for resolution. It is therefore incumbent upon the marketer to continually monitor the nature of the environment. This monitoring must include not only the response of consumers and competitors to an implemented decision, but also must include a sensing of any changes in basic dimensions of the environment (demographic, technological, etc.).

The argument for continual monitoring of the total environment made in Chapter 1 is thus reaffirmed here. Since the evaluation/control activity is an integral part of the basic managerial process, this prescription to constantly audit the environment is not a startling one. By the same token, it is a prescription that cannot be disregarded.

---

[4] J. Sterling Livingston, "Myth of the Well-Educated Manager," *Harvard Business Review,* Vol. 49, No. 1 (January–February, 1971), pp. 79–89.

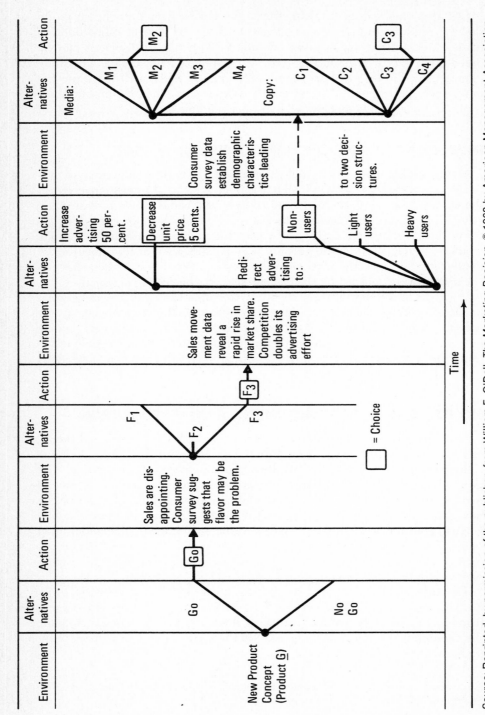

□ = Choice

Time →

Figure 5-3   Marketing Actions Change the Environment

QUESTIONS FOR DISCUSSION

1. Discuss the possible communication gap between the marketing researcher and a manager. How may such a gap be closed?
2. When in the decision process is an actionable study likely to be required?
3. What are the objectives of an actionable study?
4. What are the primary considerations that dictate the sequence of material and narrative in a business report?
5. Under what conditions should there be a return to a prior stage in the decision process (recycle)? Give an example.
6. Where does expert judgment fit into the decision process? Under what circumstances would such judgment be employed?
7. What is the purpose of postimplementation environmental monitoring? When would this type of monitoring take place?

SUGGESTED READINGS

Aguilar, Francis J. *Scanning the Business Environment*. New York: Macmillan Publishing Company, Inc., 1967.

Boettinger, H. M. *Moving Mountains: Or the Art and Craft of Letting Others See Things Your Way*. New York: Macmillan Publishing Company, Inc., 1975.

Campbell, Stephen K. *Flaws and Fallacies in Statistical Thinking*. Englewood Cliffs, N.J.: Prentice-Hall, Inc., 1974.

Huff, Darrell, and Irving Geis. *How to Lie With Statistics*. New York: W. W. Norton and Company, Inc., 1954.

Wallis, W. A., and H. V. Roberts. *The Nature of Statistics*. New York: The Free Press, 1965. Chapter 4, "Misuses of Statistics."

Zeisel, Hans. *Say It With Figures*. New York: Harper and Row, Publishers, Inc., 1968.

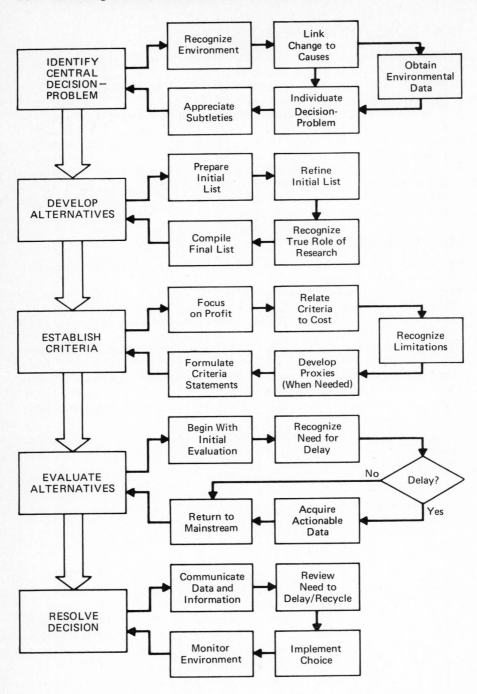

Summary Flowchart, Chapters 1–5

GRANDIN LABORATORIES

A Comprehensive Case

This case is unique in several ways. First, it is divided into five parts, each of which illustrates designated chapters and phases of the decision process. Second, it is a "worked-out" case, with each of the five parts being analyzed separately according to the five steps of the basic flowchart. Third, the case develops the decision makers' thoughts early in the decision process, long before the need for data is apparent. The entire decision flow and related decisions are illustrated in the case.

It is suggested that the parts of the case and analyses be read following the completion of the reading of the chapters to which they relate. In particular the recommended reading sequence is:

Chapter 1, Grandin Laboratories—Part A, Analysis Part A
Chapter 2, Grandin Laboratories—Part B, Analysis Part B
Chapter 3, Grandin Laboratories—Part C, Analysis Part C
Chapter 4, Grandin Laboratories—Part D, Analysis Part D
Chapter 5, Grandin Laboratories—Part E, Analysis Part E, Summary

This basic issue must always be addressed at every point in the analysis of any case or business problem: Where are the decision makers in the overall decision structure? Where should they be?

Have the decision makers located and agreed upon the central decision-problem? If so, are they now in the process of developing possible marketing alternatives? Or have they agreed upon the options available to them and are now attempting to set up the criteria for selecting one of those alternatives?

If the decision makers have proceeded through those phases, it may be that they agree on the need for more data and are now assessing the costs of obtaining various levels of accuracy of the data they seek. Or have they gone through all those steps and are now resolving the issue through the data obtained? In any event, it is essential that decision makers clearly understand where they are in the decision process so that there will be a minimum of confusion and wasted time in moving forward toward decision resolution.

GRANDIN LABORATORIES—PART A

Grandin Laboratories, producers of ethical drugs and pharmaceuticals, was established in 1894 in Canton, Ohio. Its headquarters and manufacturing plants are still located there. The company was founded by Dr. T. R. Grandin, at the time a practicing physician, for the purpose of manufacturing better "pills" which were then the most common form of medication.

During those early days most drugs were dispensed by the physician. Drugstores handled drugs and other medicines, but for transportation and communications reasons the physician did most of the dispensing to the patient. The pharmacist was largely a source of drugs for the doctor.

As drugstores became more widespread and the telephone eliminated communications problems, physicians gradually relinquished their dispensing role. Pills were declining in popularity, and patients were given prescriptions by their physicians to be filled by pharmacists.

Grandin adjusted well to these changes. It gradually moved toward its present line of ethical drugs and pharmaceuticals. The company acquired a reputation for outstanding research and high-quality products. At the same time Grandin adapted its marketing policies to the changing environment. Much of the selling effort was directed to the drug retailers. Pharmacists held Grandin in high esteem due largely to the fact that the company had continued directing its marketing efforts to the physician, who in turn often listed a Grandin drug in the prescription. Grandin's marketing strategy, up to about 25 years ago, was to restrict its laboratory research efforts to ethical products. This policy was tacitly approved by physicians as evidenced by their frequent use of Grandin products. This physician endorsement was reflected by pharmacists.

Ethical pharmaceutical houses are distinguished from proprietary drug firms by the fact that their promotional efforts are aimed at the professional buyer (physician, druggist, hospital buyers) rather than the ultimate consumer. Generally speaking an *ethical drug* can be described as one for which a physician's prescription is required. A *proprietary drug* is one which is branded and sold over the counter without a doctor's prescription. Over the years Grandin has followed the basic distribution policy of selling directly to retail druggists. In accordance with the ethical formula, the Grandin sales force has been responsible for "creating" a demand for the firm's prescription drugs by "detailing" the physicians (i.e., by missionary sales work with the doctors) and by selling the retail druggist on stocking Grandin products.

Physical distribution of Grandin products is handled through 16 company-owned sales branches and warehouses located throughout the United States.

No account is farther than two days' delivery service from any branch warehouse. Most trading centers receive either same-day or following-day service.

Several of Grandin's competitors had digressed from the ethical product to the making of proprietary drugs, marketing both to the druggists. This move was not necessarily viewed with disfavor by the pharmacists because their sales were increased by the new promotional emphasis being placed on over-the-counter products by the manufacturers. However, many physicians took a negative stance, feeling that such ethical companies would not devote the necessary research effort to the development of new drugs. They feared, too, that the profits from proprietary drug marketers would create a consumer demand for over-the-counter drugs which in many instances would result in improper use of medicines by uninformed persons. This contention was documented by national studies showing a higher proportion of self-medication being practiced by lower-income, less-educated persons. Self-medication, many physicians contended, should be discouraged.

Jealous of its high reputation among medical professionals, Grandin held to its policy of producing and marketing only ethical products—until some 25 years ago. At that time it placed its Grandin Vitamins on an over-the-counter (OTC) basis. The company's vitamin brand soon was producing a very healthy share of total corporate income and profit. The timing of the OTC product was excellent; vitamins were fast becoming a popular item for maintaining an individual's health. They were endorsed and well publicized by the medical profession as a valuable supplement, especially during winter months when certain body deficiencies were more likely to be prevalent.

Within a few years Grandin Vitamins were second in sales only to those produced and marketed by Greene Drug Company of Kankakee, Illinois. Greene markets only proprietary products, and during the past 25 years has shown vigorous growth and profitability. Grandin, however, as one of the country's leading ethical houses, was able to match Greene's growth and profitability with only a relatively small portion of total sales in the proprietary field, as shown in Table 1.

Table 1 Comparison of Grandin and Greene Sales (In Millions of Dollars)

	1963	1968	1972
Grandin Laboratories	179.1	339.2	401.5
Greene Drug Company	111.4	251.3	359.3

A substantial contribution to the growth of these and other companies serving the ethical and proprietary fields was the dramatic increase in the use of drugs and related sundries. Table 2 shows consumer expenditures for both ethical and proprietary drugs and related sundries.

Table 2 Drug and Drug Sundries Per Capita, Annual Private Consumer Expenditures

	1960	1965	1970	1972
Drugs and drug sundries	$ 19.9	$ 24.5	$ 35.6	$ 40.6
All health services	102.0	141.8	203.1	242.5

Source: Department of Health, Education, and Welfare, Social Security Administration.

Grandin's distribution of their vitamin brand was virtually 100 percent among independent and chain retail drug outlets, but among other types of dealers they were less well represented by a considerable margin. Their detail people (sales representatives) were already calling on drugstores and Grandin distribution among pharmacists was easily achieved. The company's sales-people were not, however, experienced at obtaining large grocery chain distribution, nor did they feel at this time that such distribution would be advisable.

Grandin's entry into the proprietary field years ago had little effect on the company's general reputation among physicians and pharmacists. Apparently Grandin was not viewed in the same light as Augusta, Merck, Amherst, and others who had attempted to straddle the line with a wide range of both ethical and over-the-counter products. The Grandin management was determined to hold their reputation high, and for this reason had rejected several strong internal moves to place additional Grandin products on an over-the-counter basis.

Grandin's Marketing Committee, however, has long held the opinion that this highly professional attitude on the part of top management is a constraint that cannot be justified in view of the successes of other drug houses which have made the transition. The committee has argued that Grandin should move with gradual transition toward a range of proprietary offerings to the drug retailer. Grandin's top management has listened to the Marketing Committee's arguments on several occasions during the past several years, fully recognizing that the committee is comprised of qualified and experienced people. Moreover, the committee's successful launching of the Grandin Vitamin years ago has not been forgotten. Indeed, the contribution of the company's vitamin to total corporate profit is a constant reminder.

The Marketing Committee's responsibilities relate to the allocation of the marketing dollar for both ethical products and Grandin Vitamins. The marketing vice-president heads the committee. Other members are the marketing vice-presidents for the Ethical and Vitamin Divisions, the marketing services vice-president, the sales manager, the advertising and promotion manager, the marketing research manager, the manager of marketing budget and controls, and the chief economist. (See Figure 1.)

The Marketing Committee often draws on several outside marketing research firms, but most of the work is conducted by Market Facts, Inc. (Market

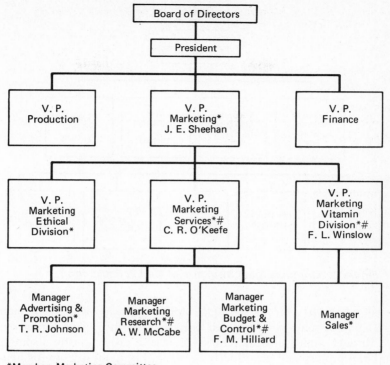

```
                    ┌─────────────────────┐
                    │  Board of Directors │
                    └─────────────────────┘
                              │
                    ┌─────────────────────┐
                    │      President      │
                    └─────────────────────┘
```

*Member, Marketing Committee
#Member, Planning Committee, Vitamin Division

Figure 1   Basic Organizational Structure of Grandin Laboratories

Facts' organizational structure is shown in Figure 2.) Grandin has been working with this company for more than ten years and has developed a close working relationship. Market Facts maintains a wide range of data collection facilities, including national personal and telephone interviewing, a national mail panel comprised of some 70,000 families, and an in-store retail testing facility comprised of both drug and grocery retail outlets. The nature of Market Facts' relationships with its clients varies. With some firms its personnel perform the role of data collection and analysis only. With other clients they participate at the problem-formulation level, gathering and analyzing the necessary data and making marketing recommendations. It is in this latter manner that they work with Grandin. A Market Facts vice-president, Francine Standish, is a specialist in the medical marketing field. Standish and Jack Avery, Market Facts' president, are the principals in charge of marketing research and counsel for Grandin.

The sales and profitability of Grandin Vitamins reached their peak during the middle 1960s. By 1969 Grandin Vitamins had a 33 percent share of the market; price and private-label brands accounted for only 11 percent of all vitamins sold in terms of dollar sales. Since that time Grandin Vitamins sales have

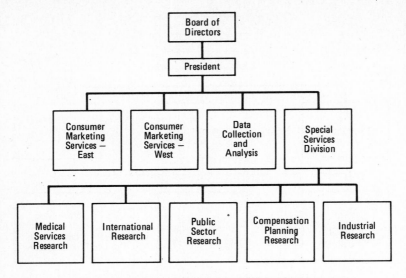

Figure 2   Organizational Structure of Market Facts, Inc.

declined nearly 40 percent, although total corporate sales have increased. Greene vitamin sales have declined only slightly since 1969. Other data obtained through audits of drug retailers showed a rather drastic decline in the sales of the professional, or ethical, vitamins. The ethical vitamins held a 59 percent market share in 1969; this figure dropped to 46 percent in 1972. At the same time, the total consumption of vitamins began to decrease somewhat after the 1966–1968 peak, as seen in Table 3.

**Table 3 Industry Sales of Proprietary
            Vitamins by Year**

1963	$15,444,000
1966	18,040,000
1969	17,202,000
1972	15,909,000

Source: Department of Health, Education, and Welfare, Social Security Administration.

In view of Grandin Vitamins' drop in market share, absolute sales, and profitability to the company, the advertising department has been requesting and receiving increased funds in an attempt to reverse the decline. The number of marketing dollars allocated to Grandin Vitamins has more than doubled during the past five years. At the same time, the marketing funds allocated to Grandin's ethical products have been lowered by approximately one fourth. There has been no reversal of the sales decline in Grandin Vitamins. Timothy R. Johnson, Grandin's advertising manager, was concerned about the inability of advertising to stem this trend and recently questioned the advertising copy and media approaches employed during the past year.

Before the regularly scheduled meetings with Grandin's advertising agency, when plans for the forthcoming year were to be drawn up, Johnson and his assistant took a critical look at the basic advertising theme as well as several of the media employed. If not acceptable by some criterion, they would then be well fortified with ammunition when their meeting with their agency took place. Normally, advertising copy and media research are conducted by the advertising agency at their expense. However, in this case, on an *ex post facto* basis, Johnson and his assistant agreed that they would have a research study conducted to determine the "worth" of the theme and media recently used.

Such a request by Johnson for advertising research was entirely within his realm of authority. His channel of communications for the research study, however, was through Grandin's own marketing research manager, Arthur McCabe. Johnson's interoffice letter to McCabe appears in Figure 3.

GRANDIN LABORATORIES
Interoffice Communication

From: Timothy R. Johnson, Advertising Manager

To: Arthur W. McCabe, Marketing Research Manager

Date: February 3, 1973

Subject: Advertising Survey of Grandin Vitamins

As you well know, Grandin Vitamins have long been an important part of our company's profit picture. During the past ten years our annual proprietary vitamin sales have dropped from more than $5 million to something above $3 million. This decline is apparently a function of two things: first, the entire proprietary vitamin industry is declining, and, second, our share of market is being reduced each year.

To counteract this, as you know, the Marketing Committee authorized a $1 million consumer advertising campaign on Grandin Vitamins. This campaign got underway last October and has now run its course. Unfortunately, you will recall, our audits by International Marketing Services of America, Ltd. do not show any reversal of the downward trend. I am hopeful of convincing the Marketing Committee of the value of repeating the advertising effort beginning this fall.

One of the problems with the campaign just completed was our inability to develop effective copy. Moreover, it could very well be that we are not aiming our messages at the right market segments. We do not want to make these mistakes again.

Would you therefore give some thought to the conduct of a market or advertising survey which will aid us in these advertising decisions. Please let me have your recommendations as soon as possible.

Figure 3   Interoffice Letter Requesting Advertising Survey

Grandin's marketing research department is comprised of ten persons: seven professionals, including Art McCabe, and three secretaries (see the organization chart in Figure 4). This is a small department when compared, for example, to the mass marketers in the food industry. However, it is the policy of Grandin to use professional research firms such as Market Facts, Inc., rather than maintaining a large in-house research staff.

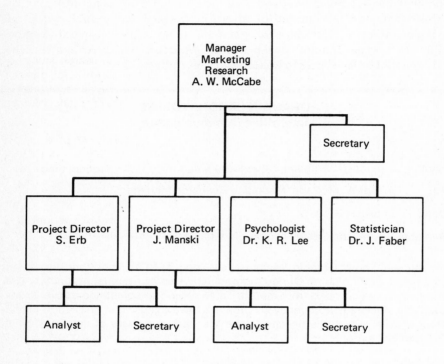

Figure 4   Organization of Grandin's Marketing Research Department

McCabe, along with the representatives of the research organizations, has always participated in the design of research studies. He works with agency people in deciding on the data collection methods, sample type and size, and the nature of the data processing and analysis. Upon receipt of Johnson's letter, McCabe sent a letter (Figure 5) to Jack Avery of Market Facts asking Avery's help in setting up a marketing research study. McCabe pointed out that the objective of the study would be data to aid the advertising department in selecting a copy theme and target audience. He enclosed data that he considered to be of interest and value to Avery (Exhibits A, B, C, and D).

GRANDIN LABORATORIES

Canton, Ohio 44701

February 5, 1973

Mr. Jack Avery
Market Facts, Inc.
100 South Wacker Drive
Chicago, Illinois 60606

Dear Jack

We are considering the conduct of an important marketing research study on our Grandin Vitamins. As you can readily appreciate, the study is of considerable importance to us in view of the role vitamins have played in contributing to our corporate profits over the past several years. Tim Johnson's letter of February 3 to me is enclosed and is self-explanatory.

The decline in vitamin sales is not unique to our own company. All other major brands have suffered sales losses. We have some data on vitamin sales and some of the attendant problems which have developed during recent times. This material is enclosed and I am sure you will find it helpful in your approach to the problem.

I would like to have your ideas on how we should go about the conduct of a study with the broad objective being to aid us in determining what basic copy theme will be most effective as well as to whom we should be directing our advertising messages.

Vitamin advertising, as you know, begins during the early part of November and is carried on intensively for about four months. Some 80 percent of all vitamin advertising purchases are made during those four months.

As far as the study is concerned, it is apparent that we must agree on procedure and cost, and then complete the entire project by the end of July so that we will be able to work with our advertising agency in the development of our program for the forthcoming season.

Cordially yours
GRANDIN LABORATORIES

Art

Arthur McCabe
Marketing Research Manager

AM/km
Enc.

Figure 5   Letter to Market Facts Requesting Advertising Study

Exhibit A   Growth in Market Share of Proprietary Vitamins

	1969	1970	1971	1972
Proprietary (unit sales)	41%	46%	50%	54%
Professional (unit sales)	59%	54%	50%	46%

Exhibit B   Sources of Consumer Purchases

	1969	1970	1971	1972
Drugstores (independent and chain)	68%	64%	61%	56%
Mail order	10	11	13	15
Department store	4	4	5	5
Grocery	3	4	5	9
Door-to-door	3	4	3	2
Discount stores	1	2	5	9
All other outlets	11	11	8	4

Exhibit C   Grandin Data *(Millions of Dollars)*

	1969	1970	1971	1972
Total company sales	$357.0	$367.4	$389.5	$401.5
Operating profit	61.2	73.3	74.5	89.1
Grandin proprietary vitamin sales	$ 5.7	$ 4.2	$ 3.6	$ 3.4
Total marketing dollar allocation	$ 4.5	$ 4.5	$ 4.2	$ 4.0
Proprietary vitamins	.5	.5	.7	1.0
All ethical products	4.0	4.0	3.5	3.0
Share of proprietary vitamin market				
Grandin Vitamins	33%	30%	26%	22%
Other major brands	56	55	54	49
Price and private-label brands	11	15	20	29

Avery discussed the letter and the attendant material with Francine Standish, his medical and pharmaceutical specialist. They recognized the specificity
of the request from McCabe, but decided to reject his suggestion of submitting
a study plan at this time. Instead, they prepared a response, in letter form, requesting a meeting with Grandin's entire Marketing Committee.

Exhibit D Dollar Sales and Market Share of Proprietary Vitamins, by Company (000s Omitted)

| | Greene Drug | | Grandin | | Fluvanna | | Augusta | | Amherst | | All Others | | Total $ |
	$	%	$	%	$	%	$	%	$	%	$	%	
1963	7,429	47	5,405	35	463	3	1,082	7	772	5	463	3	15,614
1966	8,659	48	6,675	37	541	3	902	5	721	4	541	3	18,039
1969	7,741	45	5,677	33	1,204	7	1,032	6	860	5	688	4	17,202
1972	7,506	47	3,438	22	2,532	16	687	4	516	3	1,230	8	15,909

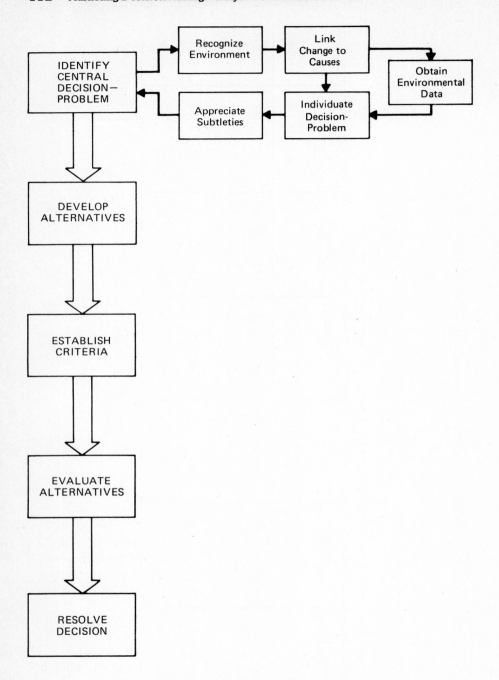

Summary Flowchart, Chapter 1

ANALYSIS OF PART A—
IDENTIFYING THE CENTRAL DECISION-PROBLEM

One should begin by using the five-step basic flowchart as an analytical framework. The five steps, to review, are:

1. Identify the central decision-problem.
2. Develop alternatives.
3. Establish criteria.
4. Evaluate alternatives.
5. Resolve the decision.

With regard to this framework one should ask: Where do the Grandin decision makers appear to be in the five-step process? Grandin's management seems to be seeking alternatives in the advertising area. Do they explicitly recognize the five-step process (or some reasonable variant)? No.

Having ascertained where the participants appear to be in the decision-making/problem-solving process, the next and key question to raise is: Where should they be? In the Grandin illustration management should be at the first step—identifying the central decision-problem. Market Facts' request to meet with Grandin's entire Marketing Committee indicates that they felt Grandin had jumped ahead without a clear definition of the decision-problem and its environment or context.

As Chapter 1 suggests, identifying the central decision-problem is facilitated by executing these substeps:

a. Recognize the environment.
b. Link changes to causes.
c. Obtain environmental data.
d. Individuate the decision-problem.
e. Appreciate the subtleties.

These five substeps are now examined in turn.

Recognize the Environment

The environment was one of declining sales in the vitamin industry, declining Grandin Vitamin sales, and a declining Grandin share of the vitamin market. The source of consumer purchases of vitamins had shifted; an increased share of vitamins were being sold through grocery, mail order, and discount retailers.

Link Changes to Causes

Here is where Grandin management's analysis comes up short. They detected changes in the environment but failed to interrelate them. A summary of environmental elements and their changes is provided in Table 4.

Table 4 Summary of Environmental Elements and Their Changes, 1969–72

Environmental Element	Source	Nature of Change
Sales Share		
Grandin vitamins	Exhibit C	Down approx. 16%/yr.
Industry vitamins	Table 3	Down approx. 3%/yr.
Market Share		
Grandin	Exhibit C	Down 11 pctg. points
Other major companies	Exhibit C	Down 7 pctg. points
Price/private label	Exhibit C	Up 18 pctg. points
Distribution Share		
Drugstores	Exhibit B	Down 12 pctg. points
Mail order	Exhibit B	Up 5 pctg. points
Grocery stores	Exhibit B	Up 6 pctg. points
Discount stores	Exhibit B	Up 8 pctg. points
Grandin Vitamin		
Marketing Outlays	Exhibit C	Up approx. 26%/yr.

Grandin management recognized that their decreasing vitamin sales stemmed from declining industry sales and faltering market share. They failed to ask *why* industry sales and market share were declining. Also, they failed to notice some interesting changes in retail sales patterns. The preceding table suggests that the decline in market share that Grandin and similar companies were experiencing was due to gains made by price and private-label vitamins. Further, the fall-off in the distribution share (i.e., share of retail sales) of Grandin's mainstay outlet, the drugstore, had been to the gain of discount stores, groceries, and mail-order operations. Clearly, the causes of the unsatisfactory, unplanned-for changes that Grandin was experiencing are price- and place-related, and not promotion-related as the advertising manager seemed to feel.

Obtain Environmental Data

From a review standpoint it is worthwhile to recap the nature of the data already supplied in Part A. The tables of Part A yield the following data classifications:

Table 1: Environmental—accounting.
Table 2: Environmental—nonaccounting.
Table 3: Environmental—derived from the accounting data of industry members, but from Grandin's perspective it is nonaccounting data.
McCabe's Enclosures (Exhibits A, B, C, and D): Environmental—accounting and nonaccounting data.

No actionable data appear in Part A because no alternatives and criteria were explicitly defined to permit actionable data to be compiled and a choice to be made. The data tell only of Grandin's environment. Environmental data provide clues as to what is going on. Actionable data permit choices to be made. Additional environmental data are called for when no, or poor, explanations of observed changes are present, i.e., when better or additional understanding is called for. Grandin can therefore be criticized for not seeking additional environmental data. Operating on the wrong track, Johnson, the advertising manager, proceeded instead to request data concerning the impact of the completed one-million-dollar ad campaign.

A speculation or hypothesis may be formed about the decline in consumer expenditures for vitamins. Looking at the data of Table 2 in Part A, this hypothesis might be developed as follows. Line 1, Table 2, could be restated as:

	1960	1965	1970	1972
Drugs and sundries as a percentage of all health services	19.5	17.3	17.5	16.7

The restated data suggest, among other things, that consumers have been spending less, or have less to spend, on drugs and drug sundries out of their budgets for health services. That is, the decline in total vitamin sales may in part be attributed to vitamins having been squeezed out of the consumer's health budget. Another explanation might be that consumers have been buying the same (or more) quantity of vitamins but they have been buying them at discount or reduced prices and, therefore, have been spending less in aggregate as observed. These are only hypotheses. The true situation with regard to the consumers' declining outlays is pertinent to identification of the central problem. Obtaining some additional data seems warranted. Grandin management did not pursue this point. Had they done so, they would have found reduced prices to be a principal reason for reduced vitamin outlays by consumers.

Individuate the Decision-Problem

The central decision-problem was not identified by the case protagonists. It could be stated from the above findings as follows:

> The erosion in vitamin sales and market share appear due to shifts in consumer purchase behavior—shifts that advertising alone will not correct; shifts that call for a planned, strategic response on Grandin's part. Examination of Grandin's distribution and pricing policies/practices appears necessary.

Johnson, the advertising manager, was trying to "put out a growing brush fire" with essentially short-term measures. The decision-problem is clearly serious enough to require a more enduring solution. As such, it is likely to involve more than just the marketing unit. For example, if expanded distribution (more specifically, adding a new channel of distribution) is seen to be the answer, then nonmarketing involvement might play out as follows:

Production: Develop appropriate packaging and packing for new channel; determine the need for additional in-plant inventory.

Accounting: Integrate new customers into billing system; prepare for expanded accounts receivable scope.

Finance: Determine to what extent additional funds from outside the company will be required; make plans to secure such funds.

Clearly, major decisions such as distribution or product modification require the cognizance of all the firm's major functions.

Appreciate the Subtleties

A starting point here is to list the participants in the case, noting their viewpoints, biases, vested interests, etc.

Major Participants	Viewpoints, Biases, Interests
Timothy R. Johnson Advertising Manager	Concerned about advertising effectiveness; had a $1 million campaign "fail"; wary of budget cuts.
Arthur McCabe Marketing Research Manager	Research technician; concern for detail and procedures; tends to take narrow view.
Jack Avery Market Facts President	Cautious about engaging in research without problem clarification; desire to sell services; an "outsider."

While it does not appear that Johnson was acting from political motives, nevertheless, one should understand his position and views on the apparent decision-problem.

Johnson revealed his thinking in his letter to Art McCabe, the company's marketing research manager. Johnson questioned the "correctness" of past advertising copy and media decisions. In a sense, he was saying that this was the basic, unresolved issue. He could be quite correct, if one views the issue from the standpoint of his department and the goals set for his department.

What are these advertising department goals and objectives? In a broad sense, Johnson's department is charged with the responsibility of administering an advertising budget in keeping with corporate goals. More specifically, the department is expected to develop effective advertising copy, aimed at the "right" people, within the budget restraints of a stated advertising appropriation. In this climate Johnson can be quite right in questioning past advertising copy and media decisions. Such questioning is basic to his department's objectives.

But Johnson, in his letter to McCabe, went a step further. He said that not only had he determined the basic issue, but he also needed information to aid him in the making of new decisions. Moreover, McCabe tacitly supported him. In his letter to Market Facts, McCabe asked the research firm to make some suggestions as to the design of the study concerning the advertising. This strongly implies that the basic, unresolved issue has been located and agreed upon, and that what is now needed is some creative thought regarding how a study can be designed so as to obtain the needed data at minimum cost. Thus, Johnson was saying that he knew the basic, unresolved issue and that there was a need for data before the final decision could be made. McCabe went along with Johnson and did not question whether or not this would be a good expenditure of marketing research money.

But was Johnson correct in his diagnosis of the basic, unresolved issue? No one can really question his desire to develop the most effective advertising copy and to direct this message to the "right" people. That is his responsibility. But Jack Avery, president of Market Facts, had a broader view of Grandin's marketing problems. He had the advantage of being an "outsider" and as a result was not influenced by "intraorganizational conflict." Johnson, subconsciously, sought to maintain the growth of his department. He most likely would resist any budget reduction which, in turn, could imply that either he was not performing well or his function within the company was becoming less essential.

Both Avery and Standish studied the data provided by Art McCabe. They viewed these data in a light that tended to eliminate advertising as the basic issue. The decline of the drugstore in the distribution role of Grandin Vitamins is apparent. Private label and price brands have increased their market share dramatically. Surely these areas cannot be understated in terms of basic issues. Consumer vitamin outlays are declining. What does this significant fact mean to Grandin? Advertising of vitamins by Grandin has doubled over the past several years, yet their sales and market share are declining. Can one really expect advertising to achieve the impossible, to overcome a forceful trend that would appear to transcend any one company's advertising effort?

These are the real basic issues to Grandin. Johnson saw the issues from his narrow, self-imposed vantage point as advertising manager. The Market Facts representatives apparently had some appreciation of such subtleties. Instead of launching headfirst into a study, Market Facts requested a meeting with Grandin's Marketing Committee; they wanted a fuller understanding of the decision situation.

DISCUSSION QUESTIONS FOR PART A

1. Assume each of the participants listed was knowledgable about the five steps of the basic flowchart of the decision-making, problem-solving process. Each participant would feel that he or she was at what step? What justification might they have for their beliefs in this regard? What evidence is there, if any, that would seem to contradict their views?
2. Several *planned* changes were brought about and contemplated by Grandin in Part A of the case. What were they?
3. How might the data in Tables 1 and 2 be displayed to reveal changes more effectively?
4. Some of the sales data in the case came from audits of drug retailers. What precautions need to be taken in the use of such data?
5. Does the case material suggest what the nature of the basic issue(s) is?
6. Grandin's market research department has a psychologist in it (Figure 3). What would be the role of this person?
7. Little detailed description is provided in the case concerning the advertising program employed by Grandin. What might such a program involve? What media would be employed? What specific vehicles might be used? What might Grandin say in its advertising, i.e., what copy might be employed?

GRANDIN LABORATORIES—PART B

(*Note to Reader:* You should have read through Chapter 2 and Grandin Laboratories—Part A to this point.)

Jack Avery, president of Market Facts, fully recognized the fact that Timothy Johnson was viewing the situation from his narrow vantage point. Avery was able to assess the total situation in a broader, more objective manner. As an outside consultant, he could be more rational in his approach to Grandin without fear of risk to himself or to his research consulting firm. And, unlike several management people at Grandin, his position was not being threatened in any way.

Avery and Standish composed a letter to McCabe. The letter, signed by Avery, did not immediately initiate a discussion of research methodology as it related to the particular advertising problem. Instead, Avery decided to broaden the subject, but without taking a strong point of view contrary to that expressed by McCabe. So he did not stress his disagreement in his letter, but instead requested a meeting with the Grandin Marketing Committee. His letter follows in Figure 6.

MARKET FACTS, INC.
Chicago, Illinois 60606

February 7, 1973

Mr. Arthur McCabe
Grandin Laboratories
Canton, Ohio 44701

Dear Art

You can be sure that we will be glad to participate with you on the study described in your letter of February 5. Certainly there is no question about the importance of vitamins to Grandin. And one can readily appreciate the desire for efficient advertising efforts in view of the presumed lack of success of the campaign being concluded.

The data you enclosed with your letter are most revealing. I was impressed with the shifting buying behavior of the American public. While the drugstore in the past has garnered the great bulk of the vitamin volume, there is no denying the inroads being made by other outlets such as grocery stores and discount houses. The decline in the share of your own brand of vitamins could very well be a function of the movement away from drugstores which, to you, is much more acute in view of the fact that over the years Grandin has derived a large measure of support from the pharmacists.

Figure 6   Letter Suggesting a Meeting Between Market Facts and Grandin

Grandin Laboratories
February 7, 1973
Page 2

One can argue that if people are switching to grocery stores and discount houses for the vitamins, to be purchased at lower prices, they are not really differentiating your brand from others. In other words, vitamins today may be viewed as a nondifferentiated item and any brand is as good as another, regardless of price.

This may or may not be true, but I am wondering whether you should be advertising at all. Perhaps the marketing funds should be directed to developing grocery outlets. Or, what would happen if you dropped the price of your brand at the pharmacy level, and communicated the low price to consumers rather than striving for some unique advertising approach attempting to convince the public that Grandin is better—although the differences among brands is not great, and perhaps nonexistent?

My question is: Should we be talking about an advertising survey at this point in time? Perhaps there are other decisions which are more important. Here are a few possibilities:

1. Should the price of your brand be decreased?
2. Should a new brand be introduced and distributed only at the grocery store level?
3. Should funds be allocated to bolster the support of the pharmacists?

In a broader sense, to what extent has Tim Johnson communicated with his own management to determine whether there is agreement or disagreement on some of these basic marketing decisions? If there is agreement, and there is still the need for more efficient advertising, then a study along the lines you suggest could very well be in order.

I recommend, however, that we all make certain we are spending the survey money for the right purpose. It could very well be that we should be researching price or channels of distribution, rather than advertising.

Francine Standish and I would very much like to have the opportunity of meeting with your entire Marketing Committee—hoping to be able to discuss several of these basic issues. I look forward to hearing from you.

Cordially yours

MARKET FACTS, INC.

Jack

Jack Avery
President

JA/km

*Figure 6   Letter Suggesting a Meeting Between Market Facts and Grandin
(Concluded)*

When Art McCabe, Grandin's marketing research manager, telephoned Jack Avery of Market Facts in response to the letter, it was agreed that it would be well to broaden the discussion of the advertising issue—perhaps to more basic areas of concern. Avery again stressed that he would like to meet with the entire Marketing Committee. He made a strong point of this to Art McCabe, feeling that unless he could express his views to Grandin management people above the level of Johnson, the advertising manager, he would find his thoughts falling on deaf ears.

With Avery's support McCabe returned to Tim Johnson and related Avery's desire to meet with the entire Marketing Committee. Johnson was well aware of Avery's stature among the top marketers at Grandin and did not feel it wise to stand in the way of his insistence upon meeting with the Grandin marketing management. He asked McCabe to set up the meeting. The memorandum announcing the meeting pointed out that Avery had asked for the meeting because he felt that more than just vitamin advertising was at stake.

In essence, the purpose of the meeting, as stated in the announcement memo, was to make some basic decisions as to the future of the Grandin vitamin business. Specifically, the memo stated, ". . . It is hoped that out of this meeting will come decisions that will enable Grandin to move forward in making the Grandin Vitamin Division a more profitable phase of the company. . . ." The memo was sent by Joseph E. Sheehan, Grandin's marketing vice-president. The fact that he sent the memo suggested to committee members that this was to be an important meeting. Thus, without exception, all members of the committee attended, along with Avery and Standish of Market Facts, who had received carbon copies of the memo.

At the meeting, Avery was introduced to the group by Joseph Sheehan. He pointed out that Avery was known to almost everyone in the room, and that Avery had suggested this meeting in order to discuss various courses of action which might be taken to enhance the profit position of Grandin Vitamins.

Avery responded: "I appreciate this opportunity to talk directly with so many Grandin executives who are influencing the future of the Grandin Vitamin. I did suggest this discussion to make certain that our research firm was engaged in meaningful effort for your company. There is little benefit to be derived from our researching problem areas that have little or no effect on your corporate or divisional revenue and profit.

"The future of Grandin Vitamins is related to many marketing efforts, advertising being an important one. But it would be well to review the role of advertising in a market place that virtually defies greater penetration for Grandin. I refer to the fact that Grandin's traditional retail channels are becoming less and less important in the distribution of vitamins. I would like to remind you once again that the nonprescription vitamin market share has declined dramatically during the past several years. Too, it is essential that we again recognize that price and private-label brands have virtually doubled their share of the market just during the past five years.

"Grandin's dollar sales, as well as market share, have declined during this period despite a substantial boost in the advertising support of the Grandin Vitamin. The advertising appropriation has been doubled during a time when

Grandin Vitamin sales and market share have dropped about one third. One cannot sit idly by and hope that something will occur which will result in a correction of the situation. The stark fact is that Grandin must take some drastic action in order to turn its vitamin profitability picture around.

"I would like to suggest, then, that you take a thorough look at the Vitamin Division's long-range goals and objectives. What do you really want this division to do for the total corporation? Are the goals and objectives set forth and last reviewed some ten years ago still appropriate for today?"

After some interim discussion, Sheehan reviewed the Vitamin Division goals. He recalled the revised goals of some ten years ago at which time the Vitamin Division was to realize a before-tax return on investment (ROI) of 20 percent—after start-up costs had been written off. The Vitamin Division had reached this goal, but during the past several years had been falling short; and the decline, as everyone in the room knew, had steepened.

It was necessary, then, that either this goal be readjusted or some new steps be taken to meet the objective. Sheehan pointed out that corporate management would not tolerate a downward revision on the ROI. Instead, he predicted that management would look for other uses of corporate funds. It would appear mandatory, he contended, to develop some strategy for Grandin Vitamins that would reverse the trend and result in the attainment of the existing goal. After further discussion, Sheehan concluded the meeting on the note that members of the Planning Committee should develop some marketing alternatives that would be in keeping with total corporate goals and marketing strategy. He specifically referred to the fact that the Grandin top management would not permit any Grandin product other than Grandin Vitamins to be marketed over the counter. The company, according to long-time policy, would continue to emphasize ethical products; only Grandin Vitamins would be identified with the proprietary field.

The Planning Committee was comprised of Fred Winslow, vice-president, Vitamin Division; Florence Hilliard, financial head of the Vitamin Division; Carolyn O'Keefe, vice-president of marketing services; and Arthur McCabe. The committee met over a period of a month and then returned with its suggestions to be considered by the Marketing Committee.

Winslow proposed a dramatic departure from Grandin's past marketing program. He described a plan for Grandin to produce a "price brand" or private-label vitamin to be distributed through grocery, discount, and department stores. The new product would not carry the Grandin name, nor would Grandin be identified as the producer and distributor. Instead, a subsidiary would be set up and the new product would be produced and marketed under the subsidiary's name. The marketing funds would be drawn from the marketing dollars currently being allocated to Grandin Vitamins. The pricing policy would call for a lower unit price, some 25 percent below the level of the Grandin Vitamin. The existing Grandin Vitamin would be continued, but left to drift with minimum marketing support.

Private label describes a retailer's own brand which carries a brand name used only by the retailer. The product is usually made for the retailer by another company, but the brand name is the exclusive property of the retailer.

Price brand refers to a brand marketed by a manufacturer at a retail price well below its nationally advertised brand. The price brand is normally not supported by advertising, with the manufacturer using price as the principal appeal. Price brands are sometimes not identified with the manufacturer; in other cases the manufacturer lists its company name on the label.

The Marketing Committee found itself engaged in heated discussions over the suggested courses of action. Sheehan, the committee's chairman, was unable to move the committee toward any resolution. The leaning of the committee was to reject the Planning Committee's thinking, but the reasons for such a rejection were not articulated at any point in time.

ANALYSIS OF PART B— DEVELOPING ALTERNATIVES

As in the analysis of Part A, this analysis will draw upon the basic flowchart and the substeps associated with each major phase.

In Part B the participants came to a better understanding of the environment confronting Grandin and realized that advertising was not linked to the sales decline. While they did not individuate or otherwise make explicit the decision-problem, they did realize that price and distribution seemed to be at issue. Thus, they began to formulate alternatives. With that development in mind, recall the substeps associated with developing alternatives:

    a. Prepare the initial list.
    b. Refine the initial list.
    c. Recognize the true role of research.
    d. Compile the final list.

Prepare the Initial List

There are three initial lists of alternatives appearing in the case thus far. Johnson had an implied list; Avery put forward some suggestions in his reply letter to McCabe; and the Planning Committee had a list. Each of these lists will be examined in turn.

The initial list of alternatives apparently being considered by Johnson had to do with advertising. Unrefined, the list might include the following:

    1. Use advertising with improved copy.
    2. Use advertising better aimed at target audiences.
    3. Do both of the above together.
    4. Continue existing program.

Not being precise as to what "improved copy" and "better aimed" mean, these statements of marketing alternatives are inadequate for decision process treatment. They are, of course, also inadequate alternatives because they are

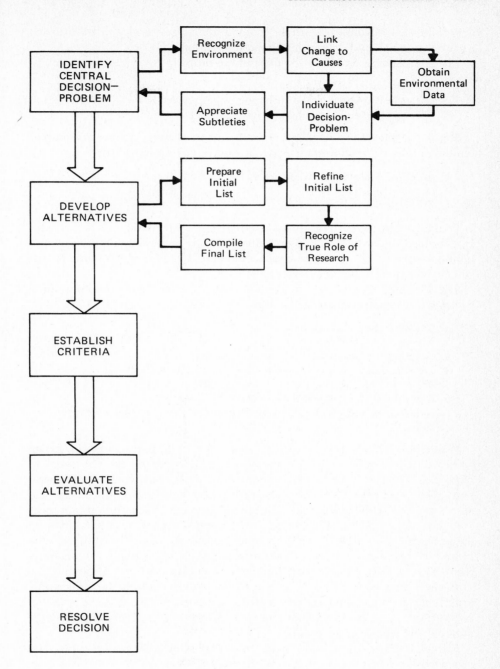

Summary Flowchart, Chapters 1–2

inappropriate to Grandin's central decision-problem concerning distribution of a price-competitive vitamin. Johnson did not see this.

The alternatives implied by the possibilities raised in Avery's letter are:

1. Decrease price.
2. Introduce a new brand for distribution by grocery stores.
3. Allocate more dollars to pharmacist support efforts.

All of the previously listed statements are marketing alternatives and in terms of a ranking from most change to least change they would be:

1. Introduce a new brand (strategic).
2. Decrease price.
3. Allocate more dollars (tactical).

Working with this diverse list of alternatives, at this point, is not a fruitful task. Indeed the presence of diverse alternatives is generally symptomatic of a failure to identify clearly the central decision-problem. Avery was trying to suggest this diplomatically in his letter to McCabe.

The Planning Committee, in Part B of the case, seems to be proposing a package of alternatives along these lines:

1. Market a price-brand vitamin.
2. Market a private-brand vitamin.
3. Do not identify Grandin with the new product.
4. Distribute through grocery, discount, and department stores.
5. Set up a subsidiary to market the new product.
6. Reduce the retail price of the new brand by 25 percent.
7. Reduce marketing support of the traditional Grandin Vitamin to near zero.

While closer to Grandin's main problem, these alternatives are not articulated with the requisite clarity to permit the group to move on. They need to be refined. But before addressing their refinement, let's briefly review the marketing environment and the framework of objectives leading up to the suggested options developed by the Planning Committee. Grandin Vitamin sales and profits were declining. Industry and corporate sales figures plus financial data revealed a situation showing that the traditional marketing approach employed by Grandin was causing this continuing and sagging trend. Top management had set some broad strategy or policy constraints on the Vitamin Division when it stated some ten years ago that vitamins would be Grandin's only proprietary product, and that only traditional pharmacies would serve as the retail outlets. These dealers would embrace all drug outlets, including the large national and regional drug chains.

Although Grandin corporate management set achievable goals for the Vitamin Division when it required a before-tax return of 20 percent on the investment (ROI), the Vitamin Division had fallen well below the goal set for it by the corporate financial management years ago. In a sense this goal of 20 percent return on invested capital was a "control point." When the return for two successive years dropped below the set goal, this was a significant deviation and it should have resulted in a review of the marketing program. (The catalyst was Johnson's request for an advertising research study and Avery's urge for a complete review.)

The Planning Committee for the Vitamin Division operated within the objectives' framework when it returned to the Marketing Committee with its suggestions for possible action. However, the inability of the latter committee to move forward was at least in part due to the fact that the marketing alternatives were perceived by some committee members as a departure from company policy.

Would brainstorming have helped the Planning Committee? Possibly. Brainstorming and other idea-generation schemes work best when there is agreement on the problem requiring solution. Grandin does not yet have such agreement. Therefore, brainstorming is inappropriate for Grandin at this point, although a genuine brainstorming effort might have revealed the true problem. Remember the manner in which brainstorming is conducted: namely, no explicit criticism of ideas is allowed until the session is over and suggestions should try to build or spinoff on other suggestions already made by participants. Quantity, not quality, is the first goal of brainstorming.

No matter which initial set of alternatives is dealt with—the advertising manager's, Avery's, or the Planning Committee's—the next step is to refine the alternatives until a mutually exclusive set is achieved.

Refine the Initial List of Alternatives

Having ruled out the lists of Johnson and Avery, one may attempt to work with the Planning Committee's list. Specifically, the Planning Committee proposed the following:

1. Market a private-label or price-brand vitamin not identified in any way with Grandin, to be distributed through grocery, discount, and department stores at a price 25 percent below the current suggested retail price for Grandin Vitamins and supported by marketing funds drawn from the existing appropriation now allocated to Grandin Vitamins.
2. Let the existing Grandin vitamin offering "drift with minimum marketing support."

A check of the above alternatives reveals that they are not exhaustive and not independent (the marketing support for the new brand was to come from funds drawn from those allocated to the existing brand). In a basic sense the above list could be made collectively exhaustive by adding:

3. Do something else.
4. Do nothing.

In a fuller sense, however, to create truly collectively exhaustive lists of *initial* alternatives, while desirable rationally, is not practical. In reality, a reasonable set of alternatives is considered. Presumably this was what the Planning Committee did to come up with the first two alternatives presented above. A closer look at alternative No. 1 reveals its compound nature and argues clearly for some type of refinement. In particular mutual exclusivity must be injected. Separating the branding options in No. 1 leads to alternatives of the format:

1. Market a price brand with Grandin identification through grocery chains, co-ops, drug chains, and independents.
2. Do not market the above.

Recognize the True Role of Research

The Planning Committee did not include (and correctly so) "engage in marketing research" as one of its proposed marketing alternatives. This issue will surface again in Part C, however.

Going back to Part A, one might point out that Johnson had as a set of marketing alternatives: (1) implement new, improved advertising program, and (2) conduct some marketing research; and that he opted for the latter. Again, it is stressed that "To do some research first" is *not* a marketing decision alternative. Marketing research is a process by which one gathers data and information for understanding the marketing environment or for producing candidate marketing action alternatives or, more usually, for evaluating a set of clearly stated alternatives. Research itself is not a marketing alternative.

Compile the Final List

The protagonists in Part B have obviously not progressed this far; considerably more refinement is necessary. This will occur in Part C of the case. Had Grandin's management progressed to the final-list stage in B they might have developed alternatives having the following generic form:

1. Market a vitamin with approach X (meaning with a particular marketing mix).
2. Do not market a vitamin as in No. 1.

Joseph Sheehan is pictured at the end of Part B of the case as having difficulty moving Grandin's Marketing Committee toward any resolution. A knowledge of the steps of the decision process would have helped him in this matter. Had Sheehan been more cognizant of the steps in the decision process he might have realized that the group was getting ahead of itself. It was trying to evaluate some proposed alternatives, primarily on the basis of personal opinion rather than on quantitative evidence. Sheehan, armed with decision-process knowledge, could have channeled the group's energies into the question of how those final alternatives would be evaluated. By displaying the steps of the decision process to the group he could have shown them where they actually were with regard to the problem at hand and what needed to be done next. As was pointed out previously, the five-step framework of the basic decision process is a powerful device for focusing group attention and discussion, thereby making committee and related meetings more efficient and effective.

DISCUSSION QUESTIONS FOR PART B

1. Avery's letter to McCabe of February 7 suggested that consumers have low brand differentiation for vitamins. Into what general product category or type, therefore, would marketers place vitamins: convenience good, specialty good, or shopping good? Is there any advantage in placing vitamins in a product category? Explain.
2. Knowing who the real decision makers are is important to outsiders called upon to advise a company. Why is this so and how did Jack Avery demonstrate that he recognized this requirement?
3. Grandin's Vitamin Division had a target pretax ROI of 20 percent. Given the life-cycle pattern of sales and profits of typical product groups, is a constant, annual pre-tax ROI target realistic? What might be a better way to state such targets?
4. Firms often put considerable effort into new product introduction decisions, but little advance thought and effort with regard to old product elimination decisions. Why do you suppose this is the case? How should product elimination decisions be handled?
5. One pricing alternative appearing in the case was to market vitamins at 25 percent below the Grandin Vitamin level. Why 25 percent? Why not 10 percent?
6. A companion suggestion was to let the existing Grandin vitamin offering "drift with minimum marketing support." Is this a good idea? What repercussions, if any, might there be?

GRANDIN LABORATORIES—PART C

(*Note to Reader:* You should have read through Chapter 3 and Grandin Laboratories—Part B to this point.)

After considerable haggling among the committee members, Sheehan began to recognize why no progress was being made. He asked Fred Winslow, chairman of the Planning Committee, to state in simple terms just what he considered to be the one thing that should be resolved first. Winslow responded by pointing out that to his way of thinking the committee should first decide on whether the private label should be adopted. He was then queried as to why he left out the price brand. He then agreed that the price brand should be a part of this decision. Still not satisfied, Sheehan reminded him that they could market both; thus, why should this option not be a part of the decision being considered? Winslow agreed that it should. The marketing alternatives, basic at this point, were agreed upon. They were:

1. Market a private-label brand.
2. Market a price brand.
3. Market both.

The complications of attempting at the outset to market both were quickly recognized. Private-label marketing is quite different from marketing a price brand, and the Marketing Committee members agreed that they should not market both, thus rejecting the third alternative.

Carolyn O'Keefe voiced her hesitation regarding the feasibility of making a decision until she knew whether the Grandin name would be identified with either or both of the two types of brands under consideration. Specifically, O'Keefe stated that she could not pass judgment on whether to enter the private-label or the price-brand field unless the identification of the Grandin name with the new product was considered a part of the issue in question. This thinking was supported, members nodding agreement, without obvious dissent.

Winslow, moving to the front of the conference room, wrote four options on an easel display sheet:

1. Market a private-label vitamin—no Grandin identification.
2. Market a price-brand vitamin—no Grandin identification.
3. Market a private-label vitamin—identified with Grandin.
4. Market a price-brand vitamin—identified with Grandin.

A lengthy discussion followed. Gradually the committee members seemed to favor a price brand over a private-label brand. The reasons were several. First, they felt that the major national retailers already had their own private labels, and any opportunities for replacing existing private-label manufacturers would be on the basis of lower costs. This, Hilliard thought, would be an unlikely happening in view of Grandin's known higher cost structure. Second, to manufacture a private label meant that Grandin would lose marketing control over the effort. With a price brand Grandin would have control over the distribution and marketing support.

But there still was not agreement on whether the Grandin name should be identified with the price brand. Sheehan pointed out that there was no conflict between a price brand and Grandin identification, although it appeared obvious to him that the brand could not be called Grandin Vitamins, the present brand name. He suggested that perhaps the extent of the identification should be simply "Manufactured by Grandin Laboratories."

Perhaps because Sheehan, with his rank within the company, seemed to suggest Grandin identification or because the committee thought it would really be the best decision—or both—it was agreed that the new price brand would carry the Grandin name on the label, but in an unobtrusive manner.

Sheehan then turned to Winslow and asked him, "What's next?" Winslow pointed out that no decision had yet been made on the mode of distribution—how the new price brand would be marketed. The initial recommendation of the Planning Committee was to distribute "through grocery, discount, and department stores." Winslow stated that he still felt that these would be good outlets for the new vitamin. However, Sheehan argued that there appeared to be no other options even offered for consideration. He suggested that Winslow list viable distribution choices. This he did, writing them on the easel flip page at the front of the conference room. The distribution choices he listed were:

1. Distribute the price-brand vitamin only through regional and national grocery chains, discount stores, and department stores.
2. Distribute only through regional and national grocery chains and voluntary co-ops.

3. Distribute only through Grandin's current drug outlets (independent and national and regional drug chains).
4. Distribute through both grocery and drug outlets as well as discount and department stores.
5. Distribute only through regional and national grocery chains and co-ops and drug chains and independents.

With a degree of ease which surprised even Sheehan, the Marketing Committee agreed to distribute the price brand through grocery chains, co-ops, drug chains, and independents. The principal reason for the quick agreement was the feeling, first, that grocery outlets were obviously becoming more and more important to proprietary drug manufacturers, and, second, that Grandin was already calling on drug chains and the company's representatives were well acquainted with the buyers of both regional and national drug chains.

O'Keefe reminded the group that while the Marketing Committee had agreed on marketing this new price brand, the committee had in fact stepped out of bounds as far as corporate policy was concerned. She pointed out that it was the company policy to restrict distribution largely to drugstores, and quoted from the policy statement of some ten years ago which contained the phrase "only traditional pharmacies would serve as the retail outlets for Grandin Vitamins." This policy, interjected Sheehan, could apply only to the existing Grandin Vitamin brand and not to the new price brand. However, the Marketing Committee felt that it would be well to clear their decision to market the price brand through grocery as well as drug outlets before proceeding with the tactical efforts required to commercialize a new brand.

Sheehan volunteered to talk with the company's Executive Committee, the policy-forming body of Grandin Laboratories. To his surprise the Executive Committee did not quarrel with the proposed grocery distribution, but they did question the wisdom of entering the price market with a Grandin-identified brand. Their contention was simply that the market was now saturated with vitamin brands of all types and sizes and that the vitamin industry as a whole was a declining one. Why, they asked, would Grandin want to enter a field already crowded with brands and a declining field at that?

Sheehan was not prepared to answer these top management questions. They queried him as to what the basis was for the Marketing Committee reaching such a decision. He had no ready answer, saying only that it was the estimate of his Marketing Committee that this new price brand would return more to the company than the Grandin Vitamin now on the market. Again they asked what his evidence was for the basis of such an assertion. Sheehan then agreed that before they moved ahead with commercializing the price brand they would conduct a thorough study to determine just what would be the chances of succeeding with the new brand.

Sheehan reassembled the Marketing Committee and reported the reaction of the company's Executive Committee to the introduction of the price brand. He recommended to the Marketing Committee that they hold off any introduction commitments until they had conducted a study which would aid them in determining what they could expect the new price brand to do. This, said Sheehan, "is where we stand at the moment."

McCabe asked what time constraints seemed to exist. He pointed out that the vitamin market develops late in the fall and carries on through April, and that there would be little time for marketing research if the coming fall was to be the introduction target date.

This, according to Winslow, would not be a problem for two reasons. First, some of the tactical decisions could be in the making during the conduct of the study; e.g., the product's name, the design of the label, advertising copy and media decisions, total advertising effort, and the like. And, second, the survey need not be very comprehensive because not only did time not permit, but he was certain that the new product would succeed, despite the feeling of the Executive Committee. Moreover, Winslow insisted that "all we have to do is to get Art McCabe and some outfit such as Market Facts to do a little interviewing and find out what people would think of a new vitamin at a given price manufactured by Grandin."

McCabe was less sanguine than Winslow on the future success of the price brand. He learned that other members of the Marketing Committee shared his view. Now that the Executive Committee had questioned the decision to enter what was termed a saturated market, most members of the marketing group leaned toward a study that would "nail down just what this new brand could do." Winslow said he certainly would not object to a comprehensive survey, but he still thought that it was largely a waste of time and money. "We would do better," grumbled Winslow, "to spend the survey time and money on getting the new product on the market and then finding out just what it would really do."

Sheehan responded by reminding Winslow and the others that the Grandin top management was not at all interested in risking the funds for this new product and then having it fail. "One must remember," declared Sheehan, "that our Vitamin Division is in mild trouble and a market failure is not what we are looking for."

The group then turned to McCabe and asked for his suggestions on how such a study should be conducted. McCabe reminded the group that highly precise data require time to acquire and that there did not appear to be an abundance of time remaining between the day of this meeting and the date on which the company must say "GO" if Grandin planned to introduce this new product during the coming fall. The best possible type of data, according to McCabe, would be a sales prediction, so that a reasonably accurate measure of revenue could be obtained. Such a study, he revealed, would take a minimum of three months, and probably as long as six months. Sheehan asked McCabe to work something up and to be prepared to present his specific recommendations to the Marketing Committee within two days. Sheehan commented that he knew this was too brief a period for preparing a comprehensive proposal, but that time was now of the essence and he would have to meet the deadline. McCabe said he would get together with the people at Market Facts at once.

A meeting with Francine Standish of Market Facts was held the following day. The project committee was headed by McCabe, assisted by Susan Erb, McCabe's senior project director. Florence Hilliard, manager of the Vitamin

Division's Budget and Control for Marketing, was also asked to participate in the study.

McCabe reviewed the status of the possible marketing of a price brand by Grandin. He explained why a study was deemed advisable—that Grandin's Executive Committee was not in favor of the price brand, at least not until some data could be produced which would support Grandin's entry into the price brand field. McCabe stressed the need for some sales forecasts based on test marketing. He said he thought only this type of data would satisfy the Executive Committee.

Hilliard pointed out that Grandin was now getting about 22 percent of the vitamin business nationally, which amounted to something under $3.5 million in sales. This figure, she reminded the committee, was falling short of Grandin's goal of a 20 percent return before taxes. Hilliard said that she hoped the new price brand would bolster the traditional brand's revenue so that the required ROI could be reached. To achieve this goal would require sales for the new price brand of one million dollars, assuming a unit price 25 percent below the traditional Grandin brand, and marketing costs some 50 percent below the current Grandin Vitamin spending.

In brief Hilliard said that if the new price brand could reach a sales level of one million dollars a year or more under these conditions, then Grandin should go ahead and market the product nationally. McCabe pointed out that before such a sales test could be run, a number of decisions would have to be made— and soon. For example, the product must be named. There must be agreement on precisely how many marketing dollars were to be placed in support of the vitamin. Also, the label and package must be designed and any changes in the product itself must be acted on at once. All this was necessary, plus a production run of the product, so that the test item could be supplied to an appropriate number of retail outlets and marketed under real-life conditions.

Susan Erb was asked to meet with the production and marketing people and to move forward on all these fronts. In the interim, McCabe and Standish would design the study itself.

ANALYSIS OF PART C— ESTABLISHING CRITERIA

Because Grandin managers were not cognizant of, or at least did not explicitly use, a decision-process model such as the basic flowchart (see page 132), there was still work to be done in refining the alternatives and compiling the final list.

Complete Refinement and Final List of Alternatives

The need for agreement on alternatives was recognized. The following list emerged:

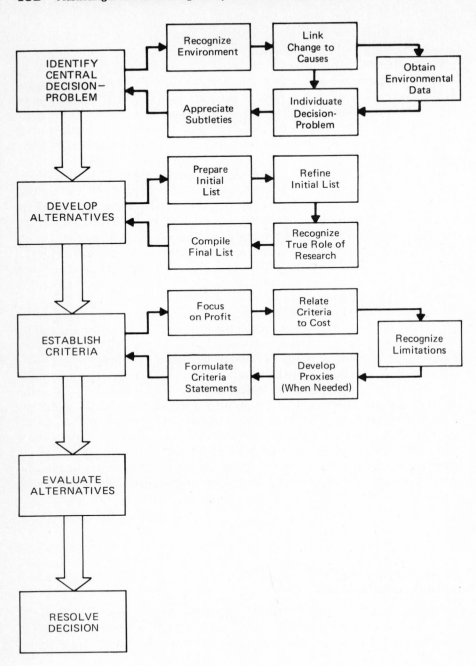

Summary Flowchart, Chapters 1–3

1. Market a private label.
2. Market a price brand.
3. Market both.

These three options were later altered, with "market both" being dropped. Then, whether the Grandin name should be identified with the new brand became an integral part of the marketing alternatives.

	No Grandin Identification	With Grandin Identification
Private label	Alternative #1	Alternative #3
Price brand	Alternative #2	Alternative #4

This set was mutually exclusive but, in a somewhat look-ahead posture, the Marketing Committee began to speculate on how the private label alternative would fare. Implicitly they were using profit as a criterion, i.e., revenue minus costs. Opportunities for significant revenue from a private label were not many, for as it turned out the major national retailers already had their own private-label vitamins. And further, Grandin would probably not be able to induce a retail chain to use Grandin as a private-label vitamin source of supply because its costs were too high; the retailer would not have an attractive margin.

After some discussion, the Marketing Committee with the aid of the Planning Committee agreed on the following set of marketing alternatives:

1. Market a price brand with Grandin identification through grocery chains, co-ops, and drug chains and independents.
2. Do not market the price brand as in No. 1.

The final list contained two decision choices which were mutually exclusive. The alternatives were reviewed with the Executive Committee in order to make certain that the options under consideration were in keeping with corporate policy and strategy. The policy of not marketing a Grandin product through nondrug retail outlets was rescinded, thus opening the door for possible grocery distribution.

The basic decision emerging during this part of the case concerns the marketing of a price brand. The evaluation of this marketing alternative involves estimating the proposed brand's revenue prospects, with test marketing chosen as the desirable way to develop data that would assist in making such an estimate. Winslow, Vitamin Division vice-president, recognized that many of the tactical marketing decision-problems (product name, advertising details, etc.) that would flow from the strategic decision regarding price-brand introduction could be addressed during the test marketing effort. A logical strategic-tactical decision sequence was therefore beginning to crystallize. The next step was explicit formulation of the pertinent criteria.

Establishing criteria is facilitated by these substeps:

      a. Focus on profit.
      b. Relate criteria to cost.
      c. Recognize limitations.
      d. Develop proxies (when called for).
      e. Formulate if-then criteria statements.

Focus on Profit

That attention was being properly given to profit considerations was apparent in the committee's rejection of the private-brand alternative. The Executive Committee also had profit in mind when they prodded Sheehan about the Marketing Committee's rationale (read: criteria) for suggesting a move into an already crowded vitamin market. Sheehan, in responding to the Executive Committee's questioning of the committee's choice, said the Marketing Committee estimated the "price brand would return more to the company" than the Grandin Vitamin brand. Hence, Sheehan was implicitly using ROI, although he had no data to support the view that the price brand would do better. The Executive Committee made him realize that hard evidence was required before one alternative could be selected over another. The need for marketing research to supply that evidence was thus recognized.

In a sense, Grandin's Executive Committee embarrassed the Vitamin Division's marketing people by asking them on what basis they had made the important decision to market the price brand. As it turned out, the marketing department had not developed even a criteria statement, much less data to support their decision to proceed with the price brand if the Executive Committee approved the corporate policy change of distributing through nontraditional drug retailers.

After Sheehan had his meeting with the Executive Committee, he reconvened the Marketing Committee and explained the sudden need for data. In a strict sense, this discussion of data was out of sequence. Adherence to the basic flowchart requires a statement of the marketing alternatives, then a statement of the criteria. Sheehan moved the committee along the road through the alternatives, but the group jumped to a decision to market the price brand without stating a criterion as the basis for making the decision. This is often done in unimportant decisions (when the obvious criterion is implied), but in this instance the commercializing of a price brand by a high-level, ethical house such as Grandin cannot be classed as an "unimportant decision."

The Marketing Committee finally found itself in a discussion of criteria, with the aid of Hilliard. It was she who talked in terms of a sales and revenue level that must be reached if a decision to market the product was to result. Certainly she stated the if-then phrase clearly enough. However, the criterion centered on absolute sales and revenue for the new price brand. Hilliard stated that the product must ultimately produce annual revenue of one million dollars or more to justify the product's introduction. She was guilty of suboptimization.

Suboptimization is often a necessary evil, but in this instance Hilliard viewed the new item only in terms of what it alone should produce, assuming that this amount could simply be added to the revenue of the traditional Grandin Vitamins. She did not recognize that the price brand could take sales away from the Grandin Vitamin, and that a sales figure of one million dollars could not be tacked onto the existing or expected revenue of the current Grandin products. In other words, the new brand in itself could actually decrease the total profitability of the Vitamin Division, even though the former produced an annual revenue of one million dollars.

Fortunately this suboptimization was within one division of the company. The situation could be corrected by developing a new criterion for the decision. The entire Vitamin Division's profits would be the ultimate test, and should have been the basis for the criterion. It was unwise to consider only the new price brand's sales revenue.

Relate Criteria to Cost

It is desirable here, from a review standpoint, to examine and classify the various criteria suggested or implied in Part C. Examples of monetary criteria are:

1. Return on investment—as implied in Sheehan's reply to the Executive Committee that the new price brand would return more to the company than the Grandin Vitamin now on the market.
2. Sales dollars—McCabe's recommendation regarding the type of data the study should generate. (Presumably if one has cost data in addition, ROI can then be calculated.)
3. A 20 percent ROI—per reminder by Hilliard of this corporate goal.
4. Sales dollars—Hilliard's formulation of an if-then criterion statement for the price brand.

Examples of nonmonetary criteria are:

1. Market share—as implied in the Executive Committee's critique of the Marketing Committee's suggestion to market a price brand. That is, the Executive Committee said that the market, a declining one, was "saturated with vitamin brands of all types and sizes," implying that it would be difficult to gain a significant share of the market with any new brand.
2. Consumer-stated likes and dislikes—as reflected in Winslow's suggestion to get Market Facts "to do a little interviewing and find out what people would think." (This might also be treated as consumer attitudes.)

Grandin should, of course, employ a monetary criterion. The emerging set of alternatives does not involve choices of equal cost; to introduce a price brand versus not to introduce one are two very different actions. The first is clearly more costly and its merit can only be evaluated after some measure of revenue generation is obtained. An ROI measure, specifically, would be the preferred criterion type.

Recognize Limitations on the Criteria

Two limitations were present: time and feasibility. It was not feasible to predict ROI unless revenue were known. This called for an estimate of sales, and whether there was sufficient time available to produce such an estimate before a decision was to be made suggested a possible inadequacy of a sales criterion. The time limitation arose from the need to introduce the price brand by the late fall—the beginning of the strong vitamin-buying period.

Develop Proxy Criteria When Needed

Sales was in essence the proxy criterion for ROI in that the latter could be predicted only with a knowledge of total product costs and predicted revenue. A sales or monetary measure, then, was necessary to forecast revenue and ultimately ROI. Winslow apparently felt that interview data would serve Grandin's purpose. But interview data that revealed consumers' feelings toward a reduced-price vitamin made by Grandin would not be adequate. What people say about how they feel and what they would do if such-and-such were marketed are usually not one and the same. Grandin needs some quantitative measures of what people actually do in response to their price-brand marketing efforts, i.e., they need unit and dollar sales data obtained under expected marketing conditions and with simultaneous measurements of industry activity.

Formulate Criteria Statements

Hilliard did utilize the recommended if-then format in stating what she felt to be the basis for a Go-No Go decision regarding national marketing of the price brand. She stated it in dollar rather than ROI terms:

> ". . . if the new price brand could reach a sales level of one million dollars a year or more under these conditions, then Grandin should go ahead and market the product nationally."

But a criterion statement in ROI terms is preferable, especially since Grandin has explicit ROI targets. However, to produce ROI measurements one must have revenue, cost, and investment data. At this stage in the development of the price brand, alternative cost and investment estimates are not much more available than are the revenue estimates. Hilliard was perhaps going on the assumption that cost and investment data in more precise form would be ready when revenue estimates derived from the price brand's test marketing results became available.

One could argue that the criterion statement in profit or ROI terms should be translated into equivalent test marketing results to speed the interpretation of those results. Going the other way, i.e., translating test outcomes into criterion statement units, offers the opportunity for conscious or unconscious inflating or fudging of the results to meet or exceed the standard.

In Part D it will be seen that Vitamin Division profitability is the criterion basis. Computing combined ROI here, for old and new vitamins, is probably easier than computing ROI separately because one avoids allocation issues. In particular, the criteria statement will be:

> If the annual operating profit of the Vitamin Division can reach $1.2 million with the price brand, then the price brand will be commercialized nationally. Implicitly, if the annual division profit cannot reach the $1.2 million level, then the price brand will not be commercialized nationally.

DISCUSSION QUESTIONS FOR PART C

1. Grandin's corporate policy favoring a limited distribution strategy came under some question. How does a company know when to change policy?
2. What does a diagram of the several committees involved in the case indicate with regard to communication and reaching agreements?
3. Hilliard hoped there would be a salutary effect on regular Grandin vitamin sales by the introduction of the price brand. Of course, just the opposite could occur. What implications does recognition of this fact have for formulating the decision criterion?
4. A favorite display device of the logician is the Venn diagram. How does the Venn diagram portray the concept of mutual exclusiveness? (Illustrate using Part C material.)

GRANDIN LABORATORIES—PART D

(*Note to Reader:* You should have read through Chapter 4 and Grandin Laboratories—Part C to this point.)

McCabe and Standish recognized that the data needed to satisfy the decision criterion could be obtained best through retail store audits of proprietary vitamin sales. Specifically, a sample of stores would be selected and research auditors would check the sales of all brands of vitamins at specified intervals. Sales in each store would be determined by employing the following procedure:

> Closing inventory (from prior audit),
> *Plus:* Purchases by retailer since last audit,
> *Less:* Current inventory,
> *Equals:* Sales during period.

Both McCabe and Standish were in agreement that all brands should be audited, including the new Grandin price brand. Data on only the latter brand would fail to yield fully usable information because the decision makers wanted to view the total profitability of the Vitamin Division—not just the sales and profitability of the new price brand. McCabe and Standish thus realized that Hilliard's earlier criterion of $1 million in sales for the price brand was inadequate.

They checked with Hilliard and after some discussion agreed that the operating profits of the entire Vitamin Division must reach at least $1.2 million in order to justify the addition of the new brand. In other words, the combined profitability of the existing Grandin Vitamin and the new price brand must exceed $1.2 million to warrant the marketing of the new vitamin.

The marketing research assignment, therefore, was to gather data that would aid in predicting whether this profit level could be reached. Moreover, the management was desirous of an "early" answer. McCabe and Standish were well aware of the high research cost of studies of the sales-audit type—if reliable data were to be obtained. Just how costly could not be determined at this point because many of the major research decisions had yet to be made. However, both researchers realized that the managerial level of disagreement was high. Moreover, the profit consequences of a wrong decision were also high in view of the approaching jeopardy to the Vitamin Division caused by a relentless decline in the division's profitability. And there was still another reason for the high level of profit consequences. If Grandin did proceed with a price brand distributed through nontraditional drug channels, their professional standing might be significantly diminished as a result. It would be difficult to reestablish that standing and the profit outlook for the entire firm, not just the Vitamin Division, would be cloudy.

With that backdrop, McCabe and Standish knew that the cost of the study would not be an issue. They talked about attempting to set some outside limits by employing a probabilistic approach whereby they would determine "perfect" data and the value of the added information to be uncovered by the study. However, this was rejected for several reasons. First, management did not participate in assessing the probabilities of reaching certain sales and profit levels. It would be unwise now, the researchers reasoned, to go back and reopen the entire subject at a time when speed was uppermost. Moreover, they thought they might be accused of "playing games," when instead they should be moving forward in gathering the data.

In addition, both researchers realized that the accuracy of the data could not be measured precisely. There were many reasons why "perfect" data could not be obtained, and McCabe and Standish thought it well not to dwell on this in any communication with top management.

Two research alternatives were posed by McCabe and Standish: (1) to use a "controlled" store audit panel, or (2) to use an "uncontrolled" store audit. The first approach could be handled by the Marketest Division of Market Facts, in that this firm could guarantee product placement in selected cities and could "overnight" set up an auditing operation among participating stores. Marketest maintained relationships with both independent and chain drug and grocery retailers. It had its own warehouses and panel trucks through which the test product was distributed to stores. The percentage of distribution agreed upon could be obtained in a realistic manner. Field representatives of the company audited the stores' sales and maintained agreed-upon stock situations. This situation could be created by Marketest and "controlled" for the duration of the study. It would be a simulation of the market place.

The other store audit option involved marketing the test product in a real-life manner. In other words, the new Grandin price brand would be distributed through normal wholesale and retail channels, and the retail sales audited. The cities would not be preselected as was the case with Marketest. The principal advantage of this approach was that it would measure both trade and consumer acceptance.

The Marketest Division approach was chosen. It was felt that the "controlled conditions" could be made to simulate real life in terms of percentage of stores handling the product as well as out-of-stock conditions. Moreover, the employment of full-time field employees, with distribution guaranteed within "days," all aided McCabe in opting for Marketest.

The second major research consideration centered on sample size—the number of cities and the number of stores within each city. Marketest maintained on-going facilities in four cities: Wichita, Kansas; Fresno, California; Erie, Pennsylvania; and Dayton, Ohio. This constraint virtually dictated the number of cities, although the option of test marketing in two cities was an alternative. Using the accuracy criterion, the greater coverage offered by four cities was deemed essential, especially when the possible time limitation was recognized.

The sample size alternatives (number of stores in each city) varied from half of the Marketest stores to all of them. The maximum number was chosen, again for the reason that Grandin was striving for maximum accuracy within a limited time constraint.

Grandin management was striving to make the price brand decision before the latter part of the year, at which time consumer buying of vitamins gains momentum. It was now early April, and with all the activities required in making the tactical decisions on brand name, packaging, and marketing effort it would still be June before the test marketing could get under way. It appeared to McCabe and Standish that a three-month minimum audit could be undertaken, with a fourth month added if needed. The weakness of conducting a market-testing operation on vitamins during the summer months was well known, but there appeared to be no alternative. Management wanted the data prior to the winter season, and, as a result, it was necessary to compromise. It would be possible, however, to adjust the sales audit data for seasonality and this approach was thought to be far superior to holding or postponing the study until the winter season.

While these research decisions were being made, Susan Erb, the research project director, was making excellent progress with the production, packaging, and marketing people. It was a relatively easy task to have the product ready in time for the early June distribution. The packaging decisions were resolved by assigning the package design to an industrial design firm and accepting its recommendations.

The brand name decision was initiated with four final candidate names: Healthmore Vitamins; Vita-Health Vitamins; Nutri-Vit Vitamins; Vigorvitamin. The criterion for selecting a name was consumers' stated intention to buy. After a sample of 250 vitamin consumers was presented with pairs of names, the name Vita-Health was chosen.

It was already agreed that the price was to be 25 percent less than the traditional Grandin Vitamin. The promotional effort was restricted to normal sales calls, with emphasis on obtaining 90 percent distribution, a figure Grandin thought easy to attain. Grandin Vitamin advertising funds would be reduced to zero immediately. All in all, according to Erb, the tactical decisions had been made and the real-life conditions for the four Marketest cities would be established by early June.

The cost of the study was estimated at $120,000, including biweekly auditing of the Marketest stores. Sample size and dispersion are shown in Table 5.

Table 5 Retail Store Sample

	Number of Stores
Wichita	
Grocery	63
Drug	39
Fresno	
Grocery	56
Drug	41
Erie	
Grocery	54
Drug	29
Dayton	
Grocery	69
Drug	50

The auditing would begin June 4 and continue through August 25. Field auditors would check out-of-stock conditions and shelf conditions twice weekly, in addition to the regular biweekly audit visit.

The problems associated with obtaining accurate and valid store audit data were well known to Susan Erb and H. Ralph Metcalf, Market Facts' analyst assigned to the study by its Medical Services Division. Very real sources of error centered on the possibility of great differences in vitamin sales between sample stores, between the test cities, or between the audit periods. If vitamin sales (and Grandin products in particular) remained reasonably constant across stores of similar size, greater confidence could be placed in the resultant data. Similarly, if the test sales data were consistent among all four sample cities, it would be possible to project the test data with a higher degree of accuracy. And, with regard to test data obtained from one biweekly period to the next from all stores in all four cities, the predicting of national sales from the sample data could be made with greater confidence if there were little variance from one time period to another. The analysts had a "gut" feeling on these error sources, but no solid evidence on vitamin sales variations.

Anticipating these problems, McCabe, Standish, and others agreed on as large a store sample as possible in order to counteract any great between-store variance. Four Marketest cities were employed instead of two so that a better measure of between-city variance could be obtained. All the researchers in charge of the study agreed, however, that the study should be of longer duration than 12 weeks in order to obtain a better measure of the between-period variance. It was pointed out as the study was being designed that the first several weeks of data collection could not be used in that the Vita-Health product would have to be given an opportunity to establish itself. The *exact* number of weeks required for Vita-Health to reach its "normal" sales level was not known, but the researchers were hopeful that, even without advertising, it would reach its plateau within four weeks. The data for projection would be available from only those weeks following a leveling off of the sales of the two Grandin products. The risk of terminating the study too early was great. However, pressure from top management for an early fall report virtually forced the researchers to gamble on the reliability of the data, hoping that between-period variance would be small enough to permit sales predictions within tolerable limits.

Another source of error in the survey data was the possibility of one or more retail outlets in the initial sample not being in business at the conclusion of the study. Such causes of store dropouts could be due to fire or bankruptcy. (One sample store was to fall out of the sample because of fire, but its subsequent elimination from the sample did not have a great effect on the data in that it was one of the smaller stores in the sample. Had it been a large outlet, and had the store sample been small, the damage to the data accuracy could have been serious indeed.)

Still another data accuracy problem was the maintenance of conditions within the sample stores. Certain independent variables within the store had to be controlled so that their effect on the data would be minimal. Examples of in-store maintenance included elimination of any out-of-stock condition of the two Grandin products, simulation of real-life shelf facings (number of packages of each brand visible to customer), and a holding of all vitamin brand prices constant during the study. All of these independent variables were the subject of Market Facts' regular distributor-auditor's twice or thrice weekly service calls on each store in the sample. The price maintenance was made possible through the arrangements between the Marketest Division and the store managements and was maintained on a regular basis through time. Price maintenance is legal for test marketing purposes.

It was agreed that Standish and Metcalf would develop the raw data and then meet with McCabe and Erb, at which time they would begin the organization of the report to Grandin's management.

ANALYSIS OF PART D— EVALUATING ALTERNATIVES

The pattern of the substeps for each of the first four phases in the basic flowchart has been one of getting a "draft" and then revising and improving it, with the help of additional information where needed. (See the flowchart on page 142.) In step one the decision-problem begins with statements of changes and ends with an explicit, individuated statement of the problem. In step two an initial list of alternatives is generated and then distilled into a final list. In step three one begins with a core profit criterion, which is subsequently modified to reflect the constraints on data collection, and then is cast in very explicit if-then form. What takes place now in step four is an initial evaluation or assessment of the designated alternatives (an assessment that generally will be very hazy) followed by appropriate data collection to permit a more complete evaluation to be made.

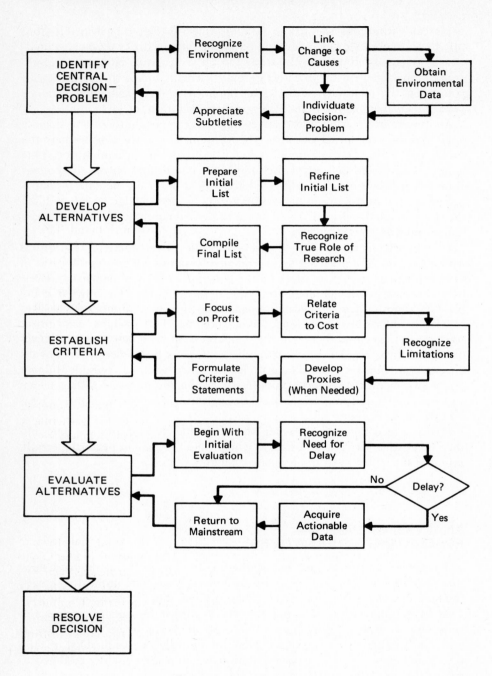

Summary Flowchart, Chapters 1–4

A point worth noting is that while marketing researchers might do much of the data acquisition and the computations to complete the evaluation of alternatives, it is the marketing manager (or managers) who will make the choice of a course of action. The *final* evaluation of any marketing alternative acted upon is, of course, made by the market.

The substeps connected with evaluating the alternatives are:

a. Begin with initial evaluation.
b. Recognize the need for delay.
c. Acquire actionable data.
d. Return to the mainstream.

Begin With the Initial Evaluation

The alternative being evaluated is the introduction of a price brand. The criterion statement reads: If divisional profits for vitamins can exceed $1.2 million per annum for the first year after the price brand's introduction (and for 'X' years after that), then the price brand should be introduced. Implicitly, if the annual division profit cannot reach the $1.2 million level, then the price brand will not be commercialized nationally. The nature of the contemplated alternative generated a high level of uncertainty as to whether the price brand would contribute to the profitability of the Vitamin Division. It was, after all, a departure from the marketing traditions and practices of Grandin.

Recognize the Need for Delay

It is fairly obvious that a decision on marketing the price brand cannot be made right away. A delay in making the choice must await the gathering of data that will permit an explicit evaluation of the price brand scheme. Nevertheless it is fruitful to play out the factors leading to the need for delay. These factors, or warning signs that delay is called for, are:

1. management disagreement.
2. profit consequences of a wrong decision.
3. pressure to act.

Management Disagreement. To find evidence that managerial disagreement was high one must turn to prior parts of the case. Winslow, in Part C, was sufficiently optimistic about the price brand's prospects that he was even willing to dispense with marketing research, or at least to undertake only a modest consumer survey. McCabe and some members of the Marketing Committee, on the other hand, were pessimistic, as apparently were members of the Executive Committee. The point of voiding established policy on product distribution was certainly viewed differently by the various participants and was a central element in the disagreement that existed.

With Grandin's Executive Committee questioning the wisdom of introducing a price brand, and the Vitamin Division's Marketing Committee nevertheless favoring such a move, the disagreement level was considered high among responsible and experienced persons.

Profit Consequences of a Wrong Decision. While not quantified, the profit consequences of a wrong decision were great. Grandin's Vitamin Division in its present form probably could not survive a product failure, or even have it fall short of its expected contribution to profit.

A two-dimensional array, or matrix, was recommended in Chapter 4 (Figure 4–2) for use in "quantifying" the disagreement-consequences "content" of a decision-problem situation. What does use of that matrix scheme reveal in this part of the Grandin case? The two factors (management disagreement and profit consequences) each would receive a score of 4 or 5 placing their combined score from 8 to 10 and clearly suggesting that some delay to acquire disagreement-reducing information is needed (see Figure 7).

Pressure to Act. The seasonal pattern of vitamin sales was a principal source of pressure to act. Much preliminary work was necessary (such as arrangements for grocery store distribution) prior to rolling out the product at the start of the winter season. This work could be delayed only so long (there was some *slack* in critical-path network terms). There was also the pressure to improve the Vitamin Division's profitability.

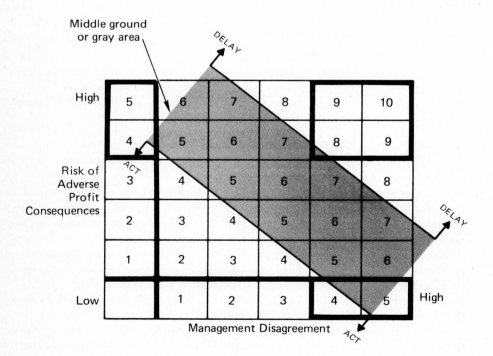

Figure 7   ***Combined Disagreement and Profit Consequences Scales as Applied to Grandin Price Brand Decision***

The need to act was apparent, but so great was the uncertainty, as reflected by the decision makers' disagreement and the high profit consequences, that a delay of several months was agreed to. During this period, data could be obtained which hopefully would reduce the uncertainty and lead to managerial agreement on either marketing the new price brand or rejecting it.

Acquire Actionable Data

Of course the decision to delay to acquire data had already been made. The ensuing decision related to how long the delay was to be and was linked to when the data would be collected. In other words, would the data be sufficiently accurate for use this coming winter if the data were gathered during the summer? Or was the risk of inaccurate information great enough to deter the demand for speed?

Length of Decision Delay. The obvious advantage of full delay (gathering data during the winter season) was greater accuracy. The disadvantage was largely incurring the opportunity cost of one year's lost sales of Vita-Health. The researchers were being strongly influenced by management decision makers with regard to the speed with which the data were to be gathered. The alternatives facing marketing management and the data collection team were: (1) gather the data as quickly as feasible so that the final marketing decision on Vita-Health could be made prior to the forthcoming winter season; or (2) gather data during the peak vitamin consumer buying season, from November through April, for use a year later. The observant reader will quickly recognize that a separate decision situation has arisen—one related to the research activity. The basic flowchart of course applied here as well. In this case we are at the state of evaluating the two research alternatives posed above.

Quantifying the evaluation of these marketing research alternatives is virtually impossible for the statistician. The issue centers on the predicted accuracy level of the data being sought—in advance of the data collection. Such levels of accuracy cannot be measured in advance; even after the study has been completed, they can be measured only with difficulty. Thus, the researchers and the management people had to work out some compromise. The researchers, by agreeing to conduct the study during the summer, were in essence saying that in their opinion they could develop data that would have an "acceptable" degree of accuracy. This phrase is vague to be sure, but in view of the circumstances it is the best that can be said.

Whether this decision is "correct" in this particular situation can be argued effectively on both sides. The most telling argument focuses on the levels of managerial disagreement and profit consequences of a wrong decision and it suggests that all efforts should be made to gather highly precise data. McCabe and Standish recognized this. With that line of reasoning, however, it can be argued quite plausibly that the risk of inadequate data should not have been taken by plunging into the study at midsummer. In other words, the risk of imprecise data was greater than the cost of delay. Despite all of this, the two researchers proceeded with all speed, apparently confident that in their judgment the resultant data would be acceptably accurate.

Descriptive vs. Experimental Study Approach. Yet another marketing research decision confronted McCabe and Standish; it concerned whether a descriptive study or an experimental study should be conducted. They agreed to employ the descriptive approach. The criterion for this research decision was accuracy of the data. They reasoned, based on experience and empirical data from other studies, that a descriptive study with a larger, more widely dispersed sample would yield more accurate data than would an experimental study involving matched groups of stores where sampling error might be a serious deterrent establishing real differences between experimental and control groups. The researchers apparently felt that they could overcome the seasonal problem of generalizing from summer data to peak winter consumer buying levels by adjusting the study data by known factors secured from prior years' sales information.

As in the situation involving the length of the decision delay, there is no way in which one can quantify, in advance, the levels of accuracy of the study data—i.e., comparing descriptive data with experimental data. Accuracy levels are not predictive in a precise sense. Instead, the researchers rely on their experience, as well as on data from other studies in which they have been engaged or with which they are familiar.

The experimental approach, however, could have been discussed by McCabe and Standish. The research alternative of employing the experimental design was never voiced. It is a reasonable design and should have received serious consideration. The underlying key to experimentation is the realization that the primary interest of the marketing decision makers and the researcher is providing a comparison of alternatives (treatments), rather than the establishment of absolute values.

The essential advantage of the experimental design approach is that a causal relationship between the marketing of Vita-Health and the profitability of the Grandin Vitamin Division can be established. Through an experimental study, cause and effect can be measured in unambiguous terms. With the descriptive approach the role of Vita-Health in altering the Grandin profit level can be confidently assumed, but there is always the lingering doubt that a three-month data collection effort during the "off-season" would not provide a solid base for projecting sales of Vita-Health on a national basis.

In theory at least the experimental design offers the superior method of predicting national Vita-Health sales. An appropriate design would involve what is termed a "before-after with control group." In brief, a "before" measure would be taken of sales of all vitamins in the sample stores. This auditing would be undertaken early in May while the several decisions were being made on Vita-Health's packaging, pricing, and other tactical decisions. Thus, the "before" measure would provide a base for subsequently determining the effect of the experimental variable—the marketing of Vita-Health. In addition, from a research design viewpoint these "before" data would enable the researchers to divide the stores into two well-matched samples based on total vitamin sales and on Grandin's (pre–Vita-Health) market share.

At the start of the test period, Marketest would have already distributed Vita-Health. Sales in both store groups would be audited weekly. The impact of the experimental variable, Vita-Health, could be determined by comparing the sales and revenues of Vita-Health and Grandin Vitamins in the test stores with the sales and revenues of only Grandin Vitamins in the control stores. If the store groups were well-matched, and other independent variables were either randomized or controlled, the revenue difference between Vita-Health plus the traditional Grandin Vitamin combination and Grandin Vitamin could be attributed only to the marketing of Vita-Health. Such resultant data could then be translated into a national sales and revenue estimate by adjusting the traditional Grandin Vitamin national revenues so as to reflect the Vita-Health impact. Implicit here is the assumption that June-August percentage revenue differences can be applied to the vitamin market on a year-round basis. However, the same assumption would have to be made for analyzing descriptive study data. Moreover, with the latter data a further adjustment for seasonality would have to be made.

Recognizing these considerations, Market Facts opted for a descriptive study with a larger and more dispersed sample with the aim of holding down sampling error. (Remember, sampling error is but one type of error that can arise in a study; though measurable it can often be swamped by other errors, even though the latter may be impossible to measure.) Again an experimental study of the basic "before-after with control group" type could have been employed if the time and funds (mostly time) were available. An important consideration would be matching the stores so that the influence of factors other than the ones being consciously manipulated in the experiment could be accounted for in assessing the changes. Cost and time constraints could hold down the allowable sample size for such an experimental study, thereby increasing the sampling error and so reducing detection of real changes or differences between the experimental and control groups.

The planned study did intend to utilize before and after measurements of product movement, i.e., before and after the introduction of the price brand. But the contemplated study did not make an explicit attempt to match stores nor was a control group of stores used. Further, a specific cause-and-effect relationship was not sought. What control meant in the study was that the research team could physically control the product marketing effort all the way up to the grocer's shelf. Such control reduces auditing errors and permits a more rigorous maintenance of the agreed-upon marketing climate.

Both design alternatives—descriptive and experimental—are acceptable. The decision is made on which of the options is believed will better satisfy the criterion of higher accuracy. Research cost is not a criterion constraint here because the researchers agreed at the outset that because of the magnitude of the marketing decision, and in order to provide the highest level of accuracy, no funds would be spared.

In attempting to optimize the research dollar for this study, McCabe and Standish were in reality engaged in a decision-making effort of their own. They had a series of research decisions to make, outgrowths of research environments and research alternatives. The broad environment consisted of the basic need for the data, coupled with the known levels of managerial disagreement and profit consequences. The research decision-problems were related to setting up the sales audit test market, the size and dispersion of the sample, and the duration of the data collection phase of the study.

All of these decisions were made without the benefit of gathering data. Both McCabe and Standish well knew that the most efficient sample stems from pilot data-gathering efforts. In this study, however, they exercised their judgment based on studies for other types of products and made the sampling decisions without the benefit of gathering additional research data.

Return to the Mainstream

In an extensive data acquisition effort such as the one just discussed, considerable energies can be expended on research decisions. Indeed these research decisions can divert the attention of participating marketing managers from other marketing decisions that they may be involved in and from environmental developments. Clearly "the show must go on." Improving the profitability of the Vitamin Division should be an on-going effort, one that should not be deferred until the test marketing results come in. For example, profitability can be improved by cost reduction. Grandin management wasted little time in cutting back on advertising for their regular vitamin.

The mainstream, like Heraclitus' river, is one of constant change. The marketing decision maker has to stay abreast of that change, even when working to bring about planned change.

DISCUSSION QUESTIONS FOR PART D

1. Retail store audit data were selected by the marketing researchers. Store audit data are frequently used in marketing decision making. What adjustments should be made when a major retail chain refuses to allow marketing research auditors into its stores?
2. Audit data were to be gathered on both Grandin vitamin brands due to the criterion employed. But why were data on all vitamin brands needed?
3. An approach involving determining "perfect" data and the value of added information with subjective probabilities was considered but rejected by McCabe and Standish. What does such an approach entail? Were McCabe and Standish right in their rejection?
4. How would test distribution of the price brand through normal wholesale and retail channels complicate interpretation of the retail sales audit data?
5. McCabe and Standish recognized that having pilot data would contribute to the design of a more efficient sample. Why is this so? (Hint: Recall formulas for interval estimates of population parameters from sample data.)
6. What was the nature of the brand name decision (i.e., how does the decision fit into the framework of the decision-making flowchart)?
7. Grandin's advertising for the regular vitamin was curtailed as soon as plans for the market test were begun. Is this a good or a bad idea? Why?

GRANDIN LABORATORIES—PART E

(*Note to Reader:* You should have read through Chapter 5 and Grandin Laboratories—Part D to this point.)

With test market data collection completed and tabulations made, Standish and Metcalf decided to arrange their report in terms of secondary and primary data. The purpose of the Marketest report was to submit the data in some logical form and sequence, to be accompanied by a description of the method of data collection and the formulae used in the calculation of the national sales predictions of Grandin Vitamins and Vita-Health Vitamins. The summary data appear in Tables 6 and 7.

Table 6 Summary of Secondary and Primary Test Market Data

Secondary Data

Industry Vitamin Sales, 1972	$15,900,000
Predicted industry decline (1966–72 average)	350,000
Predicted industry sales, 1973	15,550,000
Industry sales, June–August, 1972 (12 weeks)	1,908,000
Industry share of year, June–August, 1972	12%
Grandin Vitamin Division Sales, 1972	$ 3,438,000
Grandin market share	22%
Grandin sales, June–August, 1972 (12 weeks)	618,840
Grandin share of year, June–August, 1972 (12 weeks)	18%
Grandin national level of distribution among chain and independent retail drug outlets	90%
Marketest sample stores' vitamin share of national sales	2%

Marketest Data (Primary Data)

Test Study National Projections:

Share of Market:	
Grandin Vitamins	20%
Vita-Health Vitamins	16%
Total, Grandin Vitamin Division	36%
National Sales Projections:	
Grandin Vitamins	$ 2,799,000
Vita-Health Vitamins	2,239,000
Total, Grandin Vitamin Division	$ 5,038,000

Using the formula for the projection method to determine the operating profit for Grandin Vitamins and Vita-Health, the data in Table 6 yield the following results:

Table 7 Industry and Grandin Dollar Sales in Marketest Stores (June 3–August 26, 1973)

Dollar Sales for Bi-Weekly Periods Ending:

	June 17		July 1		July 15		July 29		August 12		August 26		Final 8 Weeks	
	No.	%	No.	%	No.	%	No.	%	No.	%	No.	%	No.	%
Grandin Vitamins	1879	21	2016	22	1932	21	1792	19	1837	20	1800	20	7361	20
Vita-Health	302	3	600	6	1252	14	1616	18	1508	16	1500	16	5876	16
Grandin Total	2181	24	2616	28	3184	35	3408	37	3345	36	3300	36	13237	36
All other brands	7013	76	6631	72	6015	65	5866	63	5847	64	5914	64	23636	64
(Industry Total)	(9194)	100	(9247)	100	(9199)	100	(9274)	100	(9192)	100	(9214)	100	(36879)	100

	Share of Market	×	Industry Sales	×	Level of Distribution	×	Return on Sales	=	Operating Profit
Grandin Vitamins	20%	×	$15,550,000	×	90%	×	27%	=	$ 756,000
Vita-Health	16%	×	$15,550,000	×	90%	×	21%	=	$ 470,000
					Total Predicted Division Operating Profit =				$1,226,000

Adding the operating profits for Grandin Vitamins and Vita-Health thus yields the total projected division operating profit of $1,226,000. This forecast is for the 12-month period following the introduction of Vita-Health, presumably after distribution has been completed. "Level of distribution" is part of the formula because the Marketest study was conducted in 100 percent of the stores in which they arranged for distribution. Grandin forecasts about a 90 percent distribution level for Vita-Health after introduction. Thus, the forecast should be reduced by the 10 percent of the stores in which there would be no distribution.

A general review of the Marketest data took place at the meeting at which Standish and Metcalf submitted their report containing the four-city data plus the secondary data to McCabe and Erb. The report also contained a description of the methodology, accompanied by all research forms and field auditor instructions. Several analyses of variance were included to indicate the extent of statistically significant differences.

McCabe and Standish met a day later to discuss the meaning of the data and to formulate the nature of their recommendations to the Grandin management. Both agreed that from a statistical point of view the projection from the test data did not assure the meeting of the required $1,200,000 combined operating profit for the two Grandin products. While the prediction was $1,226,000 based on the study, there was no denying that the sampling and nonsampling errors, as estimated, were such that the true profit figure could be below $1,200,000.

The two researchers thus were faced with making a decision as to whether to go with the existing data or continue the study for another month or so to sharpen the precision of the test data results. To delay the presentation of the data seemed unwise in view of management's desire to act. Moreover, the data were most encouraging to Grandin in that the new price brand did not appear to be taking any substantive portion of vitamin sales away from the traditional Grandin Vitamin. The evidence was that market share of the Grandin Vitamin was around 20 percent *after* Vita-Health; *before* the Grandin Vitamin share was 22 percent. In other words, Vita-Health sales were almost entirely a source of new revenue to Grandin. And while the minimum criterion figure of $1,200,000 may in fact not be met, the introduction of Vita-Health did contribute to the profitability of the Grandin Vitamin Division.

"The important thing," commented McCabe, "is that there is a degree of consistency in the Grandin and Vita-Health data that is very encouraging. Eliminating the first four weeks when Vita-Health was still in the 'climbing stage,' the Grandin and Vita-Health market shares hold very well. This data is convincing and leads me to believe that we can accept the data as conclusive evidence that the addition of the price brand will enhance the division's profits to the point where it should be added to our division's line."

"I agree," said Standish. "Let's talk about the report, and then we can get specific when we start working the data into the final presentation. Do you plan a visual type of report, Art?"

"Yes, I think so," replied McCabe. "In view of the fact that we will have two levels of persons viewing our findings, I feel that a chart presentation would be appropriate."

"What do you mean—two levels of persons?" queried Standish.

"Well, we will have the members of the Executive Committee present," responded McCabe. "The marketing management of the Vitamin Division will be there although we will of course show the presentation to them prior to the meeting with the Executive Committee. Having both the marketing people and the Executive Committee members attending the subsequent meeting will result in some sort of a communications problem. A graphic portrayal of the data along with our recommendations on Vita-Health can, in my opinion, be better handled with a visual report. Questions can be frelded as they arise. One that we should anticipate concerns the adequacy of the sample size. The written report can be submitted about a week later, after we make certain that the visual has been accepted."

"Well, we can use some of the data tables for both reports. Those that appear in the graphic can appear also in the written report," suggested Standish. "For sure, we don't want to get tangled in a lot of research jargon and hedge on every figure we show. The data are convincing, and I suggest that we forget all the statistical hedges for the graphic report at least. In the written story we can of course always have an appendix showing our statistical measures of significance, along with the details of the research methodology."

"Let's talk about the sequence of the report, Francine," suggested McCabe. "Perhaps some outline of how we will unfold the story would be in order. At the outset, I feel that we should summarize the data and present our recommendations very early in the story. After all, as you know, we want to get our point across at the beginning while we have their attention and while everyone is there."

"Well, that could be," replied Standish. "However, I feel that there is always some risk in opening with a marketing recommendation. Keep in mind that a good number of people seeing the presentation—and reading the report—are going to take exception to your recommendation simply because they took an opposite stand before the study was conducted. These people will resist accepting your recommendation merely because they do not want to be on the losing side of the argument. Also, Art, remember that there are varying levels of management to be at the meeting. And several of those who opposed the price brand expressed themselves in front of their superiors. They will strongly resist recommendations made at the outset, although they may not express themselves openly. They will, however, remain hostile.

"I would urge you to unfold the story gradually, starting with a description of the origin of the price brand and how it got into the act in the first place. I would review the marketing alternatives and the criterion the finance people offered as the basis for making the decision. Then, after you have shown that the criterion has been satisfied through projection of the test market data, there can be little argument as to the acceptance of your recommendations.

"After all," continued Standish, "presenting research data requires some selling. You just can't show a lot of figures and expect everyone to understand and buy them. You must convince the management people that these data are valid and reliable, and that they can be projected to a national picture. This will take some explanation, and it should follow your discussion of the criterion and why there was some uncertainty as to whether the needed sales figures could be met. If you wish, I'll be glad to outline the report as I see it."

McCabe quickly took Standish up on her offer. They agreed to get together again within two days, at which time Standish was to have her thoughts on paper so that they could then start "hanging" some data on the report model.

At the subsequent meeting, Standish presented McCabe with the following report outline:

 I. Purpose of meeting (or report)

  A. To act on whether to market or not to market the price brand vitamin
  B. To view data obtained by Marketest Division of Market Facts, Inc., relating to the marketing of the price brand

 II. Why the price brand was considered as a possible addition to the Grandin Division line

  A. Description of competitive brand sales
  B. Figures showing Grandin's decline in absolute sales and market share
  C. Portrayal of how the Grandin Vitamin Division was failing to meet the corporate minimum financial requirements set for the division

 III. The marketing alternatives

  A. To market the new price brand—Vita-Health—nationally through grocery chains, co-ops, drug chains, and independents
  B. Not to market the price brand

 IV. Criterion for decision

  A. Explanation as to why absolute sales of Vita-Health Vitamins would be an inadequate basis for making the decision
  B. The criterion finally agreed upon—profitability of the entire Grandin Vitamin Division: Grandin Vitamins plus Vita-Health Vitamins

V. The Marketest Study

    A. Why it was needed—to reduce the uncertainty

    B. Why the audit method

    C. Basis of national projection

    D. The data and how it leads to the recommendation that the price brand be launched nationally

VI. The recommended course of action—introduction of Vita-Health Vitamins

VII. Appendix—research and statistical details

McCabe agreed to the sequence and content, and the report was developed and presented to management in graphic and written forms. The Executive Committee and the Vitamin Division's marketing management were enthusiastic about the findings, and agreement was reached for the marketing of the price brand on a national scale.

ANALYSIS OF PART E—
RESOLVING THE DECISION

In achieving closure on the decision-problem the additional data sought has to be interpreted and then communicated in an unambiguous way to the decision makers. Only then can they make an informed choice or delay the decision for further data. (See the substeps associated with resolving the decision on the flowchart on the next page.)

The test market study revealed a predicted annual profitability slightly in excess of the minimum amount stated in the criterion—$1.2 million. However, the true figure could fall below the stated criterion.

The formula used to arrive at the projections (share of market industry sales) is one of the simpler approaches. This formula has validity when the test market audit includes all brands, which was the case in this study. In addition, reliable data on total industry sales were available through Grandin's subscription to the continuous audit data of International Marketing Services of America, Ltd.

The main block of actionable data, that which permits the choice of an alternative under prespecified criteria, is found in the Marketest Data section of Table 6, specifically the line dealing with division total profit—here $1,226,000. In addition, those Table 6 data employed in computing the division total profit are more actionable than environmental in nature (those used in conjunction with the "projection method"). Similarly, the primary data in Table 7 are actionable in the sense that they contribute directly to the computation of the operating profit (the ultimate criterion).

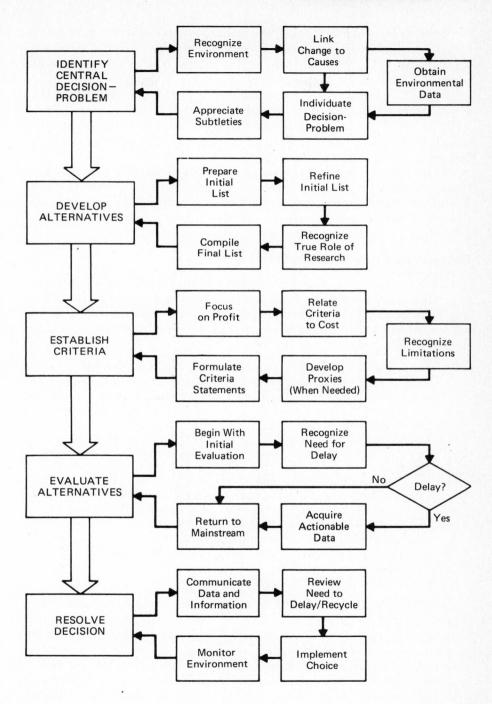

Summary Flowchart, Chapters 1–5

Additionally no evidence that cannibalization took place, i.e., that regular Grandin's vitamin sales were lost to Grandin's price brand, is found in the market shares of Table 7. If "Grandin regular" dropped in market share, while competition's share went essentially unchanged and the share of Grandin's price brand rose, then the obvious conclusion would be that price brand sales growth came at the expense of the regular brand. The market share data in Table 7 do not suggest that this cannibalization has occurred. Grandin Vitamins held relatively steady at 20%, while competition dropped from 76% to 64% giving Vita-Health sufficient sales to get up to 16%.

The Grandin research group, in a sense acting for the decision makers, agreed that the company would be better served by not delaying the marketing decision further. Thus, a continuance of the test marketing operation was rejected. Before continuing with the analysis of the test results communication activity, a closer look at the decision not to delay further is warranted.

Review Need to Delay/Recycle

The test market data, while encouraging, did not establish conclusively that the stated criterion would be met if the price brand were marketed nationally. The researchers, then, in effect acting for the decision makers, had to decide whether to recycle in the decision process and, if so, to what extent. Several options were viable to one degree or another.

1. They could delay further by extending the data collection another six or eight weeks. This move would have increased the reliability of the data. If this alternative had been selected, it would have meant that the researchers were recycling back through the area of obtaining additional data to resolve uncertainty.
2. The researchers could go ahead with the data they had in their hands (as they did), and recommend commercializing the price brand. This action also involves recycling in that they have in a sense revised management's criterion. They, in essence, said that "we will recommend marketing Vita-Health Vitamins because it does add to the profitability of the company." This recommendation falls short of the initial criterion which required a minimum operating profit figure of $1,200,000. The new criterion implicitly employed was "If the addition of Vita-Health to our line, marketed through grocery and drug channels, increases the profitability of the Grandin Vitamin Division, then we will add Vita-Health." The test data did establish solidly that this criterion was met.

Choosing option 2 was wise, for to delay further would make it difficult to achieve national distribution in time to meet the seasonal upsurge in vitamin sales. Delaying further could also give competitors additional time to make appropriate marketing countermoves.

Of course there is nothing to prevent Grandin from continuing the test in the four cities for a few more weeks while beginning national-level distribution. Most likely, however, their "license" to use resale price maintenance in the test stores will expire.

Communicate Data and Information

The researchers recognized the need to present findings to Grandin management free from technical jargon and in proper sequence.

Two reports were in the making, one revealing environmental data and the other revealing actionable data. The report prepared by the Market Facts staff and submitted to McCabe and his group was not actionable in normal use of the term. The purpose of the report was to submit data in an organized manner, but not with the intent of resolving a marketing issue. Thus, the reporting of the data was in some logical sequence, but not built around the making of a recommendation for action. The sequence agreed upon by the Market Facts researchers was related first to secondary data, then to primary data, leading to an explanation of how the final projection of Grandin and Vita-Health sales was determined. Then followed an explanation of methodology.

It can be argued that in preparing a report of this type the research methodology should be early in the report. The research technicians, the readers of the report, are interested in determining the accuracy of the data and a complete description of the methods of data collection and analysis reassures (or disturbs) them before they examine the data themselves. In defense of Market Facts' decision to place the methodology at the close of the report, it can be assumed that they knew that the Grandin people were thoroughly familiar with the research methods employed, and that to place this description at the outset of the report would slow the reader.

The actionable report presented by McCabe to his management required an entirely different approach to content and sequence. McCabe and Standish both resolved the content and sequence issues, recognizing the nonresearch composition of the audience plus the actionable nature of the report. Standish argued against opening the oral presentation with marketing recommendations, noting that some people in the audience will need to be "sold" first.

Those people needing preselling would include those Grandin managers who supported the policy of restricting distribution to drugstores and/or felt a price brand demeaned the reputation of Grandin. They would likely need a convincing argument, logically structured, to overcome their bias and to engender their support for introduction of a price brand. A review of the secondary data on the industry situation and on Grandin's profit predicament regarding vitamins should begin the argument, followed by a recap of how the alternatives were generated and how the need for additional data was recognized. The rationale behind the data-gathering approach should be presented next, then the findings, and finally the conclusions those findings suggest. The presenters should be prepared to answer, in a sound and diplomatic way, any questions that may be asked during the course of the session. (See Discussion Question 6.)

Management had been continually insistent on introducing the new product in line with the agreed-on schedule, in order to benefit by the seasonal demand. So the test market data were received by the decision makers with the full realization that the product's contribution to profit could be less than the initially stated criterion.

No additional judgment by outside experts was deemed necessary. The data resolved the disagreement among members of the Executive Committee and the Marketing Committee.

Implement Choice

After the disagreement on the course of action to be taken was resolved, a decision was made to market a price brand. The national roll-outs of the price brand would have to be done quickly so as to be ready for the seasonal upsurge in vitamin sales. Presumably during the 12 weeks of test marketing Grandin made preparations to commence national distribution as soon as the decision to do so was made. Production schedules should have been drafted; sales-contact, warehousing, and transportation plans should have been worked up; and promotional support for salespeople should have been laid out. Once the decision to go national was made these plans and schedules would be carried out by line management.

Monitor the Environment

While not explicitly mentioned in the case, the need to monitor the new, changed environment resulting from Grandin price brand introduction should be obvious to the reader.

DISCUSSION QUESTIONS FOR PART E

1. Erb and Metcalf were understandably concerned about the magnitude of error associated with the audit study. How might the two classes of error (sampling and nonsampling) apply in this instance?
2. Resale price maintenance was a control requirement for the study and fortunately the law permits such use for test marketing. What complications might have been introduced into the study were price maintenance not possible?
3. What does the sales trajectory of Vita-Health look like? Is it typical or atypical of new product introductions in general? Does market share stability appear to have set in?
4. Should McCabe and Standish place the sales estimate they derive from the study results in a confidence interval form? Why?
5. Good results regarding repurchase rates are important to successful new product introduction. Why is this so? What data, if any, are there in the case on this score?
6. In developing their reports of the test market study McCabe and Standish were rightly concerned about the kinds of questions they could expect from the marketing committee. If you were on that committee, what questions would you ask?

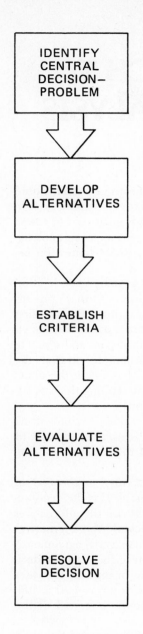

IDENTIFY CENTRAL DECISION— PROBLEM	Grandin vitamin sales and profitability declines are due to changes in consumer and competitor behavior relative to vitamin prices and place of purchase — lower prices, wider availability.
DEVELOP ALTERNATIVES	1. Market a price-brand vitamin with Grandin identification through grocery chains, co-ops, drug chains, and independents. 2. Do not market a price-brand vitamin.
ESTABLISH CRITERIA	*If* the annual operating profit of the entire Vitamin Division can reach $1.2 million with the price brand (and regular brand), *then* the price brand will be commercialized nationally.
EVALUATE ALTERNATIVES	A test market study for the price brand projects annual operating Vitamin Division profit at $1.226 million.
RESOLVE DECISION	The Executive Committee accepts the study findings and chooses to commercialize the price brand nationally. Marketing management implements this choice.

Summary of Grandin Laboratories: A Comprehensive Case

APPROACH TO CASE ANALYSIS

The case method of instruction is widely, but by no means universally, used in business schools. A variety of ways exists for an instructor to employ cases in any course—one professor has described more than twenty such uses of cases.[1] The cases offered in this book are intended to be used as vehicles in applying the five-step decision model. The analysis resulting from that application becomes the basis for class discussion and written assignments.

Case material is intended to be a *descriptive* portrayal of some episode in organizational activity. Case analysis is the *prescriptive* approach to that same situation. It is the analyst who must specify what *should* be done. But the first task for the analyst is to comprehend the descriptive material of the case. In effect, the analyst must redescribe the case in more insightful terms and separate the significant elements from the insignificant. Having accomplished that, the analyst can proceed to offer a prescription—an idea of what should be done. The five-step flowchart provides a framework both for redescribing the case situation and for prescribing the appropriate courses of action.

The cases that follow are for the most part based on real-life business situations. They are, however, altered in some instances to disguise the identity of the firms involved. Fictitious names are sometimes used to preclude revealing the companies providing the information.

It is important to adhere to the decision model described in the text in analyzing each case. The reader should ask such questions as: Has the decision-problem truly been clearly identified by the participants? Are the alternatives spelled out? Are meaningful criteria explicitly stated? How do the alternatives stack up with regard to profit consequences and level of managerial agreement?

Only after addressing these questions should one begin to focus on the decision makers' need for data, its collection, and its analysis. In some of the cases that follow, a mistake early in the decision-making process has caused a difficult situation to be compounded so that confusion reigns. The goal of the analyst, therefore, should be to locate where the decision makers went awry.

In other cases the central thrust should be the correct phrasing of the alternative courses of action or perhaps determining whether the environmental data are sufficiently significant to justify working up a list of marketing options in the first place. In still other cases the real discussion should relate to the appropriateness of the criteria for the decision in view of the profit consequences,

---

[1] Harold W. Fox, "Two Dozen Ways of Handling Cases," *Collegiate News and Views* (Spring, 1973), pp. 17–20.

the level of managerial disagreement, and the realities of data collection. To what extent should a proxy criterion be employed—or should a monetary criterion be used? Where supposedly actionable data are presented, the following question should be asked: Do the data match the criterion agreed upon? Obviously, if the criterion has not been stated, the usefulness of the data is diminished and often is of no value at all.

The reader should resist the ever-present temptation to examine case data and then immediately rationalize on behalf of one particular course of marketing action. More often than not, when difficulty is encountered in analyzing data it is because one or more of the following situations are present:

1. There is confusion as to whether the data are environmental or actionable.
2. The marketing alternatives have not been clearly spelled out and/or are not mutually exclusive.
3. Meaningful and feasible criteria have not been agreed upon by the decision makers.
4. The level of profit consequences and/or level of managerial disagreement has not been ascertained.
5. The data collected have not been related to the criteria.

It does not follow that simply because substantial data appear in a case those data are meaningful and contribute to a "solution" of the case. Very often, in real-world situations participants in the decision charge off and gather data that are really not essential to making the decision. Or, in other instances, the wrong data are collected. Good cases, like real-world situations, do not usually come neatly packaged. Too much data but too little real information are more the rule than the exception. The student will very likely become frustrated by the lack of certain data that, in the student's view, must be available to fully understand the case and to render a meaningful solution. Such frustrations should not be allowed to hinder applying the decision framework to the case— i.e., don't get "turned off" by the apparent lack of "real" data. If some industry data are desired to broaden one's understanding of the setting of a given case, consider using such sources as *U.S. Industrial Outlook*, published annually by the U.S. Department of Commerce, and Standard and Poors' *Industry Surveys*. It is strongly recommended that the reader *not* spend time engaging in library research to uncover data that might reveal the identity of the company disguised in the case and the actions taken by the firm. The search will generally be fruitless and so that time is far better spent trying systematically to apply the five-step model to the case itself. Make any reasonable assumptions necessary to proceed with the analysis.

This concept of case analysis is difficult to master. But once one has become skilled and adept in employing the basic decision framework and in carrying out the creativity, reasoning, and data handling required, one can approach any decision with assurance of making a positive contribution to its resolution.

Decision making requires skill. A study of the decision-making process will improve that skill. It is important to remember, therefore, that the cases presented in this book are to be attacked from the standpoint of an *analysis of the decision process* employed by marketing participants.

CASES

Architectural Design, Inc.

The practice that evolved into Architectural Design, Inc., was started in 1950 by Jackson J. Barwick. The practice was located in, and largely confined to, a small city of 35,000, the seat of a county largely rural and agricultural in nature. For its first 20 years, the firm was a single proprietorship, bearing very much the stamp of Barwick's talents and personality. During this period, all of the firm's projects were designed by Barwick and construction documents (working drawings and construction specifications) were produced by him, assisted by varying numbers of drafters working under his close supervision. Construction administration—that is, ensuring that projects were built in accordance with design and specifications—was also handled by Barwick, assisted by one drafter/inspector. Engineering services—design of electrical, plumbing, heating, and air-conditioning systems—for projects were acquired from outside consultants.

Although this approach limited the volume of work the practice could handle, it enabled Barwick to maintain strict quality control on his projects, and clients during this period seemed pleased that their work received the constant personal attention of the principal of the firm.

Barwick had numerous personal contacts with community leaders and potential clients. He enjoyed a considerable advantage over his competition in this regard, since he came from an old and well-known family of the area, and had lived in the town all his life except for college and naval service in World War II. His brothers were prominent local businessmen, active in civic affairs. In the mid-1950s, Barwick served a term as a city councilman, and this favorable public exposure enhanced his practice (although, of course, he did not seek or accept commissions from the city during his term of office).

His competition during this period consisted primarily of two other local, one-proprietor firms (since reduced to one by the retirement of one of the architects), neither of which enjoyed Barwick's extensive contacts or his full membership in the city and county establishments.

Clients of the firm were largely local public bodies, and projects fell typically in such categories as municipal structures, schools, public housing, and county

Material for this case was prepared originally by E. Cameron Williams, University of North Carolina at Chapel Hill, and George M. Dupuy, University of Virginia. Used with authors' permission.

offices and miscellaneous structures. Barwick also worked for local private clients on such projects as light industrial buildings, churches, clubhouses, offices, and, occasionally, a custom residence. The bulk of the firm's income, however, was derived from projects for local government, principally schools and public housing. Barwick acquired a reputation for expertise in the last two project types, and, although his practice was generally confined to his home city, the boom in low-income public housing during the late 1960s brought in some profitable commissions from housing authorities in nearby counties.

Francis P. Mayo joined the firm in 1965 as a drafter, after earning his architectural degree and serving four years as a naval officer. (Registration laws for architects require architecture graduates to serve an apprenticeship under a practicing architect before taking the professional examination; passing the exam is the last step toward registration, or licensure to practice architecture.) During Mayo's apprenticeship, Barwick came more and more to rely on Mayo's flair for contemporary design to lend the firm's projects the aesthetic qualities clients were beginning to demand. Although Barwick was confident of his technical skills as an architect, he had worried for some time that his designs were cold and sterile; workable and efficient, but prosaic. By the end of Mayo's apprenticeship, Barwick had gradually turned over to him responsibility for aesthetic design, reserving for himself the more technical decisions regarding structure and materials. They thus evolved a team approach to project design.

Mayo passed the professional exam in late 1969 and became a registered architect. Barwick encouraged his drafters/apprentice architects, on becoming registered, to go into practice for themselves—preferably, of course, in another city. But he saw Mayo as a valuable asset to the practice, and thought their team approach promised both better design and a more efficient design process. Accordingly, he offered Mayo a partnership in the firm, and Mayo accepted. Barwick became president, Mayo, vice-president.

Acting on the advice of Barwick's attorney, they incorporated their partnership and named it "Architectural Design, Inc." Effective January 1, 1970, their partnership agreement called for Mayo to be, initially, a junior partner with a lesser share of the firm's profits, but for the proportion to be automatically adjusted annually in Mayo's favor until, in 1975, they would share equally.

On becoming a partner, Mayo immediately took a more active part in the affairs of the firm, particularly in dealings with clients and potential clients. More inclined toward innovation and creative approaches than Barwick, he advocated a more aggressive approach to client relations; rather than a relatively passive acquiescence to client desires, he favored persuading clients to allow more innovation in design and materials and more flexible building budgets. He was aware of the possible dangers involved in taking this tack in a small and conservative community, but was convinced that it would pay off handsomely in the long run in the form of more satisfied clients and a reputation for the firm of being up to date and design oriented.

Meanwhile, the practice of architecture in the United States was undergoing great changes. Traditionally, American architects have practiced in a manner similar to that of physicians, dentists, and lawyers. The American Institute of Architects (AIA), following trails blazed by the American Medical Association and the American Bar Association, attempted to insulate its membership from "excessive competition" by restricting entry into the profession and establishing a code of ethics that forbade advertising, competition on the basis of fee, and related promotional activities.

A number of architectural firms practice on a regional, and even national, scale, with very large staffs and networks of branch offices, and utilize the latest managerial techniques. Many of these firms offer services far beyond those traditionally thought of as architectural; in addition to in-house engineering (now almost universal among larger firms), these include such services as master-planning, city planning, site selection, landscape design, interior design, feasibility studies, land-use planning, and recreational facilities design. The rapid growth of such firms was facilitated by their willingness to promote themselves to the fullest extent allowed by the AIA canons.

Along with these trends came the beginning of an erosion of similar professional "rules" that tended to restrict competition. The case of *Goldfarb vs. Virginia State Bar* in 1975 effectively abolished local bar association fee schedules for legal services and, by extension, the similar fee schedules for local AIA chapters, thereby opening the door to competition among architects on the basis of fee. (The AIA chapter to which Barwick and Mayo belonged had, however, ceased publishing fee schedules several years before.) There was a general feeling in the profession that the ban on advertising would be the next to go.

Barwick and Mayo had felt that aggressive self-promotion was detrimental to the dignity of their profession. They avoided using the term "selling" or even "marketing," preferring instead the term "client acquisition." For years, they held the position that their professional reputation, coupled with their best efforts to satisfy their clients, would ensure ample work for the firm. For example, Mayo and Barwick insisted on daily visits to job sites to assure quality control.

The 1970s saw ADI's gross fee income slip annually; it dropped each of the three years from 1971 through 1973, inclusive. (See Figure 1.) Since these same years saw a considerable inflation in building costs, and the firm's fees were generally computed as a percentage of project cost, the true situation was actually worse than the already-alarming picture painted by the gross fee income trend. Barwick felt the slippage in revenues was partly his fault; he had relaxed his attention to the personal relationships with past and potential clients that he had built up over the years before Mayo was ready and well-enough known in the community to take up the slack. Mayo thought the firm needed firmer, more energetic direction, tauter project administration, and better business management than he felt able to provide without sacrificing his efforts to build a reputation for the firm of design excellence, creativity, and innovation. They both sensed an erosion of the firm's public image, and both agreed that they each spent too much time on tasks too important to delegate to a drafter or secretary, yet not of a nature to require the attention of one of the principals.

Accordingly, they hired Edward C. Lassiter in mid–1974 and gave him the title of Administrator. His assigned duties were quite varied; they included: the

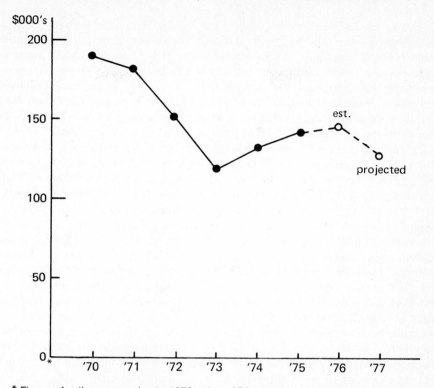

* Figures for the years prior to 1970, when ADI was a single proprietorship, are not available, but analysis of project records suggests a steady growth in fee income throughout the 1960s.

Figure 1   Gross Fee Income for ADI

day-to-day business management of the firm; project administration, including routine contacts with clients and contractors, and daily field observations of work in progress; writing and preparation of project manuals (books that include all project documents, such as contracts and construction specifications, with the exception of the working drawings); and the institution of a public relations program to polish up the firm's image in the community. He was also expected to come up with fresh ideas, either original or borrowed, for the overall direction of the firm.

Lassiter's background didn't precisely fit him for this far-reaching assignment. He had a B.S. in transportation, had served four years as a naval officer, worked two years as a line supervisor for a manufacturing firm, and two years as administrator of a federally funded municipal housing rehabilitation project. However, Barwick and Mayo were impressed by his intelligence and enthusiasm, thought that he would learn quickly, and realized that people with experience in all of the varied duties they wanted to delegate were rare, if not nonexistent. Since Barwick and Mayo were both ex-naval officers, they also regarded Lassiter's navy background as a plus.

Lassiter made considerable progress toward mastering the various facets of his job during the next two years. His public relations program grew rapidly, culminating in local and state newspaper attention to their projects, and coverage for one particularly newsworthy project on three TV stations. He was somewhat handicapped in the more technical aspects by his lack of background and had to learn specifications, construction terminology, and inspection from scratch. But, in general, he did perform capably enough to free Barwick and Mayo from many routine duties, and they were satisfied with his work.

The overall picture wasn't improving, however. Gross fee income in current dollars rose somewhat in 1975, but double-digit inflation erased most of the real gain. Changes in federal government housing policy had dried up big public housing projects, which had been a large part of their workload during the late 1960s and early 1970s. School design and construction, the other large portion of their practice, was being eroded by intense competition from big out-of-town firms that practiced on a state-wide or national scale. One client, a school system which had given Barwick and ADI all of its business for 25 years, switched to one such firm. Most disturbing, perhaps, was the fact that ADI had even lost two desirable projects to a local competitor. This small firm—one architect and a drafter—had never before been a serious threat, and had subsisted mainly on minor renovations, small country churches, and the like. There was some evidence that this firm made these gains, at least in part, through cutting its fees. Now the situation seemed to be reversing, with the bulk of ADI's practice now tending more and more to just that sort of small low-profit work. The recession of 1974–75 intensified the competition; many firms similar in size and scale of practice to ADI folded during this period, according to AIA data.

Barwick, Mayo, and Lassiter all agreed that the survival of their firm was at stake and that some form of "marketing" was needed. They also realized, however, that they knew nothing about marketing. After some discussion, they decided to relieve Lassiter of some of his duties, take up the slack themselves, and assign him the task of designing a marketing effort and directing its execution.

Lassiter tackled this new task methodically, beginning with a review of the firm's history and past projects and a classification of past projects by general type. He read several books on marketing architectural and engineering services, and subscribed to a newsletter, published by a firm of marketing consultants to the profession which attempted to forecast construction volume and project-type trends by regions of the United States.

Lassiter had observed that clients consistently asked, at interviews, about the extent of ADI's experience with the particular building type contemplated. Lassiter was convinced that the firm had lost two recent jobs for which it had interviewed—a public safety complex and a public library—at least in large part because the clients felt ADI lacked experience in these building types. Since the main point in any marketing effort would be to secure an interview with the prospect and thus a chance to make a presentation, and since proper preparation for an interview involved a considerable outlay of time and money (architects rely heavily on elaborate graphics, such as color slides, as presentation aids), Lassiter felt that common sense dictated that they should seek to be interviewed only when they had a reasonable chance of being selected.

Lassiter's research among the firm's records confirmed that ADI was most experienced in educational facilities and low-income public housing. Public housing construction was practically nil, but ADI's experience in this type was directly transferable to privately developed, multi-family residential projects. ADI's experience in designing churches for the major denominations was limited, but Lassiter foresaw a boom in new construction and renovation of churches, particularly among the fundamentalist protestant denominations.

Lassiter was convinced that one great selling point ADI had, which its national and regional competitors didn't share, was the fact that ADI was a local firm, immediately available for client consultation, crisis management, and "service after the sale." He had heard some clients grumble that their high-powered architects in Chicago or New York forgot them as soon as the building was up; they became difficult to reach. Lassiter intended, therefore, in selling ADI services, to bear down hard on ADI's hometown status; but, obviously, the effectiveness of this point would vary inversely with the prospect's distance from ADI's office. Any expensive frills like branch offices or a company plane were out of the question, at least for the short run.

Lassiter wondered just how far he could go, in terms of marketing activity, without jeopardizing the firm's membership in AIA. In reading the AIA code of ethics, and interpretations of them, he was somewhat surprised to learn that there was a considerable range of "legal" marketing activity. Although advertising and promotions (in the classic marketing sense) were *verboten*, personal selling was allowed. (At its national convention, held in Philadelphia in May of 1976, a proposal to allow members to advertise, with restrictions, was considered and rejected by the AIA.) Firms were also allowed to prepare and distribute (but not through mass mailing or other blanket distribution methods) a brochure describing the composition, history, philosophy, and past projects of the firm. Lassiter found that these brochures, in the case of some firms, were quite elaborate and expensive.

Another legitimate device was a periodic newsletter, factual in content, with news of the firm and its activities. The mailing list for the newsletter could include past clients and prospects with whom personal contact had been made.

Finally, as Lassiter had already determined, a public relations effort, such as ADI had been mounting, was permissible.

QUESTIONS FOR DISCUSSION

1. How would you begin the analysis of the decision-problem confronting ADI?
2. Categorize the available data concerning the situation using the types of data and information discussed in Chapter 1.
3. Based upon what you can surmise about the project records and files that ADI has kept, what additional data or information might you want from them? What type of data and information would this be?
4. Is "a general, downward trend in fee income" a satisfactory way to articulate ADI's decision-problem? How would you improve it?

5. What are the apparent causal factors behind the general downward trend in ADI's gross fee income? Why is it important to know this?
6. Off the top of your head, so to speak, what are the alternatives that ADI should consider? (I.e., prepare an initial list.)
7. What data and information in the case lend support to your list of alternatives?
8. What additional information (information that could reasonably be expected to be compiled) would you like to have to aid in refining your list of alternatives?
9. What criterion do you propose as the basis for evaluating your final list? Is it a realistic one in light of ADI's resources and capabilities?

Bay Baking Company

The Bay Baking Company of San Francisco was founded in 1879 as a family bread-baking firm serving the Bay area. It restricted its distribution to the San Francisco trading region for about 50 years. In 1931 the company's management expanded its distribution to the three Pacific Coast states, with bread-baking facilities being established in Seattle and Los Angeles.

The company's sales and profits grew somewhat continually during the 50-year period. The addition of the Seattle and Los Angeles plants boosted Bay Baking's sales and profits. By 1938, having survived the Great Depression, the corporate earnings were at an all-time high.

The large grocery chains, such as Oakland-based Safeway, began to gain ground during the late 1930s. Subsequent to World War II they were a significant factor in grocery product distribution. The independent grocer, unable to cope with the pricing and merchandising efforts of the chains, fell by the wayside as a significant factor in the distribution of food and other grocery products. Many large chains offered their own private-label canned goods, paper products, and baked goods. The bakery products were well received by consumers, and the chains moved more aggressively into the fresh baked goods field, establishing their own plants and distributing bread and other baked goods daily to their retail outlets.

Recognizing this threat to the independent bakery, Bay Baking's management moved into the packaged "store" cookie field. The bread volume by 1965 was only ten percent of the company's sales volume, and declining. In 1968 Bay Baking sold its bread-baking facilities to a national baking company. Full emphasis was now placed on its packaged cookies. Distribution by 1970 was in 11 western states. Bay Baking's sales and profits enjoyed steady growth.

The cookie line of Bay Baking was comprised of three brands of chocolate chip cookies, a creme sandwich, and a vanilla wafer. Past market studies of the West Coast territory had shown that among all brands the chocolate chips and creme sandwich outsold all other types combined. Bay Baking's three chocolate chip brands' contribution to profit in 1970 was three times that of the creme sandwich and vanilla wafer combined. The three chocolate chip brands were

Cookie-Anne, Bay Chips, and Bay Drops, each representing a different price level. Distribution of Bay's products was largely in grocery chain outlets of the western states. Bay Baking produced no private-label cookies for any of the chain operators.

The company's merchandising efforts were considered highly effective. Their packaging was viewed by the industry as ingenious and appealing to consumers. Prices were exceedingly competitive, not only with other manufacturers' brands but with the chains' own brands as well. By 1972 Bay Baking's brands held a 30 percent share of packaged cookie product category sales—up from a 21 percent level only five years earlier. The total consumption of cookies by an increasingly affluent consuming market was at an all-time high.

Sales plateaued somewhat during 1973 and 1974, even dipping in a small degree during the latter months of 1974. Profits for 1974, however, dropped 18 percent compared to the previous year. This decline in profitability was largely a function of the increased direct material costs that were reflecting a severe inflationary condition throughout this country, as well as most industrialized countries of the world. While it was true that direct labor costs and financial costs had risen during this two-year period, these increases were not of the magnitude of those for ingredients such as sugar, chocolate, flour, shortening, and eggs.

The spectacular increases in these costs can be seen below by comparing the invoiced prices of the goods purchased by Bay Baking for chocolate chip cookies over the 1972–1974 period:

	June 1972	June 1973	June 1974	Percentage of Total Cost of Raw Material
Sugar	$10.10 cwt.	$13.10 cwt.	$63.50 cwt.	44%
Blended corn syrup	7.92 cwt.	8.40 cwt.	19.00 cwt.	4
Chocolate chips	.58 lb.	.64 lb.	.75 lb.	6
Vegetable shortening	.11 lb.	.13 lb.	.44 lb.	21
Powdered eggs	.70 lb.	1.01 lb.	1.25 lb.	6
Flour	5.10 lb.	5.39 lb.	11.10 lb.	14
Flavoring, milk, etc.	. . .	. . .	. . .	5
Total				100%

Faced with such a radically altered cost and profit picture, Bay Baking management sought to cut costs. One option was a drastic reduction in the firm's marketing effort. This option was rejected, however. Such a move was considered ill-timed in view of Bay's own recent retail price increases that had gone into effect during the latter part of 1974, some six months earlier. This price increase was a substantial one, amounting to an average of 34 percent for the three chocolate chip products:

Cookie-Anne	From 39¢ to 55¢ or 41%
Bay Chips	From 33¢ to 44¢ or 33%
Bay Drops	From 29¢ to 37¢ or 28%

This boost in retail prices resulted in a decline in sales during the latter part of 1974, and the decline accelerated during the first several months of 1975. To curtail marketing efforts at this time would, in the opinion of the management, only exacerbate the decline. The marketing strategy should embrace a plan to boost sales via a more aggressive marketing effort in order to compensate for the predicted continued sales decline occasioned apparently by the price increase.

Peter Ellingson, Bay Baking vice-president in charge of marketing, recommended reducing the number of units per package while holding the price constant or even lowering it slightly. He pointed out that several mass marketers of other packaged goods had adopted such tactics. Kathryn Freemound, Bay's production manager, pointed out the cost problem of redesigning their packaging machinery. She stressed, too, that such a move had certain ethical overtones and she thought such action could be construed as a device to mislead consumers. There was the risk that their customers might even rebel at such a maneuver, Freemound pointed out. After a brief discussion this possible course of action was discarded.

A further price boost was viewed with extreme hesitancy, although it was agreed that an increase could be justified in light of the constantly growing cost of the finished products. An analysis of overhead, financial costs, and general and administrative costs revealed that opportunities for reductions in these areas were minimal at best.

Watkins Branch, Bay Baking's sales manager, posed the possibility of lowering the quality of the products. He suggested the substitution of different types of ingredients, which he presumed were available at lower prices. He admitted that this was not his field, but it was at least another approach to meeting the profit squeeze being faced by the company.

Ralph Aikman, the company's president, took a strong negative position, stating in no uncertain terms that the quality of Bay's products would be maintained at any cost. The company must locate some other alternative. Branch, risking a possible confrontation with Aikman, pointed out that consumers of their brands might not be able to detect substitute ingredients. If such a situation were true, he argued, there would be little or no risk in substituting several less costly ingredients.

Other management people in the meeting were not willing to take a stand openly. Ellingson suggested that it would be unwise to postulate on consumer acceptance. If consumers could detect differences, a sales decline could be expected. He wondered if it were possible to determine in advance whether consumers could in fact differentiate between the current Bay chocolate chip brands and a product containing substitute ingredients. The management members responded with enthusiasm to this thought. They were able to endorse the conduct of a marketing research study without openly disagreeing with Aikman.

Aikman asked Freemound what substitute ingredients could be considered. She recommended three possibilities, pointing out the cost saving for each:

Current Ingredient	Substitute	Saving
Sugar	Liquid corn sweetener	37%
Wheat flour	Rye flour	48%
Chocolate chips	Cocoa bits	34%

It was quite feasible, according to Freemound, to substitute the suggested items. She rejected the substitution of lard for the presently used vegetable shortening. Substituting the above three items would result in a substantial saving. Freemound presented a picture of the wholesale and retail prices in order to demonstrate the cost reduction:

		Prices	
	Materials Cost	Wholesale	Retail
Cookie-Anne	18¢	43¢	55¢
Bay Chips	17¢	34¢	44¢
Bay Drops	16¢	28¢	37¢

Branch took the position that to initiate production of Bay's chocolate chip cookies and test consumer reaction through normal retail channels would have a high risk level for several reasons. First, he argued, it would be months before one could determine whether the substitute ingredients were affecting sales. Bay might lose a good portion of its existing market if the new cookies were rejected. Secondly, it would not be appropriate to relate the new ingredients to a sales decline if one were in fact to occur. Other factors, he claimed, also could be affecting sales. For example, a deterioration in the economy or continued inflation could curtail consumption of selected food items. He posed the possibility that the substitute raw materials could even enhance sales but that other variables, more causal in nature, would result in an overall sales fall-off.

Ellingson insisted somewhat to the contrary that any determination of whether to employ substitute ingredients must be related to sales and revenue. "How," he questioned, "could we know with any degree of certainty what the effect of the substitute ingredients on sales will be unless we measure the sales and the resultant revenue?"

Freemound, well-versed in experimental design studies in Bay Baking's production department, inquired about some type of experimental study in the market place. Ellingson described a market testing service that would conduct experiments at the retail level by testing current products against contemplated products. This type of service, however, would require a minimum of three months, and should the data not be statistically significant at that time an additional one or two months could be required. The cost of such a study was estimated to be upwards of $30,000.

Aikman, while not objecting to the cost of the project, contended that they could not allow six more months to pass before making this decision. He surmised that perhaps one month or even more would be necessary to prepare the test cookies, another five months for the research effort, and another month or so before the data could be translated into a decision. The delay in making the decision could not be tolerated; some other method for resolving the issue must be located.

Few members of management were inclined to disagree with Aikman, and none expressed an opposing view. Ellingson and Branch both recommended engaging an independent marketing research firm to secure their thoughts on how a prediction of the effect of the substitute ingredients on Bay's chocolate chip cookie sales could be determined within a relatively short period of time, say, six weeks.

Harriet Golden of the marketing research firm met with Ellingson and Branch and explained the problem of predicting sales without an actual market test. She pointed out that any comparison of consumer preferences would not yield completely reliable data in that the precise relationship between the preferences and sales would not be known. It would be feasible, however, to conduct a sophisticated study of preferences and, in essence, there would be three separate studies, one for each of the three brands—Cookie-Anne, Bay Chips, and Bay Drops. Golden was authorized to conduct the study, and it was agreed that the final product decisions would be based on stated consumer preferences.

The data were collected from a sample of 921 homemakers in the communities of Walnut Creek and Los Angeles, California; Pullman, Washington; and Salt Lake City, Utah. Interviewers in each area, operating under staff supervisors, were assigned randomly selected geographic areas within which they were to seek qualified respondents—homemakers who had purchased one or more packages of Bay Baking's chocolate chip cookies during the past six months.

In order to obtain estimates of discrimination levels among respondents, a "repeat pair design" was employed. Initially, the respondents were screened to obtain background information concerning their cookie purchasing behavior. Each respondent was then given two packages of cookies. One of the packages contained the current formulation of Cookie-Anne for example, and the other package contained the test formulation. The products were identified only by code numbers.

Respondents were asked to try both formulations at the same time. They were instructed to serve the cookies to other family members. All respondents were given a questionnaire to complete after trying both the current and test products. Homemakers were provided with a shorter form for family members participating in the project.

Approximately five days after the products were placed in the homes, follow-up interviews were conducted with the homemakers to obtain additional information about any differences that might have been noticed. Respondents' completed questionnaires as well as those of family members were collected at this time. Homemakers were then given two more packages of the same cookies, but with different code identifications. The trial procedure was then repeated with homemaker and family member preferences again being obtained. Thus, two tests were conducted with each respondent family. Another sample of homemakers was exposed to a similar repeat pair procedure for Bay Chips, and still another sample for Bay Drops. Thus, three separate subsamples were used, involving 921 respondents in all. The identical two-stage testing—Test #1 and Test #2—was followed for all three Bay Baking chocolate chip brands and the test products with the substitute ingredients.

The breakdown of the sample in terms of location and number of brand purchasers is shown in Table 1.

Table 1 Number and Location of Brand Purchasers

	Total	Cookie-Anne		Bay Chips		Bay Drops	
		Pur-chaser	Nonpur-chaser	Pur-chaser	Nonpur-chaser	Pur-chaser	Nonpur-chaser
Walnut Creek	236	53	28	50	27	24	54
Los Angeles	244	52	29	46	36	41	40
Pullman	212	42	28	53	21	17	51
Salt Lake City	229	48	31	34	37	19	60
Total	921	195	116	183	121	101	205

Note: Nonpurchaser is a respondent who buys Bay Baking's cookies but not that brand.

The report from the marketing research firm described the rationale for employing the repeat pair test design. The following is quoted from the report:

> In a standard blind product test, preferences alone may not provide as much information as is needed to suit the objectives of the research. For example, in a hypothetical test of two products, if Product A is preferred by 51 percent and Product B is preferred by 49 percent (ignoring the "no preferences"), this could have occurred for either of two reasons:
> 1. Virtually no one could detect a difference between Products A and B, so their preferences were simply educated guesses which divided about evenly on a simple random basis, or
> 2. Many people could actually detect a difference between the test products, but about half preferred A and about half preferred B.

If it is important in the objectives of the study to determine which of these explanations is the correct one, a repeat pair approach provides an opportunity for doing so. The technique permits an estimate of the actual discrimination level as well as the preference distribution.

Assume, for purposes of illustration, that Products A and B are subjected to a repeat pair test and that both products are actually identical. The percentage of all respondents who prefer Product A in Test 1 and prefer Product B in Test 2 would be theoretically distributed as follows:

	A	B	Total of Test 2
A	25%	25%	50%
B	25%	25%	50%
Total of Test 1	50%	50%	

It is assumed that one who "preferred" a different product in each test (AB or BA) could not detect a difference between the two products. Thus, the proportion of people in either the AB or BA cells are nondiscriminators.

When products are in fact different, one cannot assume that *all* of those who preferred the same product both times (AA or BB), could actually tell the difference between the two products. The proportion of testers who expressed a consistent preference includes some people who *could* tell the difference and some who *could not* tell the difference and simply "got into" an AA or BB cell on the basis of chance alone.

The model that is used in a repeat pair design takes this fact into account. The total proportion of people falling into either of the "inconsistent" cells (AB or BA) provides an estimate of the proportion who fell into one of the "consistent" preference cells on a basis of chance. The actual formula is: (AA + BB) – (BA + AB) = estimated discrimination level.

To further illustrate, assume that the percentages of all respondents who prefer Product A in Test 1 and prefer B in Test 2 were distributed as follows:

	A	B	Total of Test 2
A	36%	20%	56%
B	20%	24%	44%
Total of Test 1	56%	44%	

The resulting estimate of the proportion who could tell the difference between Products A and B in this case would be 20 percent. Furthermore, these findings would suggest that of the 20 percent about 16 percent prefer Product A and only 4 percent prefer Product B.[1]

If the only information available indicated that Product A was preferred over Product B by a 56 to 44 margin, this may be a perfectly adequate basis for many decisions. However, if Product B were the current formulation, one could argue that a change to Product A (the test formulation) would run the risk of alienating as many as 44 percent of the current product's existing users. By utilizing the repeat pair design, with the resultant estimate of the discrimination level, the hypothetical data on the preceding page suggest that only 4 percent might be alienated by a change to the new formulation.

A subsequent section of the market researcher's report contained a description of the data uncovered. First, data are presented on the Cookie-Anne repeat pair overall preferences. Then follow data on Bay Chips and Bay Drops.

COOKIE-ANNE VS. TEST FORMULATION

In this test the current Cookie-Anne was compared to a revised formulation with three substitute ingredients: liquid corn sweetener, rye flour, cocoa bits. Of the homemakers expressing preferences in each replication of this test, 40 percent preferred the current Cookie-Anne both times, while 22 percent preferred the test formulation each time. A total of 38 percent fell into either of two "nondiscriminator" cells (AB or BA). The findings show that 76 percent could not discern a difference; thus, 24 percent *could* differentiate. The best estimate of preferences within this 24 percent is that 21 percent really prefer the current Cookie-Anne while 3 percent prefer the test formulation.

The repeat pair test for Cookie-Anne showed the following percentages of those interviewed who preferred the current formulation in Test 1 and those who preferred the test formulation in Test 2, viz., 57 percent and 39 percent.

	Test	Current	Total of Test 2
Test	22%	17%	39%
Current	21%	40%	61%
Total of Test 1	43%	57%	

---

[1] These percentages may be found by using the formulas: $AA - \dfrac{BA + AB}{2} = EDL$ for Product A, and $BB - \dfrac{BA + AB}{2} = EDL$ for Product B.

Test product	6.38	6.22
Current product	6.55	6.17
Differences for test	− .17	+ .05
Bay Drops Test		
Test product	7.03	6.92
Current product	6.80	6.58
Differences for test	+ .23	+ .34

An analysis of the same data, but among only purchasers of Cookie-Anne, reveals that the threshold of discrimination does not seem to vary when contrasted with all consumers of the three brands of cookies. Twenty-four percent of Cookie-Anne buyers could discriminate between the current and test products, and 21 percent actually preferred the current formulation.

RATINGS OF CURRENT AND TEST PRODUCTS ON SPECIFIC ATTRIBUTES

The homemaker was also asked to rate selected product attributes on a five-position scale. The attributes and scale points are shown in the summaries that follow (see Figures 1, 2, and 3). The mean ratings are plotted (C = current product, T = test formulation).

The findings disclose a high similarity on all attributes when the current and test formulations are compared. There are, however, product weaknesses revealed that may be of a correctable nature. For example, all three current products as well as the test cookies are viewed as being "not quite moist enough." Similarly, all products are thought to be a "little too crispy."

Test #1	Much Too Much	Little Too Much	Just Right	Not Quite Enough	Not Nearly Enough
Sweetness			T C		
Crispiness		T	C		
Moistness			C T		
Texture		T	C		
Richness			C/T		

Test #2	Much Too Much	Little Too Much	Just Right	Not Quite Enough	Not Nearly Enough
Sweetness			T C		
Crispiness		T	C		
Moistness			C T		
Texture		T	C		
Richness			C/T		

Figure 1   Ratings on Specific Attributes—Cookie-Anne

Test #1

	Much Too Much	Little Too Much	Just Right	Not Quite Enough	Not Nearly Enough
Sweetness			Ⓣ Ⓒ		
Crispiness		Ⓒ Ⓣ			
Moistness			Ⓣ Ⓒ		
Texture		Ⓒ Ⓣ			
Richness			Ⓒ Ⓣ		

Test #2

	Much Too Much	Little Too Much	Just Right	Not Quite Enough	Not Nearly Enough
Sweetness			Ⓒ Ⓣ		
Crispiness		Ⓒ Ⓣ			
Moistness			Ⓣ Ⓒ		
Texture		Ⓒ Ⓣ			
Richness			Ⓒ Ⓣ		

Figure 2   Ratings on Specific Attributes—Bay Chips

Test #1

	Much Too Much	Little Too Much	Just Right	Not Quite Enough	Not Nearly Enough
Sweetness			Ⓒ Ⓣ		
Crispiness		Ⓣ	Ⓒ		
Moistness			Ⓒ Ⓣ		
Texture		Ⓣ	Ⓒ		
Richness			Ⓣ Ⓒ		

Test #2

	Much Too Much	Little Too Much	Just Right	Not Quite Enough	Not Nearly Enough
Sweetness			Ⓣ Ⓒ		
Crispiness		Ⓣ	Ⓒ		
Moistness			Ⓒ Ⓣ		
Texture		Ⓣ	Ⓒ		
Richness			Ⓒ Ⓣ		

Figure 3   Ratings on Specific Attributes—Bay Drops

QUESTIONS FOR DISCUSSION

1. After Bay Baking's price increase during the latter part of 1974 and the resultant sales decline in 1975, what marketing alternatives were formed by management? List these marketing options for each separate decision structure—where *one* marketing decision will result (a decision area). List also the criteria statements for each decision area, and show what marketing action was taken in each decision area.
2. When Ralph Aikman "took a strong negative position" in opposition to lowering the quality of Bay's products, just where were the decision makers in the decision process?
3. Where were the decision makers in the decision process when Branch suggested obtaining some measure of consumer acceptance?

4. On the basis of an explicit "consumer acceptance" criterion that you have developed, which of the marketing alternatives posed did the survey support for action?
5. The decision makers tacitly agreed that they would rely on consumer preference/ acceptance data rather than dollar sales data. In what basic way did this decision affect the data collection method employed by the firm conducting the study?
6. Why was the monetary criterion *not* used by management?
7. What are the logical arguments in favor of a monetary measure for the Bay Baking management?
8. Even though the monetary criterion was rejected by management, what contributions to the formulation of the consumer acceptance criterion would of necessity have to be made with the assistance of Bay Baking's accounting or financial people?
9. Where does the taste/flavor rating of the existing and test products enter into the total decision-making area as it relates to Bay's cookie products?
10. If you had been a member of Bay's management, what would you have done differently?

Brady-Bushey Ford, Inc.

Warren Bushey has been the head of a highly successful Ford agency in central Virginia for eleven years. He assumed control of the agency when it was moderately profitable. At that time it was located on a congested street in a community of 35,000. He soon moved the agency's operations to the city's outskirts on a major highway. He modernized both the sales and service areas.

Brady-Bushey has a sales staff of 12 people. During recent years the agency's retail sales have averaged more than 2,000 new and used vehicles. Bushey recognizes the importance of customer satisfaction, and he constantly strives to maximize the performance of both his sales and service personnel. He realizes that the customer holds the key to ways in which he could improve retail performance even more. It could be possible that the agency might be losing prospective customers because the sales department is overly aggressive or because of customer problems at the servicing level.

Bushey thought information on these and other aspects of customer relations would be of help in continuing his efforts to improve the overall position of his agency. He had learned the value of marketing research from the Ford Motor Company headquarters and is aware of some of the customer attitudinal studies aimed at predicting the success of alternative exterior passenger car designs being considered by Ford. Bushey has also seen research reports on the effectiveness of Ford's advertising efforts.

But could a study be conducted for an individual dealer? He talked with a professional marketing research firm and learned that such a study was feasible but expensive. Bushey explained to the research company that he did not have any preconceived notions as to what information should be sought. In general, he thought, a rather broad spectrum of data would give some indications as to where he had problems. He hoped, too, that out of the contemplated survey would come some things to do that would strengthen his new car sales and improve the service department. Said Bushey: "There are always the obvious things to do, such as improve our service, or increase our advertising. I don't need a survey to tell me that. What I am looking for is something that will be specific and tell me what we should do to achieve improved service and greater sales." After several conversations with the research firm the survey was authorized.

The marketing research study was essentially a gathering of descriptive data. As the term implies, such a study attempts to describe something—in this case, the attitudes of Ford and Chevrolet owners toward the sales and service departments of their dealers. In addition, the study attempted to define what changes might be desirable to increase new car sales at Brady-Bushey Ford and improve the agency's service department. Pantops Chevrolet is the competing dealership covered by the survey.

The data in this study were collected in personal, face-to-face interviews. A highly structured questionnaire was used for interviewing purposes, insuring uniformity and reliability of responses. Subjective observations by the interviewer were eliminated. The questionnaire utilized a psychological measurement device called the semantic differential[1] to measure customer attitude.

A sample of 502 Ford and 595 Chevrolet passenger car owners was drawn at random from a list of automobile registrations provided by R. L. Polk, Inc., an independent listing service in Detroit. This sample resulted in completed, usable interviews from 188 Ford and 207 Chevrolet owners. Only those who visited and/or bought and/or have had their cars serviced at Brady-Bushey or Pantops Chevrolet were included in the final sample. The following tables are taken from the study report.

Table 1 Assessment of Dealers by Ford and Chevrolet Owners

	Percentage of Purchasers	
View of Dealers	Brady-Bushey	Pantops
Very favorable	25%	13%
Somewhat favorable	46	48
Unfavorable	29	39
Number of owners interviewed	143	136

---

[1] The semantic differential is a method for obtaining degrees of attitudes or opinions on given products or subjects. A number of bipolar scales consisting of two opposing adjectives are submitted to respondents who are asked to "scale" their feelings regarding each item. Most marketing research texts provide a description of this technique.

Table 2 Customer Opinion of Brady-Bushey Ford Correlated With Miles Driven

	Miles Driven		
View of Brady-Bushey	Under 10,000	10,000–20,000	Over 20,000
Very favorable	29%	25%	15%
Somewhat favorable	53	48	40
Unfavorable	18	27	45
Number of owners interviewed	38	66	41

Table 3 Probability of Repurchase

Owner's chances of buying another automobile from these two dealers are:

Brady-Bushey	Pantops
57 out of 100	54 out of 100

Table 4 Probability of Repurchase Related to Car Mileage

	Number of Owners Who Would Repurchase From	
Miles driven	Brady-Bushey	Pantops
Under 10,000	66 out of 100	56 out of 100
10,000–20,000	55 out of 100	53 out of 100
Over 20,000	51 out of 100	52 out of 100

Table 5 Customers' Attitudes Toward Brady-Bushey Sales Department

Characteristics	% Holding Attitude	Favorability Index*
Showroom hours		
were most convenient.	81	78
were not convenient at all.	3	
The salesperson		
answered all my questions extremely well.	69	63
did not answer at all well.	6	
The showroom was		
extremely attractive.	59	55
not attractive at all.	4	
The overall salesperson's approach was		
low pressure.	51	40
high pressure.	11	
I think I got		
a great deal dollarwise.	50	40
a poor deal dollarwise.	10	
The available selection of new cars was		
most adequate.	50	40
inadequate.	10	
The sales literature was extremely		
informative.	50	39
uninformative.	11	
The types of cars that interest me were		
always in the showroom.	39	24
never in the showroom.	15	
There was		
no parking problem at the dealership.	45	20
a parking problem at the dealership.	25	

*The favorability index is arrived at by subtracting the percentage of strongly unfavorable responses from the percentage figure of strongly favorable customer responses. The resulting number, the favorability index, shows the number of percentage points by which the favorable attitudes exceed the unfavorable ones.

*Table 6 Comparison of Customer Attitudes Toward Sales
Departments of Brady-Bushey and Pantops*

	Brady-Bushey Favorability Index	Pantops Favorability Index	Brady-Bushey Net
Sales department hours of operation	78	78	—
Ability of salesperson to answer questions well	63	67	− 4
Attractiveness of showroom	55	54	1
Pressure of salesperson	40	31	9
Deal: dollarwise	40	33	7
Selection of cars on lot	40	53	−13
Informativeness of literature	39	39	—
Cars in showroom interest the customers	24	23	1
Parking facilities	20	46	−26

Table 7 Importance of Dealer's Service Reputation in New Car Buying Decision

	Percentage of Ford and Chevrolet Owners
Service reputation was:	
A very important factor	90%
A somewhat important factor	8
Not at all an important factor	2
Number of owners interviewed	352

*Table 8 Comparison of Brady-Bushey and Pantops on
First-Visit Success of Car Repair*

Success of Car Repair	Brady-Bushey	Pantops
Always fixed the first time	47%	39%
Sometimes fixed the first time	33	42
Never fixed the first time	20	19
Number of service customers interviewed	169	156

Table 9 Comparison of Service Customers' Trust in Brady-Bushey and Pantops

Customers' Attitudes	Brady-Bushey Customers	Pantops Customers
Great trust in department	44%	37%
Some trust in department	44	43
Little trust in department	12	20
Number of service customers interviewed	170	156

Table 10 Miles Driven Correlated With Trust in Service Department

	Under 10,000	10,000– 20,000	Over 20,000	All Service Customers
Brady-Bushey Ford	58%	50%	37%	44%
Pantops Chevrolet	30	48	51	37

Table 11 Customers' Attitudes Toward Service of Brady-Bushey and Pantops

	Brady-Bushey Index	Pantops Index	Brady-Bushey Net
Reasonableness of prices	20	8	12
Warranty explained clearly	43	34	9
Service department hours of operation	48	41	7
Performance of mechanics	28	28	—
Service department's competence	51	54	–3
Car ready on time	47	51	–4
Service manager's promptness	31	37	–6

Table 12 Customers' Attitudes Toward Brady-Bushey Service Department

Characteristics	% Holding Attitude	Favorability Index
The service manager is		
very competent.	58%	51
not competent at all.	7	
The hours of operation of the service department		
are very convenient.	57	48
are not at all convenient.	9	
The car is		
always ready when promised.	58	47
never ready when promised.	11	
The warranty was		
explained very clearly.	57	43
not explained clearly.	14	
The service manager		
is prompt when the car is brought in.	44	31
is not prompt when the car is brought in.	13	
The mechanics do		
an excellent job.	44	28
a poor job.	16	
The service prices		
are reasonable.	35	20
are not reasonable.	15	

Table 13 Relationship Between Selected Service Attributes and Trust in Dealer

Dealer	Percentage of Those Very Favorable About:			
	Service Manager's Competence	Service Manager's Promptness	Reasonable Charges for Service	Quality of Mechanic's Work
Brady-Bushey Service Department	53%	53%	68%	76%
Pantops Service Department	45	51	51	65

**Table 14 Probability of Repurchase Correlated With Customers'
Trust in Dealers' Service Departments**

Dealer	Attitudes of Customers		
	Complete Trust in Their Dealer's Service Department	Some Trust in Their Dealer's Service Department	No Trust in Their Dealer's Service Department
Brady-Bushey	72 out of 100	52 out of 100	20 out of 100
Pantops	73 out of 100	52 out of 100	35 out of 100

**Table 15 Percentage of Customers Having Brady-Bushey Perform Repair
Work Correlated With Miles Driven**

Service Performed at Brady-Bushey	Miles Driven		
	Under 10,000	10,000– 20,000	Over 20,000
Transmission fixed	86%	91%	83%
Tune-up	83	68	64
Body work	83	68	51
Ignition/starter fixed	75	79	80
Brakes adjusted	73	67	61
Generator replaced/adjusted	63	71	77
Front end aligned	61	59	58
Muffler replaced	44	46	41
Oil change and lubrication	36	40	38
Fanbelt replaced/adjusted	27	27	25
Tires rotated	16	19	16
Battery replaced	13	15	19

Table 16 Service Preferences of Brady-Bushey Customers

Type of Service	Dealer	Gas Station	Them-selves	Other
		Customer Preference		
Transmission fixed	88%	1%	2%	8%
Ignition/starter fixed	76	10	7	8
Tune-up	71	17	8	4
Body work	69	—	2	30
Generator replaced/adjusted	69	12	10	9
Brakes adjusted	65	19	8	8
Front end aligned	56	9	—	35
Muffler replaced	44	24	10	21
Oil change and lubrication	37	48	12	3
Fanbelt replaced/adjusted	28	47	22	4
Tires rotated	17	39	17	27
Battery replaced	15	33	16	36

Warren Bushey and his sales and service managers read the report with great interest, noting that the survey did point up some apparent weaknesses in both sales and service. Bushey asked his two managers to digest the data and return to him with their thoughts as to what should be done with the newly uncovered information.

QUESTIONS FOR DISCUSSION

1. In a broad sense, would you say the data contained in the report are largely environmental or actionable? Why?
2. What contribution is made by the findings uncovered in the first four tables?
3. How would Bushey use the data in Table 5?
4. If you were Bushey, what would you do with the data in Tables 7 through 10?
5. Select five pieces of information (from any of the tables not mentioned in questions 1–4) that you consider worth pursuing, and develop them into alternatives for Bushey to consider. Would these alternatives have surfaced if the study had not been conducted?

Charlottesville Central Business District

The political and business leaders of Charlottesville had long recognized that the Central Business District (CBD) was facing rapidly increasing competition from outside the core of the city. This trend continued until there was an obvious loss of retail sales market share in the CBD relative to competitive shopping areas such as the Barracks Road Shopping Center.

The engineering firm of Harland Bartholomew and Associates was called upon for consulting advice, which they presented as a plan for the revitalization of the Charlottesville downtown area. This plan proposed a series of three improvements for the Central Business District and provided for their implementation.

The Bartholomew Plan was praised by community leaders. It was comprehensive in scope and highly professional in nature. Nevertheless, the city did not take immediate action. The basic problem seemed to be one of sequence. There was still uncertainty in the minds of the Charlottesville City Council and the downtown merchants (the decision makers) as to which improvements recommended by Bartholomew should be undertaken first.

To Bartholomew's three recommended improvement areas, a fourth was added when it became apparent that an additional study was to be made. Thus, four basic alternative courses of action were ultimately formulated. The four alternative action areas were:

1. Beautification of the CBD.
2. Access to the CBD.
3. Parking in the CBD.
4. Merchandising practices of CBD merchants.

The second study, by a marketing research firm, was commissioned to gather reliable data for predicting the relative beneficial impact of the alternatives on the city's downtown area, thus enabling the council and the merchants to move ahead on the more critical improvements. Major extracts from the report of this study follow.

HOW THE STUDY WAS CONDUCTED

Data in this study were collected through personal (face-to-face) interviews. A highly structured questionnaire was used for interviewing purposes. The questionnaire was unbiased and utilized the semantic differential to measure shopper attitudes. A sample of 438 shoppers from the Charlottesville-Albemarle County area was drawn on an area-probability basis. The female head of the household was interviewed whenever possible.

Although it provided vast amounts of interesting data about the CBD and competing shopping areas, the study primarily was designed to provide reliable information about the best sequence for implementation of the four basic alternatives. Thus the study was designed to describe what consumers actually want for the Central Business District and how they will react to the various alternative improvements.

EXISTING SHOPPING BEHAVIOR

There are two types of data that may be gathered in a marketing research study. The first type of data describes conditions as they presently exist. These data served two useful purposes in terms of this study. First, they quantified a number of relationships that had long been suspected to exist, but were now substantiated. In addition, these data provided enlightening new information.

The second type of data gathered in this study is actionable data. These data lead to specific action on a set of existing alternatives. In this case, they would provide information that, hopefully, would allow the best alternative to be selected for the benefit of the Central Business District. Examples of actionable data are data about specific beautification, access, parking, and merchandise mix preferences.

First, look at the shopping behavior of the residents of the Charlottesville-Albemarle County area. To what extent do shoppers go outside the area to make purchases? Do areas such as Washington, Richmond, and Waynesboro draw much business out of the Charlottesville area? This study traced the purchase of over 3,300 selected items in nine product categories. As shown in Table 1, 94 percent of all items are usually purchased in the Charlottesville-Albemarle area. Two percent are purchased in Washington or Richmond, and 4 percent are purchased in other areas. This data indicate that shoppers are able to find what they want in the Charlottesville-Albemarle area.

Table 1 Areas in Which Selected Items Are Usually Purchased

Area of Purchase	Percentage of Items Purchased
Charlottesville-Albemarle	94%
Washington-Richmond	2
Other areas	4
Total items purchased	3,382

Table 2 shows the purchases of the nine specific items: hardware, drugs, dresses, gifts, men's clothing, electrical appliances, toys, furniture, and children's clothing. When the shoppers who did not ordinarily purchase the specified items are eliminated, more than 85 percent of each of the items is purchased within the Charlottesville market area. CBD competition is from inside the area, not from outside it.

Table 2 Purchase Points of Specific Items

Shopping Area	Departments in Which Items Are Purchased								
	Hardware	Drugs	Dresses	Gifts	Men's Clothing	Electrical Appliances	Toys	Furniture	Children's Clothing
Charlottesville-Albemarle	99%	96%	88%	93%	85%	80%	64%	63%	64%
Washington-Richmond	—	—	2	1	2	1	2	5	1
Other areas	0	3	3	2	5	5	3	9	2
Did not ordinarily purchase	1	1	7	4	8	14	31	23	33
Total sample	438	438	438	438	438	438	438	438	438

Of basic interest is the extent to which shoppers use Barracks Road Shopping Center relative to the Central Business District. The data in Table 3 indicate that three out of ten shoppers said that they spend most (70 percent or more) in the CBD. Four out of ten spend most in the Barracks Road Shopping Center.

Table 3 Relative Use of Central Business District and
Barracks Road Shopping Center

Area of Purchase	Percentage of Shoppers
Purchase 70 percent or more in the Central Business District	31%
Use both areas about equally	29
Purchase 70 percent or more at Barracks Road Shopping Center	40
Total sample	438

Where people spend most of their money does not have much significance unless one knows who these shoppers are. How long have they lived in the Charlottesville-Albemarle area? Where do they live? What is their "buying power"? Segmenting the market along these lines will aid in pinpointing the problem.

First, what about length of residence? As shown in Table 4, 41 percent of all shoppers have lived in the Charlottesville-Albemarle area less than ten years. These people are the newer residents and tend to be younger in age. If a shopping area cannot attract these younger people and newer residents, then they can expect a decline in older, loyal customers as the years pass.

Table 4 Shopper Grouping by Length of Residence in
Charlottesville-Albemarle

Years of Residence	Percentage of Shoppers
Four years or less	28%
Five to nine years	13
Ten years or more	59
Total number of shoppers interviewed	438

Barracks Road has much greater attraction for newer residents. For example, of those shoppers who have lived in the area for four years or less, 15 percent purchased 70 percent or more in the CBD while 54 percent purchased most in

Barracks Road. On the other hand, of those older residents having lived in the area for ten years or more, the trend is just the opposite. Forty-two percent of the shoppers spent most in the CBD while only 28 percent spent most in the Barracks Road area.

These data indicate that Barracks Road Shopping Center has much more attraction for shoppers who have lived in the area for less than ten years. The Central Business District is not attracting the newer residents and younger shoppers. This fact is detailed in Table 5.

Table 5 Use of Shopping Areas Related to Length of Residence in Charlottesville-Albemarle

	4 Years or Less	5 to 9 Years	10 Years or More
Purchase 70 percent or more in CBD	15%	11%	42%
Use both areas about equally	31	35	30
Purchase 70 percent or more in BRSC	54	54	28
Total number of shoppers interviewed	123	57	258

Where do people live in relation to both shopping areas? How does where people live relate to their shopping behavior? About the same number of shoppers live close to Barracks Road as to the Central Business District. Table 6 relates the use of both shopping areas to where shoppers live. One third of the shoppers who lived closer to the CBD went away from the CBD to do most of their shopping at Barracks Road. On the other hand, only one sixth of those who lived closer to Barracks Road spent a majority at the less convenient CBD. Thus, Barracks Road Shopping Center is attracting not only those living closer to it, but also a substantial portion of those living closer to the Central Business District.

Table 6 Use of Shopping Areas Related to Shopper's Distance From Area

	Area of Residence		
	Closer to CBD	Equidistant from CBD and BRSC	Closer to BRSC
Purchase 70 percent or more in CBD	44%	30%	16%
Use both areas about equally	22	32	32
Purchase 70 percent or more at BRSC	34	38	52
Total number of shoppers interviewed	169	106	161

In assessing shoppers and various shopping areas, it would be misleading to give all shoppers equal weight. For example, it would be much more beneficial for the CBD to attract a shopper with an income of $25,000 per year and four children than a shopper with an income of $2,500 per year and no children. All shoppers were divided into three groups—high buying power, middle buying power, and low buying power—with approximately the same number of people in each group. This judgmental classification is based on several factors such as income, car ownership, family size, age range of children, and location of residence. These groups are shown in Table 7.

Table 7 Shopper Grouping by Buying Power

Buying Power	Percentage of Shoppers
High	38%
Medium	27
Low	35
Total number of shoppers interviewed	438

Even though the high buying power group is only roughly one third of all shoppers in terms of the number of people, it might command two, three, five, or even eight times as much buying power as the low buying power group—the precise amount cannot be determined. It is apparent that this high buying power group is essential to a shopping area's success.

Table 8 relates this buying power to place of purchase. In the important high buying power group, four out of ten shoppers spend 70 percent or more at Barracks Road in contrast to two out of ten spending a greater portion in the CBD. The same is true for the middle buying power group: one out of every two at Barracks Road vis-à-vis one out of every four at the CBD. The reverse is true for the low buying group, where three out of ten spend a majority at Barracks Road while four out of ten spend most at the CBD. Thus, not only do more people shop at the Barracks Road Shopping Center, but they also spend more money there.

Table 8 Use of Shopping Areas Related to Buying Power

	Buying Power		
	High	Medium	Low
Purchase 70 percent or more in CBD	19%	26%	44%
Use both areas about equally	37	22	24
Purchase 70 percent or more in BRSC	44	52	32
Total number of shoppers interviewed	167	118	153

Why is it that high and middle buying power shoppers do not shop at the Central Business District? One reason could be that Barracks Road is more convenient to these higher buying power shoppers. Table 9 shows where shoppers in the three buying power groups actually do live. In the high buying power group twice as many shoppers live closer to Barracks Road than to the CBD. The trend is just the opposite for the low buying power group. In this group, twice as many shoppers live closer to the CBD than to Barracks Road.

Table 9 Shopper Groupings—Distances Within Buying Power Groups

	Percentage of All Shoppers
High buying power	38%
Live closer to CBD	10
Live equidistant	9
Live closer to BRSC	19
Medium buying power	27
Live closer to CBD	12
Live equidistant	6
Live closer to BRSC	9
Low buying power	35
Live closer to CBD	17
Live equidistant	9
Live closer to BRSC	9
Total sample	438

Table 10 carries this analysis a step farther—the use of shopping areas related to both buying power and shopper's distance from shopping area. In the low buying power group there is a definite tendency to shop in the area that is the most convenient, probably because of a lack of mobility in this group.

Table 10 Use of Shopping Areas by Low Buying Power Families, in Relation to Distance From Shopping Area

	Area of Residence		
Shopping Area	Closer to CBD	Equidistant	Closer to BRSC
In the CBD (70 percent or more)	59%	42%	19%
In both areas	20	29	26
In BRSC (70 percent or more)	21	29	55
Number with low buying power	73	41	38

This tendency to shop in the most convenient area is not so evident in the high buying power group. People with high buying power are more mobile. They have the ability to shop in the area that appeals to them, and they do not mind leaving the area that they live in. The Central Business District is not attracting the high buying power shoppers—those shoppers with a greater freedom of choice who would and could go to the CBD if it sufficiently attracted them. The high buying power data are shown in Table 11.

Table 11 Use of Shopping Areas by High Buying Power Families, in Relation to Distance

Shopping Area	Area of Residence		
	Closer to CBD	Equidistant	Closer to BRSC
In the CBD (70 percent or more)	33%	16%	13%
In both areas	29	45	38
In BRSC (70 percent or more)	38	39	48
Number with high buying power	45	38	85

WHAT THE CBD COULD DO—FOUR COURSES OF ACTION

Whenever an important decision is to be made, it is essential that the alternative courses of action be carefully spelled out. Four basic options for the improvement of the Central Business District are offered (alternatives 1, 2, and 3 are drawn from the Bartholomew report):

1. Beautification—exterior feeling
2. Access
3. Parking
4. Merchandise—sales personnel

It should be understood exactly what these alternatives mean. The *beautification* alternative would include such items as improvements of store fronts, development of malls and plazas, elimination of overhead wiring, and the like. For this alternative to be selected, should it prove to be sufficiently important, it is essential that implementation be a *collective* joint effort as well as an individual effort.

There are two basic considerations under *access*—access to and from the Central Business District, and access to the CBD once within the fringe of the area.

The *parking* alternative includes many considerations. A few examples are metered parking, reducing walking distance from car to stores, parking garages, correct change for meters, and increased number of spaces.

The *merchandise* alternative includes items such as quality level of merchandise, variety of merchandise, interior attractiveness of stores, and attitude of sales personnel. This course of action primarily requires individual action by the merchants for its successful implementation.

CRITERIA FOR DECISION

The importance of formulating good alternatives to make a well-informed decision has already been stressed. In addition to a clear statement on the various decision choices, there must be some criteria or standard on which a decision can be made regarding the selection of the best course of action. In other words, the criteria state on what basis the decision will be made. Agreement on criteria helps minimize the risk of collecting vast amounts of data and then being unable to use these data to make an intended decision.

For a study as complex as this project, it is not a simple matter to determine exactly what final action to recommend—even after all the data are ultimately collected and analyzed. The decision process is not so simple as "plugging in" a few inputs and "cranking out" the output recommendations by computer. However, the goal of this study is to select that course of action that will bring the most buying power downtown, relative to its cost of implementation. But the answer is still not that simple. The data could indicate the need for more than one alternative inasmuch as it is highly unlikely that only one alternative could completely solve the problems facing the CBD. In other words, which blend of these alternatives is the most likely to result in an enhancement of volume for CBD enterprises? Which one should be considered as having top priority? What other actions should be taken later and with what degree of emphasis? Predicting the relationship between these possible courses of action and their "buying power pull" will aid considerably in making the decision.

Essentially this attempt at predicting such a relationship will be based upon how the shoppers perceive each of the two major shopping areas—CBD and Barracks Road—and how well these perceptions correlate with where the shoppers in fact spend most of their nonfood shopping money. One of the questions on the questionnaire concerned where the family shopping money was spent, and each shopper was given a scale from 100 percent to zero percent. Table 12 shows this distribution of the shopping dollar between the two principal areas.

Shoppers' perceptions of the two areas were correlated with the Table 12 data. In this way it is possible to learn a great deal about the importance of various attributes of the two areas as they relate to where the shopping dollars are spent. This correlation, in essence, enables one to determine the importance of the areas' basic attributes, such as general appearance, merchandising, access, and parking, as they tend to influence where a person shops. These four attributes are the basic decision areas for the CBD.

But that is only part of the story. Knowing what influences important segments of the shopping public to spend money in one area rather than another is desirable, but it does not prescribe what the CBD should do. There would be little reason, for example, to stress improved merchandising if it were found that little difference between the two areas existed on this issue. Thus, part of the criteria for the CBD action will be based on how well the CBD fares on each of the four basic decision areas—in contrast to Barracks Road.

Table 12 Distribution of Shopping Dollar

Percentage Spent		Percentage of Shoppers Interviewed
At CBD	At BRSC	
100%	0%	6%
90	10	9
80	20	10
70	30	6
		31%
60	40	6
50	50	17
40	60	6
		29%
30	70	10
20	80	11
10	90	14
0	100	5
		40%

This contrast will be revealed by analyzing how well shoppers feel the two shopping districts perform. These data were obtained through the employment of the semantic differential. Each person interviewed was shown a list of some 80 statements—40 on the CBD and 40 on Barracks Road. Each statement contained two extremes and the interviewees were asked to show their feelings about each statement by marking one of seven boxes representing a scale of feeling. One example, drawn from the 40, appears below:

The stores carry
an ample supply   ☐ ☐ ☐ ☐ ☐ ☐ ☐   The stores carry
of merchandise   a skimpy supply
                                                                      of merchandise

The statements covered various aspects of all four decision areas. Both shopping districts were then compared by showing the extent to which the shoppers felt strongly or somewhat strongly about the different bipolarized statements.

FACTORS INFLUENCING WHERE PEOPLE SHOP— CENTRAL BUSINESS DISTRICT VS. BARRACKS ROAD

In a broad sense, there are four factors that could influence where a person shops in the Charlottesville-Albemarle area. One factor is *access*. How easily can a person get to a particular shopping area? Of course, there are many facets to this problem—distance from home, distance from work, traffic congestion, traffic lights, one-way streets, and a host of other less important considerations. However divergent these facets are, they may all be included in assessing the access to the shopping area.

Another factor is *parking*. Are there enough parking places? How long does it take to find a parking place? Does one have to walk too far after parking to get to the store area? Are parking meters a deterrent? Parking embraces a rather wide range of important and unimportant problems.

A third factor is *beautification*. The external feeling created by shopping districts is a consideration. Does the area appear old and run-down? Do the buildings need repainting or repairing? Would more greenery be desirable?

The fourth factor is *merchandise*. Considerations to this factor are quality of merchandise, variety, prices, and attitude of salespeople. All of these can be described as merchandising—a function performed by the individual store.

In Charlottesville-Albemarle, which of these four general factors is most likely to influence where a person shops? As mentioned in the previous section under "Criteria for Decision," where a person usually shops will be correlated with how that area is perceived.

The most important consideration is *ease of access*. This one factor looms well above others in determining which of the two shopping areas is visited. The fact that the shopper can get to one area more quickly than to the other is of prime importance. The next most influential consideration is parking, followed by beautification and merchandising. This evidence appears in Table 13.

Table 13 Shoppers' Perceptions of Shopping Areas Correlated With Their Choice of a Shopping Area

	Correlation
Access	
It takes too long to get to area./I can get to area very quickly from where I live.	.55
I have an extreme problem/no problem in getting to area.	.46
Parking	
After parking, I always have too far to walk/never have too far to walk to get to where I want to shop in the area.	.38
It is extremely hard/easy to find a parking place in the area.	.38
It always/never takes too long to find a parking place in the area.	.37
Beautification	
Area appears old, run-down/modern, well-built.	.18
Area is unattractive/attractive.	.18
Merchandising	
Merchandise quality is poor/excellent.	.21
I always/rarely have difficulty in finding what I want.	.19
Salespeople are not/are extremely nice and cooperative.	.22
Stores carry a skimpy/ample supply of merchandise.	.19
I rarely/always find a wide selection of articles in size for which I am shopping.	.16
Prices are much higher/not much higher.	.13

The extent to which general statements describing the two shopping areas correlate with where the money is spent is shown in the column "Correlation." For example, "Takes too long to get to shopping area/does not take too long" has a correlation of .55 with where the shopping dollars are spent. This is in contrast to a correlation of .13 between "Prices are much higher/not much higher" and where shopping money is spent. From this it can be concluded that how long it takes one to get to a shopping district is much more important than differences in price levels between the two shopping areas—if in fact such price differences do exist.

Access

The access problem, from the viewpoint of the CBD, has two parts—getting to the periphery of the downtown area and getting to the specific parking area once within the fringe of the CBD. For example, a shopper driving to the CBD from the west side of Charlottesville must travel through much traffic on either Main Street or Grady-Preston Avenues. Once Water Street or High Street is reached, the shopper must travel to some parking area near the CBD. In doing so the shopper probably would travel on one or more one-way streets.

To solve the first access problem—getting to the fringe of the CBD—several political bodies are involved. Streets can be widened; new approaches can be built from Interstate 64 to the central part of Charlottesville. Such construction would involve funds from a variety of sources. Thus, the CBD must contend with many different groups of people to remove this serious deterrent.

The second aspect of access—reaching the downtown area after arriving at the fringe—does not appear to be a serious deterrent to the shopper. There was a correlation of only .14 between "One-way streets make it difficult for me to reach the area" and where the shopping dollars were spent. This figure is in contrast to much higher correlations for statements which describe such en route problems as slow traffic, congestion, and traffic lights.

Table 14 on page 202 shows the extent to which some correlation exists between several more specific access statements and the general access statement: "There is/is not an extreme problem in getting to and from the CBD." These high correlations demonstrate the nature of the CBD access problem: shoppers' difficulties are in reaching the area and not in traveling from the fringe to the selected parking lot.

But how do the CBD and Barracks Road compare on this access problem? The study data obtained from Charlottesville-Albemarle County shoppers indicate that the CBD faces the more serious situation. In this study, some three out of ten persons definitely agreed that the CBD had an extreme problem in contrast to one out of ten who felt the same way about Barracks Road Shopping Center. Very few shoppers thought one-way streets were a problem in getting to either of the two major shopping centers. Only 14 percent agreed that one-way streets made it difficult to reach the CBD; 9 percent said one-way streets were a problem en route to Barracks Road.

It can be said, then, that access is a strong influence in determining where a person shops—the most important single factor. This problem is much more

Table 14 Correlation of Specific Central Business District Statements With General Statement on Access

Basic Statement I think that there is/is not an extreme problem in getting to and from the CBD.	Correlation with Basic Statement
Elements of Statement	
Traffic moves much too slowly/moves very swiftly on streets leading to the CBD.	.34
There are far too many/aren't many traffic lights to fight in get- ting to the CBD.	.40
There is far too much/hardly any traffic congestion along the streets leading to the CBD.	.46

serious for the CBD than Barracks Road. But the access problem for the CBD centers on the difficulties in getting to the downtown area, not in short-approach movements to a parking place once the shopper is in the general area of the downtown district.

Parking

Table 13 on page 200 showed that parking was the second most important influence determining whether a shopper went to the CBD or to Barracks Road. The question to be answered now is whether parking is more of a problem for one shopping district than for the other.

The data are convincing in demonstrating that the CBD faces a parking problem far more serious than Barracks Road. In a general sense the latter has no parking problem, whereas the CBD has inherited a problem that looms as the most immediate issue to be resolved if the downtown area is to recover its market share. The great difference between the two areas is shown in Table 15. Shoppers overwhelmingly agree that a parking problem is much more prevalent in the CBD.

Table 15 Parking Problem Comparison—Central Business District Vs. Barracks Road

Parking Problems	CBD	BRSC
Finding a parking place	92%	11%
Having to walk too far after parking	43	9

Recognizing that the CBD has the more serious parking situation, the next step is to attempt to ascertain just what is meant by a "parking problem." It could be the difficulty in locating a space, the distance one must walk after parking the car, or the parking meter situation, with the attendant problem of correct change.

All of these CBD parking issues are prevalent in shoppers' minds, but if any one appears to be most bothersome it would be the distance one must walk after parking. This fact is revealed in Table 16, in which statements describing the different elements of the parking issue are correlated with the general statement "There is an extreme parking problem in the CBD." The table also shows the percentage of all shoppers who definitely agree that parking is a problem for the CBD.

Table 16 Correlation of Specific Parking Statements With General Statement on Parking

Basic Statement There is an extreme/absolutely no parking problem in CBD.	Correlation with Basic Statement	Percentage Agreeing That This Is a CBD Problem
Elements of Statement		
I would like to see more parking places in this area.	.36	73%
Parking meters are a nuisance in this area.	.32	56
Having correct change for parking meters is always a problem.	.29	44
After I have parked, I always have too far to walk to get to the place in which I want to shop.	.42	43

It can be seen from the data in Table 16 that any solution to the parking problem is multisided. More parking places, reduction of meter parking, and bringing the shopper closer to the stores in one form or another all enter into the picture. But the last problem, reducing the walking distance, appears to be foremost in importance in view of the high correlation with the basic statement. However, none of the parking issues can be ignored and all must be solved.

Beautification

As is true with access and parking, beautification has several components. The general description of this problem was posed to all shoppers in Table 13 (page 200) and contained the term "unattractive/attractive." Beautification appeared to rank somewhat below parking as an influence in determining where people shop, and a great deal below access as a factor. But what about the CBD versus Barracks Road?

As with parking, Barracks Road Shopping Center is seen by shoppers as vastly superior in terms of this attractiveness attribute. Of all shoppers, 33 percent definitely agreed that the CBD was unattractive. This contrasts with Barracks Road where 7 percent saw the area as unattractive. It can be argued, then, that while beautification is not the most important factor influencing where a person shops, the fact remains that it is a more serious problem for the CBD in view of the low esteem shoppers have for the appearance of the CBD.

What, then, are the elements of beautification? Are they more plantings and malls, or remodeling, repainting, and repairing of the buildings? Table 17 shows that remodeling, repainting, and repairing the buildings is more important than more plants or shrubs. The table also reveals how the CBD and Barracks Road compare on these beautification scores.

Table 17 Correlation of Specific Beautification Statements With General Statement on Beautification

Basic statement The appearance of the entire area is extremely unattractive/attractive to me.	Correlation with Basic Statement	Percentage Agreeing This Is a Problem	
		At CBD	At BRSC
Elements of statement			
There should be many more plants and shrubs in the area.	.07	55%	50%
There should be some malls or small park-type areas.	.22	54	32
Most of the buildings should be remodeled, painted, or repaired.	.48	46	6

The facelifting of the exteriors of CBD buildings is by far more important to the CBD than is the introduction of more greenery and "malls or park-type areas." The correlation of the former with the general statement on unattractiveness, plus the fact that plants, shrubs, and park-like areas are deemed desirable by all shoppers regardless of the preferred area, support this statement. In other words, greenery is always nice, anywhere. But it does not influence where a person shops. Moreover, Barracks Road is seen as needing greenery as much as the CBD. But the buildings' exteriors are quite another issue. They are the important elements of beautification for the CBD.

Merchandising

The merchandising factor, it will be recalled, is comprised of a range of different influences. It embraces the quality of the merchandise, the variety available, prices, and the appeal of the sales personnel. Thus, it is difficult to settle on any one phrase that describes this decision area of merchandising.

It was shown, however, that quality of merchandise has profound influence on where a person shops (Table 13, page 200). Also, the extent to which the shopper feels that there is difficulty in finding items also ranks high as an influencing factor. Attitude of salespeople appears important. However, the issue to be resolved is whether the CBD stands better or worse on these scores when compared to Barracks Road. Table 18 reveals that the two major shopping areas are not greatly different on such merchandising issues. But even more important, very few shoppers took a dim view of either shopping area with regard to these issues.

Table 18 Comparison of Central Business District and Barracks Road on Different Aspects of Merchandising

	Percentage of Shoppers Agreeing	
Merchandising Aspects	CBD Stores	BRSC Stores
Have very poor quality merchandise	10%	14%
Rarely have a wide selection in my size	21	17
Carry a skimpy supply of merchandise	12	7
Have layouts which make it impossible to find what I want	21	17
Have much higher prices	8	19
Have impolite sales personnel	6	6

Certainly there are not great differences between these two major shopping areas with regard to the nature of the merchandise. Even though the quality of the merchandise has considerable influence on where a person shops, there is little difference between the CBD and Barracks Road. Compared to access, parking, and beautification, this merchandise decision area must be considered as the least important as an immediate course of action aimed at recapturing market share for the CBD.

CONCLUSIONS

The data presented in this report reveal new and old information. That parking is a problem for the CBD does not develop anything new. However, quantifying such information and placing it in a rank order provides a basis for its use. Such data lessen argument and uncertainty. The information enhances decision process completion.

What, then, are the salient points developed by this study?

1. The CBD attracts families with low buying power. It is most appealing to those families which on a per capita basis are spending far less than the families shopping at Barracks Road Shopping Center.
2. Newer residents of Charlottesville-Albemarle are much more likely to shop at Barracks Road. Thus, with the passage of time the size of the market segment attracted to the CBD will diminish if the present situation remains unchanged.
3. Most of the families with high buying power do not live close to the CBD.
4. Inadequate access to the CBD is the single most important deterrent to increased shopping downtown.

5. The access issue centers more around the problem of reaching the general area of the CBD, not the problem of traveling from the CBD fringe to a parking place.

6. Parking is the second most important deterrent to shopping at the CBD. The problem embraces all aspects of parking—number of spaces, distance shopper must walk from car to store, and the meter nuisance.

7. Beautification of the CBD is not an all-important action area, but it cannot be ignored. Attractiveness of the area is construed as meaning some improvement of building exteriors. The need for more greenery, malls, and park-like areas is considered desirable but not important in influencing where one shops.

8. The merchandise offered by the two shopping areas is not greatly dissimilar. It is felt by shoppers that offerings by the CBD and Barracks Road are so closely related that they can see little or no difference. The one exception is that Barracks Road Shopping Center is thought to be somewhat more high-priced. However, this perception does not influence which shopping area is visited.

QUESTIONS FOR DISCUSSION

1. Phrase the marketing alternatives facing the City Council and the downtown merchants.
2. What is the criterion for the decision?
3. Describe briefly the decision environment that led to the formulation of the four marketing alternatives.
4. In what sense do the data showing the relative priority of the options under study (access, parking, beautification, merchandise) serve as environmental data? Give two examples.
5. How would the decision makers (City Council and downtown merchants) use the data in Tables 1 through 11?
6. How would you improve the "Conclusions" section of the report?
7. How would you improve on the sequence of the report?

Consumer Products, Inc.

The new product committee of Consumer Products, Inc. (CPI), was appointed seven years ago and has had a highly successful record of grocery product innovations and developments. The committee, headed by Anne Fischer, the company's marketing vice-president, approached each new product suggestion in a systematic manner and relied heavily on marketing research to predict the ultimate success of the suggested entries.

The corporate strategy called for maximum growth through new product development, rather than through increasing market shares of its existing brands or through acquisition. The corporate management felt that the increasingly high cost of enhancing market shares would reduce the return on funds. Also, the company had experienced several unprofitable acquisitions, one of which resulted in the FTC requiring the company to divest itself of the new division in order to avoid antitrust action under the Clayton Act.

It was at this time that the new product committee was formed and charged with the responsibility of developing new consumer grocery products. The existing distribution channels of Consumer Products were to be relied upon for new product introduction.

The new product group employed a variety of practices aimed at locating product innovations. Large samples of homemakers were engaged to describe their daily household behavior over a period of weeks in order to reveal possible gaps in homemaker needs. Other samples of homemakers were asked to describe their reactions to various household duties, with the thought that negative reactions would open up new ideas for possible product innovations. The committee held brainstorming sessions on a regular basis. During these gatherings all ideas were deliberately received enthusiastically so that no one would be inhibited in making suggestions. Quantity of ideas was encouraged, not quality. In this way it was thought that the risk of overlooking a new idea would be minimized. Evaluation of the many ideas could come later.

The committee sought combinations and improvements of existing brands. Thus, two or more existing brands could be marketed on a joint basis. Or current company products could be improved in one way or another. Not only were new product innovations sought, but product combinations and improvements were also the responsibility of the committee.

One of the committee's many marketing environment studies concerned malted milk consumption. The study revealed that while malted milk was a popular drink among young persons, virtually all of the consumption of the product took place outside the home. There were two brands of malted milk powders aimed at home use, but neither of these was viewed favorably by the great majority of malted milk drinkers. One member of the CPI new product committee brought these facts to the attention of the committee and suggested that further study be made of the reasons why those trying the home-use malted milk powder did not continue to consume the product.

The data gathered by the study indicated two factors influential in reducing repeat use. First was the contention of users that the two current brands did not taste like "real malted milk." Secondly, the powders did not produce a drink having the thickness sought by most malted milk drinkers. The committee member in charge of pursuing this possible new product area recommended that CPI's research and development group be charged with formulating a powder that would overcome these two basic objections.

After several taste and thickness alternatives were subjected to trial by malted milk drinkers, a formula was agreed upon by R&D. This formula was submitted to the new product committee. The costs of the product, at varying levels of production, were estimated by the manufacturing division. The product was named "Maltamix."

Two marketing elements still had to be resolved: price and package size. The options developed by the packaging people were:

4 packages for 89¢.
3 packages for 69¢.
4 packages for 79¢.
3 packages for 59¢.

Fischer stated that the decision to be made was clear: which one of these combinations would produce the highest level of profitability? In view of the high degree of uncertainty surrounding the decision, it was decided to employ a store auditing division of a marketing research company to provide data to reduce the uncertainty. This division maintains panels of stores in a small number of cities. Stores are compensated for their cooperation in permitting the marketing research personnel to "force" distribution, maintain shelf stock, check sales of brands at frequent intervals on products or marketing variables being measured. The marketing researcher, in effect, acts as a middleman. It maintains its own warehouses and trucks. Drivers distribute and place the products in the cooperating panel stores in accordance with instructions appropriate to the study being conducted.

Every attempt was made to hold all independent variables constant during the study or at least to randomize them to the greatest extent possible in order to net out their effects. In this study involving Maltamix, the following variables were held constant to the extent feasible within the cost limitations:

Shelf position of Maltamix.
Number of facings.
Prices of competing malted milk powders.
In-store merchandising of Maltamix.

Store panels were matched so as to create groups of stores that were comparable in terms of chain membership, total sales volume, and malted milk powder sales volume. The only promotional effort on behalf of Maltamix was in-store banners, aisle displays, etc. These were identical in each panel store. The factor being measured—price/package size—was permitted to operate freely within this real-life setting. The design of the study, then, aimed at measuring the response to the four price-package options in terms of number of units sold and gross revenue.

The marketing research studies of this type do not measure trade acceptance. Distribution extent is artificially created and can be adjusted to simulate existing distribution on other Consumer Products brands or to a specified distribution level. In this way, within the limitations of known and unknown survey error, panel store sales can be projected on a national basis.

The scope, location, and scheduling of the study was as follows:

1. Four panels of 12 stores each were selected in the Dayton, Ohio, area (SMSA).
2. Each panel was assigned a price/package combination.
3. Audits of the number of units sold and gross revenues were obtained for each of the four panels for each audit period.

The data collection pattern is shown in Figure 1.

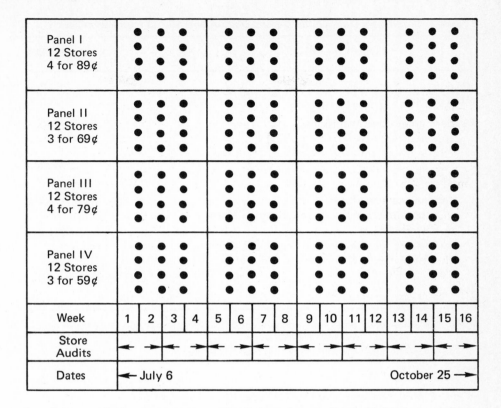

Figure 1   Schedule of Audits (16-Week Test Period—Dayton, Ohio)

During the conduct of the study the drivers maintained stock so that all stores were constant with regard to inventory and no out-of-stock condition ever existed. Most stores were visited on an every-third-day basis, assuring rigorous control of the in-store variables not being measured.

The marketing research company selects panel stores in test cities on the basis of representation of the All-Commodity Volume (ACV)—total sales in a market area. In the Dayton area, all stores used by the marketing researcher represented 70 percent of the ACV. The stores selected for the Maltamix study accounted for 50 percent of the ACV. These same stores accounted for 60 percent of malted milk powder sales in terms of units and 64 percent in terms of dollar volume as shown in Table 1 on page 210.

Brand share data in terms of units sold showed that the 4-for-79¢ combination outsold the other three. Also, the brand share captured by the 4-for-79¢ combination was slightly higher than the 4-for-89¢ mix. And total units sold during the final 12 weeks of the study showed the 4-for-79¢ combination outselling the other three options under consideration. The data, shown in Table 2, cover only the final 12 weeks of auditing. The first four weeks of data

Table 1 Significant Data on the Dayton Market and Stores Involved in Study

	SMSA*
Population	852,700
Households	258,200
Supermarket sales (in millions)	$280.3

Food Stores	Number	Percent ACV
Maltamix sample stores:	48	50%
Corporate chains (Liberal, Kroger, Marsh, Big Star)	32	36
Voluntary co-ops and independents (Super Duper, I.G.A., Foodtown, Super Value)	16	14
Other stores	60	50
Total Dayton area	108	100%

Source of SMSA Data: *Sales Management Survey of Buying Power* and *Progressive Grocer Marketing Guidebook.*

*SMSA: Greene, Miami, Montgomery, and Preble Counties.

Table 2 Maltamix Unit Sales by Package / Price Combination

Audit Period	4-for-89¢ Units Sold	Brand Share	3-for-69¢ Units Sold	Brand Share	4-for-79¢ Units Sold	Brand Share	3-for-59¢ Units Sold	Brand Share
July 6–July 19	1,006	4.7%	628	3.3%	1,597	6.6%	993	5.7%
July 20–Aug. 2	3,018	8.9	1,692	6.1	2,624	7.1	2,589	6.9
Aug. 3–Aug. 16	2,535	12.5	1,777	11.0	2,879	11.4	2,307	15.1
Aug. 17–Aug. 30	2,472	11.2	1,806	7.4	2,532	10.6	2,177	9.3
Aug. 31–Sept. 13	1,858	9.9	1,717	9.9	1,901	10.3	1,854	9.0
Sept. 14–Sept. 27	1,553	9.1	1,083	8.9	1,991	13.5	1,423	10.5
Sept. 28–Oct. 11	1,670	13.0	1,143	9.6	1,506	11.5	1,209	9.6
Oct. 12–Oct. 25	1,453	9.9	1,203	11.3	1,269	11.0	1,254	8.1
Total for final 12 weeks of test period	11,541	11.1%	8,729	8.6%	12,078	11.4%	10,224	10.6%

are considered unreliable inasmuch as several weeks are required to develop a test market from initial distribution to normal sales movement. The initial distribution of Maltamix was not complete until the end of the first week.

The dollar sales comparisons for the four combinations are shown in Table 3. Here, too, the data cover only the final 12 weeks. Dollar share represents the percentage of consumer dollars spent on Maltamix in contrast to the two malted milk powders already on the market.

Table 3 Maltamix Dollar Sales by Package/Price Combination

	4-for-89¢		3-for-69¢		4-for-79¢		3-for-59¢	
Audit Period	Dollar Sales	Dollar Share	Dollar Sales	Dollar Share	Dollar Sales	Dollar Share	Dollar Sales	Dollar Share
July 6–July 19	221.3	17.2%	144.4	12.5%	319.4	19.7%	198.6	16.7%
July 20–Aug. 2	663.9	28.1	386.1	21.3	525.0	20.5	517.8	19.4
Aug. 3–Aug. 16	557.7	36.0	408.7	32.7	575.8	29.9	461.4	37.2
Aug. 17–Aug. 30	543.8	33.6	415.4	24.7	506.4	29.2	435.4	27.8
Aug. 31–Sept. 13	408.7	29.2	394.9	30.3	380.2	27.5	370.8	25.8
Sept. 14–Sept. 27	341.6	27.2	249.1	27.4	398.2	33.0	284.6	27.8
Sept. 28–Oct. 11	367.4	35.4	262.9	28.7	301.2	29.1	241.8	24.9
Oct. 12–Oct. 25	319.6	28.8	276.7	32.1	253.8	27.5	250.8	22.6
Total for final 12 weeks of test period	2538.8	32.2%	2007.7	29.3%	2415.6	29.5%	2044.8	28.6%

The data shown above and other related audit information were presented to the new product committee. A discussion of the significance of the sales and revenue information was held.

QUESTIONS FOR DISCUSSION

1. What marketing decisions directly related to Maltamix were made by Consumer Products prior to formulating the price/package options—decisions that were to become a part of the marketing environment for the decision choices on price and package?
2. Anne Fischer states that the criterion for the price/package decision was to be highest level of profitability. Why could that be considered a weak criterion?
3. The audit information was presented to the new product committee. On the basis of the material presented in the case, why would the committee have difficulty in making the decision?
4. In addition to product and marketing cost information, what specific figure not provided in the case would be essential for national dollar sales and profitability for Maltamix to be projected nationally?

Dotsan Grill Guide Thermometer

Dotsan Instrument Company manufactures and markets a variety of technical instruments for a wide range of applications. Best known to the general public are the Dotsan thermometers for home use. Annual sales have exceeded $55 million over the past five years. A Consumer Products Division was established and a new plant built in Asheville, North Carolina, to produce and market the full line of Dotsan consumer items. The company has engaged in a new product development program that has resulted in several successes.

The Dotsan Grill Guide was the most recent creation from the new product development program. It was designed to aid the home outdoor grill or barbecue user when grilling meats and other foods. The user would place the Grill Guide on the grill after the coals had greyed and it would measure the radiant heat felt by the meat. The user could then adjust the grill height or disperse the coals until the desired temperature was obtained.

A temperature chart was supplied with the Grill Guide, listing the appropriate temperatures for various foods including steak, hamburgers, sliced ham, frankfurters, poultry, and fish. It was recognized, however, that a "backyard chef's" need for the Grill Guide was less when preparing steak or hamburger because the meat thickness and time for heating on the grill were the important variables affecting the result. With other foods, such as poultry, roasts, and fish, the longer grilling times placed greater importance on correct and constant temperatures of the grill.

Because the Grill Guide measured only radiant heat, the "kettle" or covered type of outdoor grill was not satisfactory for Grill Guide use. However, most of the grills in use were not of this kettle type and the Consumer Products Division did not feel that this factor would seriously limit the sale of the product.

The company's management reacted enthusiastically and quickly made the decision to produce and market the Grill Guide. Dotsan obtained the approval of the National Livestock and Meat Board, an endorsement they thought to be of considerable value. The main selling themes emphasized perfection in charcoal grilling, elimination of guesswork, and perfect results every time. The product was mounted on a pegboard display card with the thermometer itself contained in a transparent "bubble" or "blister pack"; the temperature chart was on the back.

A retail price of $3.98 was established and was printed on the display card. This price was determined largely by estimated production and marketing costs and was related to a minimum annual sales movement. Dotsan's production people stated that their costs were based on an anticipated annual production level of 22,000 units.

The Grill Guide received virtually overnight distribution among those outlets handling Dotsan's consumer line. Hardware and department stores which already displayed the Dotsan pegboard with the various consumer thermometers placed the new Grill Guide on this board as another Dotsan product. This distribution took place during the fall, in time for the holiday gift-giving season as well as the following spring when the demand for thermometers of this type was presumed to reach its peak.

One of the first promotional moves was the placement of a listing for the Grill Guide in the gift catalog of Miles-Kimball. This catalog has a distribution of more than one million. Some manufacturers of low-cost gift items depend solely on this type of promotion for their products.

The Grill Guide was also advertised on a cooperative basis in the *Chicago Tribune* by Marshall Field & Company, a leading Chicago department store located in downtown Chicago and in several suburbs. One of the largest Philadelphia hardware stores listed the item in a newspaper advertisement and gave it a special display. A west coast distributor ran a small amount of display advertising in *Sunset* magazine, a publication having mass circulation in the western sections of the United States.

In general, however, Dotsan did not support the Grill Guide with any sustained advertising or promotional program of its own. As with other Dotsan products, the emphasis in advertising was on the Dotsan thermometer line, and the virtual saturation of their distribution and display cards in hardware and department stores was considered sufficient marketing effort.

After two years on the market, the Grill Guide had fallen far short of its anticipated sales. Sales during those two years amounted to 2,400 units, 1,200 per year. (Remember that the production department at Consumer Products Division had stated a requirement of 22,000 annual sales if they were to maintain their production costs at a satisfactory level, permitting a $3.98 retail price.)

A meeting of the marketing committee has been called by the divisional vice-president to discuss the future of the Grill Guide. Members of the marketing committee are the marketing manager, the marketing research director, the sales manager, the advertising manager, and the divisional vice-president.

QUESTIONS FOR DISCUSSION

1. In what phase of the decision-making process is Dotsan's marketing committee?
2. What was the decision criterion when management first decided to produce and market the Grill Guide?
3. In retrospect, what should the Dotsan management have done differently in deciding to market the Grill Guide?
4. What marketing alternatives now face the marketing committee in its meeting about to get underway?
5. Assuming you were a member of the marketing committee and you had great influence on what the committee was to do, what would you recommend as the next move of the decision makers, after agreement on the marketing alternatives?

Ethical Drug Marketing Association, I

During most of the years following World War II, the U.S. pharmaceutical industry prospered. The return on common equity ran close to 20 percent during the early 1970s. The average profit margin on sales of manufacturers and marketers of ethical and proprietary drugs was close to 10 percent during that period, compared to 5.7 percent for U.S. industry overall.

In 1974, several industries were approaching the drug manufacturers' performance on return on common equity. Steel, for example, jumped from less than 5 percent in 1970 to 15 percent in 1974. Paper, at 6 percent in 1971, vaulted to 18 percent for 1974. (See Figure 1.) The trucking industry actually passed the drug makers during the latter year.

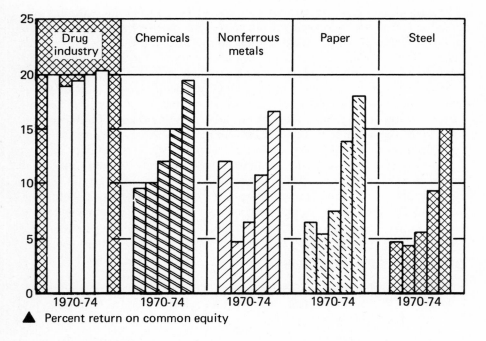

Source: "The Drug Industry's Clouded Future," reprinted from the November 23, 1974, issue of *Business Week* by special permission. © 1974 by McGraw-Hill, Inc.

Figure 1   The Drug Industry Stalls While Others Make Big Leaps

In a broad sense, pharmaceutical products can be divided into two groups—ethical and proprietary. The former are those that can be issued to customers by prescription only. The latter type can be sold over the counter; e.g., aspirin, cough medicine, some tranquilizers, and antihistamines. Proprietary drugs are "primarily advertised or otherwise promoted to the general public."[1]

The U.S. ethical drug sales volume for 1974 approximated $5.5 billion a year, up from $3 billion for 1967. Most leading manufacturers marketed both prescription and over-the-counter drugs. Abbott Laboratories and Richardson-Merrell, for example, derived about one third of their sales revenue from ethical products; Warner-Lambert, 39 percent; and American Home Products, 38 percent.

The failure of the drug industry to increase its return on common equity in the early 1970s caused some industry leaders and financial analysts to wonder about the industry's emergence from this stalled position. Prices of drugs had risen more slowly than the consumer price index. Profit margins for many leading companies had fallen.

Business Week, in its November 23, 1974, story on the drug industry, listed four problems of a unique nature that were faced by the ethical drug makers:

1. New regulations from the Department of Health, Education, & Welfare that required reimbursement of recipients of Medicare, Medicaid, and other federal health care programs at the lowest price at which the drug was available.
2. Greater difficulties in developing new drugs and in pushing them through extensive and costly clinical testing.
3. A reshaping of the market, with much more emphasis on high-volume, low-profit products at the expense of the companies' traditionally low-volume, high-profit drugs.
4. A rising tide of foreign competition as overseas companies, largely European, sought to exploit the lucrative U.S. market.

Those who argued that the drug industry was headed for financial trouble or at least minimal growth contended that those four problems would all be at work to varying degrees. They felt that the federal government's new pricing regulations could well result in the drug firms cutting back on their new product research. Historically, laboratory research had led to new ethical products and large profits that had in part been reinvested in further research.

Many of the 200 top-selling branded prescription drugs faced losing their patent protection by 1984, at which time they would become exposed to multi-source (generic) competition (i.e., from products of identical chemical composition). The multi-source brands would then fall in price, it was contended, and foreign competition would place an even greater squeeze on corporate profitability. The Federal Drug Administration required that new drugs be tested for eight or nine years and, as laboratory research costs got even higher, it was less likely that new product research could be maintained at its present 1974 level. During the several years prior to 1974, six companies brought out 29 of the 69 drugs introduced to the market and only nine of these made it to the top-200 drug list.

---

[1] As defined by the U.S. Department of Commerce.

The result was that few drug manufacturers garnered big profits on new ethical products, something industry leaders asserted was necessary if adequate laboratory research was to be conducted. Furthermore, said these industry spokespeople, the life cycle of a drug had been shortened considerably. Not too many years ago, they pointed out, the 17-year patent life would have afforded ample protection. But recently, they noted, this period was reduced to about ten years, resulting in a company's inability to recoup its cost and derive a profitability level that would support additional research. This decline in new drug products introduced by the industry is shown in Figure 2.

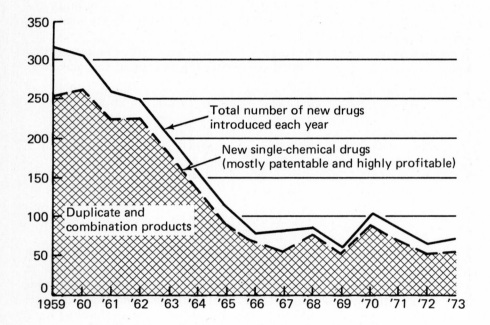

Source: "The Drug Industry's Clouded Future," reprinted from the November 23, 1974, issue of *Business Week* by special permission. ©1974 by McGraw-Hill, Inc.

Figure 2   How High-Profit Drug Lines Have Declined

For some years the cost of marketing ethical drugs had been under fire. While laboratory research usually ranged from 10 to 20 percent of sales revenue, marketing costs would sometimes exceed that level. Government officials, consumer protectionists, and many individual members of the medical profession insisted that the high marketing costs of prescription drugs were unnecessary, and that if a profit squeeze were taking place, a reduction in the marketing efforts would be more appropriate than a lessening of laboratory research.

There are three major components of ethical drug marketing. First are the "detail people" who represent the individual manufacturers and devote virtually all their time to calling on doctors, nurses, pharmacists, and hospital staffs. A second marketing effort is direct mail. A third is space advertising in various medical journals. These publications are many and varied, ranging from the nationally distributed *Journal of the American Medical Association* to smaller and highly technical publications directed to the medical specialties. In addition are the many state medical publications plus those of a regional nature. The drug marketer also uses publications covering the retail pharmacist and hospitals.

Much of the criticism of the scope of the marketing effort was directed at direct mail and publication advertising. The latter in particular was denounced. It was asserted that elaborate four-color advertisements in a wide variety of magazines, for example, were unnecessary and that members of the medical profession could be reached with equal effectiveness through the use of direct mail, systematic listing of new products in publications, detail people, and the wide range of conventions and seminars. It was contended by the fault finders that magazine advertising was not effective and was an inefficient use of the manufacturers' marketing funds. They urged publication retrenchment as a means for bringing marketing and laboratory research costs more into line.

The Ethical Drug Marketing Association,[2] formed several years prior to 1974, had as its basic purpose the role of providing industry marketing data and conducting cooperative marketing research that would aid in more effective marketing of ethical drugs. Its membership was comprised of virtually all of the leading ethical drug manufacturers.

At the 1974 annual conference of EDMA a discussion centered on the high cost of drug marketing. It was pointed out, among other things, that doctors were one of the most difficult and expensive professional groups with which to communicate. On the other hand, it was stressed, it was vital that those in the medical profession be well versed in the latest product developments. The goal was to communicate with the profession in as efficient a manner as possible. A sizable group attending the conference argued that those marketing efforts found to be ineffective should be dropped. It was hoped that some joint effort sponsored by EDMA could be undertaken in order to determine what could and should be done.

The individual member EDMA companies were already subscribing to several syndicated market data collection services. The offerings of these services were discussed, with several members arguing that no additional data were needed. The syndicated services and the type of information they yield include the following.

> *National Journal Audit*—IMS America, Ltd. Subscribers to this audit are entitled to:
>
> 1. Data describing the size of new and old product promotional campaigns.
> 2. Comparisons of expenditures by companies and therapeutic classes.
> 3. Journal usage by company, class, and product.
> 4. Analysis of individual advertisements according to the use of color, inserts, position, size of advertisements, frequency, and pattern of insertion, circulation, and expenditures.

---

[2] A fictitious organization.

National Prescription Audit (NPA)—IMS America, Ltd. This audit has been conducted since 1952 and measures prescription drug usage on a national basis. Data are collected biweekly from a panel of 400 pharmacies selected so as to be projectable to the national level. An average of 100,000 new and re-fill prescriptions are audited monthly. Data are reported in terms of number of prescriptions dispensed and dollar volume by brand name.

Drug Distribution Data—Subsidiary of IMS. This organization collects sales and distribution data on the movement of pharmaceutical and ethically pro-moted over-the-counter products from warehouse to retail outlet. It gathers this information from wholesalers, drug chain warehouses, and prescription mail order houses throughout the country. The service costs approximately $250,000 a year. It does not include direct-from-manufacturer sales data. Sub-scribers receive these types of data:

1.   Nationwide sales statistics with share of market in a given locality.
2.   A market index by territory providing a comparison between subscribers' sales by product and 41 companies' total sales.
3.   Reports on therapeutic classes of products enabling subscribers to measure how their products compare with competition—by individual sales terri-tories, supervisors, regions, and nationally.

Audatrex—IMS America, Ltd. Data generated for this service are derived from a panel of 700 doctors across the country in private practice. Reports in-clude such information as brand loyalty, brand switching, company loyalty, intensity and breadth of product uses, and product displacement at the *pre-scriber* level. These data are presented by physician age groups, medical spe-cialty, and geographic region.

Post-Script—Market Measures, Inc. (not syndicated). This service measures the sales effect of ethical pharmaceutical promotion campaigns, i.e., direct mail, journal advertising, and sales force programs. Data are gathered from pharmacists by auditing new prescriptions written. This particular service of Market Measures is not syndicated and can be conducted on city-by-city bases as special studies for individual client companies or as organizations warrant.

After the discussion of the offerings of the syndicated services, a committee was appointed to determine whether EDMA should rely on the existing syndi-cated data, or design a special research study of some type. The purpose of the latter approach would be to attack some specific issue relating to the effective-ness of the industry's marketing efforts, with the focus to be on the marketing endeavors of the industry aimed at communicating with the medical pro-fession.

The committee decided to meet during the annual conference. They held a five-hour meeting on one evening of the conference but they could not reach an agreement on what to do. Committee members could not agree on the type of research data needed.

QUESTIONS FOR DISCUSSION

1. The case states that some 200 top-selling branded prescription drugs will lose their patent protection by 1984. What type of information is this: actionable or environmental? If you were a member of the top management of one of the leading ethical drug companies, what use could you make of that information?
2. How does EDMA contribute to the marketing effectiveness of its member companies?
3. If the members of EDMA at their annual conference feel that the communication expenditures are lacking in efficiency, what steps are in order?
4. The case describes several syndicated market data collection services. How could the information provided by any one of these services be of value to EDMA in attacking the claimed inefficiency of ethical drug marketing?
5. Develop a set of promotional alternatives and the relevant criteria that EDMA might reasonably consider on behalf of its members.

Ethical Drug Marketing Association, II

Of the three principal components of ethical drug marketing—detail salespeople, direct mail, and medical journal advertising—the EDMA research committee opted to study journal advertising. The objective of the study, as stated by the committee, was to determine whether medical journal advertising was effective as a marketing device for their member companies.

There was considerable disagreement among committee members as to how the study should be conducted. Several favored a "brand awareness" study, aimed at measuring the extent to which there was a greater awareness of brand names of advertised drugs than of nonadvertised products. Other members opted for some measure of sales.

The committee took their problems to Elaine Okemo, director of research for *Modern Medicine,* a publication nationally distributed and well respected among physicians. Okemo was known to be a sophisticated marketing researcher who could provide them with sound counsel on research feasibility and procedure. Okemo was most enthusiastic about cooperating, even though her publication, and perhaps medical journal advertising in general, would be subjected to severe scrutiny as to its effectiveness in communicating with the medical profession.

Okemo recommended some form of controlled experiment where some measurement of actual sales resulting from advertising could be made and contrasted to sales when the products were not advertised. The particular experimental scheme chosen was to insert selected advertisements into a subset of *Modern Medicine*'s copies. The results of ethical sales would then be compared with sales achieved when products were not so advertised. It was to be a "controlled experiment," employing a test and a control group.

Okemo suggested that EDMA talk with Market Measures, the firm offering the Post-Script service. It was ultimately agreed that EDMA would engage Market Measures and that *Modern Medicine* would participate in the study.[1]

Four products were selected for the research—Eli Lilly's Seconal (SECK-o-nal), Upjohn's Pamine (PAM-een), Pfizer's Tyzine (TY-zeen), and Lederle's Varidase (Var-i-DACE). None of the four products had been extensively advertised during the previous three or four years. The nature of each advertisement (copy theme, color, number of pages, etc.) was left up to the manufacturer. The advertisements appeared in 13 consecutive issues of *Modern Medicine* for seven months beginning in July and ending in January.

The study was conducted in two cities—Buffalo, New York, and Tucson, Arizona. The advertisements were inserted into copies of *Modern Medicine* and distributed to the regular circulation list for all physicians whose last names began with the letters "A" through "K" in both cities. Those physicians having last names beginning "L" through "Z" received the unaltered copies. The test advertisements were bound into the magazine copies in a way that readers would not realize a special insertion had been made. Thus, the test copies (going to the A–K physicians) were identical to the normal copies in every way except for the four advertisements. Copies to both the test (A–K) and control (L–Z) groups were mailed simultaneously. The advertisements were randomly dispersed throughout each of the 13 issues over the seven-month test period.

The products, scope of advertisements, and the national prescription sales and dollar volumes for the four products are shown in Table 1.

Table 1 Data on Products Used in Modern Medicine Study

Product Brand	Therapeutic Category	Advertisement Scope	Prior 12-month National Prescription Sales	
			Number	Dollar Value
Seconal	Hypnotic sedative	2 page, 2 color	3,204,000	$2,933,000
Varidase	Enzyme	1 page, b & w	219,000	525,000
Pamine	Antispasmodic	3 page, 4 color	291,000	434,000
Tyzine	Topical nasal decongestant	3 page, 4 color	242,000	222,000

None of the products had any appreciable promotion for several years prior to the undertaking of the study. Moreover, each of the manufacturers agreed

---

[1] In reality *Modern Medicine* was the instigator of the study, not EDMA. For classroom use, EDMA has been created and actually does not exist. *Modern Medicine* employed Market Measures, released the data, and should receive full credit for the study. The research effort was praised by academicians and practitioners.

not to engage in any special promotions on the test brands during the research effort.

New prescriptions for the four products were audited monthly in 100 pharmacies in the two cities. The data collection was supervised by members of schools of pharmacy in the two metropolitan areas. Prescription files of pharmacies that filled more than 60 percent of all prescriptions were audited.

A pretest measurement in all drug outlets audited was conducted for five months prior to the actual start of the test itself. This measurement took place from February through June. The data emerging from this pretest period revealed that the two groups of doctors (A–K and L–Z) were quite similar in terms of new prescriptions filled as well as the areas of specialization of the doctors. The specialties for the two groups were tabulated as shown in Table 2.

Table 2 Areas Of Specialization for Test Groups A–K and L–Z

	A–K Test	L–Z Control
Internal medicine	17.2%	18.5%
General practice	17.1	19.7
General surgery	11.5	10.8
Obstetrics-gynecology	7.3	6.7
Pediatrics	5.7	6.8
Osteopathy	5.2	5.0
Anesthesiology	4.3	4.0
Ophthalmology	4.3	4.6
Orthopedics	3.3	2.4
Radiology	3.3	3.7
Otolaryngology	3.2	2.5
Psychiatry	3.2	2.7
Neurology	2.5	1.2
Urology	2.5	2.7
Dermatology	2.4	1.9
All others	7.0	6.8
	100.0	100.0

The survey information was gathered and processed by Market Measures, Inc., and submitted to *Modern Medicine* for release to EDMA members. In a summary statement under "Findings," Market Measures commented on the data contained in the report:

> The findings show that each of the four advertising campaigns had a postive effect on the prescribing habits among the physicians receiving issues (of *Modern Medicine*) containing the advertisements. The effect ranges from +2.6 percent to +57.4 percent. That is, during the seven months of test measurements, prescriptions for the test products were written more frequently by physicians who were exposed to the advertisements in *Modern*

Medicine compared to the physicians who were not. This positive effect seen refers to the number of prescriptions we would expect the two groups to write based on the pretest measurements. In this analysis, we compare a pretest period of February through June with a test period of July through January.

Some of the tables included in the report issued by *Modern Medicine,* plus one exhibit, appear below and on the following page.

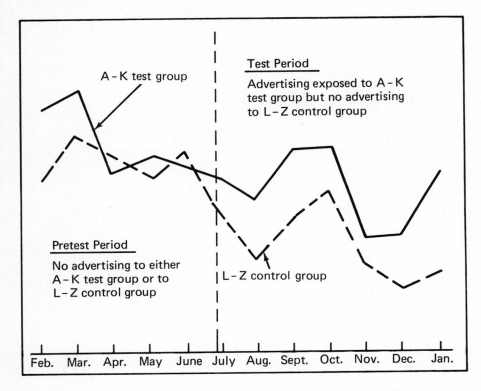

Figure 1   *Trend in Monthly New Prescriptions—Test Versus Control Group Doctors*

Table 3 *Comparison of Number of New Prescriptions Written*

	5-Month Pretest		7-Month Test	
	Number	Percentage	Number	Percentage
Prescriptions written by:				
Test group doctors, A–K	3,015	52%	3,718	53%
Control group doctors, L–Z	2,780	48	3,294	47

Table 4 New Prescriptions Written by Brand, Test Vs. Control

| | New Prescriptions (Test Period) As a Percentage of New Prescriptions (Pretest) | | | |
	Seconal	Pamine	Tyzine	Varidase
Test doctors, A–K	87.1%	96.0%	123.4%	86.2%
Control doctors, L–Z	84.9	83.9	78.4	78.3
Test over control	+2.6	+14.4	+57.4	+10.1

Note: Measured in average prescriptions per month.

Table 5 Projected Contribution of Advertising*

Four products combined NPA** U.S. total new prescriptions, July–January test period with no advertising	2,220,000
Increase in prescriptions as projected effect of advertising	161,000
Total new prescriptions if products had been advertised nationwide	2,381,000
Percentage of increase in prescriptions due to advertising	+7.2%
Return to manufacturer for each new prescription added	$2.185
Gross contribution of advertising	$352,000
Less cost of advertising	$321,000
Net contribution of advertising to date	$31,000

* While the sample in this study is not presented as representative of the country as a whole, this projection will be useful in understanding the significance of sales possibilities at the national level—*Modern Medicine.*
** National Prescription Audit—IMS America, Ltd.

QUESTIONS FOR DISCUSSION

1. The research committee made two basic errors at the very outset. What were they?
2. Why would "brand awareness" be a poor criterion?
3. Assume the advertising alternatives for EDMA are:
   a. To recommend that EDMA members drop or greatly reduce advertising in national medical journals.
   b. To recommend that members retain their advertising levels in national medical journals.
   What does the criterion seem to be, based on data presented in the case?
4. What basic omission creates some difficulty in interpreting the data presented in Figure 1?
5. It can be said that the data appearing in Table 3 are neither environmental nor actionable. How could this be? Why are the Table 3 data shown in the report? Where would the data be used within the context of the decision model?

6. There are several aspects of Table 4 that can be criticized. What are they? What additional data would you add to Table 4 in order to increase the acceptability of the data?
7. On what bases could you challenge the data shown in Table 5?
8. Would you be willing to accept the data developed by the research study as a basis for making the advertising decision facing EDMA's research committee?

Glessner Breweries, I

Jacob Glessner founded his brewing company in 1871. Locating in east central Pennsylvania, he established a successful family operation based on a brewing formula developed in Munich, Germany, a century earlier.

Glessner Breweries today maintains distribution in eastern Pennsylvania, southeastern New York State (outside of New York City) and in much of New England. Shipments reached an all-time high in 1974 when 5,000,000 barrels were sold. (A barrel in the brewing industry contains 31 gallons.)

Consumption of beer in the United States has steadily increased over the years. According to the United States Brewers Association (U.S.B.A.), consumption of malt beverages since 1964 has increased as shown in Table 1.

Table 1 Consumption of Malt Beverages

Year	Barrels (in Millions)
1964	97,851
1965	99,453
1966	103,853
1967	106,786
1968	111,049
1969	115,793
1970	121,601
1971	126,438
1972	130,166
1973	136,822
1974	144,174
1975	148,341

This consistent increase in consumption has been due to several factors, most important of which have been the growth in population and the steady increase in per capita consumption. The per capita figures from the U.S.B.A. are shown in Table 2 for all persons in the United States 21 years and older.

Table 2 Per Capita Consumption of Malt Beverages by Persons 21 Years of Age and Over

Year	Gallons
1964	27.2
1965	27.0
1966	27.9
1967	28.4
1968	28.9
1969	29.7
1970	30.8
1971	31.4
1972	31.6
1973	32.7
1974	33.9
1975	34.2

Per capita consumption of beer has varied greatly during the past several years from one part of the country to the other. In Alabama and Arkansas, for example, per capita usage has hovered around 20 gallons per year. This is in contrast to Nevada and Montana where the consumption has been approximately 45 gallons per person 21 years or older. In the Glessner territory per capita consumption has also been high. For example, in the two New England states of New Hampshire and Vermont the per capita figure for the past few years has exceeded 46 gallons. Total shipments for the industry for the Northeast (Pennsylvania, New York State, and New England) has held steady at about 23 million barrels.

With the exception of only two years, Glessner has outsold all nationally distributed brands in its area. This margin, however, has declined over the past four years, with both Anheuser-Busch and Miller making consistent inroads into Glessner's market share. Glessner's share dropped from 20.5 percent in 1974 to 16.6 percent in 1977. At no other time in the company's history has this market penetration figure been so consistently in decline. Shipments have dropped from the 5 million barrels during 1974 to 4.4 million barrels in 1977, resulting in a corresponding profit sag. And this decline took place during a three-year period when beer sales in the country were increasing.

The management of Glessner Breweries was well aware of the dismal fate of several hundreds of local and regional breweries over the past 30 or 40 years. Only those smaller breweries with a strong consumer franchise and sophisticated marketing skill had been able to survive the unrelenting growth of the nationally distributed brands. The decline in the number of breweries operated in the U.S. over the past several decades as reported by the U.S.B.A. is shown in Table 3. On the basis of that historical pattern, the future of local and regional breweries seemed far from bright.

Table 3 Number of Breweries Operated in U.S.

Year	Number of Breweries
1940	611
1950	407
1960	229
1961	229
1962	220
1963	211
1964	204
1965	197
1966	187
1967	176
1968	163
1969	158
1970	154
1971	148
1972	147
1973	122
1974	111
1975	102
1976	95
1977	94

Twice during the past five years national breweries had approached the Glessner people concerning possible purchase of the Glessner name and facilities. In both instances the Glessner management rejected the proffers.

Jacob Glessner, IV, the brewery's young president, modernized its brewing process when he assumed the presidency three years ago. At that time he brought into the organization a brewing chemist who made the final decisions on the use of hops and barley malt which, with other variables, altered the taste of the final product somewhat. The role of the old-time brewmaster, so long accepted by the brewing industry, was minimized considerably. At Glessner the brewing chemist controlled the brewing process, a practice that was already being followed by brewers of the nationally distributed brands.

Several members of the Glessner management voiced concern that without the artistry of the former brewmaster, the taste of Glessner beer had been changed and that consumers in the northeastern market were turning away from the brand. They argued that a brewing chemist could not adequately replace the brewmaster, whose years of experience provided a quality that would never be equalled by the more modern, sophisticated quantitative methods. This management group felt strongly that a substantial portion of the Glessner sales decline was due to formula alterations instituted by the brewing chemist, resulting in flavor and taste changes. Jacob Glessner, however, was not about to be dislodged from his commitment on behalf of his brewing chemist.

Glessner Breweries had been packaging its beverage in both bottles and cans over the past 15 years. Approximately 30 percent of their sales were in cans with the balance in bottles. This proportion had not changed significantly over the 15-year span. Several modifications were made in their packaging during that time, however. In each instance experiments were conducted among consumers before adopting the modifications. The screw-type bottle cap and the so-called "easy-open, tab top" can were adopted as a result of such market tests. Recognizing the problem of disposal and the much-publicized environmental issue of nonreturnable bottles, Glessner did switch to the use of returnable bottles accompanied by a deposit at the time of purchase. This was one of Glessner's first moves after he assumed the brewery presidency.

This early decision by Glessner proved costly, and it was readily apparent after only nine months' experience with the returnable bottle program. Even though the switch to the returnable bottle required costly cleaning equipment and created warehousing problems not fully anticipated, the choice was made to revoke the returnable bottle decision and revert to the original package of nonreturnable bottles. Most of the Glessner management felt that they had caught the packaging error in time and that it had had little or no long-run effect on the brand's sales. Only Jacob Glessner, IV, opted for continuing with the returnable bottle, but he acquiesced when he realized he had little support.

The Glessner advertising effort revolved around the maintenance of an image of Glessner Beer having the "old-time German flavor." This theme was promulgated through print and radio advertising and the bottle/can label. The label featured an illustration of a Munich brewery with statements briefly describing the brewery's use of the best in malts and hops. The label was adopted 15 years ago and had remained unchanged ever since.

Several years ago a few members of Glessner's marketing group questioned the use of this Munich label, contending that because a good portion of their total market was in southeastern New York State and most of New England, beer consumers in those geographic areas were not especially susceptible to the German imagery approach. They supported their thinking with data that revealed a higher Glessner market penetration in eastern Pennsylvania, which has a higher German population, than in Massachusetts, southern Vermont, and southern New Hampshire. It was pointed out two years ago that the Glessner share in eastern Pennsylvania was 22.8 percent of dollar sales, while at the same time in Massachusetts and the southern parts of Vermont and New Hampshire their penetration was 14.1 percent. When these data were presented some two years ago, however, the point was made by several management people that this variance in penetration by geographic area was a function of the caliber of the distributors involved and was not due to any differences in the demographics of the beer-consuming public. This point was never seriously challenged, although those asking for the survey data on market share held a contrary view. They believed that the Munich label and the entire German beer image could be an obstacle in the path of greater sales in those sections of New York State and New England having Glessner distribution.

The Munich label issue later surfaced again and this time the marketing department assumed the responsibility of commissioning an industrial designer to create two alternative labels. One of these new designs featured a group of trees framed by an ornamental wreath; the second one had a lake as its distinctive characteristic, surrounded in the distance by trees. Both labels aimed at creating the image of the outdoors, healthfulness, refreshing feeling, and coolness. This change in the communications strategy would be basic to Glessner Breweries, if it were approved.

The marketing committee, headed by Thelma D. Kaiser, met with the management group and presented its proposed plan of changing the Glessner communications strategy from the Munich German formula brew to that of a refreshing, outdoors, cool beer. They would aim at the 21–40 age group, that market segment known from past market research to consume disproportionately high amounts of beer.

Kaiser, anticipating some opposition, recommended that Glessner conduct a thorough study to determine whether the "tree" or "lake" label would have greater acceptance than the existing Munich label. She contended that there was little reason to argue the merits or demerits of the new strategy until some consumer data could be obtained.

Glessner, possibly hesitant to drop a century-old identification with family tradition, advocated a continuance of the current strategy. His argument was twofold. First, he felt that a change, at this or any time, would throw away the many years of German identification which has enabled the brewery to be successful and, at least up to this time, withstand the threats of the nationally distributed brands. Second, he would be disinclined to accept the data from a consumer study because, to his way of thinking, it would be impossible to measure the worth of the existing label in contrast to the two alternatives. He felt that in such a study the Munich label would always have the distinct advantage of familiarity. "After all," he stressed, "the current Munich label has been around for more than a dozen years and the Glessner-Munich story has been told again and again for more than a century." Any survey conducted at this time, he asserted, would not be able to overcome this familiarity problem.

QUESTIONS FOR DISCUSSION

1. Are the data describing the uninterrupted decline in the number of small breweries (Table 3) environmental or actionable? If environmental, would the data relate to a strategic or tactical decision-problem? If actionable, what were the marketing alternatives?
2. When Glessner Breweries decided not to entertain offers from national breweries regarding the purchase of their facilities, what would the alternatives have been?

3. What were two of Jacob Glessner, IV's early decisions after becoming the brewery's president? How did the personal equation enter into those decisions?
4. What do you consider to be the most basic decision-problem faced by the Glessner management? What were the environmental data that led to an awareness of that decision-problem? Was the decision-problem strategic or tactical in nature? Why?
5. What four tactical marketing decisions were made by the management and/or the marketing people? List the environments and marketing alternatives for each.
6. Glessner's marketing committee said the company would aim at the 21–40 age group. Would this decision have been made prior to or simultaneously with the selection of the "tree" or "lake" label? How would this decision to target the advertising effort to that market segment enter into the development of the criterion for the label selection issue?

Glessner Breweries, II

After extensive discussions covering a four-month period, the management of Glessner Breweries decided to alter drastically the communications strategy, i.e., identification with the Munich formula some two centuries old. This decision, in a sense, was an overruling of Jacob Glessner, IV, who, for perhaps subconscious and sentimental reasons, had opposed the departure from an old family association. Young Glessner, however, agreed to the new strategy when it appeared that the majority favored the move. Included among those favoring the change were long-time brewery executives, and Glessner was astute enough not to force his rank on his management.

The new promotional strategy stressed Glessner Beer as modern, healthful, refreshing, masculine, light, and good tasting. This image was in contrast to the old Glessner Beer, which was promoted as strong tasting, full-bodied, and old-fashioned.

Management agreed that a new label was needed. The two labels developed by the industrial designer several months before were those considered for adoption. A marketing research firm was called in for advice on how to conduct a study that would reveal information necessary to decide which label would better reflect the new Glessner image. Thomas Payle was the research company's vice-president assigned to work on the Glessner account. He recommended that the current Glessner label be included in the study as a reference point.

Glessner's marketing strategy aimed at increasing market share at the expense of the two leading national brands in their area, Budweiser and Miller. Payle recommended that the sample for the survey be drawn from Budweiser and Miller drinkers. A drinker was defined for purposes of this study as a person who drank two or more bottles or cans of beer a week during the summer months. The study itself was conducted during July and August when beer drinking was at its yearly peak. Interviewing was conducted during evenings and weekends in order to increase the chances of locating beer drinkers. Both male and female beer drinkers were included in the study.

Glessner distribution was bounded on the west by a line drawn approximately from Harrisburg, Pennsylvania, north through Williamsport, and into New York State through Elmira and Syracuse. From Syracuse the line followed Interstate 90 to the Schenectady area and then north to Rutland, Vermont, and east through New Hampshire. In brief, the Glessner market was comprised of southeastern New York State, excluding New York City, all of Connecticut, Massachusetts, Rhode Island, and the southern portions of Vermont and New Hampshire. Total population of the area was approximately 24,000,000. Payle urged that the study be conducted in middle Atlantic areas not being served by Glessner so that any bias caused by label familiarity could be overcome. In other words, the three labels would have equal opportunity to be favored because none of the respondents from whom the attitudinal information would be obtained would have had any great exposure to Glessner, if any.

The sample size was 1,200, dispersed equally among the communities of Montpelier, Vermont, and Rochester and Jamestown, New York—all outside Glessner's market area. Technically known as a probability sample, it was divided equally between Budweiser and Miller drinkers, both brands having strong distributors in the Glessner market area. Prior studies had shown that Budweiser outsold Miller almost three to one in Glessner's market. Schlitz, a close third to Miller, was not included in the study because of the added complexities and the attendant higher survey costs.

The drinkers were shown the current Glessner label (Munich = M) and *either* the trees (T) or the lake (L) label. The dispersion of the sample is shown in Table 1.

Table 1 Sample Distribution by City

	Montpelier		Rochester		Jamestown		Total		
	Male	Female	Male	Female	Male	Female	Male	Female	Total
Munich + Trees	147	46	140	55	154	50	441	151	592
Munich + Lake	153	54	160	45	146	50	459	149	608
Total sample	300	100	300	100	300	100	900	300	1200

The questionnaire was designed so as to develop both environmental and actionable data. The latter aimed at obtaining an overall measure of "likelihood of buying" when shown two labels—the Munich label and either the trees or lake label. This predictive measurement was accomplished through a series of scaling questions, the respondent having the opportunity to reveal different degrees of opinion ranging from "very likely to buy" at one end of a continuum to "very unlikely to buy" at the other extreme. The choice was between only two labels, and did not take into consideration the extent to which respondents would be more likely to buy brands other than Glessner. The intent of the research was to measure the differences between two Glessner labels—the trees label and the lake label. The Munich label was included simply to eliminate a direct confrontation between the trees and lake labels.

While the overall preference was revealed by the attitudinal scaling approach, Jacob Glessner, IV, was desirous of determining whether one or both of the new labels communicated the particular beer image set forth by the management group. Even though one may have had greater across-the-board acceptance, which of the two under consideration best communicated the image desired by Glessner?

Thomas Payle of the research firm presented the survey data to the Glessner management. He pointed out the closeness of the preferences, with all three labels (including the current Munich label) sharing virtually equal support. In view of sampling and other errors inherent in surveys of this type, he pointed out, there was no statistically significant difference between the trees and lakes labels. He further explained that because of this lack of a clear-cut "winner," the Glessner management could select either of the two with minimum risk. (The data appear in Table 2.)

Table 2 Trees Label Vs. Lake Label

Label Preferred	Budweiser Drinkers		Miller Drinkers		Total Budweiser and Miller Drinkers
	M vs. T	M vs. L	M vs. T	M vs. L	
Munich label	60%	48%	42%	56%	51%
Trees label	40		58		49
Lake label		52		44	48
Number of drinkers interviewed	300	300	300	300	1,200

Jacob Glessner and Thelma Kaiser, the brewery's marketing manager, were somewhat perplexed by the data. Intuitively, they hesitated to accept Payle's findings. Glessner asked that Kaiser and others take a few days to review the data, including the so-called imagery data that were also included in the report. It was agreed that the management would meet again within a week because it was essential that the new label be agreed upon. After all, Jacob Glessner commented, "this is a most important decision and we must make certain that we do the right thing."

The imagery data uncovered by the study appear in Table 3 on page 232. The percentages describe those beer drinkers who felt that the adjectives shown to them during the interview at the time they were viewing the labels were "very descriptive" or "somewhat descriptive" of a beer having the label under consideration.

Table 3 Images Communicated by All Three Labels

Images	Munich	Trees	Lake
Masculine	70%	55%	34%
Healthy	29	40	38
Light	18	32	40
Modern	18	38	27
Good taste	61	30	41
Refreshing	32	60	52
Number of drinkers interviewed	1,200	600	600

QUESTIONS FOR DISCUSSION

1. Support the argument that the Glessner management should flip a coin and go with either the trees or lake label.
2. If the management were to adopt the coin-flipping approach, what would be necessary within the context of the decision model—as far as the Munich label is concerned?
3. Support the argument that the data are not sufficiently accurate for the making of the label decision.
4. Now that the data are in, and looking back with 20/20 hindsight, would you have employed a sales criterion rather than the "consumer-stated preference." Why?
5. It is apparent that the imagery data in Table 3 do not lean heavily in favor of one label over others. What use could be made of these data?
6. If you were Jacob Glessner, IV, what would you do, now that you have had an opportunity to study the survey data?

Indiana Structural, Inc.

Indiana Structural, Inc., has been manufacturing above-ground water storage tanks since 1956. Forming tank heads has been an important part of the total fabrication process. For more than a year the management of ISI has considered greater utilization of its productive plant capacity by making its cold pressing facilities available to firms now purchasing their tank heads from other sources.

To allocate a portion of its productive capacity to outside customers would involve considerable cost, and would risk disruption of production scheduling.

Moreover, a marketing staff would have to be recruited, trained, and then sent out on its sales mission.

The productive capacity that would be available to outside customers varies from season to season, and it would not always be predictable. During the past two years the excess capacity ranged from 40 percent to 9 percent. Arguments were propounded for and against the move to seek outside tank head business, and the management committee agreed there was a paucity of available information for making a decision. They, therefore, authorized a study aimed at determining whether they should make this move.

The research firm employed to make the study has been conducting analyses for ISI's top management for many years. The company has served as a marketing consultant to ISI and, when necessary, has gathered data on which to make their recommendations. The research firm's role in this study was no different from their role in the past. The research people were called in, the problem explained, and the study undertaken. A new account executive within the research organization was assigned to the study. The report was presented to the ISI management, but was not considered satisfactory. The report follows.

Report to the Management of Indiana Structural, Inc.

BACKGROUND AND OBJECTIVES OF STUDY

Indiana Structural, Inc., is a leading manufacturer of above-ground water storage tanks used by municipalities, institutions, and private industry. The company has cold press capabilities for forming tank heads as large as 140 inches in diameter and 2.5 inches thick. These capabilities are utilized solely for the production of heads used in the fabrication of tanks for ISI's customers. This internal demand, however, is not sufficient to insure full utilization of these facilities.

It is ISI's feeling that existing excess press capacity might efficiently and profitably be put to work by entering the commercial tank head market. This market consists of steel plate and tank fabricators. They produce a variety of tanks requiring dished or curved tank heads as opposed to flat, steel plate ends.

These steel plate tank fabrication companies utilize two processes in the forming of larger diameter heads—flanging and spinning. Both processes generally are more economical for small production runs than is cold pressing, the method employed by ISI. However, as runs approach and exceed 40 heads, the break-even point for cold pressing is reached. Thus, in larger runs the cost per cold-pressed head is less than with competitive processes because fixed costs comprise a relatively larger portion of production expenses.

In order to determine the opportunity and advisability of entering the commercial tank head market, ISI has authorized a study among tank fabricators and manufacturers of other equipment utilizing tank heads.

The specific objectives of the study are:

1. To identify those segments of the market that utilize tank heads of the type produced by ISI by:
   a. configuration,
   b. diameter,
   c. material,
   d. gauge.
2. To identify specific customers within each of the market segments and to learn general characteristics including:
   a. type of heads and quantity used,
   b. customer's in-house capabilities for head fabrication,
   c. location,
   d. required delivery time.
3. To estimate the number of commercial tank head customers by volume of usage.
4. To learn the reaction of tank head users to current suppliers' marketing effectiveness.
5. To determine the degree to which the needs of the market are satisfied by current products.
6. To determine where ISI's capabilities fit into the commercial tank head market and how entry could most effectively be approached.

METHOD OF STUDY

This report is based upon a two-phase study conducted among various influences within tank fabrication and other companies that utilize tank heads in the manufacture of their products. Purchasing influences interviewed for this study included plant superintendents, purchasing agents, and design engineers.

The sample of this study was selected from several sources. These sources included: *Thomas' Registry, Dun and Bradstreet's Million Dollar* and *Middle Market Directories,* and respondent referrals. Companies included in the sample typically had a Standard Industrial Classification (SIC) code of 3443—steel plate fabricators and boiler shops. The majority of them also had sales in excess of $1,000,000. Representative products fabricated by these companies included: carbon steel and other steel alloy tanks, heat exchange and transfer equipment, chemical or refinery processing, and electrical utilities equipment.

A total of 152 interviews was obtained for this study. Personal, in-depth interviews were completed with qualified purchasing influencers in 63 companies. These personal interviews were distributed geographically as follows:

Chicago	7
Cleveland	6
Dallas–Fort Worth	8
Buffalo	3
Houston	7
Los Angeles	6
Philadelphia	19
Kansas City	7
Total personal interviews	63

In addition to the personal interviews, 89 semi-structured telephone interviews were conducted with companies widely dispersed geographically covering 27 states. In the process of interviewing, another 31 companies were contacted. However, they were not users of tank heads and were not interviewed.

The total number of contacts completed via the two interviewing techniques is as follows:

Personal	63
Telephone	89
Additional contacts	31
Total number of contacts	183

A pilot phase was incorporated to reduce the possibility of misdirection and irrelevancies at an early stage in the study. By using in-depth, open-ended, personal interviews with 25 companies, the important issues and patterns inherent in the market were examined. Resulting information provided an insight into:

1. The type of relevant information obtainable.
2. The best research methods useful in reaching the qualified respondents.

Pilot research indicated that the most significant markets, in terms of volume tank head usage, existed in the smaller 30- to 60-inch diameter range. The remainder of the market, users of larger diameter heads, was seen at this point to consist primarily of custom or job-shop tank fabrication operations. Characteristics of these larger diameter head users appeared as follows:

1. Orders were placed in small lots.
2. Frequency of orders and type and size of heads were solely dependent upon specifications for tanks or equipment by customers of the fabricator.

The volume market identified during the pilot study consisted of tank fabricators having a relatively standardized product line. A typical fabricating firm manufactured tanks between 18 and 60 inches in diameter. Primary end-use areas for these products were water treatment, liquefied petroleum gas, truck fuel, and other types of storage tanks. An interesting characteristic of these volume users of small diameter tank heads was that the typical delivery time expected for in-stock heads ranged from one day to a maximum of three weeks. Approximately 65 percent expected delivery within a period of one week. Deliveries expected for special order heads within this same size range varied from one week to eight weeks. About 60 percent expected delivery within four to five weeks and approximately 35 percent expected delivery by the end of three weeks.

Although this segment appeared to be the only volume market in terms of total head usage and large order lot sizes, it was felt that ISI's capabilities were not compatible with the needs of the market for the following reasons:

1. ISI's tank head forming capabilities were competitive in terms of cost only for heads larger than 60 inches and in runs of approximately 40 or more.
2. Short delivery times required for under 60-inch heads were not within the company's capabilities.

Thus, it was decided that the study should be directed toward those market segments requiring heads 60 inches in diameter and larger.

The final phase of the study consisted of the in-depth, personal interviews with 38 companies and semi-structured, telephone interviews with 89 separate companies. Interviews were completed only with those fabricators using heads 60 inches or larger in diameter. If a company used heads smaller than 60 inches, this fact was noted; however, the respondent was questioned only about specific usage in the larger diameter ranges. This procedure was followed to reduce the difficulty of obtaining specific data for the broad range of head sizes that may be used by typical custom fabricators whose requirements are determined by their customers' design specifications.

Interviews were pursued primarily with companies belonging to the 3443 SIC group because few companies outside this category were volume head users.

SUMMARY OF THE FINDINGS

1. Of the 152 tank head users interviewed, approximately two thirds (102 companies) had some requirements for tank heads 60 inches in diameter and larger. The vast majority of these users belonged to SIC group 3443. They typically were tank fabrication and engineering firms doing custom or job shop fabrication. No definitive market segments in terms of head usage were apparent among these users of larger diameter heads.
2. Usage of tank heads among the 102 larger diameter users can be broken down as follows:
   a. Hemispherical heads 60 inches and larger were used by 40 percent of the fabricators.
   b. Elliptical heads of the same size were used by 75 percent.
   c. ASME Code F & D heads were used by 82 percent.
   d. Standard F & D heads were used by 49 percent.
3. Total yearly usage of these heads generally did not exceed 50 for either the 60- to 80-inch or 90- to 130-inch diameter ranges. Furthermore, approximately two thirds of these use categories consisted of less than 25 heads per year. ASME Code F & D heads were the only ones that enjoyed usage in higher quantities. However, there were virtually no firms that used more than 250 of these heads.
4. Regardless of the type or size of head ordered, lot sizes were small. Approximately 65 to 75 percent of all orders placed consisted of lot sizes of five units or less. An additional 15 to 23 percent of the orders consisted of six to ten units, meaning that 90 percent of all orders were for less than ten units.
5. Required delivery time for in-stock heads was typically less than three weeks. For special order heads, 60 to 89 inches and 90 to 130 inches, required delivery was four to five weeks and four to seven weeks, respectively.
6. It is estimated that a total of 400 establishments are users of tank heads 60 inches in diameter and larger.

7. Approximately 65 percent of all tank head customers indicated that they were serviced directly by factory technical representatives (Table 15). Distributor servicing was cited by 22 percent and local sales servicing by 36 percent. Distributor and local sales servicing were most prevalent in the Southwest. The East depended more heavily on local sales organizations. It appears, however, that factory servicing will remain the principal sales method within the industry.

8. The marketing and servicing effectiveness of suppliers is generally good. The vast majority appeared completely satisfied with all aspects of servicing. Only 21 out of 102 companies had some complaint about suppliers. Slow delivery times represented 17 of these complaints. Poor fitting tolerances were mentioned by four respondents; however, two of these indicated that it was a significant problem. Three mentioned a need for better cleaning of heads.

9. Generally, the needs of this market are being satisfied by products currently available. The most important criteria for the purchase of heads seemed to be availability and cost. Pricing within the industry appears very competitive for the more standard sizes of heads. Where special materials and sizes were used, pricing varied greatly. Availability of heads is an area that could be improved. Hemispherical heads, for example, were said to be difficult to obtain when needed. This same situation existed with other special order heads in the larger sizes. Demand for close fitting tolerances does not appear to be great. Current product tolerances were perceived by the majority of respondents to be sufficient for most of the job shop type of fabricators.

DISCUSSION OF THE FINDINGS

Market Segments

There does not appear to be any stereotyped segmentation of tank head usage by specific configuration, diameter, material, and gauge in the larger diameter heads. The general pattern is usage of all four types of tank heads for pressure vessels and tanks, heat exchange and transfer equipment, and utilities' tanks and equipment. The most prevalent material is carbon steel with stainless steel following with a very small use percentage. Some of the other materials used in very small quantities are nickel, other steel alloys, aluminum, and titanium. For those heads not produced by ISI, other market segments are discernable:

1. Truck tanks are 60″ to 90″ elliptical and ASME Code F & D heads that are generally 12- to 8-gauge carbon and stainless steel.
2. High pressure boiler and steam drums are 30″ to 90″ hemispherical, elliptical, and ASME Code F & D heads that range in thickness from 2″ to 8″ carbon steel and steel alloys.

Head Usage

Hemispherical Heads

Forty percent of the firms using heads larger than 60 inches have requirements for hemispherical heads (Table 1). Total yearly usage for these heads is not great. For heads 60″ to 89″ and 90″ to 130″ total usage is 50 or fewer heads per year for virtually all of the user companies (Table 2).

The majority of these use less than 25 hemispherical heads yearly. Several companies are recorded as using between 100 and 500 of these heads. Three of these companies form their own hemispherical heads in-house.

Thus, usage of hemispherical heads is not great by those companies buying from head suppliers.

Table 1 Companies Using Hemispherical Heads

	Percentage of Companies Using Heads 60″ and Larger
Use hemispherical heads	40%
Do not use hemispherical heads	60
Number of companies	(102)

Table 2 Volume Usage of Hemispherical Heads

Number of Hemispherical Heads Used Per Year	Percentage of Companies Requiring Heads With These Diameters		
	60″ to 89″	90″ to 130″	Over 130″
1– 25	22%	16%	13%
26– 50	14	14	13
51–100	—	1	—
101–250	—	2	—
251–500	3	—	—
None Used	61	67	74
Number of companies	(102)	(102)	(102)

Elliptical Heads

Elliptical heads are used by three fourths of the fabricators of larger diameter tanks (Table 3). Virtually all of these fabricators use fewer than 100 elliptical heads in a year (Table 4). Usage is greatest in the 60″ to 89″ range with 52 percent of the companies using less than 100 heads. The 90″ to 130″ range includes approximately 55 percent of the firms using less than 100 heads. In both size categories, however, 45 percent and 43 percent, respectively, use fewer than 25 heads per year. Use in excess of 250 heads per year amounts to only 3 percent of the companies interviewed. In-house forming is not as extensive in elliptical heads. Two firms form approximately 200 heads per year. One company purchases nearly 750 elliptical heads.

Table 3 Companies Using Elliptical Heads

	Percentage of Companies Using Heads 60″ and Larger
Use elliptical heads	75%
Do not use elliptical heads	25
Number of companies	(102)

Table 4 Volume Usage of Elliptical Heads

Number of Elliptical Heads Used Per Year	Percentage of Companies Requiring Heads With These Diameters		
	60″ to 89″	90″ to 130″	Over 130″
1– 25	45%	43%	40%
26– 50	10	10	3
51–100	7	2	—
101–250	3	1	—
251–500	1	2	—
More than 500	2	1	—
None	32	41	57
Number of companies	(102)	(102)	(102)

ASME Code F & D Heads

ASME Code F & D heads are the most utilized heads in the market. Eighty-two percent of larger diameter tank fabricators use these heads (Table 5). Seventy-two percent of these companies use up to 250 heads between 60″ and 89″ while 60 percent of them use up to 250 heads between 90″ and 130″ (Table 6). Approximately half of the companies in each of these groups use fewer than 25 heads per year; however, usage is fairly evenly distributed between groups of 26 through 250 heads. The companies using between 251 and in excess of 1,000 heads amount to approximately 4 percent. In-house forming does not appear to be prevalent for ASME Code F & D heads.

Table 5 Companies Using ASME Code F & D Heads

	Percentage of Companies Using Heads 60" and Larger
Use ASME Code F & D Heads	82%
Do not use ASME Code F & D heads	18
Number of companies	(102)

Table 6 Volume Usage of ASME Code F & D Heads

Number of ASME Code F & D Heads Used Per Year	Percentage of Companies Requiring Heads With These Diameters		
	60" to 89"	90" to 130"	Over 130"
1– 25	38%	35%	42%
26– 50	14	13	2
51–100	10	7	1
101–250	10	5	1
251–500	1	1	—
More than 500	3	1	—
None	24	38	64
Number of companies	(102)	(102)	(102)

Standard F & D Heads

Approximately half of the larger diameter tank fabricators are users of Standard F & D heads (Table 7). Usage is nearly equal in the 60" to 89" and 90" to 130" diameter ranges. About 30 percent of these companies are users of up to 100 heads per year with more than half of these using fewer than 25 heads annually (Table 8). In the 60" to 89" range, 101–250 and 251–500 are used by 5 percent and 3 percent of the companies, respectively. Usage in excess of 250 heads is quite small for both groups. There is a certain amount of in-house forming conducted for Standard F & D heads.

Table 7 Companies Using Standard F & D Heads

	Percentage of Companies Using Heads 60″ and Larger
Use Standard F & D heads	49%
Do not use Standard F & D heads	51
Number of companies	(102)

Table 8 Volume Usage of Standard F & D Heads

Number of Standard F & D Heads Used Per Year	Percentage of Companies Requiring Heads With These Diameters		
	60″ to 89″	90″ to 130″	Over 130″
1– 25	23%	24%	15%
26– 50	5	5	2
51–100	2	3	1
101–250	5	1	—
251–500	3	—	—
More than 500	1	1	—
None	61	66	82
Number of companies	(102)	(102)	(102)

Typical Order Size

To improve insight into tank head usage and purchase requirements, Table 9 has been constructed. It illustrates the percentage of typical order lot sizes for all companies involved in the study. Regardless of the type of head ordered, 64 to 75 percent of order lot sizes consist of five units or less. Orders of six to ten units occur only 15 to 23 percent of the time. This means that approximately 90 percent of all orders never exceed ten units.

Lot sizes for ASME Code and Standard F & D heads are slightly better than for hemispherical and elliptical heads. However, the difference is not significant. These data would appear to support the contention that the majority of users of heads 60″ and larger are custom shops generally ordering as need dictates.

Table 9 Typical Order Size for Heads 60" and Larger

	Percentage of Orders Placed			
Quantities Ordered	Hemispherical	Elliptical	ASME Code F & D	Std. F & D
1– 5	77%	70%	64%	66%
6–10	15	20	23	23
11–15	4	3	3	2
16–20	4	3	3	5
More than 20	—	4	7	4
Total number of orders	(27)	(59)	(61)	(40)

Required Delivery Time

Virtually all stock heads between 60" and 130" are expected to be delivered before the end of two to three weeks (Table 10). The bulk of heads in the 60" to 89" range are expected within a week. It appears that the few stock heads in this largest size range do not typically exceed 96 inches.

Delivery of special order heads 60" to 89" in diameter is generally expected within a period of two to seven weeks. The majority of these customers appear to demand a four- to five-week cycle (Table 11). For 90" to 130" heads approximately 86 percent of the fabricators expect delivery within a four- to seven-week period. Only 7 percent expect two- to three-week service, while 7 percent do not look for their heads until eight or more weeks have elapsed.

Table 10 Expected Delivery Times for Stock Heads

	Percentage of Companies Requiring Stock Heads in These Size Ranges		
Delivery Time	60" to 89"	90" to 130"	Over 130"
1 Week or less	88%	69%	64%
2–3 Weeks	10	10	20
4–5 Weeks	1	8	10
6–8 Weeks	1	13	6
Number of respondent companies	(52)	(42)	(27)

Table 11 Expected Delivery Times For Special Order Heads

Delivery Time	Percentage of Companies Requiring Special Order Heads of These Size Ranges			
	30″ to 59″	60″ to 89″	90″ to 130″	Over 130″
1 Week	8%	2%	—	—
2–3 Weeks	44	15	7%	5%
4–5 Weeks	46	66	20	40
6–7 Weeks	2	10	66	50
8 Weeks or longer	—	7	7	5
Number of respondent companies	(84)	(90)	(42)	(20)

Estimated Size of the Market

The initial hypothesis concerning users of tank heads was that the vast majority would be members of the Standard Industrial Classification (SIC) group 3443—steel plate fabricators and boiler shops. This hypothesis was found to be correct.

Although some companies not listed under the 3443 SIC code are tank head users, their significance to total head usage does not appear to be great. Therefore, in estimating the number of firms in various usage categories, data from the Census of Manufacturers concerning employment size of boiler shops, SIC 3443, have been utilized as the base point.

In Table 12, column two (adjusted for nonhead usage), is an estimate of the number of plants using tank heads in the fabrication of their products. Establishments having fewer than nine employees were completely eliminated as users of tank heads because experience of contacts with very small shops gave substantial indications that very few, if any, have any requirements for heads of the type produced by ISI. Shops in the 10 through 250 employee range were estimated by a 65:35 ratio with the former representing tank head users and the latter nonusers. Establishments in the remaining two categories were estimated with a 70:30 ratio. These ratios were developed by evaluating the number of companies classified as 3443 that could be eliminated by inspection of their description and combining them with those interview contacts that proved companies to be nonusers of tank heads.

The third column in Table 12 (adjusted to usage of heads over 60″) was developed in a similar manner. The average ratios were determined for companies interviewed that are users of heads less than 60″ and those that are users of heads 60″ and larger. Ratios of 70:30 in terms of users of heads 60″ and larger versus users of heads less than 60″ were utilized for the categories having 10 through 249 employees. For the remaining two employee categories ratios of

85:15 and 90:10, respectively, were used. These ratios were then applied to the numbers of firms in column two of Table 12 and resulted in column three, the estimated number of firms using tank heads 60″ and larger.

Table 12 Number of Establishments by Employee Size—SIC 3443, Boiler Shop Products

Number of Employees	Number of Plants	Adjusted for Non-Head Usage*	Adjusted to Usage of over 60″
1– 4	314	—	—
5– 9	208	70	
10– 19	260	170	120**
20– 49	304	120	140**
50– 99	134	130	70**
100–249	114	60	42**
250–499	21	14	12***
500 & over	28	19	17****
Total plants	(1383)	(583)	(401)

*Estimates based on 65% to 70% portion for users of tank heads.
**Estimates based on 70% portion of users of heads over 60″.
***Estimate based on 85% portion of users of heads over 60″.
****Estimate based on 90% portion of users of heads over 60″.

Finally, the number of firms using heads 60″ to 89″ and 90″ to 130″ was estimated by projecting actual usage figures to the 400 companies estimated to be users of tank heads 60″ and larger. The results are contained in Tables 13 and 14. Table 15 presents data on sales and servicing.

Table 13 Estimated Number of Firms Using Heads Between 60″ and 89″ by Volume of Usage

Volume of Annual Usage	Hemi-spherical	Ellip-tical	ASME Code F & D	Std. F & D
1– 25	90	180	170	92
26– 50	15	40	35	20
51– 100	3	8	40	15
101– 250	3	8	40	12
251– 500	6	4	4	10
501– 750	—	4	4	2
751–1000	—	—	6	2
Total number of companies	(117)	(244)	(299)	(153)

Table 14 Estimated Number of Firms Using Heads Between 90" and 130" by Volume of Usage

Volume of Annual Usage	Hemi-spherical	Ellip-tical	ASME Code F & D	Std. F & D
1– 25	65	170	140	90
26– 50	15	40	50	20
51– 100	8	8	25	15
101– 250	4	5	20	5
251– 500	—	4	4	2
501– 750	—	2	2	2
751–1000	—	—	—	—
Over 1000	—	—	—	—
Total number of companies	(92)	(229)	(241)	(134)

Table 15 Sales and Servicing

Agency Providing Service	Percentage of Companies Using Heads Between 60" and 130"
Local sales representatives	13%
Distributor	22
Factory	65
Number of companies	(102)

CONCLUSIONS

ISI must produce heads by using specific dies for each head of a different configuration and size. Production runs must consist of approximately 40 heads in order to be competitive. Very few fabricators require the same head in order lot sizes in excess of ten, let alone a large annual volume of any specific head.

If, however, ISI feels it is important to pursue this market, one or any combination of the following strategies will be useful.

1. Locate a large number of firms using the same head.
2. Locate a few volume users of relatively standardized heads that do not fabricate in-house.
3. Locate users of heads willing to enter into die ownership agreements in order to ensure a source of heads.
4. Promote the concept of standardized tanks and tank heads to engineering firms and other design influences.

QUESTIONS FOR DISCUSSION

1. Within the context of the decision model, where did the decision makers and the research marketing consultant err?
2. Using Appendix A, Guidelines for Writing a Business Report, as a reference, what did the research consultant do wrong in preparing the report?
3. How would you go about rewriting this report? (Your instructor may choose to require you to rewrite it.)

Juice-Ade, Inc.

Juice-Ade, Inc., is a regional bottler of soft drinks, with distribution in Illinois, Iowa, Missouri, southern Minnesota, and southern Wisconsin. The company was organized during the late 1960s by Jeanne White and Lillian Juleman, former sales representatives for a cola company.

The company has shown substantial growth from its humble beginnings when White and Juleman were confident that they could "out-market" the major soft drink companies. Their reasoning was that mass bottlers of cola and other soft drinks were often too unwieldy for effective applications of marketing effort and that, with an acceptable formula for their product, Juice-Ade could develop into a highly profitable venture.

The company's founders did not contend at any time that they could outspend the mass bottlers in terms of advertising dollars. Instead, they felt they could conduct a more efficient marketing program and, in time, outsell the major brands in their region. To what they hoped would be a successful advertising effort they added their own knowledge of distribution. Thus, during the first several years of the company's life they were personally involved in establishing relationships with dealers of all types and developing an aggressive sales organization.

Sales last year amounted to $22 million, with profits of $2.1 million. Juice-Ade had grown considerably indeed! White, the company's president, and Juleman, executive vice-president, were no longer active in the day-to-day distribution problems. They did, however, perform the role of an advertising committee inasmuch as this marketing effort was the single most important expenditure made by the company. Advertising costs during the past year were nearly $1.8 million. Both White and Juleman participated in all advertising decisions: theme, media selection, media mix, and dealer cooperative advertising. It was in this advertising area specifically that White and Juleman felt they could gain on the mass bottlers by measuring the worth of their various advertising decisions through marketing research. By participating actively in these advertising matters, they brought to bear a dimension they contended was not present in the larger companies.

That this approach was fruitful was evident by their constant sales growth and increased share of the total soft drink market in their region. In some areas they actually outsold either Coca Cola or Pepsi Cola, and with a smaller per capita advertising expenditure. Most of their advertising appropriation was allocated to spot radio and television commercials, supplemented by billboards. As billboard advertising began to come under some environmental fire, they gradually withdrew from use of this medium.

This retreat from billboards took place at a time when Juice-Ade had decided to expand its bottling and distribution efforts into Indiana, a state not yet covered by the company. As was its normal practice, the company would introduce Juice-Ade with abnormally heavy advertising expenditures. Based on past performances, its share of market would begin to plateau after about two years of marketing effort. This was true in several Indiana cities where Juice-Ade first undertook distribution. In Ft. Wayne, for example, store audits conducted over a four-week period showed the following market share of ounces sold:

Pepsi Cola-Diet Pepsi	28.0%
Juice-Ade	18.4
Coca Cola-Tab	16.2
All other brands	37.4
	100.0%

After about a year in Ft. Wayne, Juice-Ade gave serious consideration to increasing newspaper advertising expenditures. The usual type of display advertising was rejected. Instead, some form of cooperative advertising with the grocery retailer was being examined. The purpose of the cooperative effort would be to promote a lower price of Juice-Ade in a portion of retailers' newspaper advertisements. The cooperative effort was not aimed at obtaining more distribution, because Juice-Ade had already achieved a successful level of distribution. It would, however, enable the company to secure local advertising rates, a by-product reason for cooperative advertising.

White and Juleman were interested in determining whether cooperative advertising would produce sufficient revenue to justify its use. If worthwhile, they would broaden its use to other company markets where cooperative advertising opportunities were available.

Juice-Ade was not in a position to conduct research itself, but the management thought it advisable to secure some research information because they had no way of determining how effective the advertising would be. If they did expand this cooperative advertising to other areas, it would involve considerable funds, and Juice-Ade did not proceed with new marketing efforts without first measuring their worth. More than that, the decision involved more than one fourth of their total advertising expenditure. Added to that was the possible loss of sales should they make a wrong decision.

White and Juleman had in the past used a Chicago-based marketing research firm for much of their product testing involving consumer attitudes. Juice-Ade had heard that this research company maintained a store auditing operation in Ft. Wayne. They called in Christine F. Jonas, an account representative, and discussed possible procedures for obtaining the necessary research information to measure the cooperative advertising's effect.

Jonas recommended an experimental design, specifically a "before-after with a control group." A base period of three weeks would measure the sales of soft drinks at the retail level, providing a reference point for later data. The stores in the sample would be divided into two matched panels or groups of stores, with one group running cooperative Juice-Ade advertisements in the Ft. Wayne *News-Sentinel* three days a week while the other group, the control, would not carry the Juice-Ade advertisements. After a test period of four weeks, the cooperative advertising would be withdrawn and the sales again audited to determine what aftereffect the cooperative effort had on Juice-Ade sales. During the four-week test period the 16-ounce, returnable 8-pack for 94¢ would be featured in special displays. The advertisements would be one column, two inches in size.

The purpose of the research, then, was to enable Juice-Ade to determine whether cooperative newspaper advertising should be employed. The experimental design approach was considered appropriate, and Juice-Ade was willing to pay for the extra precaution of conducting a base period audit aimed at making certain that the store panels were well matched, plus having the advantage of a double check by comparing both the before and during periods as well as comparing the two store groups during the test and post-measurement periods.

The market research firm could hold many in-store variables constant. They could make certain that no store ran out of stock, for example, because they acted as the distributor during the study. The firm's personnel had their own trucks and delivered the test products as needed. They also maintained the shelves so that display differences would not contaminate the data. The firm maintained relationships with the participating chains and independents, compensating them for their willingness to permit research of this type.

Schematically, the experiment for Juice-Ade was as follows:

	Base Period	Test Period	Post Period
Test Store Panel A	No Display	Display + Adv.	No Display
Control Store Panel B	No Display	Display Only	No Display
Week No.	1 2 3	4 5 6 7	8 9 10

In addition to auditing the beverage sales in the panel stores and designing the general nature of the experiment, the marketing research firm had the responsibility of selecting the stores and matching them for test purposes. There were two local chains in Ft. Wayne—Rogers and Maloleys. Through split-run newspaper advertising, it was possible to divide the stores into two matched panels of ten grocery retailers each, with the Juice-Ade advertisement running for the Maloleys stores in the north zone where it did not run for Rogers. In the south zone the Juice-Ade advertisement was included in the Rogers advertisement, but not in the Maloleys. Special displays of Juice-Ade were placed in all stores (control and test) during the four-week test period. The store locations and treatment pattern are shown in Figure 1.

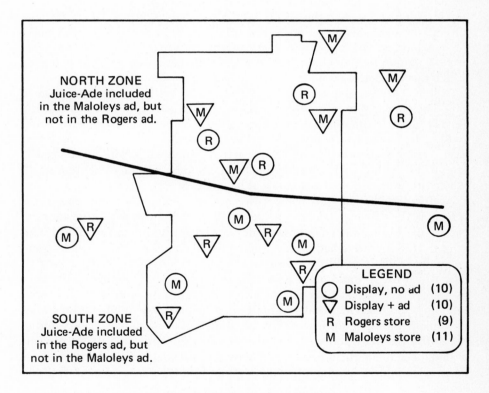

Figure 1 Panels of Grocery Retailers—Ft. Wayne Study

It was essential that the test and the control store panels be matched as closely as possible, for the obvious reason that the goal was to isolate the impact of that variable or those variables of interest to the decision makers. Cooperative newspaper advertising was the variable whose impact White and Juleman wished to measure. The experiment, then, would have to be conducted between two groups of stores that were as comparable as possible so that any sales differences uncovered between the retail panels would not be the result of store group differences.

The market research firm, which audited the sales movements of a total of 50 stores in Ft. Wayne, compiled data on each store, so that selecting outlets for matched panels was a relatively simple matter. The All-Commodity-Volume (ACV), square footage, checkouts, and the unit and dollar sales on many product categories were a part of the data bank on the 50 stores. In this study, then, all that was necessary was to select the Rogers and Maloleys outlets that had as much geographic dispersion (isolation) as possible, arrange for the split-run newspaper advertising, and initiate the data collection.

The market research firm acted as the distributor during these research studies, so comparable distribution of leading beverages could be controlled. While the market place, such as this set-up in Ft. Wayne, does offer a "laboratory condition" for experimental purposes, it is still a far cry from the physical sciences or a manufacturing operation where unwanted variables can be truly controlled, randomized, or eliminated. A list of store panels showing the extent to which this "laboratory condition" can be met is shown in Table 1.

Still another variable that had to be observed and hopefully controlled or randomized was the promotional activity of competitive bottlers. While the market research firm, through the cooperation of the store managements, could reduce the amount of competitive effort, it was unreasonable to expect that over a ten-week period all competitive activity would stop. This was especially true in this study, which was conducted from July 8 through September 14 when soft drink sales were seasonally at high sales levels.

As Jonas explained, this competitive activity was one of the reasons for spreading the data collection over a period of several weeks, with store auditing each week. In this way any unusual sales movement during one week was minimized. If the auditing had been restricted to only one week, for example, some competitive effort could have distorted the findings by introducing a variable over which there would have been little or no control. By gathering the data over a period of weeks the effect of such competitive promotion tended to be randomized. Observing what was happening helped explain any unusual sales movement during a given week. By auditing weekly sales movements during the entire ten-week period, the market research firm provided its statisticians with data enabling them to compute between-week and between-store analyses of variance, which went far in telling how significant the data were—statistically speaking.

Jonas stressed that all of these design decisions, such as weekly audits over a ten-week period and thrice-weekly checking on stock and displays added to the cost of the research. But she insisted that without these refinements they could not be at all certain about the reliability of the final data.

Upon completing the data collection, processing, and analysis, Jonas submitted a report to the Juice-Ade management. In it she elaborated on the reasoning behind the agreed-upon use of "controlled store testing" procedures in the study. She pointed out that a *traditional* test marketing operation employs

Table 1 Characteristics of Store Panels A and B for Ft. Wayne Juice-Ade Study

Store Number	Chain	Estimated ACV (In Millions of Dollars)	Store Size (In Thousands of Square Feet)	Number of Checkouts Regular	Express	Total
Panel A (Feature Advertisement)						
V17	Rogers	$32.5	12.5	5	0	5
V20	Rogers	62.5	14.5	7	0	7
V21	Rogers	37.5	18.0	6	0	6
V22	Rogers	50.0	15.0	8	0	8
V23	Rogers	52.5	12.0	6	0	6
V27	Maloleys	25.0	20.0	6	1	7
V29	Maloleys	34.5	14.0	4	0	4
V30	Maloleys	23.0	2.0	3	0	3
V32	Maloleys	55.0	14.5	7	0	7
V38	Maloleys	72.0	19.0	7	1	8
Averages — Panel A		$44.4	14.2	6	—	6
Panel B (No Feature Advertisement)						
V16	Rogers	$17.0	7.0	4	0	4
V18	Rogers	85.0	14.0	10	0	10
V19	Rogers	52.0	17.0	7	0	7
V24	Rogers	35.0	18.5	7	0	7
V28	Maloleys	35.0	12.0	5	0	5
V31	Maloleys	70.0	15.5	9	0	9
V34	Maloleys	27.0	20.0	6	0	6
V35	Maloleys	25.0	20.0	6	1	7
V36	Maloleys	39.0	14.0	5	0	5
V37	Maloleys	27.0	13.0	4	0	4
Averages — Panel B		$41.2	15.1	6	—	6

a large number of stores, selected for the specific purpose of auditing the movement of a product class that includes the brand of interest. The data obtained from the traditional audit test are often inaccurate for a variety of reasons: (1) store relationships are on a one-time basis and managements tend to lose interest or do not cooperate; (2) invoice sets describing store purchases are often incomplete; (3) data collection is not always handled by personnel experienced in auditing procedures; (4) distribution of the test product often must bypass large chain grocery operations because of their policy of refusing to permit one-time data collection activities; and (5) in-store variables are difficult to control under a one-time relationship atmosphere.

Jonas pointed out that her firm's *controlled store testing* was handled by researchers experienced in auditing and involved cooperative retailers who benefited from the continued compensation paid to them by the firm. It attempted to simulate the marketplace and held this simulation constant during the periods of data collection. She quoted C. S. Muije of Brown and Williamson Tobacco Company who stated before the American Marketing Association:[1]

> In a controlled store test the researcher deliberately attempts to control as many variables as he can. The researcher seeks to measure consumer response (sales) under known marketing conditions. In a controlled store test, distributional reactions are *not* measured. In fact, distributional conditions are imposed (thus achieving the control over some variables).
>
> The major weakness of controlled store testing is the extrapolation of its results to real-world conditions having different characteristics than those existing during the controlled test. For example, a researcher can determine sales of a new brand of soap priced at 7¢ a bar. The researcher has controlled one of the variables—price to be 7¢. Shelf positions, facings, and absence of out-of-stock are also controlled. . . .
>
> . . . if a management is considering policies in which a 7¢ retail price could be obtained, then the researcher's data are most useful. The point is that controlled store tests are designs where as many of the merchandising variables as possible are specified and implemented in groups of stores. Great care should be exercised to specify and implement realistic controls to improve utility of the resultant sales data. . . . The use of controlled store testing has markedly increased in the United States. . . . The results suggest [this type of testing] can yield actionable research results. . . . Controlled store testing is another valuable research tool.

Jonas, in preparing her report, thought such additional discussion was appropriate because Juice-Ade, Inc., had always relied on the more traditional store audits. The report, she reasoned, should devote some portion to convincing the readers that the controlled experiment data were more accurate and reliable.

After covering the study approach, Jonas then presented the data. The report revealed sales movement in terms of 8-ounce equivalents, for easy comparisons. In addition to summary tables, detailed tabulations listed sales movement in ounces by size of bottle or can. The methodology discussion explained the research design, with tables covering store selection, data on each of the panel retailers, and in-store competitive display activity.

Table 2 reduces all sales data to 8-ounce equivalents. The effect of the cooperative advertising, as shown in Table 3, is revealed as +21 percent for Juice-Ade, with the base period weekly sales equal to 100.

---

[1] Spring Conference, American Marketing Association, May 25, 1971, Montreal, Canada.

Table 2 Average Weekly Sales in 8-Ounce Equivalent Cases
(Test vs. Control Stores)

	Control Store Panel			Test Store Panel		
	Base Period No Display	Test Period With Display	Post Period No Display	Base Period No Display	Test Period Display + Ad.	Post Period No Display
All brands	10,334	13,338	8,317	9,488	13,554	7,792
Juice-Ade	1,894	6,680	1,509	1,686	7,166	1,395
Pepsi–Diet Pepsi	2,333	1,671	1,822	2,568	1,959	1,942
Coca Cola–Tab	1,590	1,470	1,299	1,402	1,230	1,311
All other brands	4,157	3,517	3,687	3,832	3,199	3,144

Table 3 Summary of Advertising Effect *(Indices of Unit Sales Changes in 8-Ounce Equivalent Cases from Base Period to Test Period)*

	Control Panel (Display Only)	Test Panel (Display + Ad)	Estimated Effect of Ad
Total beverage category	136	143	+ 5%
Juice-Ade	352	425	+21%
Pepsi–Diet Pepsi	71	76	+ 7%
Coca Cola–Tab	92	87	– 5%
All other brands	85	83	– 2%

Note: Base period weekly sales = 100.

Table 4 lists in-store special promotions for competitive brands during the 10 weeks of the Juice-Ade study.

Table 4 **Competitive In-Store Promotion**

| Week(s) | Store No. | Panel | Competitive "Specials" | |
			Brand	Activity
1–2	V34	B	Elf 12 oz. cans	Display—180 cases at 8¢/can (regular 13¢)
1–2	V35	B	Elf 12 oz. cans	Display—40 cases at 8¢/can (regular 13¢)
3	V17	A	Canada Dry 28 oz. mixes	Display—8 cases at regular price
3	V21	A	Canada Dry 28 oz. mixes	Display—50 cases at regular price
3	V22	A	Fanta 16 oz. cans	Display—100 cases at regular price
5	V27	A	Canada Dry 28 oz. mixes	Display—15 cases at regular price
5	V16	B	Pepsi 16 oz. cans	Display—15 cases at regular price
5	V19	B	Faygo 32 oz. flavors	Display—12 cases at regular price
6	V24	B	Faygo 32 oz. flavors	Display—20 cases at regular price
6	V17	A	Coke 16 oz. return	Display—20 cases at 8 bottles/79¢ (regular 8/98¢)
7	V17	A	Elf 12 oz. cans	Display—43 cases at regular price
7	V20	A	Pepsi 16 oz. return	Display—23 cases at 8 bottles/79¢ (regular 8/98¢)
8–9	V21	A	Coke 16 oz. return	Display—100 cases at 8 bottles/79¢ week 8, regular price of 8/98¢ week 9
8–9	V24	B	Coke 16 oz. return	Display—50 cases at 8 bottles/79¢ week 8, regular price 8/98¢ week 9
10	V23	A	Pepsi 16 oz. return	Display—30 cases at 8 bottles/79¢ (regular 8/98¢)
10	V22	A	Faygo 32 oz. flavors	Display—15 cases at regular price
10	V27	A	Faygo 32 oz. flavors	Display—30 cases at regular price

QUESTIONS FOR DISCUSSION

1. Without getting into detail, where did White and Juleman go awry in their approach to making the decision on cooperative newspaper advertising?

2. Why did Jonas stress the greater reliability and validity of the controlled store test in contrast to a traditional store test?

3. Why would a statistician desire to see the sales data presented on a week-by-week basis, shown for each individual store?

4. List the marketing, experimental, dependent, and independent (uncontrollable) variables in this case.

5. Assume that White and Juleman are unwilling to accept the data collected in the study as a basis for making their cooperative advertising decision. Justify their hesitancy.

6. What contribution do the data in Tables 1 and 4 make to the deliberations of the decision makers?

7. Develop arguments for and against conducting the study in 20 test markets instead of only one.

Kanine Dog Food, Inc.

Kanine Dog Food, Inc., processes and distributes both dry and canned dog food in the Northeast—the Middle Atlantic and New England states.[1] It has been the leading dog food marketer in that part of the country for over 12 years, holding a greater market share than leading nationally distributed brands such as Purina, Ken-L-Ration, Alpo, and others.

Over the past four years, however, the leading national brands were beginning to close the gap. Kanine's lead in market share was gradually diminishing—and at a time when the industry was growing steadily. Thus, while their gross sales and their profitability were showing increases, the management recognized that Kanine's decline in market share was a cause for real concern.

---

[1] Although based on an actual study, the data and brand information for this case have been altered to protect the identity of the sponsoring company.

(Market share data were obtained from the A. C. Nielsen retail grocery store audit service.)

The Kanine top management called for a meeting with the marketing committee to discuss the basic strategies that had been employed by the marketing people over the past several years. In general the marketing strategy centered on gaining a greater market share through intensive marketing efforts: pervasive distribution and heavy advertising. New product efforts were not a part of the strategy, nor was there any plan to develop extensions of the two existing products by introducing various flavors. The basic long-run strategy was straightforward: out-market the competition in the Northeast, the area which Kanine knew best and covered well.

The meeting between marketing and top management people was lengthy and at times somewhat heated. The marketing committee did not underestimate the possible long-run implications of the decline in market share and stressed the need for more marketing dollars to intensify the effort. They were able to document that the national brands were allocating increasing amounts of financial resources to advertising. Thus, argued the marketing people, more Kanine marketing dollars could reverse the market share trend.

Charles Williams, Kanine's president, retorted that such a request reminded him of the oft-told story of the salesperson who constantly insisted that more goods could be sold with a larger expense allowance. Obviously critical of the company's marketing effort, Williams continued by saying that while the national brands could be out-advertising Kanine, such an argument did not recognize the sales cost Kanine incurs in maintaining their high level of distribution throughout their market area. Williams stated in firm terms that no additional marketing funds would be made available for the rest of the current fiscal period, and that he personally would urge his management not to increase the advertising effort for the subsequent fiscal period. Instead, he contended, greater mileage must be gleaned from the present level of expenditure.

Allison Rickard, Kanine's advertising manager, voiced the opinion that the dog food industry had undergone changes of some magnitude during the past three or four years with the introduction of a wide variety of new products. Purina now had five dry dog food products: Purina Chuck Wagon, Dog Chow, High Protein Meal, Liver Chow, and Puppy Chow. Alpo was making great strides with heavy advertising support of their all-meat canned food. General Foods' relatively new Gravy Train had garnered a market share approaching 10 percent. New product formulations and extensions of current lines were being introduced almost daily and these, argued Rickard, were the true threat to Kanine's market position.

Margaret Black, a newly appointed outside director of Kanine, happened to be sitting in on the meeting. She voiced the thought that Kanine, in her opinion, had been too willing to settle for successes of the past. The company, she asserted, had not adjusted to the many new marketing moves of its national brand competition. Kanine, Black pointed out, has only two branded products: Kanine Dog Food (the canned food) and Kanine Meal (the dry product). Black said she knew of no discussion in which the marketing people had seriously considered additional items for the line. For example, she asked, should Kanine introduce a puppy line in either canned or dry form, or both? Kanine's pricing policy, Black further contended, had not been under review for at least 24 months. And the basic advertising theme ("Your dog will be more healthy with Kanine"), which had been used for three years, also had not been reconsidered.

In summary, said Black, there have been many decisions which should have at least been considered and on which, as far as she knew, no action had ever been taken one way or the other. She leveled the criticism at the marketing group that they had been lacking in creativity, restricting their thinking to the past.

Verne Eden, Kanine's marketing research manager, posed the thought that possibly the company should conduct a large-scale study among dog owners in their market area to aid both the management and marketing groups in the making of some marketing decisions. He pointed out that he was aware that not many options had been under serious consideration during the past three or four years. Such a study, he felt, would aid Kanine to a great extent.

Eden's suggestion was well received. He was asked to develop some survey plans and to come back with an estimate of their cost. This he did, and his budget figure of $40,000 for the study was authorized.

The study itself took three months to conduct. Upon its completion the report was distributed to all management people as well as to all members of the marketing committee. One week following the distribution of the report, a meeting was held to allow Eden to discuss the meaning of the findings.

The report was rather lengthy, containing some 120 pages. It was detailed, but the opening pages summarized the important findings as well as provided a brief description of how the data were collected and analyzed. The opening pages of the report follow. Detailed tabulations simply support the summaries and are not included here.

BACKGROUND AND OBJECTIVES

Kanine Dog Food, Inc., has a significant franchise in the dog food business in the northeastern United States. For the purpose of strategy planning, the company commissioned a thorough, large-scale consumer survey of the dog food market.

The fundamental objectives of the study were:

1. To learn how dog food brands are perceived with respect to strengths, weaknesses, similarities, etc.
2. To learn how the market is segmented in terms of consumer preferences.
3. To measure brand trial and usage levels within the various market segments.

4. To integrate these findings for the purpose of appraising the existing market strategy and determining whether or not the product image should be modified to produce sales gain.

HOW THE STUDY WAS CONDUCTED

The total research effort consisted of three stages. The nature and purpose of each stage may be summarized as follows:

1. *Exploratory Study* (group interviews)
   To develop a long list of product characteristics and attributes and to insure that every ramification of the dog food market is covered.
2. *Data Reduction* (self-administered by dog owners)
   To reduce the long list of items developed in Phase 1 into a manageable list and to identify those characteristics which are responsible for discrimination among brands.
3. *Final Study* (self-administered by dog owners)
   To obtain a rating of dog food brands on characteristics identified in Phase 2 and to measure consumer preferences. Also, to record brand trial and usage data.

The final study consisted of a quota sample of dog owners drawn from households representative of the northeastern United States population in terms of family income, age of female head, and city size. The sample size was as follows:

	Number	Percentage
Total mailed	2,817	100
Usable returns	2,086	74

The core of the questionnaire dealt with brand image measurements. It consisted of asking each respondent to describe a selected number of dog food brands on 19 brand/product characteristics. Furthermore, the respondents were asked to describe their notion of a "perfect" dog food. The brands included in the measurements were:

	Dry	Canned
Alpo		X
Gaines Meal	X	
Gaines Gravy Train	X	
Kanine Dog Food		X
Kanine Meal	X	
Ken-L-Ration		X
Purina Chuck Wagon	X	
Purina Dog Chow	X	

All of the brands, including the "ideal" brand, were rated on the following seven-point semantic differential scale.

	1	2	3	4	5	6	7	
1. Is very nutritious	☐	☐	☐	☐	☐	☐	☐	Is not too nutritious
2. Smells and looks like meat	☐	☐	☐	☐	☐	☐	☐	Doesn't smell or look like meat
3. Provides lots of energy	☐	☐	☐	☐	☐	☐	☐	Doesn't provide much energy
4. Less expensive than most other brands	☐	☐	☐	☐	☐	☐	☐	More expensive than most other brands
5. Consistently high quality	☐	☐	☐	☐	☐	☐	☐	Sometimes poor quality
6. Doesn't give a dog diarrhea	☐	☐	☐	☐	☐	☐	☐	Tends to give a dog diarrhea
7. Has everything a dog needs	☐	☐	☐	☐	☐	☐	☐	Has to be supplemented with other foods
8. Made by a well-known company	☐	☐	☐	☐	☐	☐	☐	Made by a less well-known company
9. Makes a dog look healthy	☐	☐	☐	☐	☐	☐	☐	Dog does not look healthy
10. Good for active, outdoor dogs	☐	☐	☐	☐	☐	☐	☐	Good for less active, indoor dogs
11. Does not contain much cereal or grain	☐	☐	☐	☐	☐	☐	☐	Contains a lot of cereal or grain
12. Good for younger dogs	☐	☐	☐	☐	☐	☐	☐	Good for mature, grown-up dogs
13. Good value for the money	☐	☐	☐	☐	☐	☐	☐	Poor value for the money
14. Contains a lot of protein	☐	☐	☐	☐	☐	☐	☐	Is low in protein
15. My dog likes it very much	☐	☐	☐	☐	☐	☐	☐	My dog doesn't like it
16. Has a pleasant smell	☐	☐	☐	☐	☐	☐	☐	Has a disagreeable smell
17. Contains a lot of meat	☐	☐	☐	☐	☐	☐	☐	Has no meat in it
18. The vet recommends it	☐	☐	☐	☐	☐	☐	☐	The vet never mentions it
19. Made by a company that is more reputable than most	☐	☐	☐	☐	☐	☐	☐	Made by a company that is less reputable than most
	1	2	3	4	5	6	7	

SUMMARY AND CONCLUSIONS

Brand Image Summary

1. Kanine Meal is perceived as one of the lowest priced brands of dry dog food, including national and local/regional brands.
2. Kanine Dog Food's image appears to be strongly tied to the profile of Kanine Meal.
3. The Kanine brand occupies a strong middle ground in terms of product quality where it is rated lower than most of the national brands.
4. Kanine is strongly associated with all-grain, cereal properties. Conversely, it is least associated with meat either in terms of appearance or content.

Market Segments Summary

1. Dog food purchasers differ from one another in terms of their needs and expectations. An analysis of these needs reveals four market segments:
   a. Indoor-pet households which are oriented toward well-known, widely accepted national brands. Consumption of dry dog food is relatively low on a per-household basis.
   b. Dog food buyers who profess to buy without regard to brand popularity or company's reputation but who want a lower priced product that is good for active, outdoor dogs. They buy relatively large quantities of dry dog food.
   c. Dog-owning households who prefer meat-oriented products and expect to pay a high price. Dry dog food potential is slightly below average in this segment.
   d. Households who want a grain product that is of reputable quality and less expensive than most others. Dry dog food consumption is very high.
2. Kanine's brand development in terms of trial and usage is highest in the second and fourth segments, as was described in the preceding paragraphs.

Brand User Analysis Summary

1. Kanine Meal is most popular in those households where the ownership profile indicates a demand for large quantities of dry dog food, e.g., households with hunting dogs, three or more dogs, outside dogs, large breeds, in rural areas, etc.
2. Kanine Meal users differentiate most strongly between their brand and leading competition on the basis of price. Price is the single, most pronounced factor separating Kanine's image from the nationally advertised products.
3. In terms of overall image, Kanine's franchise is more vulnerable to Purina Dog Chow than to other leading brands. On the other hand, Dog Chow users show only a remote preference for the Kanine product.
4. An analysis of all the discriminating attributes shows that consumers tend to judge the brands on combinations of attributes rather than on individual items independently of other data. These combinations of items may be called attitude dimensions on which brand discrimination takes place. The following significant dimensions are identified:

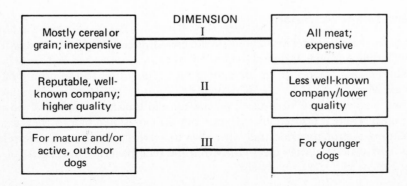

These three dimensions are the most dominant in explaining existing discrimination among the brands. Together they account for nearly 90 percent of the perceived differences.

Dimension I is relatively more important in explaining differences among canned brands than among dry brands. The largest amount of discrimination among dry brands takes place on Dimension II. A brief review of brand positioning on each attitude dimension follows:

Dimension I

Of the dry brands included in the study, consumers identify Gravy Train and Purina Dog Chow as higher priced, protein-oriented products. Conversely, Kanine Meal was the dry brand considered least expensive and mostly made up of cereal or grain.

Dimension II

On the second attitude dimension—which arrays the brands from (a) most reputable/popular, of higher quality, and well-liked by dog to (b) less well-known, of less consistent quality, and not necessarily endorsed by the vet—is this line-up:

> Purina Dog Chow
> Gaines Meal
> Purina Chuck Wagon
> Gravy Train
> Kanine Meal
> Kanine Dog Food

In general terms Kanine occupies a strong middle ground only a slight distance away from Gravy Train and Purina Chuck Wagon. Kanine Meal rates particularly high in terms of its value for the money, where it is surpassed only by Purina Dog Chow.

Dimension III

On this attitude dimension Kanine Meal and particularly Kanine Dog Food are viewed as mostly limited to mature, grown-up dogs.

Market Segments: A Closer Look

In addition to brand image measurements, the study explored what optimum values and preferences consumers hold about the product category. Hence, the respondents were asked to describe their notion of a perfect brand of dog food.

The purpose of gauging these values was to see whether or not meaningful market segments can be identified that have significantly different expectations. The hypothesis is that, if such segments can be found, they can be expected to react more favorably to marketing appeals directed at their respective desires. The analysis reveals four significantly different segments of dog food buyers:

Segment A

Dog owners in this segment, which comprises almost one half (42 percent) of the dog-owning households, place above-average emphasis on the following:

1. They want a dog food that is good for mature indoor pets that spend a good part of their existence indoors getting little, if any, exercise.
2. They need a vet's approval of the dog food since in all probability a vet plays an important role in their pets' lives.
3. They prefer a brand that is manufactured by a reputable, well-known company.
4. Pleasant smell and, to some extent, meat-like appearance carry a somewhat stronger appeal to this segment than to most others.

An analysis of usage and demographic profiles shows these distinguishing characteristics about those dog owners comprising Segment A:

1. Their per capita purchasing of dry dog food is significantly lower than in the other segments.
2. Their trial and usage of Kanine Meal is well below average. Kanine Dog Food has made a relatively better penetration in this segment than Kanine Meal.
3. They are concentrated in city and suburban areas; they are somewhat older and feel stronger about brand loyalty than most others.

Segment B

This segment contains about 35 percent of dog owners surveyed. They are least concerned about brand popularity. Their description of a perfect dog food demonstrates willingness to accept a dog food that is never mentioned by the veterinarian and is made by a company that is less well-known and less reputable than most others. To some extent they dismiss the need for a pleasant-smelling product; nor are they concerned about meat-like properties in a perfect dog food. They prefer less expensive, economy products.

Some other differences can be noted about dog owners in Segment B:

1. Their usage of dry dog food is very high, making them the most important segment in terms of sales volume potential.
2. The reported business levels for Kanine Meal are relatively favorable.
3. They do not appear to be particularly brand loyal.
4. The incidence of hunting dogs is exceptionally high among them.
5. They tend to live in rural communities, are somewhat younger than average, and have near median incomes.

Segment C

About 15 percent of dog owners fall in this segment. The benefits or values which separate them from other groups are:

1. The expectation that their preferred brand is more expensive than most others.
2. A preference for all-meat products—products containing a lot of meat, not much cereal or grain and smelling and looking like meat.
3. The company's reputation and popularity are quite significant. It is also important that the veterinarian has a high opinion of the brand.

In terms of usage and demographics, these observations may be made about Segment C dog owners:

1. They purchase relatively large quantities of dry dog food considering that their attitudes favor canned, all-meat types.
2. They are below-average prospects for both Kanine Meal and Dog Food.
3. They profess strong brand loyalty to premium-priced national brands.
4. They are older and mostly in the below $10,000 income brackets.

Segment D

This segment accounts for 8 percent of the dog owners surveyed. Their description of a perfect dog food reflects the following:

1. Unlike any other segment, they approve of a product that contains mostly cereal and no meat and which has no resemblance to meat in terms of odor or appearance.
2. They are much more cost conscious than other segments, i.e., they prefer a brand that is less expensive.
3. At the same time the vet's approval is relatively important.
4. The brand they buy must be particularly good for active, outdoor dogs.

Usage and demographic data highlight these characteristics of Segment D:

1. The incidence as well as the rate of purchase of dry dog food is higher in this segment than in any other segment.
2. While this segment accounts for only 8 percent of the households as opposed to 42 percent in Segment A, it matches Segment A (both 23 percent) in terms of dry dog food tonnage bought per month.
3. Kanine's franchise is strongest in this segment. Both Kanine Meal and Dog Food have developed highly favorable trial and usage levels relative to other segments.
4. A high proportion of dogs in this segment are used for hunting. The incidence of show dogs also is above average.
5. The dog owners are younger. The majority have incomes of $10,000 or more. Many live in rural and less densely populated areas.

Determination of Most Discriminating Items

The first step required in multiple-discriminant analysis is the selection of those attitude variables that cause differences in the perception of brands. In other words, the analysis seeks to identify those factors which contribute most to the discrimination among the brands included in the study.

Tables 1, 2, and 3 show the variables that were used to describe the brands ranked in order of "F" ratios. The higher the "F" value, the more important that variable is in explaining perceived differences among the brands. The statements in the upper portion of the list are the most potent in terms of discriminating among brands. The statements near the bottom of the list are relatively less discriminating, i.e., contributing considerably less to the perceived differences in brands.

The top statement dealing with company popularity separates the brands by a greater extent than any other statement. However, there are many other attributes on which brand images are perceived to differ dramatically.

All of the statements have "F" ratios exceeding the number required to be statistically significant at a 99 percent level of confidence. In other words, for all statements included in the study there is a significant level of discrimination among brands.

Table 1 Most Discriminating Items of Dry and Canned Brands Combined

No.	Attribute	F Ratio
8	Made by well-known company	214.8
19	Made by reputable company	175.0
17	Contains a lot of meat	170.4
2	Smells/looks like meat	155.3
11	Does not contain much cereal	138.9
4	Less expensive	130.7
1	Very nutritious	82.4
14	Contains a lot of protein	70.0
5	High quality	63.8
3	Provides energy	58.1
9	Makes dog look healthy	50.4
16	Has a pleasant smell	40.2
12	Good for younger dogs	38.1
10	Good for active dogs	38.0
15	Dog likes it	38.0
7	Has everything a dog needs	32.5
13	Good value	28.6
18	Veterinarian recommends it	24.1
6	Doesn't produce diarrhea	18.3

Table 2 Most Discriminating Items of Dry Brands by Dry Dog Food Users

No.	Attribute	F Ratio
8	Made by well-known company	220.1
19	Made by reputable company	186.1
1	Very nutritious	98.3
5	High quality	50.0
9	Makes dog look healthy	42.5
3	Provides energy	41.9
12	Good for younger dogs	35.4
14	Contains a lot of protein	33.0
10	Good for active dogs	32.9
13	Good value	32.6
4	Less expensive	28.5
7	Has everything a dog needs	26.2
18	Veterinarian recommends it	25.1
16	Has a pleasant smell	25.0
6	Doesn't produce diarrhea	24.1
15	Dog likes it	22.1
11	Does not contain much cereal	14.9
2	Smells/looks like meat	14.0
17	Contains a lot of meat	6.4

Table 3 Most Discriminating Items of Canned Brands by Canned Dog Food Users

No.	Attribute	F Ratio
11	Does not contain much cereal	181.2
17	Contains a lot of meat	180.4
4	Less expensive	100.9
2	Smells/looks like meat	95.4
8	Made by well-known company	91.9
14	Contains a lot of protein	74.2
1	Very nutritious	73.1
19	Made by reputable company	73.0
3	Provides energy	70.5
16	Has a pleasant smell	50.5
5	High quality	48.2
15	Dog likes it	40.0
9	Makes dog look healthy	39.0
7	Has everything a dog needs	32.7
10	Good for active dogs	24.7
18	Veterinarian recommends it	10.1
6	Doesn't produce diarrhea	6.2
13	Good value	4.1
12	Good for younger dogs	3.5

While the report revealed much interesting data which evoked discussion among the management and marketing people, there was unmistakable disappointment in Eden's marketing research report. Williams seemed to speak for those attending the meeting when he commented: "I'm not sure just where we go from here."

QUESTIONS FOR DISCUSSION

1. Why were the Kanine management and marketing committee members disappointed in Eden's research report?
2. Was Eden justified in requesting funds for the study he conducted?
3. How did the research data contribute to furthering Kanine's marketing efforts?
4. If you had Eden's job as marketing research manager of Kanine, would you have spent the $40,000 differently? Why? In what way?
5. Assuming Eden's data are valid and reliable, where did he err in presenting the data to his company's management and marketing people?
6. Before a marketing research study is authorized, what questions should the marketing research director ask of the decision makers?
7. In terms of marketing alternatives, state three basic decision areas already discussed by management and not developed by Eden's research study.
8. What tactical marketing alternatives are suggested by the research study?

Mario's Frozen Pizza

Mario's Foods is one of the most successful manufacturers and marketers of foods of all types. Originally best known for its cheeses, the company has branched out over the years into a wide variety of foods. The corporate name was changed from Mario's Cheese Company to Mario's Foods several years ago to reflect this broadening of its product line.

A good portion of its success stems from the systematic manner in which many of its marketing decisions are made. Marketing research is frequently employed by the various brand management groups to aid them in making marketing decisions. This effort has reduced new product and marketing strategy failures to an almost irreducible few.

Mario's Foods has a highly successful frozen food item—Mario's Frozen Pizza. This product has always had a good market share and profit contribution. Long packaged in a square box, the frozen pizza itself comes with a cooking pan. The pizza, in the pan, must be removed from the box and placed in the oven for cooking.

Currently, a new pizza package is under consideration. This new package, round in shape and made of aluminum, can be placed *directly* into the oven from the freezer. Thus, the sales display package also performs the role of the cooking pan.

The brand management group in charge of Mario's Frozen Pizza feels that the new package will have strong consumer appeal. However, there is some hesitation on the part of the decision makers regarding introduction because the new package will be a rather radical departure from the normal square box. In view of the fact that Mario's Frozen Pizza is already a highly profitable item and holds a sizable share of the frozen pizza market, the brand management is unwilling to make the decision without some evidence that greater sales will result.

Brand management, therefore, has decided to conduct a survey to aid in making this decision. Before undertaking the survey, however, there is considerable discussion among members of the management group as to the basis on which the decision will be made. A meeting is called, with Mario's marketing research director in attendance, to reach some understanding as to what the decision criteria will be.

QUESTIONS FOR DISCUSSION

1. What are the product (packaging) alternatives?
2. Marketing research managers are often participants in decisions of the type described in this case. If you were the research manager for Mario's Foods, what questions would you ask of the marketing management or brand manager before agreeing to a particular criterion (suggested by management) for making this packaging decision?
3. State the criterion for this decision with a complete if–then statement. Support this criterion by listing the factors that entered into its selection.

Piedmont Furniture Company

In April, 1971, Piedmont Furniture Company participated in the annual Spring Market furniture exhibition in High Point, North Carolina.[1] This exhibit is an important one for furniture manufacturers. To make it convenient for retailers and dealers to view new furniture items and basic offerings in a producer's line, manufacturers cooperate in displaying their wares at key locations at set times throughout the year.

Because of the costs, most furniture manufacturers do not exhibit at every exposition. Considerable intra-industry debate has taken place concerning the desirable number of showings per year, with several retailers and manufacturers now favoring just one showing a year.

The desire for one market per year stems not so much from holding down display costs as it does from the interest in keeping down the number of style changes. There is considerable pressure on the furniture manufacturer from retailers, salespeople, and the trade press for "something new." In some cases the changes are minor, causing retailers to complain about the ordering and stocking problems such changes generate. Even in the case of more significant modifications retailers sense that the average customer is unaware of them, but at least they serve to revitalize the retailer's floor-selling effort.

The premier showing for many years was the Chicago International Home Furnishings Market. However, the October and April exhibits at the Southern Furniture Exposition Building (SFEB) in High Point, North Carolina, have since taken the top spots.

As many as 10,000 retail buyers from the 50 states come to view not only the displays of some 300 manufacturers in the SFEB, but also those of furniture manufacturers in the neighboring cities of Lexington, Thomasville, Hickory, Drexel, Lenoir and also southside Virginia. The area contained by these cities is the source of most U.S. furniture. Specifically, the region produces more than 60 percent of all wood bedroom furniture, 52 percent of all wood dining room furniture, and 28 percent of all upholstered furniture.

The regional showings to the trade, such as those in Dallas, Atlanta, New York, and Los Angeles, draw buyers from a considerably smaller area. These markets are often used by the larger producers when their High Point shows have been less than successful, order- and image-wise.

In the past, furniture markets were closed to the general public. Industry leaders, however, felt that the industry needed to stimulate greater consumer interest in furniture and furniture styling changes. People were moving away from an attitude of furniture purchases being made for life. Redecoration was increasing. The trade association moved to open the April, 1971, exhibit to the general public after the regular trade show period as a test; they called it "Furnitureland Show USA."

---

[1] Portions of this case reprinted by permission from Walter B. Wentz (ed.), *Cases in Marketing Research* (New York: Harper & Row, Inc., 1975), pp. 70–76. Original version prepared by A. C. Ruppel and J. E. Littlefield, University of North Carolina, Chapel Hill.

Among the general public, there often exists some confusion about furniture style and fashion terminology. A furniture style denotes that a piece has one or several distinctive, and therefore recognizable, characteristics that enable it to be classified in some way. Implicit in this definition is the major role played by the classifier's perception and judgment. The subjective nature of styles is the major source of difficulty in dealing with them in furniture marketing. Education and experience play a major role in shaping an observer's style recognition capability and aesthetic sense. This capability varies greatly among the participants in the furniture marketing process, with the extremes represented by the designer at the "expert" end and the general consumer at the other. Any treatment of style trend patterns and opinions must be evaluated in light of this wide variation.

Usage of the term *style* in connection with art forms (of which furniture is one) came about in the 18th century. Particular styles may bear the name of the artisan involved (e.g., Chippendale) or of the patron (e.g., Queen Anne). The roster of furniture styles, like the styles in art, generally reflects a progression of *period styles*.

The main lines along which a furniture style is classified are the time and the place of origin. Figure 1 on the following page diagrams a generally accepted "hierarchy" of style categories.

Confusion often arises in the use of the term *fashion*. This label refers to the style in current favor, the one which tends to induce a great deal of emulative activity. Some people will be heard to say, "I want to be in style" when the more appropriate phrase is, "I want to be in fashion."

Similarly, there is frequent mention of the *fashion cycle,* a term representing the apparent growth and decay of different styles. Some styles peak and decline in popularity rapidly, i.e., they are fads. A few die permanently more slowly. Still others reappear with varying degrees of modification. Often a shift from simplicity to complexity and back to simplicity can be discerned. Furniture fashion cycles may be less volatile than those associated with apparel and other facets of personal adornment.

If one confines the use of fashion to denote only the currently most-preferred style, then "fashion cycle" is more accurately "style cycle." Since there are strong colloquial pressures for the former, continued use of "fashion cycle" is likely. But it is important to remember that style is essentially a supply-side phenomenon, while fashion occurs on the demand-side. And, as with all aspects of the marketplace, fashion and style are interactive.

The relative prominence that different furniture styles receive in advertisement and floor displays influences a consumer's perceptions of what is fashionable. Thus, there is the problem of the self-fulfilling prophecy. That is, on the belief that a given style will be popular, the decision may be made (by manufacturer and retailer) to display furniture lines giving emphasis to that style. The consumer, in turn, incorporates this emphasis as *one* piece of information as to what is, or is likely to be, fashionable. While many other factors, such as ego or self-concept and reference group behavior, shape the consumer's fashion judgment, the impact of actual displays cannot be discounted.

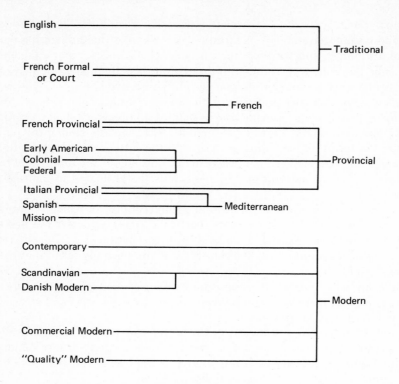

Figure 1   One Classification of Major Furniture Styles

At the "Furnitureland Show USA" in High Point, Piedmont Furniture Company's display sales group conducted a survey, the results of which caused concern among Piedmont's three vice-presidents (sales, merchandising, and manufacturing). The survey was conducted during the four days after the April, 1971, Spring Market when the exhibits were opened to the general public. Many visitors from the surrounding area toured the Piedmont display, which was unchanged from what the trade had seen—four new groups, two bedroom suites and two living room suites, plus three seemingly perennial favorites. The attending salespeople requested the visitors to complete a short questionnaire concerning their reactions to the four new groups.

What puzzled the Piedmont executives was that more than three fourths of the respondents expressed a clear dislike for three of the four new offerings. This reaction was in sharp contrast to the favorable reception given to all four by the representatives of the "shelter magazines" (periodicals focusing on home furnishings and decorations) and, more importantly, by retailers and buyers representing the key metropolitan market areas. Both of these groups felt that the buying public would be receptive to the modern styling of the new pieces. (Note the comments in Table 1.)

Table 1 Selected Data From the Home Furnishings Daily 1970 Mail Survey Among Department and Furniture Stores
(Top Three Styles and Percentage of Respondents Each Reporting Their Best Seller)

Item	First Place	%	Second Place	%	Third Place	%
All case goods	Spanish/Mediterranean	52	Colonial/Early American	20	Contemporary	8
Bedroom suites	Spanish/Mediterranean	49	Colonial/Early American	22	Contemporary	11
Dining room	Spanish/Mediterranean	34	Colonial/Early American	29	Italian Provincial	15
Family dining	Colonial/Early American	56	Contemporary	20	Spanish/Mediterranean	14
Wood dinettes	Colonial/Early American	62	Spanish/Mediterranean	14	Contemporary	7
Metal dinettes	Modern	43	Contemporary	37	Spanish/Mediterranean	14
Occasional tables	Spanish/Mediterranean	34	Colonial/Early American	17	Contemporary	13
Occasional cabinets	Spanish/Mediterranean	31	Traditional	21	Colonial/Early American	20
Occasional chairs	Traditional	49	Colonial/Early American	15	Contemporary	14
Bar furniture	Colonial/Early American	38	Contemporary	22	Modern	20
All upholstered furniture	Traditional	62	Colonial/Early American	16	Contemporary	12
Living room	Traditional	60	Colonial/Early American	15	Contemporary	11
Dining room	Colonial/Early American	51	Contemporary	21	Spanish/Mediterranean	14

Source: Market Research Department (New York: Fairchild Publications, Inc., August, 1970).

Note: In its Tuesday, September 8, 1970, edition of *Home Furnishings Daily*, page 12, Fairchild headlined the report from which the above data are drawn: "Modern Showing Greatest Growth." The accompanying article went on to say: "Unlike results in comparable surveys in recent years compiled among department and furniture stores throughout the country, it is significant that reporting retailers did not in most cases view Spanish/Mediterranean as the style currently showing the fastest growth in popularity.

"Contemporary fills this slot, as over a third (35 percent) of the stores—furniture stores and department stores alike—agreed that this is the up-coming furniture style. Another 20 percent find the fastest gains being made in traditional styles, while retailers are equally divided—at 18 per-cent—in reporting that Modern and Spanish/Mediterranean are showing the biggest popularity gains.

"Thirty-one percent of the stores feel that their customers are ready for modern, avant-garde plastic furniture. The big appeal is to a young, so-phisticated market with an eye for interesting room pieces.

"The 69 percent of the stores which say their customers are not ready for ultramodern plastic furniture find that their areas generally lag in ac-cepting new ideas or feel that this type of furniture is not right for the life styles, tastes, or pocketbooks of their clientele.

"Stores covered in the survey findings are distributed throughout the country. Of the 85 stores reporting, 68 percent classified their operation in regard to type of furniture handled as medium priced. Twelve percent were quality (high-priced) stores, while the balance carried a mixture of quality (medium-priced) and promotional furniture."

This table and quotations are reprinted with permission of *Home Furnishings Daily,* © Fairchild Publications.

The manufacturing vice-president was especially puzzled because he had just received additional data confirming the apparent swing to modern and contemporary. He was referring to the report in R. D. Behm's column in the April, 1971, issue of *Furniture Design & Manufacturing*, a trade journal. Behm noted that since tables are bought largely on impulse, they could probably be used as an indicator of current style and material preferences. His study of tables at the winter (January, 1971) market in Chicago revealed that contemporary/modern was up almost a fifth from its 23.4 percent showing at the October, 1970, market (see Table 2).

Table 2 Relative Representation of Styles in Table Groups Displayed at Chicago Winter Market, January, 1971

Styles	Percentage
Early American/Colonial	27.1 %
Contemporary/Modern	27.0
Spanish	19.6
Italian	11.6
French (including Court)	9.3
English	5.4
Total	100.0 %
Number of groups represented	1,341

Source: R. D. Behm, "Winter Survey Indicates Wood Choices for Tables." *Furniture Design & Manufacturing* (April, 1971), pp. 24, 26.

Note: The groups classified were those of 50 table manufacturers and of major table-producing case-goods manufacturers.

The origin of Piedmont's new product groups went back six months before the Spring Market when the top management group met to review product line performance piece by piece. Their prime internal data source was the firm's computerized sales and inventory status reports. Five groups and seven miscellaneous pieces were designated for dropping. The available stock for three of the five collections would be exhausted within a reasonable time at the anticipated rates. The other two were put down for close-out discussions with the major retail chains. Concerned with holding down the size of the overall line, the executives tentatively decided to add only four new groups to replace the five culled out. To determine where to add the four, Piedmont management next examined its offerings in terms of price categories and major style-design clusters. A matrix, or cross-tabulation, was used (Figure 2) showing not only the firm's offerings but those of prime competitors as well. The questions now were what to add and where. It was quite clear that dining room units were well covered. "Besides," observed the vice-president for merchandising,

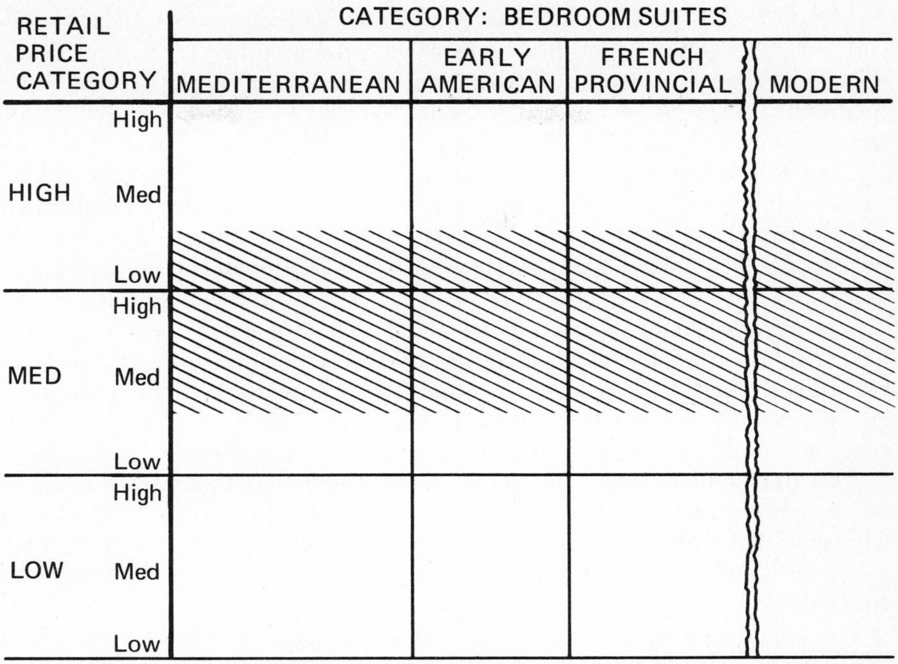

Note: The offerings of Piedmont and competing producers are listed in the appropriate cells
to uncover gaps in the various lines and so reveal possible market opportunities.
Piedmont produces in the cross-hatched area.

**Figure 2 Format of Piedmont Furniture Company's Matrix Analysis
of Furniture Lines**

"the growing trend toward apartment and other multiunit dwellings has made
the formal dining area less significant. We have to start turning out collections
appropriate to these developments."

The manufacturing vice-president stated that Piedmont's competitors were
planning some introductions in the top price segment of the medium-price category. He felt that Piedmont should try to come in first below them. He was
confident that his plants—the case-goods unit at Hartwick and the upholstery
facility at Dunn—could hold down costs on any new run.

The sales vice-president recounted her impressions from her recent visit to
the last European Design Show at Milan, and observed that in line with the
growing proportion of young marrieds and the apartment boom, Piedmont had
best bring out some modern items. This too received agreement. The meeting
adjourned with a decision to have the staff designers prepare some sketches.

The preliminary drawings, when presented at the next meeting, did not generate much enthusiasm among the executives. At the suggestion of the sales
head, they decided to bring in a freelance designer, one who was familiar with
European design trends and sensitive to developments in furniture retailing in
major U.S. cities.

The next set of sketches was well received and management had little difficulty in picking two bedroom and two living room groups for further development. Prototype pieces representative of each group were prepared and
Piedmont brought its six regional sales managers in for a one-day review of the
results. They were generally enthusiastic, but quick to point out that the designs would not do well in less-urbanized areas. The manager from the Northeast wanted to see a new bedroom suite in Mediterranean. Management
agreed that Mediterranean had been a strong contender longer than expected,
but, citing their matrix analysis, they felt that Piedmont had sufficient coverage.

One other regional salesperson remarked that now would be the time to
have a company-owned retail operation where the new designs could be tried
out on customers. Several major U.S. furniture firms were contemplating such
an approach to product development. A firm in England had actually been
running such an operation. Piedmont, of course, had noted these developments
but was reluctant to make any move on two counts: (1) there was the risk of
having new designs displayed at a test store copied by the lower price producers
who specialized in imitation; and (2) if any consumer research were needed,
Piedmont's advertising agency could handle it or find a marketing research firm
that would.

The advertising agency was called in next. Its job was to start formulating
the campaign around the new collections and to provide some layouts for showing to key customers. This step was the final one in the review process before
going to the market.

Piedmont then flew selected dealers into its plant locations to scrutinize the
contemplated offerings. These people were often quite blunt, but they brought
valuable knowledge based on their day-to-day contact with furniture shoppers.

The people from the agency were pleased to see Piedmont taking a new tack
in its offerings. The dealers were also delighted, especially when they noted the
promotional support that Piedmont was planning to provide. A few minor
modifications were suggested, subsequently made, and Piedmont proceeded to
prepare for the upcoming Spring Market at High Point.

Reflecting on staff advice, the sales vice-president decided not only to try to
record retail buyer comments on the new groups, but also to poll the general
public when they passed through the exhibit during "Furnitureland Show
USA." The merchandising vice-president suggested that, in addition to getting
consumer reactions, Piedmont should try to get some data on furniture purchase plans and shopping behavior. The advertising agency was therefore asked
to prepare an attractive questionnaire and a brochure for use at the open
house.

The response to Piedmont's survey was greater than anticipated. The tabulation of preferences regarding the four new groups took half a day and yielded
the puzzling results described earlier.

Piedmont was not the only firm that polled the public at the "Furnitureland
Show USA" during the four days and three nights. Burris Industries, Inc., permitted visitors to register for reclining chairs of their choice (first, second, third)

which were given away as prizes in a drawing. Stanley Furniture Company also used a questionnaire.

Another poll was taken during the show by a furniture industry trade group, the American Walnut Manufacturers Association. Since 1934 the AWMA (which merged with the Fine Hardwoods Manufacturers Association in 1971) had conducted surveys of the items displayed at major furniture markets. Up until 1967 the surveys were conducted in January and June at the Chicago Markets; since that time compilations have been made for the major showings in High Point, North Carolina.

Table 3 summarizes historical data for the style portion of the AWMA survey. These surveys are perhaps more correctly termed "censuses" for they count and classify all furniture on display. Classification is made of suites by wood type, by style, and by finish.

Table 3 Recap of AWMA Survey Results Regarding Style Prominence at Major Furniture Markets

Year	Modern	Early American & Colonial	Italian & Spanish	French	English	Miscellaneous
1935	36%	16%	5%	9%	25%	9%
1940	27	17	3	12	33	8
1945	37	15	3	6	27	12
1950	48	14	4	8	17	9
1955	60	15	7	10	6	2
1960	48	26	8	13	3	2
1961	39	32	12	13	3	1
1962	38	32	12	15	2	1
1963	31	33	17	16	2	1
1964	34	29	19	14	2	2
1965	31	32	23	11	2	1
1966	26	28	29	10	7	—
1967	23	32	31	11	3	—
1968	19	29	38	10	3	1
1969	22	28	37	10	3	—
1970	25	28	34	9	4	—

Table 4 displays part of the actual results of the April, 1971, and the October, 1970, surveys. These figures reflect only what manufacturers have displayed to the trade and *not* what has been sold to retail buyers and final consumers. There have been no national polls taken on a continuing basis of retail furniture sales by style. The results of those special longitudinal studies that have been made at the retail level have tended, according to industry experts, to follow the AWMA data patterns, only with more pronounced peaks and valleys.

Table 4 Southern Furniture Market Surveys by the Fine Hardwoods/American Walnut Association, April, 1971, and October, 1970
(Bedroom and Dining Room Suites)

	April, 1971 Number of Suites	Percentage	October, 1970 Number of Suites	Percentage	Change in Points
Type of Wood: (Solids and Veneers)					
Walnut	305	11.2%	329	13.6%	− 2.4
Mahogany	56	2.1	52	2.1	—
Cherry	179	6.6	192	7.9	− 1.3
Maple	296	10.9	248	10.3	+ .6
Oak	320	11.8	287	11.9	− .1
Butternut	39	1.4	43	1.8	− .4
Pecan	321	11.8	320	13.2	− 1.4
Birch	34	1.3	46	1.9	− .6
Pine	165	6.1	113	4.7	+ 1.4
Prints and Plastics	578	21.3	472	19.5	+ 1.8
Painted	319	11.7	214	8.9	+ 2.8
Other solids*	23	.8	23	1.0	− .2
Other veneers*	82	3.0	77	3.2	− .2
Total	2,717	100.0%	2,416	100.0%	

	April, 1971		October, 1970		Change in Points	
Style of Furniture:						
Modern	19.6%		22.1%		− 2.5	
Commercial Modern	.4		1.3		− .9	
Total		20.0%		23.4%		− 3.4
French Provincial	8.0		8.6		− .6	
Court	1.1		.6		+ .5	
Total		9.1		9.2		− .1
Colonial and Federal Early American		30.0		27.9		+ 2.1
Italian		15.2		12.2		+ 3.0
Spanish		20.8		22.0		− 1.2
English		4.9		5.3		− .4
		100.0%		100.0%		

*Includes elm, prima vera, rosewood, teak, avodire, laurel, wormy chestnut, acacia, ash, mozambique, and other woods not listed separately.

The results of the April, 1971, AWMA poll were not available at the time Piedmont management was trying to fathom the significance of the results of their own survey at their spring showing. And, while it would be several weeks before Piedmont would receive all the orders that the furniture retailers would place after arriving home from the market, a sufficient number of orders had been written during the showing to indicate that the four groups should be cut, i.e., manufactured in a preset quantity. The outcome of the poll during the open house generated some doubt about production activity.

QUESTIONS FOR DISCUSSION

1. Why were the Piedmont vice-presidents having difficulty interpreting the results of their survey conducted at the 1971 Spring Market at High Point?
2. In terms of the decision-making process, what was Piedmont's interest in the data in each of Tables 1 through 4? In other words, how would the vice-presidents use the data?
3. Assuming that the decision makers have agreed on the product alternatives, what would be an appropriate criterion, recognizing that "profitability" *per se* cannot be measured prior to making a decision?
4. Having agreed upon a criterion for a decision, and assuming that a decision delay cannot consume more than ten weeks because of furniture display deadlines, from whom should the actionable data be obtained?
5. At one point in the case the furniture prototypes were being viewed by several regional sales managers. One remarked that the company should own a company-operated retail outlet where "new designs could be tried out on customers." In terms of the decision model, how was this comment out of place?
6. Why should the Piedmont vice-presidents hesitate to accept the data presented in Tables 1 through 4?

Pinehurst Hosiery, Inc., I

Until the mid-fifties women's hosiery was somewhat of a stable item. Basic beige was the color offering. Virtually all hosiery was full-fashioned, a type knitted as a flat pattern and then sewn up the back with a seam and manufactured in many different sizes.

In 1955 the stretch stocking made its appearance. These stockings were manufactured in three or four sizes, stretching to fit the foot, leg, and thigh. At about the same time the seamless stocking was introduced. This type of hose was knitted as a tube with no seam except in the toe. The customer now had a choice between full-fashioned and seamless hosiery. By 1957 the seamless type had gained some market acceptance, with sales of one million dozen pairs out of a total industry shipment of 57 million. The composition of the market (in dozens of pairs) is shown below:

	Stretch	Nonstretch	Industry Totals
Seamless	1 million	0	1 million
Full-fashioned	2 million	54 million	56 million
Industry totals	3 million	54 million	57 million

Pinehurst Hosiery was organized in 1947. During its early days it manufactured the commodity-like, full-fashioned stocking for women. All of its distribution was through major department stores. While the Pinehurst hose was a nondifferentiated item, it was somewhat more sheer than most brands on the market and sold at a price higher than most of its competition. The suggested retail list price was in the $1.40–$1.50 per pair range.

The company did not experience great growth during its early years. Total sales in 1957 amounted to $5.5 million on some 380,000 dozen pairs. This amount was well under one percent of industry sales. There were no dominant companies in the hosiery field during those years, with ten companies larger than Pinehurst having in total less than a combined 30 percent of the ladies' hosiery sales.

The Pinehurst management was comprised largely of long-time technical people in hosiery manufacturing. They were thoroughly experienced in the uses of yarn, dyes, chemicals, and knitting technology. Engaged in a business of manufacturing a staple item, they gave little consideration to new products, innovative marketing efforts, and distribution. The major problems of those days related to labor, improvements in raw material supply, and holding down costs so prices could meet those of foreign competitors who were making some inroads into the U.S. market. The industry was fragmented, with little interchange of ideas on creative marketing concepts.

The introduction of stretch stockings in 1955 caught virtually all hosiery manufacturers by surprise. Its growth for the following two years was governed largely by the industry's ability to convert sufficient machinery to the new process. Even so, within two years, as mentioned earlier, the stretch product had reached a volume of 3 million dozen pairs.

The Pinehurst management had not concerned itself about the 1955 entry of stretch hosiery for several years. This apathetic posture was due in part to its lack of interest in new products and also to its contention that its own full-fashioned product would not be replaced to a great extent by the stretch version of the full-fashioned stocking. During the early sixties, however, two of the younger members of the management team urged Pinehurst to enter the stretch field. Furthermore, they argued that this entry should be with a product having some unique attribute or feature. It was decided, ultimately, to allocate several thousands of dollars to their small research and development department, with the assignment to develop a stretch stocking with a differentiating characteristic.

By 1966 there had been substantial shifts in the market shares of full-fashioned and stretch stockings. From a 5 percent share in 1957, stretch had moved up to 11 percent in 1966. DuPont's Nylon was the major fiber used in the stretch products. The full-fashioned stocking had virtually disappeared, being replaced by the seamless style. Industry shipments in terms of dozens of pairs for 1966 were approximately as follows:

	Stretch	Nonstretch	Industry Totals
Seamless	11 million	86 million	97 million
Full-fashioned	0	3 million	3 million
Industry totals	11 million	89 million	100 million

This dramatic shift in the composition of hosiery demand had a severe impact on Pinehurst Hosiery, even though it had switched over to the regular seamless stocking. Thomas Parker, Pinehurst's president, stated at a management meeting that he felt the company should seriously consider marketing a new product—depending on what the company's R&D department could develop. Other management people took a similar view.

The R&D people, after several months of developmental effort, announced that they were ready to present their recommendations. The new product was a ladies' stretch stocking, but the basic difference between the new Pinehurst product and other stretch stockings then on the market was that the Pinehurst item would be *one size and would fit all*. In fact, there was only one other stocking of this type on the market, and it was made of a different yarn that was textured, which was considered a serious shortcoming.

The new development was 15 denier (like some 95 percent of all stockings sold). It could be produced in several shades and was "bag" resistant and considerably less prone to snags than were nonstretch stockings. Possible negatives were that it looked somewhat coarse when not on the leg. Also, the welt (the very top of the stocking) was unusually heavy and required longer than overnight to dry.

The Pinehurst management was unanimous in its enthusiasm over their new stretch hosiery development. They realized, too, that the hosiery industry was experiencing dramatic changes in consumer demand and preferences and they recognized the need for adjusting to these changes. The management, however, had always relied on other companies to lead the way in new product development. To introduce an almost completely new product and be cast in the role of an innovator was a new experience that was not relished by several top Pinehurst decision makers. In the past they felt secure when making product changes because other firms led the way. Such was the case, for example, when Pinehurst switched from regular full-fashioned stockings to seamless knits several years earlier.

The hosiery industry was fast developing into a dynamic field. Past consumer purchasing patterns were outdated, within the year in many instances. The Pinehurst group was in a quandary as to whether to risk making and distributing this new stretch stocking. They would have to borrow to finance the purchase of new equipment. And then there was the plethora of manufacturing, distribution, and marketing decisions to be made once they had decided to proceed with production of their stretch hosiery. The scope of the decision confronting them therefore seemed much too broad.

The company's treasurer gathered some accounting data to aid the decision makers in determining whether to go ahead or not. The treasurer attempted to show the decision makers where their break-even point (see Table 1) would be with the new item—as yet unnamed.

Table 1 Break-Even Analysis of Pinehurst's New Stretch Fit-All Stocking

Annual fixed costs, constant and programmed		$1,509,600
Profit margin:		
Revenue from sales		100.0%
Expenses:		
Raw materials	59.7	
Direct labor	17.6	
Sales commissions	4.0	
Total expenses		81.3
Profit margin contribution		18.7%

Break-even sales:

$$\frac{\$1,509,600 \text{ fixed and programmed}}{.187 \text{ contribution}} = \$8,073,000$$

Profit at $10,000,000 sales:

$10,000,000 \times .187 - \$1,509,600 = \$361,000$

Costs presented by R&D suggested a manufacturer's selling price of $13.00 per dozen. This price would lead to a suggested retail list of $1.30–$1.40. There would be no current competition per se. Cantrece, made of a special type of nylon and which at that time had approximately 8 percent of the stretch volume, was a multiple-size hose. Other competing stretch hosiery brands were Mini-Magic by Chadbourne Gotham, Clingalon by Sears, and several produced by Agilon, using a texturizing process similar to the curling action that occurs when a knife edge is run over a ribbon. However, all those stretch brands were offered in multiple sizes, in contrast to Pinehurst's "one size fits all" variety.

Pinehurst Hosiery's gross revenue from sales for the year ending December 31, 1966, was $8 million. Profit after taxes was $460,000.

Despite the management's enthusiasm for the new stretch stocking, and Parker's tacit recommendation that they go ahead and produce and market the product, there was some hesitation on the part of several finance members of the management team. They felt that a mistake at this juncture could be a disaster. The company was not prepared to market the product on a scale thought necessary if Pinehurst was to capitalize on the innovativeness of the new item. Parker called a meeting to discuss the issue and, hopefully, make a decision. He pointed out during the meeting that Pinehurst could produce the new item, but arrange to have some mass marketer distribute and sell the item on some basis acceptable to Pinehurst.

QUESTIONS FOR DISCUSSION

1. What was the function of Pinehurst's research and development (R&D) department as it participated in the decision-making process? Should R&D make recommendations to top management?
2. What were the marketing alternatives facing top management?
3. What was the purpose of the break-even analysis presented by Pinehurst's treasurer? What were the weaknesses in the treasurer's analysis?
4. Should the criterion be monetary or nonmonetary in nature? Why?
5. Should Pinehurst proceed to obtain actionable data? Why?

Pinehurst Hosiery, Inc., II

The Pinehurst management made the decision to introduce its innovative stretch seamless stocking early in 1967.[1] Because of the myriad of line decisions to be made, actual distribution was not effected until November of that year. The stocking sold at $1.40 retail and was named Pinedex. Distribution, as in the past, was exclusively through major department stores.

Pinedex was an immediate sales success. Retailers and hosiery consumers alike endorsed the new concept of a stretch seamless with one size fitting all. The new stretch yarn that made the Pinedex possible was unique. The only competing brand of a "one size fits all" stocking was made of a different yarn and the Pinehurst management had the feeling that it was not well accepted by the trade.

Sales of Pinedex zoomed to $9 million during its first full year on the market. During the same year (1968), revenue from its old line dropped to $3 million but after-tax profit for the company rose to $580,000. The management viewed this Pinedex performance as a remarkable achievement. They had planned on a pay-out period of three years for Pinedex, but it was accomplished in one year. The industry hailed the product in glowing terms.

Pinehurst's management responded by allocating additional funds to the marketing effort for 1969. A sizable consumer-oriented advertising appropriation was budgeted. A New York–based advertising agency was engaged. Additional sales representatives were hired so that department store penetration could be enhanced and better control over store stocks could be accomplished. Management was geared for a substantial improvement in its already high-level profit performance of 1968.

The substantial improvement predicted for 1969 did not materialize. Instead of an increase, Pinedex sales revenue was down dramatically to $6 million. Total company sales were $8 million. Profits for the company were off at a

---

[1] A portion of this case is drawn from an article appearing in the March, 1969, issue of *Hosiery and Underwear*.

most disappointing $36,000. Members of management held differing views of what caused the serious decline. Several management people argued that Pinehurst had overcommitted itself in terms of its marketing effort. These marketing costs were considerably higher than any previous years in Pinehurst's history, even for 1968 when Pinedex was first introduced. Moreover, these people stressed, this commitment was at a time when competition was adjusting to Pinedex by offering several brands of stretch, "one size fits all" stockings. By early 1969 several aggressive and reputable firms were marketing a similar product nationally.

Martin W. Stone, Pinehurst's sales manager, pointed out that in his judgment the company ". . . was flogging a dead horse by restricting distribution to major department stores." He presented data from Market Research Corporation of America which revealed that a relatively small portion of women's stockings was being sold in this outlet type. Pinehurst had recently subscribed to an MRCA service, a continuing consumer reporting panel that reflected national sales of clothing and related items. There were 7,500 families on the MRCA panel with homemakers reporting their family purchases. MRCA had an excellent reputation and its data were considered highly accurate.[2] The MRCA data in Table 1 were shown to the Pinehurst management by Stone.

Table 1 Dollar Market Share of Women's Stockings by Type of Outlet

	1967	1968	1969
Major department stores	20.5%	18.6%	13.2%
Mail order	16.9	17.4	19.3
Specialty shops	14.2	15.1	13.8
Minor department stores	10.7	10.5	9.4
Dime and variety stores	8.9	9.9	11.3
Discount stores	8.7	11.7	13.1
Department chains	3.0	3.5	3.7
Vending machines	3.0	5.4	6.8
Other outlets	14.1	7.9	9.4
	100.0%	100.0%	100.0%

In addition, Stone presented the latest industry sales data that revealed 1969 stocking sales to be only 83 percent of 1968's sales. This decline, stressed Stone, was coupled by a drop in the market share being held by its one and only outlet type—the major department store. This category dropped more than seven percentage points in market share in two years. "Yet this," stated Stone, "is the outlet upon which we are depending."

---

[2]MRCA data presented in this case are illustrative and are not factual.

Stone had other data, also from MRCA. These data related to sales of women's stockings by retail price lines covering the past three years (see Table 2).

Table 2 Dollar Market Share of Women's Stockings by Retail Price Range

Price Range	1967	1968	1969
$ .00– .39	12.6%	12.9%	13.8%
.40– .49	5.7	5.3	5.8
.50– .69	19.9	21.2	21.8
.70– .79	6.5	7.7	9.0
.80– .89	5.7	7.7	8.1
.90– .95	3.6	3.1	3.3
.96–1.00	18.3	19.8	20.3
1.01–1.35	13.1	13.5	14.2
1.36–1.50	6.8	5.1	3.0
1.51 +	7.8	3.7	.7
	100.0%	100.0%	100.0%

Here again Stone developed his main point—that Pinehurst was aiming at a declining market. Its stockings, selling at $1.40 retail, were bracketed at so high a level that this contributed to the Pinehurst sales and profit deterioration. Stone argued that a complete change in their distribution and pricing policy was in order if Pinehurst were in fact to survive.

The MRCA data, new to the Pinehurst management, was startling. There appeared to be little disagreement on Stone's recommended recanting of their past strategy. The vice-president of finance stated that their cost structure would allow a reduction of their price to a point that would permit the retailer to reduce the list price to the $1.35 or even $1.25 level.

Before the discussion got too far, however, Thomas Parker, Pinehurst's president, talked about the inroads being made by pantyhose. It was his opinion that the decline in the *stocking* industry sales was, in fact, due largely to the fast-growing sales of pantyhose. The miniskirt, he pointed out, became prevalent in 1967. Several hosiery manufacturers had altered their existing equipment so that pantyhose could be produced.

On the basis of the National Association of Hosiery Manufacturers' statistics, pantyhose shipments during 1968 amounted to approximately 25 million pairs. This amount was some 17.1 percent of the total hosiery shipments, keeping in mind that the hosiery industry is comprised of both stocking and pantyhose producers. Parker further contended that the pantyhose purchaser is willingly paying for more fashion and better yarn construction. "She's paying because she wants a fashion that relates to her new way of dressing. She also wants a garment that performs, that's comfortable, that fits, that *keeps* its fit. These are the concerns of our industry," he continued. "Some of the most important developments have taken place in the areas of merchandising, knitting, and fiber and yarn production. Premium yarns, such as Cantrece, Agilon, and Actionwear, provide a maximum of aesthetics and performance."

Parker's remarks were received with little comment. Stone did remark that he thought the pantyhose market would plateau at about its present level. However, several members of management saw a decline in the offing. Pantyhose, they argued, were largely a function of the miniskirt and when the style trend called for lower hemlines, the pantyhose volume would drop likewise. Parker countered with a recent survey among department store lingerie buyers: 91 percent were of the opinion that pantyhose sales would stay near present levels. He admitted, though, that fashion trends were difficult to predict and his own forecasts were based on intuition.

Ellen Hummel, assistant sales manager in charge of distribution, explained how the regular nylon of the past complicated the retailers' inventory and display problems. With the nylon there were some 16 variables in fit for women's hosiery. "Take those 16 variables in fit and multiply them by a choice of 20 colors and you get 320 variables. But with stretch hosiery, whether stockings or pantyhose, there are three or four fit variables with the same 20 colors; and when you multiply these, you arrive at only 60 to 80 units." The stretch product, of which the pantyhose was apparently an important segment, made it possible for a retailer to have a much smaller inventory investment and yet really be in the fashion business with a flexible and appealing array of colors and styles. Hummel concluded with the assertion that Pinehurst should recognize that regardless of whether hemlines go up or down, the issue of fashion was present today as never before and pantyhose was and would be an integral part of the industry.

Pinehurst's chief financial officer, W. Randolph Shenker, expressed the view that the company could not stand the strain of entering the pantyhose field and having styles and sales turn downward. The 1969 unexpected decline in Pinehurst's revenue and profit precluded any great investment in pantyhose equipment and marketing effort if coupled with a falling off of pantyhose industry sales. Shenker thought a review of their present pricing and distribution strategies, along the lines suggested by Stone, was very much in order.

Parker and others were not convinced. They asked Stone whether there were any data on the sales of pantyhose by retail price category. They inquired, too, about any surveys that might provide some insight into consumers' reactions to pantyhose. Parker asserted that "consumer attitudes could go far in aiding our thinking."

Stone responded that he had no information along those lines, but that he would go back to MRCA and determine whether such information was available. MRCA had just completed a general study of pantyhose and Stone purchased a copy of the study report. Data contained therein were presented to the Pinehurst management, as shown in Table 3.

Table 3 Women's Pantyhose Retail Sales by Retail Price Range

Price Range	1968		1969	
	Units	Dollars	Units	Dollars
$ .00– .99	14.3%	7.6%	9.8%	5.1%
1.00–1.49	31.7	23.3	27.3	19.5
1.50–1.99	28.9	29.8	31.8	31.3
2.00–2.49	11.2	13.3	12.4	14.1
2.50–2.99	6.6	10.8	11.2	17.4
3.00–3.49	5.0	9.4	5.8	9.0
3.50–3.99	1.5	3.0	1.4	2.8
4.00 +	.8	2.8	.3	.8
	100.0%	100.0%	100.0%	100.0%

QUESTIONS FOR DISCUSSION

1. Are the data in Tables 1, 2, and 3 environmental or actionable? Why? What contribution do the data make to the deliberations by Pinehurst management?
2. Based on all the information and data provided in the case, list as many decision areas (i.e., broad families of potential alternatives) as you can think of. Start each with this phrase: "Pinehurst management should decide whether to. . . ."
3. a. What is the basic, unresolved issue in this case?
   b. Why do you select that issue as being the most basic?
   c. Rephrase the issue in terms of marketing alternatives.
   d. What environmental information leads up to those choices?
   e. What criteria would be appropriate for the making of the pantyhose decision—in terms of an if-then statement?
   f. Should there be a decision delay?
   g. Assuming that a decision delay has been thought desirable by management, how "accurate" should the actionable data be?
   h. What would be a good source of the actionable data?
4. Near the end of the case, Shenker expressed some concern about Pinehurst entering the pantyhose field, and he suggested a review of the company's present pricing and distribution strategies. Parker and others tended to disagree, and they asked Stone to obtain additional data from MRCA. Stone obtained some of the information. Support the argument that Stone erred in obtaining and presenting the data shown in Table 3.
5. Assume that the following marketing alternatives emerge from some of the discussions of the Pinehurst management:

   a. To redirect the Pinedex marketing effort to non-department store accounts, with a product priced at $1.30.
   b. To continue with the company's present distribution and pricing policies.

   Prepare an if-then criterion statement and discuss how you would evaluate the alternatives if a decision delay is called for.

Relico Steel

Relico Steel has been in the steel window manufacturing business for nearly 35 years. The principal product is of the steel casement type, selling at a price somewhat above competing types, such as the aluminum and wood windows.

The company markets through distributors who in turn sell to building material dealers (including the so-called lumber dealers). The dealers sell to builders and homeowners.

For about 15 years following World War II the company's profits reached all-time highs. Then sales and profits began to slide significantly. The company diversified into other fields, but without success. The steel casement window has always been the real breadwinner.

The top management of Relico grew up in the steel business, and at one time the company was a division of a steel-producing firm. Shortly after the war the present management acquired the company, resulting in a complete separation from the steel producer.

Relico's sales and profit picture over a 15-year period follows:

	1960	1965	1970	1975
		(000s Omitted)		
Sales	$17,000	$21,000	$16,000	$13,000
Net profit	1,500	2,100	800	400
Percentage from windows	98%	97%	90%	85%
Percentage from other products	2	3	10	15

Relico did not have accurate information on how well the window manufacturing industry fared during the above 15-year period, but it was well known from census data that construction activity increased greatly since 1960 and that the Relico decline ran contrary to the growth of the building materials industry.

Figures 1, 2, and 3 show the intracompany correspondence that led to a meeting of the marketing committee.

RELICO STEEL COMPANY
INTEROFFICE COMMUNICATION

FROM: Kay Gathron, Marketing Manager

TO: Samuel Kennedy, Sales Manager
Andrea Hicks, Advertising Manager
Jim Gillespie, Director of Marketing Research

DATE: March 2, 1976

SUBJECT: Addition of Aluminum Window to Product Line

Our next meeting of the marketing committee will be held in my office at 9 a.m. on March 9, one week from today. The purpose of the meeting will be to reach a decision on whether we should move into the area of the aluminum window. You will recall that the company's executive committee assigned us the task of making this decision and they agreed that they would abide by our recommendation.

You will find some data attached which, at my request, was compiled by Jim Gillespie. These data reveal the growth of the aluminum window frame, in contrast to steel and wood.

Also attached is a report from Chris Williams, head of our research and development department. As you will see, he provides us with up-to-date information on the two new developments which have grown out of his new product efforts—the painted, galvanized steel window and the stainless steel window.

We will want to include these new developments on our agenda for it is entirely possible that we may want to go in that direction.

Please read all of the enclosed carefully so that you will be prepared to aid us in making these decisions so vital to the future of our company.

Figure 1   Announcement of Meeting to Discuss Addition of Aluminum Window to Product Line

RELICO STEEL COMPANY
INTEROFFICE COMMUNICATION

FROM: Jim Gillespie, Marketing Research

TO: Kay Gathron, Marketing Manager

DATE: February 28, 1976

As you suggested, I am showing below the trend in window frame material usage over the past several years. These data were obtained from the U.S. Department of Labor. Please remember that the percentages are based on only new non-farm, one-family homes. Thus, the use of our products in multidwelling units and commercial structures is not reflected.

	1960	1965	1970	1975
Wood	70%	65%	60%	55%
Steel	30	32	22	14
Aluminum	—	3	18	31

I could not secure too much information about our leading steel window competition. Strong Window, as you know, markets both steel and aluminum windows and their financial reports do not reveal the product mix in any way. My informal investigation of the trade revealed nothing new along this line.

You will be interested in some new information I came upon the other day with regard to the importance of various builder sizes in this country. As you will see, the large builders are not only few in number, but control a sizable portion of the entire building material dollar. The following table may contribute to our next meeting of the marketing committee.

Size of Builder	Units Constructed Per Year	Estimated Share of Market	Number of Builders
Very large	250 or more	35%	300
Large	100–249	25	900
Medium	25–99	20	2500
Small	5–24	10	9000

Some 10 percent of the homes are estimated to be constructed by marginal builders who are responsible for four or fewer units annually.

Figure 2   Memorandum Giving Background Data Prepared for the Marketing Committee

RELICO STEEL COMPANY
INTEROFFICE COMMUNICATION

FROM: Chris Williams, R&D

TO: Kay Gathron, Marketing Manager

DATE: February 12, 1976

We have now virtually concluded our developmental work on the two new windows on which we have been working for the past 18 months. This effort, as you know, was undertaken on your behalf and with your funds to enable us to offer a more diversified line to the trade.

In response to your letter to me of February 5, I am now summarizing the results of our efforts. In essence, we have developed two new concepts in the window field. We feel that both are feasible from a manufacturing point of view and would not require an inordinate amount of new equipment.

The new products can be described as follows:

1. A painted, galvanized steel window made of light gauge metal and designed to sell at a price close to that of any conventional aluminum windows.
2. A stainless steel window entirely similar in construction to (1) and designed to sell for about 50 percent more. This product, if manufactured, would be the first of its kind on the market.

Both of these products have properties that might enable them to compete very effectively with aluminum windows. Before discussing these properties, it might be well for me to review what I believe have been the major appeals of aluminum windows in recent years:

1. Low initial cost, including installation.
2. Minimum of deterioration and maintenance.
3. A marketable feature to home buyers—the modern window, trouble free, convenient.

The painted, galvanized steel window would be approximately equal to the aluminum window in terms of strength and weight. Its protective paint hot-dip galvanizing minimizes the threat of "red rust" which is considered a serious disadvantage of other steel windows, as opposed to the more successful aluminum.

It can be argued that this window is superior to aluminum from the standpoint of deterioration. Although careless handling might cause chips and thus rust, if properly cared for such a window would never oxidize and take on the rough,

Figure 3   Memorandum Detailing New Products Under Development

Kay Gathron
February 12, 1976
Page 2

blackish look of aluminum after a decade of weathering. Moreover, it has been more than 25 years since the aluminum window boom got underway and the increasing presence of weathered aluminum might make the new window all the more attractive to the builder and the homeowner, in turn.

Such a window could be offered in a variety of colors to blend with the decor of a house. This might be a feature that would encourage builders to buy since it might make the window a salable feature when showing prospects through a model home, for example.

Thus, there are reasons why this window could be expected to compete effectively with aluminum in terms of all of the three basic advantages aluminum has enjoyed.

The stainless steel window, it is believed, has the following desirable properties:

1. An absolute end to deterioration and resulting maintenance costs— of particular interest to apartment builders.
2. More attractive appearance than other metal windows.
3. At least comparable performance in terms of strength, durability, and convenience of operation with any other kind of window.
4. The appeal of the entire concept of stainless steel—something that has been presold to the consumer as a superior material—is a very promotable feature.

The major disadvantage for this window would be its high initial cost; but even this, it can be argued, is minimized by the absence of maintenance costs and a much longer life before replacement need be considered.

It should also be pointed out that although the stainless steel window would cost in the neighborhood of 50 percent more than other metal windows, it would still be very competitive in price with deluxe wood windows. Moreover, it would probably not add more than about $200 to the cost of building most houses, and it would be expected to earn a good share of that amount in sales appeal alone.

At present, our plans for these two new window concepts embrace single-hung, double-hung, and slider types. Neither casement nor awning types have been designed. Although it is not known at this time, the fact that these products might be marketed in a limited line could prove to be a disadvantage.

As of course you know, we have not attempted to determine the potential for either of these new products. However, from my vantage point, I feel that they should be well received by the trade and would justify our entering the market with these unique windows.

Figure 3   Memorandum Detailing New Products Under Development (Concluded)

QUESTIONS FOR DISCUSSION

1. Describe the marketing environment and list the decision-problems it presents to the marketing management of Relico. (Use data presented in the case.)
2. What is the central decision-problem—the basic, unresolved issue?
3. Assuming that the Relico management has decided to adopt one of the three new window types (aluminum, galvanized, stainless steel), some decision must be made regarding the casement window. Here are three marketing alternatives available to the firm's marketing management:

   a. Withdraw completely from the traditional steel casement window business.
   b. Do not withdraw completely; reduce marketing effort to near zero.
   c. Do not withdraw; increase marketing effort by three or four times.

   Criticize this set of marketing options.
4. An obvious set of product alternatives would be:

   a. Market the painted galvanized steel window.
   b. Market the stainless steel window.
   c. Market an aluminum window.

   Criticize this set of product alternatives.
5. What is the role of Relico's R&D department in terms of its assignment from Kay Gathron, Relico's marketing manager? (See Figure 3.)
6. Assume that Relico rejects the aluminum window and is now considering the marketing of one of the two new window types: galvanized and stainless steel. In addition to selecting one of those two, the company must decide on how the product is to be distributed, and at what price. Work these options on product, distribution, and price into one set of marketing options, using a grid showing no more than six alternatives. Assume that there would be three distribution choices along with the two window types.
7. What criterion would be most appropriate for the alternatives emerging from Question 6?

Smith Chemical Company

Since 1961 Smith Chemical has been located in Chase City, West Virginia, a city of 44,000. As communities and companies through the country developed a greater awareness of air pollution, Smith Chemical too became concerned about the extent to which its plant was causing odors to settle on the city's residents.

The company's management decided in 1966 to install pollution control devices. Since then, additional equipment has been incorporated into the initial devices. These efforts to control air pollution, while effective, did not completely eliminate the odor problem, and Chase City residents (with their heightened sensitivity to pollution) became disturbed by what they thought was a failure to correct the problem. Property owners insisted to the company's management that the odors were offensive and unbearable. They contended that the pollution was causing a decline in the value of their property. In addition, there was personal discomfort, which was manifested in eyes smarting.

A small group of property owners developed a petition requesting Smith Chemical to eliminate the odor. The petition was signed by more than 1,200 property owners in Chase City and was presented to the Smith management. The central thrust of the petition was that Smith Chemical had not yet solved the pollution problem and they demanded immediate corrective action.

The company management was sympathetic to the feelings of the community's residents. They pointed out to the group's leader than since 1966 they had been adding to their pollution control equipment. A substantial and costly alteration was made in 1975. They stressed that they thought they had gone as far as they could without adopting a completely new manufacturing process, which, from a cost standpoint, would be prohibitive. They had no desire to move out of the community, they stated, but continued insistence might cause them to do so. This comment received considerable coverage in the Chase City newspaper, and charges and countercharges developed.

Smith Chemical did not wish to move from the community. In fact the management was of the private opinion that the pollution problem was being overstated by the highly vocal group that presented the petition. They therefore decided to conduct a telephone survey to measure the attitudes of the Chase City population to determine just how serious the problem was in the eyes of the community. The survey was designed to measure among other things:

> Level of awareness of odors in the air
> Degree of concern about odors
> Description of odors
> Identity of sources of odors
> Frequency of noticing odors

The resident locations of all petitioners were plotted on a map of Chase City. The vast majority lived in a broad area west of the Smith plant, which was located on the eastern edge of the city. The survey itself was conducted among petitioners and nonpetitioners—all property owners. An analysis of the data revealed that there were virtually no differences between the signers and nonsigners. Thus, the data were combined.

The survey did not reveal to interviewees that air pollution was the principal subject of the survey nor was Smith Chemical identified as the sponsor. The pollution questions were intermingled with questions on a variety of other subjects, such as property taxes, busing, law and order, education, and other local issues. The sample size was 514, divided equally among men and women of property-owning families.

An important finding is shown in Table 1. Of the eight local issues, air pollution ranked sixth in terms of the respondents being "very concerned" about the

Table 1 Property Owners' Concern for Community Issues

Level of Concern	Community Issues							
	Property Taxes	Education/Schools	Law and Order	Streets and Roads	Sewage Treatment	Air Pollution	Zoning	Parks/Recreation
Very concerned	76%	60%	62%	61%	60%	44%	25%	26%
Somewhat concerned	13	26	22	25	21	24	21	29
Slightly concerned	6	10	10	7	11	20	20	24
Not at all concerned	5	4	6	7	8	12	34	21
Total	100%	100%	100%	100%	100%	100%	100%	100%
Number of property owners interviewed	514							

particular issue. A total of 44 percent were "very concerned" about air pollution, in contrast to 76 percent being similarly concerned about property taxes. Education, law and order, streets and roads, and sewage treatment all were of greater concern to the property owners of the city than was the air pollution issue.

Another question asked of respondents related to which one of eight community issues was considered to be the most serious problem for property owners. Only 5 percent of the respondents felt air pollution to be the most serious community problem. The vast majority of the property owners interviewed said property taxes, education/schools, or law and order were more serious problems. The complete findings are shown in Table 2.

Table 2 Most Serious Community Problems

Community Problem	Property Owners Holding This Viewpoint
Property taxes	33%
Education/schools	28
Law and order	21
Streets and roads	5
Sewage treatment	5
Air pollution	5
Zoning	2
Parks/recreational facilities	1
Total	100%
Number of property owners interviewed	514

Respondents were also read several statements pertaining to the Chase City community. On each statement they were asked the extent of their agreement or disagreement. As shown in Table 3, nearly half the population agreed with the statement, "Air pollution is not a problem in Chase City." Better than three out of four disagreed with the statement, "Industries that pollute the air should be closed down even if it means putting people out of work." And three out of four property owners felt that Chase City should do all it can to attract new industry to the city.

Property owners were also asked about their reactions to several types of pollution such as noise, water, and odor from sewage treatments as well as from industrial plants. While industrial air pollution was recognized as the most prevalent of the four, water pollution was recognized as a serious problem in terms of the extent to which property owners thought the pollution "unreasonable to the degree that it interferes with life or property." Table 4 on page 296 details these findings.

Table 3 Property Owners' Agreement With Statements Regarding Local Issues

Level of Agreement	(1) Chase City has fewer problems than other cities of its size.	(2) Chase City should do all it can to attract new industry.	(3) Air pollution is not a problem in Chase City.	(4) Industries that pollute should be closed down.
		Statements and Sequence in Which They Were Read		
Definitely agree	13%	74%	22%	8%
Tend to agree	32	15	23	14
Tend to disagree	37	6	28	28
Definitely disagree	18	5	27	50
Total	100%	100%	100%	100%
Number of property owners interviewed	514			

Table 4 Degree to Which Property Owners Feel They Are Affected by Various Types of Pollution

	Noise Pollution	Odor From Sewage Treatment	Water Pollution	Odor From Industrial Plants
The pollution is reasonable, although it may be annoying.	9%	12%	10%	26%
The pollution is unreasonable, but not an interference with life or property.	8	14	20	24
The pollution is unreasonable to the degree that it interferes with life or property.	5	7	11	13
Total Aware	22%	33%	41%	63%
Property owners not aware of this type of pollution	78	67	59	37
Total	100%	100%	100%	100%
Number of property owners interviewed	514			

The complete report contained additional data, but for the most part it did not pertain to the overall attitudes of the Chase City property owners. These additional data related to such subjects as:

> Frequency of noticing odors,
> Time of day odors are most noticeable,
> Type of day when odors are most noticeable,
> Season when odors are most noticeable,
> Descriptions of odors,
> Frequency of odors compared to last year.

Smith Chemical's management, after reviewing the complete report, set aside a full morning to determine their next move. The company's president told the management people in attendance at the meeting that, if necessary, they would continue in session for the full day and that all persons invited to the meeting should plan their schedules accordingly.

QUESTIONS FOR DISCUSSION

1. If you were part of the management attending the meeting called by Smith Chemical's president, what would you recommend to be done?
2. Is the survey information environmental or actionable?
3. What environmental information was available to the Smith Chemical management prior to the conduct of the telephone opinion survey?
4. Assuming that the Smith Chemical management had formulated the alternatives before they authorized the opinion study, what could these alternatives have been?
5. Develop an if-then criteria statement for a given set of alternatives agreed upon by the management.
6. Should Smith Chemical have given thought to the attitudes of any particular segment of the Chase City population other than "property owners"? If so, how would this affect the criteria statement?
7. Assume that the telephone opinion survey had been conducted after the alternatives and criteria had been agreed upon—actionable data. What information in the survey would have aided the company's decision makers in carrying out some future action along public relations lines?

Southeastern Meat Products, I

For more than 30 years Southeastern Meat Products has been successfully packing and selling bacon, ham, and pork products in the southeastern section of the country. The packing plant is located in Emporia, Virginia, and the company's 24 salespeople cover southern Virginia, North Carolina, South Carolina, and most of Georgia including Atlanta.

The company's growth over the past six years had leveled off after consistent growth during most of its corporate life. Over the years, Charles MacMillan, Southeastern's president, had considered several suggestions for increasing growth, but each one seemed to require more capital than appeared feasible. Moreover, MacMillan was not aggressive and tended to settle for a plateau in profits rather than risk losses in new ventures. The company was closely held, and there was no stockholder pressure for increased profits.

Southeastern Meat Products' best selling and most profitable item was its bacon line, branded Southern Bacon. The brand had developed a strong consumer franchise and the national brands, even with all their advertising, were unable to make significant inroads into Southeastern's market share. Over the past eight years the bacon product had contributed nearly 40 percent to Southeastern's total profitability.

While attending a packer convention in Chicago, MacMillan heard of a bacon substitute which was being marketed in the Middle West. The product simulated the form, texture, and taste of bacon, and retailed for approximately one half the price of bacon. In addition, the substitute, according to its advertising, contained one third the calories of real bacon. Because it was precooked, the substitute would not shrink during the cooking process. It was sold as a frozen product in the freezer cases of the retail stores. The trade called it a "bacon analog."

The company originating the bacon substitute was a relatively small firm with limited geographic distribution. However, from what MacMillan could learn the product was selling well. Other than this rather general information he had no solid evidence that the bacon substitute was profitable.

MacMillan wrote to the American Meat Institute in Washington, D.C., inquiring as to whether their organization had conducted any studies on the consumer acceptance of the new product. He pointed out to the institute that a bacon substitute, if enthusiastically adopted by the homemaker, could have a profound effect on the bacon market. He knew that the institute conducted studies from time to time on behalf of its nearly 400 meatpacker members. However, the institute responded that they had conducted no research on the product, but "were watching the bacon analog carefully." This was of little help to MacMillan, who recognized that with virtually no corporate growth over the past several years he could not afford to permit a substitute product to cut into his bacon sales.

In talking with his own management group, the possibility of Southeastern marketing its own brand of bacon substitute was voiced. This thought was considered abhorrent at first, but as the discussion continued there appeared to be merit in considering such an option. The rationale was that if the bacon substitute gained a foothold it would be better for Southeastern to be marketing the product even though it might reduce their sales of "natural" bacon. Furthermore, it was recognized that Southeastern's distribution setup through their own salespeople could be readily utilized with little additional sales cost.

The favorable reaction of the Southeastern management cooled somewhat when they realized that the company did not have the money to finance the necessary production. They could possibly obtain a bank loan, but the future of the bacon substitute was uncertain and it was thought that a bank would view this departure of Southeastern into an unknown area unfavorably.

Still, MacMillan was concerned about the long-run prospects of the bacon substitute. He pointed out that if the midwestern product sold well in a small geographic area, it is quite likely that some mass marketer such as General Mills or General Foods would either buy the company or market their own versions of the analog. In either event, reasoned MacMillan, at some point Southeastern Products would be facing real competition to the regular line of bacon should the substitute develop into a successful item for its present manufacturer.

MacMillan asked his finance people to obtain the cost of getting into the production of a bacon analog. They determined that machinery would cost approximately $250,000 and that the initial advertising program would amount to $90,000 for their four-state area, including demonstrators who would be placed in stores over a period of six months.

Southeastern's management wished to know to what extent a bacon substitute would divert revenue and associated profits from the existing bacon line. How much of analog sales would be truly new sales? There was considerable disagreement among management as to what course of action to take.

QUESTIONS FOR DISCUSSION

1. Assuming the marketing alternatives are "to market the bacon analog or not," what would be the most appropriate if-then criterion statement? Justify that criterion.
2. Under what conditions would a proxy criterion be justified?
3. What would be the principal weakness of a proxy criterion?
4. Develop the argument that it is premature for MacMillan to be thinking about decision alternatives.

Southeastern Meat Products, II

Because of the uncertainty surrounding the decision on whether or not to enter the bacon substitute field, Charles MacMillan, the company's president, suggested that some sort of consumer survey be undertaken to determine what homemakers thought of the new product. Brenda Wadkins, Southeastern's sales manager, said that she had heard of surveys conducted by the U.S. Department of Agriculture on subjects such as new products. Because this bacon substitute could affect meatpackers throughout the country, perhaps the USDA would conduct some sort of study to measure what would happen to bacon sales if the substitute product were placed on the market, she reasoned.

Wadkins was asked to set up an appointment with the USDA in Washington, D.C., to discuss the possibility of such a study. She was impressed with the knowledge and technical skills of those with whom she talked at the USDA. Wadkins found them highly knowledgeable and experienced in conducting studies of this type. The USDA officials explained to her that they would consider such a study only if the resultant data could be published for the benefit of the entire industry. The data, they said, ". . . should give the decision makers in both the public and private sectors a better understanding of the impact of these new items."

Wadkins reported back to Southeastern and at a management meeting she explained the attitude of the USDA. It was agreed that such a study, which would be paid for by the USDA, would benefit Southeastern considerably and they authorized Wadkins to return to Washington and take the necessary steps to encourage the USDA to conduct the study. Two weeks later the USDA informed Southeastern that they would be undertaking the study, which would be conducted in Fort Wayne, Indiana. Both Wadkins and MacMillan argued that they would prefer to see the survey conducted in the

Southeast, but it was pointed out that the study was for the benefit of the entire industry and not solely for Southeastern Meat Products. Wadkins and MacMillan agreed that it would be better to have survey data from the Middle West at no cost to them rather than conduct their own study and encounter the high cost of gathering the data. Moreover, both of them realized that they had virtually no experience in studies of this type.

The product to be used during the study was purchased from the midwestern firm producing the bacon analog. The study required nine months to complete. Six of those months were devoted to market testing in retail stores. Additionally, a consumer attitude study was conducted. The report released by the USDA follows.[1]

Consumer Acceptance
of a New Bacon Substitute

By
Ray S. Corkern and Philip B. Dwoskin
Agricultural Economists
Marketing Economics Division
Economic Research Service

INTRODUCTION

Fabricated foods compete with traditional agricultural commodities for a share of the consumer's food dollar. These new products are generally manufactured from components of traditional agricultural commodities and non-agricultural products. Their potential effect on agricultural commodity markets is of considerable interest to all segments of the farm economy, including researchers and policymakers in the U.S. Department of Agriculture.

In recent years, a number of firms, both large and small, have been developing the capability of producing and marketing various kinds of meat analogs. Some of the products are being used as ingredients in dried entrees for the household market. Others are being developed as separate entities, such as bacon analog bits; while others are being used in the institutional market as meat substitutes in various kinds of main-dish entrees. A number of articles have been written on the development of vegetable protein materials as meat substitutes, but little information has been published evaluating the sales performance of a meat analog in an actual market test situation. This publication provides the general public and policymakers with the first realistic evaluation of the sales potential of a meat analog in the household market sector.

---

[1] Part I of this Southeastern Meat Products case is hypothetical. Part II is hypothetical up to the point of the USDA conduct of the study. Thus, the background leading up to this USDA study is fabrication. The report (ERS 454, September, 1970) is factual and is reprinted in full as released by the USDA.

OBJECTIVES OF MARKET TEST

Objectives of the market test were: (1) To determine the new product's sales potential, (2) to compare the product's sales with those of bacon, (3) to evaluate the relationships between store characteristics and sales of the new product, and (4) to assess the product's market prospects.

DESCRIPTION OF THE ANALOG

The test product simulates the form, texture, color, and taste of bacon and can be used as bacon by homemakers. Approximately 14 ingredients are contained in the product:

Wheat proteins	Salt
Soy proteins	U.S. certified color
Yeast proteins	Seasonings
Water	Monosodium glutamate
Corn oil	Vegetable gum
Egg albumen	Flavorings
Brown sugar	Nucleotides

The manufacturer's analysis of the approximate yield of nutrients from four strips (28.4 grams) of the test product is shown below:

Component	Amount
	(In Grams)
Protein	6.30
Fat	3.10
Carbohydrate	3.30
Ash	1.40
Fiber	0.30
Moisture	14.36
	(In Milligrams)
Sodium	483.00
Calcium	2.80
Iron	0.45

Source: *Manufacturer's New Bacon Analog Recipes.*

The major differences between the analog and bacon were stressed in advertisements to consumers. The analog is precooked and does not shrink during cooking. It contains little or no cholesterol, and has only one-third the calories of bacon (65 per four strips of the analog). In addition, throughout the test period, the price of the analog was held constant at 69 cents for an 8-ounce package. Newspaper advertisements stressed that the 8-ounce package contained 32 slices in contrast to the 20 slices usually found in a 1-pound package of bacon. On an as-served basis, therefore, the analog cost approximately half as much as bacon.

Another unusual feature was that the bacon analog was sold as a frozen food whereas bacon stocks were displayed as usual in refrigerated cases in a separate section of each store.

MARKET ENVIRONMENT AND METHODOLOGY

The analog was market tested in Fort Wayne, Indiana, from September, 1968, through February, 1969. Fort Wayne is located in the northeastern part of the state and has a diversified industrial economy. The city's 1968 population was estimated to be 176,000, compared with a 1960 population of 161,800.

Forty supermarkets in national, regional, and local chains were selected for the test. For analytical purposes, test stores were classified on the basis of seven major characteristics. Three of these—average weekly dollar sales, neighborhood median income, and type of store—remained the same throughout the 6-month test. These store characteristics are generally stable over short time periods. The remaining characteristics—meat case dollar sales, pounds of bacon sold, average price of bacon, and number of bacon brands available—were not the same throughout the test period. These store characteristics usually change fairly rapidly. Since the number of stores in each class was not constant during the entire test period, the analysis was based on average sales of the analog and of bacon per store as indicators of possible market relationships.

Each store's sales were audited monthly by the private market research company under contract with the manufacturer of the analog. The primary data consisted of the sales of bacon analog; bacon; imitation bacon bits; and selected meat case items, such as TV dinners, meat pies, and seafood packs. Data on the amount sold, number of brands available, and price per unit were recorded. Throughout the 6-month test, no control was exercised over factors influencing store sales of products other than the test product.

The test period was divided into two phases. During Phase I (the first 3 months), in-store displays and stocks of the analog were checked and maintained each week by contract personnel. Intensive promotion and advertisement of the analog consisted of in-store shelf talkers, weekly quarter-page newspaper advertisements, and frequent TV spot advertisements. During Phase II (the second 3 months), food brokerage and store personnel maintained in-store displays and stock. There were few newspaper, TV, and radio advertisements. Marketing of the bacon analog was similar to that for a long-established product; that is, considerably fewer inputs of promotion and merchandising.

In addition to making the store audits, the contractor interviewed buyers and nonbuyers of the analog by telephone. During the initial weeks of the study, about 500 cards were placed in the new product packages offering purchasers a small gift for filling out their name and address and mailing the card. About 300 cards were returned, and these people were interviewed to determine their reaction to the analog. A sample of 100 people who were aware of the analog but had not tried it was selected from the Fort Wayne telephone directory, and these people were interviewed. Information obtained included initial purchase rate, repeat purchase rate, intentions to buy, problems in use, reaction to price level, household use patterns, and overall satisfaction with the product. Because of the proprietary nature of the consumer data, specific tables relating to percentage-buying, problems in use, and so on, are not shown.

MARKET TEST RESULTS

Several important market relationships emerged: (1) The new bacon analog is an acceptable product; (2) the product's sales pattern is similar to that of bacon; (3) store characteristics can be used as guidelines for introducing the product in other markets and in stores within a market; (4) promotion and some measure of control over display and store stocks are necessary to maintain a high level of analog sales; (5) in the short run, the analog does not compete with bacon; and (6) market share is only a partial indicator of potential sales of the analog.

Consumer Acceptance of the Analog

In 38 test stores, the analog was purchased each month throughout the test period. In two stores, it was purchased in each of 5 months. This consistent purchasing pattern, as indicated by store audits, suggests that the bacon analog is an acceptable product.

A further indication of acceptance by Fort Wayne buyers was provided by the consumer survey results. Users were asked to rate their overall satisfaction with the analog on a five-point scale. They were also asked to discuss what they specifically liked and disliked about the product. In general, users expressed a high level of satisfaction. The product's strongest attributes were ease and speed of preparation and good cooking qualities. A large proportion of the users found nothing that they disliked about the product.

A substantial majority of analog users said they would buy the product again. Buyers' initial and repeat purchase rates as determined by the consumer survey phase reinforce the pattern noted in the audited sales data.

Sales Pattern of the Analog and Bacon

Average monthly sales of the bacon analog and bacon during Phase I, Phase II, and the entire test period are compared in Table 1.

Table 1 Average Monthly Sales of the Analog and Bacon, by Phase, Test Area, September, 1968–February, 1969

Product	Phase I	Phase II	Both Phases
		Pounds	
Bacon analog	3,051	846	1,948
Bacon	73,772	66,932	70,352
Ratio of bacon to analog	24:1	79:1	36:1

Sales of the analog and bacon declined from Phase I to Phase II but not by the same relative or absolute magnitudes. Bacon analog sales declined 72 percent, whereas bacon sales declined only 9 percent. In addition, analog sales declined in each store, while bacon sales increased in 15 stores and decreased in 25 stores. The decline in analog sales during Phase II was associated with little or no promotion, little display case control, and distribution in the hands of a food broker. Store personnel said the slight decline in bacon sales was due to seasonal and other factors rather than to the availability of the bacon analog.

One measure of the market potential of a new product is its sales compared with those of a similar product. Total poundage of bacon consumed nationally in 1968 was estimated to be 1.45 billion pounds.[2] Since the test product closely simulates bacon, the ratio of bacon sales to analog sales provides a rough estimate of the new product's potential in the market place (Table 1). Although it is extremely hazardous to make projections based on the results of one market test, these data do indicate the tremendous market that may be available to successful bacon analogs.

Relation of Sales of the Analog and Bacon to Store Characteristics

Sales of the bacon analog and bacon were not the same for all stores in the test market. Several significant relationships emerged when sales were related to specific store characteristics (Table 2).

Neighborhood Income—Bacon analog and bacon sales were greater when the median income for the neighborhood was above $6,000. Also, for each income level, sales of both products were larger in those stores with the highest total sales and meat case sales.

Type of Store—The average sale of the bacon analog per store was greater in local and regional chains than in national chains. In contrast, the average sale of bacon per store was greater in one of the national chains than in the regional and local chains, and next highest in the local chains.

Weekly Dollar Sales—Bacon analog and bacon sales were significantly greater in stores having high average weekly sales than in other stores. However, the ratio of sales of bacon to sales of the analog was also greater in these stores than in others. This result suggests that sales of the two product types respond differently to increases in weekly store sales. These patterns were consistent for Phases I and II despite the absolute decline in both products' sales in Phase II.

Monthly Meat Case Sales—Bacon analog and bacon sales increased as other meat case sales increased.

Bacon Sales—Sales of the analog per store increased as sales of bacon increased. To a limited degree, this correlation indicates that the bacon analog is considered a new product, and possibly a complementary product, by consumers who limit bacon purchases for health or other reasons.

---

[2] Federal meat inspection statistics and Household Food Consumption Survey—1965-66, Report No. 1, Agr. Res. Service, USDA.

Table 2 Average Pounds of Bacon and the Analog Sold Per Store, by Selected Store Characteristics, Test Area, September, 1968–February, 1969

Store Characteristics	Phase I		Phase II		Average, Both Phases	
	Bacon	Analog	Bacon	Analog	Bacon	Analog
Neighborhood median income						
$6,000 or less	1,524	56	1,295	17	1,409	37
More than $6,000	2,217	99	2,022	25	2,120	62
Type of chain						
National	2,429	74	2,075	21	2,252	47
National	821	58	1,013	13	917	35
Local	2,160	84	1,729	27	1,944	55
Local	2,171	91	2,126	25	2,149	58
Regional	1,344	58	1,171	16	1,257	37
Average weekly sales						
$39,999 or less	1,160	53	1,044	15	1,102	34
$40,000–$60,000	2,124	80	1,915	24	2,020	52
More than $60,000	3,061	123	2,776	33	2,919	78
Other meat case sales						
$100 or less	672	38	757	10	714	24
$101–$200	1,869	68	1,597	19	1,733	44
Greater than $200	2,561	105	2,271	29	2,416	67
Bacon sales (pounds)						
1,000 or less	1,829	30	421	7	1,125	18
1,001–2,000	1,444	66	1,429	19	1,436	40
2,001–3,000	2,445	95	2,425	30	2,435	63
More than 3,000	3,501	132	3,435	38	3,468	85
Average price/lb. bacon						
75¢ or less	1,829	69	1,662	20	1,745	44
76¢–80¢	1,842	71	1,650	19	1,746	45
81¢–85¢	2,029	89	1,664	22	1,846	56
More than 85¢	1,552	73	1,535	21	1,543	47
Brands of bacon available						
5 or less	1,397	55	991	13	1,194	34
More than 5	1,989	83	1,932	24	1,960	54

Price of Bacon—Both products showed little variation among stores when stores were grouped by average price of bacon per pound. The highest sales of the bacon analog and bacon occurred in stores in which the price of bacon ranged from 81 to 85 cents in both Phase I and Phase II.

The effect of the price of bacon on sales of the analog in individual stores could not be evaluated. The price of the bacon analog was constant, whereas the price of bacon varied because of the different brands within a store and from store to store. The price of bacon was only one of a number of marketing factors that might have influenced per store sales of the analog. Also, since the two products were not sold side by side in the stores, the influence of price differentials between them was somewhat reduced.

The consumer survey indicated that the analog's price was an important consideration for buyers. An overwhelming majority of buyers of the bacon analog regarded the price as very reasonable. Since one of the important elements of the advertising campaign was to stress how economical the bacon analog was compared with bacon, it was not very surprising to find this favorable attitude.

Brands of Bacon Available—Average per store sales of both products were larger when more than five brands of bacon were available. However, use of the number of brands of bacon as a criterion for introduction of the analog would probably be invalid. Other store characteristics, such as average total weekly sales, neighborhood median income, and meat case sales, would be better criteria to use in selecting stores for introduction of a bacon analog. These criteria are more stable than the number of brands of bacon available and are generally more easily obtained.

Promotion and Display Control

The test procedure did not permit identifying the effects of controlling promotion and display on per store sales of the analog. However, a comparison of the bacon analog's sales performance in Phase I and Phase II suggests that sales are influenced considerably by promotion and in-store inventory, and display control. The average monthly sales of the analog declined by 72 percent from Phase I to Phase II. Similar declines in its sales occurred for each store in the test market.

Competition Between the Analog and Bacon

The market test results did not clearly delineate the competitive relationships between the bacon analog and bacon. They did indicate that (1) sales volume patterns of the bacon analog and bacon were similar; (2) average price per pound of bacon did not appreciably influence the analog's sales during the test period; (3) for each selected store characteristic, changes in sales of the bacon analog and bacon were not of the same magnitude; and (4) percentage declines in bacon sales from Phase I to Phase II were less than those noted for the bacon analog.

The consumer survey indicated a greater amount of competition between the bacon analog and bacon than did the store audit data. This is reflected in the way the analog was used in the home. Most users said they used the product at breakfast, generally as the main meat course. Survey findings also indicated that many users were attracted to the analog because of its advertised low-caloric and low-cholesterol values. Probably many of those who bought the product for these reasons were not then using bacon or were not serving it to certain individuals in their families. At present the substitution effect of the bacon analog on bacon consumption is not clear. However, it is unlikely that one-for-one consumption of analog for bacon will prevail in the long run. The bacon analog may find a large share of its customers among people who are not now using bacon for dieting or health reasons. However, if the favorable price-use relationships prevailing in the market test continue during a regional or national introduction of the product, the analog is likely to acquire a share of the bacon market similar to that established in the market test.

Share of Market for the Analog and Bacon

The market shares of the bacon analog and bacon are presented in Table 3. The analog's share declined from 4 percent in Phase I to 1.3 percent in Phase II. This decline is probably attributable to changes in the method of distribution and promotion.

Table 3 Market Share of the Analog and Bacon by Selected Retail Store Bacon Sales Groups, Test Area, September, 1968–February, 1969

Average Monthly Sales of Bacon in Retail Stores (In Pounds)	Phase I		Phase II		Both Phases	
	Analog	Bacon	Analog	Bacon	Analog	Bacon
0–499	6.1%	93.9%	2.1%	97.9%	4.1%	95.9%
500–999	6.0	94.0	1.2	98.8	3.7	96.3
1,000–1,499	4.9	95.1	1.5	98.5	3.0	97.0
1,500–1,999	3.9	96.1	1.1	98.9	2.5	97.5
2,000–2,499	3.4	96.6	1.3	98.7	2.4	97.6
2,500–2,999	3.8	96.2	1.1	98.9	2.4	97.6
3,000–3,499	3.8	96.2	1.1	98.9	2.8	97.2
3,500–3,999	3.5	96.5	1.0	99.0	2.9	97.1
4,000–4,499	4.0	96.0	1.5	98.5	3.2	96.8
4,500–4,999	4.1	95.9	—	—	4.1	95.9
All stores	4.0	96.0	1.3	98.7	2.7	97.3

In Phase I, the analog's market share was highest in stores that sold an average of 0–499, 500–999, and 1,000–1,499 pounds of bacon per month, and in Phase II, 0–499, 1,000–1,499, and 4,000–4,499 pounds per month. If maximization of market shares were the only criterion for store outlet selection, these stores would be expected to perform best as outlets for a bacon analog. However, a more appropriate criterion of store selection for maximum market penetration is the average sales per store by various bacon sales groupings (Table 4). Based on this criterion, stores with bacon sales above 2,000 pounds per month would be selected for the introduction of the analog.

Table 4 Average Sales of the Analog and Bacon Per Store, by Selected Bacon Sales Groupings, Test Area, September, 1968–February 1969

Bacon Sales Groups (Pounds)	Phase I			Phase II			Both Phases		
	Stores Within Bacon Sales Group	Analog	Bacon	Stores Within Bacon Sales Group	Analog	Bacon	Stores Within Bacon Sales Group	Analog	Bacon
	Number	Pounds		Number	Pounds		Number	Pounds	
0–499	17	18	282	18	6	281	35	12	282
500–999	8	53	796	6	11	893	14	32	884
1,000–1,499	25	65	1,267	33	19	1,228	58	42	1,248
1,500–1,999	17	68	706	19	19	1,720	36	44	1,713
2,000–2,499	22	79	2,266	20	31	2,222	42	55	2,244
2,500–2,999	14	108	2,728	15	28	2,688	29	68	2,708
3,000–3,499	9	129	2,885	6	38	3,282	15	84	3,084
3,500–3,999	5	370	3,706	2	38	3,677	7	204	3,692
4,000–4,499	2	177	4,200	1	62	4,021	3	120	4,111
4,500–4,999	1	190	4,500	—	—	—	1	190	4,500

IMPLICATIONS

Analysis of the market test data implies that a relationship exists between retail store characteristics and the sales performance of bacon analogs.

Market test results indicate guidelines for placing bacon analogs in new markets and for choosing stores for promotion emphasis on this product from within a market area. For example, stores with the best sales performance for the bacon analog were those located in a neighborhood with median incomes above $6,000, with weekly sales of $40,000 or above, and with bacon sales of 2,000 to 2,499 pounds per month. The analysis also provides guidance for developing marketing strategies and distribution schemes to maintain or increase sales.

Hard estimates of the potential impact of fabricated foods, such as a bacon analog, on sales of traditional agricultural commodities could not be obtained from the limited data of this market test. No evidence during the 6-month test period indicated that the bacon analog sales had an appreciable effect on sales of bacon. However, the high sales obtained in Phase I—the period of heavy promotion—indicated that a segment of the public will accept a meat analog product if it is of good quality and is reasonably priced.

The consumer survey indicated a high level of satisfaction with the product and little or no adverse reaction to the concept of a meat analog. It also pointed up the versatility of this type of product in its appeal to important segments of the market—weight and cholesterol watchers and people interested in good buys.

Another interesting feature was the good reception the product received as a frozen food. Apparently, meat analogs may not suffer too severely in sales if sold from freezer cases rather than the traditional refrigerated meat cases. It is also significant that the test product is still being sold in Fort Wayne and in at least two other cities where the product was introduced in 1969-70. All in all, test market results, though limited, indicate a good chance for further commercial success of the bacon analog.

The Southeastern Meat management found the report interesting, but somewhat difficult to understand. They had trouble relating the data to their own decision on whether to market a bacon analog. The new information left the management group even more confused than before, and the report did not perform its desired function of reducing management uncertainty.

Accordingly, MacMillan asked Wadkins to rework the USDA report and attempt to relate the data to Southeastern's own specific issue.

QUESTIONS FOR DISCUSSION

1. In terms of the decision Southeastern Meat Products is in the process of making, what are the weaknesses of the "Objectives of Market Test" appearing in the USDA report? How would you rephrase them for presentation to Southeastern's management?

2. If you were assigned the task of rewriting the USDA report for Southeastern's management, what would be the basic outline of your report?
3. What information in the USDA report is not applicable to the Southeastern Meat Products decision? How could this information be used by Southeastern Meat, if at all?
4. Describe the methodology employed by the USDA in the study. Do you see any weaknesses in the design of the study? If so, what are they?
5. What basic information that Southeastern Meat needs for making the decision is missing from the USDA report?
6. Using the USDA report as a base, write a report for the Southeastern Meat management. Assume that you are Brenda Wadkins, Southeastern Meat's sales manager who, along with the company president, encouraged the conduct of the USDA study. In writing the report, as Wadkins, you will be forced to admit that the USDA study falls short, explaining why. Make certain, nevertheless, that you develop a recommended course of action for management.

Southeastern Meat Products, III

Southeastern's management had every reason to be disappointed in their two years of marketing Ba-Cure. Sales were running some 30 percent of predictions, and the bacon substitute effort was being challenged by many members of the company's marketing and finance people.

When Southeastern introduced Ba-Cure nearly two years ago, they followed several mass marketers into the battle for a profitable share of the soybean-based, meat-substitute market. These leading food processors, as well as USDA economists, forecasted annual sales of $1.5 billion for soy-protein products by 1980. However, 1977 sales in this category were only $160 million. While it was generally agreed within the industry that the meat substitute products introduced during the middle 1970s lacked taste appeal, meat prices were rising dramatically and so consumers were seeking some alternative. Meat prices then softened.

Ba-Cure was caught in this gloomy market condition. Charles MacMillan, Southeastern's president, was nevertheless convinced that their brand of bacon substitute did in fact have the taste, feel, and smell of the real thing. He refused to accept the contention that the company should drop the product. Brenda Wadkins, now the marketing manager, pointed out in a management meeting that there was an increasing demand for soybean derivatives by institutions and restaurants. These users had found that the substitutes could replace 30 percent of their meat servings. Wadkins argued for capitalizing on the company's know-how and for moving into this market. Moreover, continued Wadkins, schools could be expected to consume in excess of 120 million pounds of textured vegetable proteins in 1978, nearly four times the consumption of 1971.

Rather than fight a losing battle against large competitors in a mass market that had not endorsed a bacon substitute, Wadkins argued for allocating funds to their R&D department with the charge that they develop a soybean derivative using the so-called textured vegetable proteins. This product could be marketed not only to schools, restaurants, and institutions, but also to processed-food manufacturers as well. The latter group would buy them for TV dinners, frozen pizza, snacks, soups, and the like.

While MacMillan did not oppose allocating the funds to R&D, he continued to propound Ba-Cure. Just recently, he pointed out, an agriculture department economist said that soy products will replace 4 percent of the red meat production by 1980. True, this was down from an earlier estimate of 8 percent, but in the aggregate this represented a market that in some way could be tapped.

MacMillan and Wadkins decided to call in their advertising agency and pose the Ba-Cure problem to them. MacMillan discussed the current status of Ba-Cure, and stated in no uncertain terms that he was personally authorizing the advertising agency to develop a marketing program designed to turn Ba-Cure into a solid contributor to the company's profits.

Marilyn Stine, the agency's account executive for Southeastern Meat, returned two weeks later with an outline of a recommended advertising strategy. "Today," said Stine, "the American public is being warned about the healthfulness of meat. A nutritionist for the American Association for the Advancement of Science has just released data showing that meat ranks right behind tobacco and alcohol as a cause of heart disease." Continued Stine, "An associate professor of nutrition at Loma Linda University said her research showed 'the use of meat decreases life expectancy, it increases heart-attack rates, it increases cancer rates.' It is on the basis of this growing concern being communicated to the public that we recommend targeting Ba-Cure to that population segment concerned with its health and willing to overcome this insecurity through changes in diet."

"Consumer surveys," Stine submitted, "show that at least one half of all American families have at least one member concerned about heart disease resulting from excessive cholesterol. It is this market segment that will respond to Ba-Cure if the product is portrayed as a health item." "Not only can it be portrayed in that light," added Stine, "it is in fact a health item. And, just coincidentally, its name lends that aura, even though it was selected to suggest smokehouse curing. We urge Southeastern Meat to go this route on advertising strategy."

When MacMillan presented Stine's thinking to the company's top management group, he said that the company was proceeding along those lines. Ralph May, the company's treasurer and chief financial officer, asked how far along the plans were. MacMillan responded that he had authorized, only the day before, that Stine initiate the necessary activity and return with specifics as to advertising cost and implementation. Treasurer May then said that he personally opposed flaying a dead horse, and that in his opinion Southeastern should back off and drop Ba-Cure for good. "This company can ill-afford pouring good money after bad, and that would be the situation if Southeastern continued to attempt to foist Ba-Cure on a public that simply did not like the taste or feel of the product," May emphasized.

Taken back by those strong arguments presented by his highly respected chief financial officer, MacMillan said he would again talk with Wadkins and Stine.

QUESTIONS FOR DISCUSSION

1. List the marketing alternatives suggested by the situation. (Make certain they are mutually exclusive, are properly sequenced, and are within the sphere of influence of the decision makers involved. Be creative.)
2. Assume that one set of alternatives relates to whether to market Ba-Cure as a health product, stressing its worth as a meat substitute for persons concerned with high cholesterol. In view of high disagreement and high profit consequences of a wrong decision, what would be your criteria for the decision? Prepare an if-then statement.
3. If management insisted on making the Ba-Cure decision within a few weeks, would that affect your criterion listed in response to Question 2? Why or why not?
4. In what way could marketing of Ba-Cure as a health item run contrary to corporate policy?
5. When MacMillan returns to meet with Wadkins and Stine, after his mild confrontation with Ralph May, Southeastern Meat's financial officer, what basic issue will face the group at that point in time? How is that issue different from the basic unresolved issue?
6. What will be the role of Southeastern Meat's R&D if it is assigned the task of developing a marketable soybean derivative?

State Paper Company

State Paper Company is a family-owned warehousing and distributing firm with headquarters in Memphis, Tennessee. Offices are located in Nashville and Knoxville, Tennessee, and Birmingham, Alabama.

The company distributes paper products and janitorial supplies. Revenue from sales has averaged more than $8 million over the past five years, with approximately half of that volume coming from industrial supplies and the balance from consumer goods such as grocery paper products. The industrial products handled are cardboard boxes, adhesive tapes, janitorial products, kraft paper, packaging and liner paper, and styrofoam. The company employs 13 salespeople who call on both industrial and consumer accounts.

Two years ago Marian Anderson, State Paper's president, received a letter from the president of United Packaging, David T. Thomas. The letter informed her that State Paper had been selected by United Packaging as the exclusive distributor of "Synthastrap," a somewhat new synthetic binder used for strapping packages being prepared for shipping. Synthastrap was designed as a competitive item to steel strapping, a highly successful item for many years.

Thomas wrote that State Paper had been chosen because of its excellent reputation in the south central area, one of the few sales districts not being served by United Packaging. Synthastrap had been placed on the market about a year ago, and a total of nine distributors had been signed up. Five of these distributors had been selling Synthastrap for nearly a year. Two firms had signed up less than three months ago. Thomas closed his letter by saying that he hoped State Paper would study the potential of Synthastrap and upon the completion of such an investigation would become United's exclusive distributor in the south central region.

The following day, at the regular semiweekly officer's meeting, the United Packaging letter was discussed. The officers' enthusiasm was high and it was decided to have a United representative meet with them as soon as possible. An afternoon of the following week was set aside.

Lee Ann Hickock, United's assistant sales manager, attended the meeting and explained the application and advantages of Synthastrap. She pointed out that the new product was a synthetic binder used in virtually every situation where steel strapping was used. In discussing product advantages, Hickock pointed out that Synthastrap was as strong as steel, yet lighter in weight, thus reducing shipping charges somewhat. The new strap, she stressed, was safer than steel because there was no recoil danger when cut. Moreover, the product had no sharp metal edges to injure handlers or to cut into cartons.

Another advantage, according to Hickock, was that Synthastrap could be stored in a much smaller space than steel strapping. In addition, it could be disposed of more easily. And, finally, Hickock contended that Synthastrap would sell for less than any high quality steel strapping then on the market. Without going into any detail, Hickock explained that the product was priced at the same level as all of the lower priced steel strappings. United Packaging's pricing policy, Hickock argued, permitted a reasonable profit which could be substantial for State Paper if the latter supported it with aggressive selling effort. Hickock ended her presentation by stressing that State Paper would be the sole distributor in their area of a product having no similar synthetic competition.

Immediately after Hickock's departure, the officers of State Paper reconvened with the hope of reaching a decision. In attendance were Anderson; Ralph Graham, executive vice-president; Clara Hanson, treasurer; and Richard Holtzman, sales manager and secretary. While there was considerable enthusiasm for the product, there were also several reservations. One of these doubts centered on State Paper's ability to market the product inasmuch as it required calling on packaging and shipping people. This would place their sales representatives in the position of attempting to explain a product to a market segment in which they would not feel completely secure. Binding and shipping were specialized production functions in manufacturing establishments and required a high degree of knowledge on the part of sales representatives if effective selling was to result.

Another area of apprehension related to United Packaging's requirement that the first order be a minimum of $50,000. Graham and Hanson felt that this might be too great an investment for a company of State Paper's size to make in what was thought to be an unproven product. Anderson said she would attempt to determine whether this initial order size could be reduced. A telephone call to Hickock the following day was to no avail. Hickock pointed out, however, that reorders could be of any dollar amount.

Anderson reassembled the officers to tell them of her telephone conversation. That the group was uneasy about taking on Synthastrap was evidenced by continued expressions of concern. Hanson described her hesitancy by stating that the product would undoubtedly move slowly and the requirements for the initial order would tie up corporate funds unwisely.

Holtzman pointed out that the competition on paper products had been especially keen during the past year and he questioned whether they should allocate their salespeople's time away from paper products in favor of the untried Synthastrap. Holtzman contended also that the demand for Synthastrap would be low because the product was untried under extensive production conditions. United Packaging, he asserted, had not had time to develop and perfect large bindery machines to be used in applying Synthastrap to containers for shipping. Thus, the only firms that could use the product were those with small hand-binding operations. In addition, he argued, even the hand binders would be required to buy new tools. This added expense of switching to Synthastrap would deter a great number of companies from buying the new product.

Holtzman voiced his feeling that the officers were discussing marketing an untried product without really knowing the size of their potential market. He suggested that State Paper undertake a survey to determine this figure. Other members of the group embraced the thought and it was decided to survey the market.

It was agreed that the company's sales organization would conduct the survey. An explanatory letter was sent to the salespeople and at a sales meeting a week later a complete description of Synthastrap was presented. The sales representatives were told that as they made their next regular contacts they were to ascertain how much steel strapping was used, how much was machine bound, and how much hand bound. The salespeople were also to determine, if possible, when each firm would be replacing its machine and/or hand tools. Upon the completion of the survey interview they were to explain Synthastrap and report the reactions.

The data collection took about two weeks. Upon its completion, Holtzman met with Anderson and showed her the complete findings. Both were enthusiastic. The survey revealed that most of State Paper's industrial accounts now used steel binding, either machine or hand. These strapping users all felt that their present binding equipment was durable and not in need of being replaced at the time of the interview. However, hand tools were normally replaced every four to six months. A very high proportion of those interviewed were interested in Synthastrap and said they would be interested in trying it out in the hand binders.

Specifically, Holtzman's survey findings looked like this:

Companies using strapping		88%
Use machine binders only	36%	
Use hand tools only	42	
Use both machine and hand tools	10	
Companies not using strapping		12
Companies interested in Synthastrap		76%
Companies not interested		24
Number of companies interviewed		(120)

Anderson, impressed with the data, called a meeting of the officers at which Holtzman presented the survey findings. While Graham and Hanson expressed some hesitancy about the worth of the data, Anderson, however, stated in somewhat unyielding terms that she was recommending the acceptance of United Packaging's offer. Anderson summarized her thinking by reviewing the criteria that led her to make this recommendation. These criteria were the high profit margin, the lack of direct competition on a synthetic strap, the exclusivity of the distributorship, the promotional aid promised by United Packaging, and the fact that United Packaging was a highly responsible firm which would stand by its commitments.

The officers then agreed that Synthastrap should be adopted for distribution and Anderson was asked to communicate this decision to United Packaging.

QUESTIONS FOR DISCUSSION

1. How would you characterize State Paper's profit consequences of making a wrong decision, on a scale from high (5) to low (1)? Justify your position.
2. How would you assess the level of managerial disagreement of State Paper's decision-making group?
3. Was State Paper justified in having its survey conducted?
4. How could Hickock of United Packaging have improved her presentation to the State Paper management?
5. Anderson lists several criteria which led her to make her recommendation that State Paper adopt the United Packaging proposal. Was Anderson correct in her selection of those criteria?
6. If actionable data are thought desirable to resolve the issue, what proxy criteria would be feasible?
7. Both Graham, State Paper's executive vice-president, and Hanson, treasurer, voiced some doubt regarding the worth of the data gathered by Holtzman and first presented to Anderson. What justification could they have had in their hesitancy to accept the data?
8. Inasmuch as the disagreement among the decision makers was evenly divided (Anderson and Holtzman vs. Graham and Hanson), how did the decision to adopt the Synthastrap come about?

U.S. Army Recruiting Command

The role of women in the U.S. Army has grown considerably in importance since World War II. Their role in the military is likely to become even more significant in the future. The goal of the U.S. Army Recruiting Command is to attract better qualified young women into the U.S. Army so that they can continue to make an even greater contribution to the military effort.

Recruiting for the military is big business. Since the end of the Indochina conflict in the early 1970s and the advent of the 100 percent volunteer army, many millions of dollars have been earmarked for recruiting. In 1974, $40 million was allocated to the Army's 1975 recruiting program for advertising alone, including several million to be spent to attract women into the U.S. Army. This is in contrast to $120 million allotted to the Navy, Marine Corps, Coast Guard, and Reserves.

For the past several years the U.S. Army Recruiting Command has engaged the N W Ayer ABH International advertising agency to handle advertising strategy implementation. The agency and the Army Recruiting Command work closely in developing the total program. In order to provide themselves with adequate information, the Recruiting Command and Ayer conducted two research studies aimed at learning more about the problems of attracting young women into the U.S. Army. Study #1, made in 1971, developed a wide range of data concerning the thinking of women regarding their possible entry into the U.S. Army. Study #2, conducted in 1974, enabled the recruiters to measure changes in attitudes of women over the three-year period.

The advertising people were at the stage of developing a basic advertising theme to be aimed at young women of an age group qualifying them for enlistment. With the information uncovered by these studies, plus ideas from other sources, it was hoped that an effective advertising communications program would emerge. The studies were not designed to enable the advertising decision makers to select the advertising themes. Instead, the surveys sought information that would provide the advertising copywriters with some new thoughts that in turn might stimulate their creativity.

A wide range of subjects was covered by the two studies, from degree of familiarity with women's military service to perceptions of women's duties in the U.S. Army. The data from the two studies are shown in Tables 1 through 5.

Table 1 Familiarity With Women's Military Service, 1974 vs. 1971

Level of Familiarity	1974	1971
Very familiar	6%	2%
Somewhat familiar	25	21
Slightly familiar	37	40
Not at all familiar	31	37
Number of respondents	758	720

Table 2 Thought Previously Given to Women's Military Service, 1974 vs. 1971

	1974	1971
A great deal of thought	9%	5%
A fair amount of thought	13	13
A little thought	30	22
None	48	60
Number of respondents	758	720

Table 3 Overall Attitude Toward Women's Military Service, 1974 vs. 1971

Attitude Toward Women's Military Service	For Young Women Like Themselves		For Themselves	
	1974	1971	1974	1971
Very favorable	12%	6%	5%	4%
Somewhat favorable	34	27	17	13
Neither favorable nor unfavorable	24	28	19	18
Somewhat unfavorable	14	14	19	18
Very unfavorable	16	25	40	47
Number of respondents	758	720	758	720

Table 4 Perceptions of Women's Duties in the Army, 1974 vs. 1971

Perception of Type of Work Army Women Perform	1974	1971
Clerical/secretarial/office work	68%	68%
Nursing/medical/dental	65	67
Kitchen work/food planning	9	9
Entertainment/USO/public relations	2	5
Perform duties same as men	7	—
Teaching	6	5
Technician	5	3
Social work	1	2
Communications	3	2
Data processing work/computers	4	2
Recruiting	1	1
Mechanics	2	1
Officers	4	3
Can choose own career/select work	2	1
Marching, drilling	4	2
Menial or boring jobs	2	4
Number of respondents	758	720

Table 5 Things the Army Might Do to Make Itself More Attractive to
Young Women, 1974 Study

Action to Make the Army More Appealing	Young Women Generally	Respondents Themselves
Higher pay/better salary	23%	27%
Fewer rules, regulations/greater freedom	23	13
Individualism/come, go as you please	6	7
Shorter enlistment/no enlistment	7	8
Travel/overseas duty	12	10
Choice of location	8	10
Training/educational benefits/college credits	14	19
Career preparation for civilian life	6	6
More opportunity/better jobs	3	2
Choice of job or area of work	12	14
Better uniforms/no uniforms	10	4
Better living quarters/choice of living quarters	5	4
Meeting new people	2	3
Better social life/easy to meet men	1	—
More feminine image	3	1
Excitement/adventure	2	2
Better image	2	1
More paid vacation time	3	4
Job security	2	2
Health benefits/other benefits	7	6
Advertise more/provide more information	5	2
Room for advancement	3	2
Equal opportunity	5	2
Offer family life	3	3
Number of respondents	758	758

A second phase of the 1974 study was conducted among 250 new inductees, interviewed at two U.S. Army facilities: Fort McClellen, Alabama, and Fort Jackson, South Carolina. These women were all in basic training and had enlisted during the first three months of 1974.

Table 6 Summary of Importance of Reasons for Joining the U.S. Army, 1974

Reasons for Joining the Army	First or Second in Importance	Average Rate of Importance**
Opportunity to learn a job skill	36%	3.7
To get an education	35	3.6
For the pay	19	3.0
Opportunity to develop as a person and become mature	18	3.2
Opportunity to serve my country in meaningful way	17	3.3
Opportunity for travel overseas	12	2.6
Opportunity for travel in the U.S.	10	2.6
To do useful things for society	8	3.2
To get money to pay for an education when I get out	8	2.8
Had a guarantee of the kind of work I would do	8	3.1
Opportunity for excitement and adventure	5	3.2
Service offers job security	5	3.3
Opportunity to become independent and to get away from home	4	2.5
To take advantage of medical and dental benefits	4	2.7
Couldn't get a civilian job I liked	2	2.4
Didn't like the job I had	2	2.1
To make new friends	1	3.1
To meet the kind of men I would like to know	1	1.8
Annual leave or vacation	1	2.0
Nothing to do around home	1	1.6
Got tired of going to school	*	1.3
Many of my friends joined the service	*	1.3
Number of enlistees interviewed	250	

*Less than 0.5 percent.
**Maximum score = 4.0.

QUESTIONS FOR DISCUSSION

1. Why did the U.S. Army Recruiting Command authorize the conduct of the study among prospective women enlistees?
2. Summarize the principal finding from each of the tables in the research report.
3. Translate each one of the table summaries developed in Question 2 into sets of advertising alternatives. Be as creative as possible. Remember, you are not making the decision as to what options will be used. At this stage of the decision-making process you are simply striving to list as many ideas as possible in the form of advertising theme alternatives.
4. Reduce all the alternatives to two basic themes that you would consider using, remembering that only one of those will ultimately be selected.

Virginia Chemicals, Inc.

Headquartered in Portsmouth, Virginia, Virginia Chemicals, Inc., has had annual net sales growth for sixteen consecutive years. For the recent five-year period the figures are:

Year	Net Sales ($ million)	% Change From Previous Year
1972	44	22
1973	51	16
1974	69	35
1975	80	16
1976	90	24

The major portion of the company's revenue is derived from the sale of bulk and packaged industrial chemicals to various processing industries such as agriculture, food preservation, pharmaceutical, photographic, pulp and paper, textiles, and refrigeration. Mechanical equipment and parts related to refrigeration systems are also manufactured by the company. None of the company's products are sold in the mass consumer markets. Virginia Chemicals, Inc., has facilities throughout the United States and Canada.

Space advertising for the company is limited to industry business publications. With regard to media selection and scheduling, advertising manager Janet Gottfried states that in 90 percent of the cases she follows the recommendations of the company's advertising agency, Vansant and Dugdale of Baltimore. She views media selection as a decision involving the agency's recommendation and common sense.

Gottfried "inherited" Vansant and Dugdale when she joined the company as advertising manager in 1968. She feels that the relationship with the agency

This case was prepared with the assistance of C. Allan Foster, Virginia Chemicals, Inc. Revised 1977.

is good, pointing out that campaigns worked up for the company are rarely rejected. The advertising management feels that if it is paying the agency to develop appropriate recommendations, then those recommendations should be followed. In most cases the agency provides at least three different campaigns for presentation in response to an ad work-up request.

Late each August Gottfried meets with the vice-president/director of marketing, who has input from the various product managers as to each product's current status, future market potential, and advertising needs. Also present is a representative from Vansant and Dugdale. For a couple of days the three merely kick ideas around concerning various advertising strategies and possibilities for the next year. Gottfried refers to these meetings as "hopes, dreams, and ambitions" sessions. Shortly after these meetings, the advertising agency sends back a report to Gottfried outlining what the agency considered relevant, and where advertising emphasis should be. After carefully reviewing the report Gottfried goes to Baltimore to meet with the agency and to tell them where, in her opinion, they missed the mark in coming up with salient and useful advertising strategies. Gottfried has always felt that such exchanges of communication should ultimately accomplish two things:

1. Succinctly state the goals of advertising in the order of their importance.
2. Determine the amount of money needed to reach these goals.

Gottfried regards these sessions as beneficial. Because specific needs and reasons for advertising in each product area are carefully predelineated, the agency has been able to come up with good advertisements.

On the question of how much to spend on advertising, Gottfried relies heavily on experience and what she feels she can justify to management. There are no fixed rules for budget preparation. The budget, by necessity, is somewhat nebulous. Typical breakdown of the budget is shown in Table 1.

Table 1 Advertising Budget Breakdown—Virginia Chemicals, Inc.

Item	Percentage of Total Advertising Expenditures
Ad space, national	41%
Salaries	15
Sales promotion	15
Annual report	12
Ad production costs	9
Conventions	5
Travel and entertainment	1
Price list printing	1
Other printing	1
Total	100%

Though it is not practiced at Virginia Chemicals, Gottfried thinks that the most intelligent and efficient way to determine an advertising budget is on a percentage of net-sales-billed basis. Her rationale is that this procedure ties advertising directly to overall operation plans and gives a fix on advertising levels and allocations.

QUESTIONS FOR DISCUSSION

1. In terms of the five-step decision model, what do the "hopes, dreams, and ambitions" sessions accomplish?
2. What does a ranking of advertising goals (one of the two accomplishments Gottfried feels is of value in having the meetings) mean in terms of the five-step process? What might some of those goals be?
3. A recurring marketing decision-problem is the determination of how much to spend on advertising. Two approaches to such determination are presented in the Virginia Chemicals episode. What are they? Which is more in harmony with the five-step decision model? Which would you use? Why?
4. What seems to be the involvement level of "expert judgment" in the various decision situations described in the case? Do you feel this level is appropriate? Explain.
5. What data, if any, do you think the decision makers should be acquiring to enhance the profitability of those decisions? How would you determine whether the data should be obtained?

WCOM Radio Station, I

WCOM is a radio station in Sterling, Illinois, a prosperous and cultural community having a trading area of approximately 67,000. The University of the Midwest, located in Sterling, has a student enrollment of approximately 16,000.

WCOM began broadcasting in 1964. The station, incorporated as WCOM, Inc., is managed and owned by virtually the same persons. Of the corporation's eight stockholders, five are employed by the station.

WCOM-AM has a signal strength of 2,000 watts. It broadcasts 18 hours daily. There are two local competing radio stations. One of the other AM stations, WZYX, has a signal strength of 2,000 watts. The other, WCBA, operates on a power of 1,000 watts. These strengths are for all stations' full broadcasting period of 18 hours. All three local stations broadcast on both the AM and FM bands.

WCOM-AM, like other commercial radio stations, derives almost all of its revenue from the sale of advertising time. Approximately 90 percent of the station's profits result from advertising on the AM band. Advertising time is sold largely to local merchants, dealers, or bottlers of nationally distributed products. Approximately 80 percent of the advertising sales are made locally, with the remaining 20 percent handled by station representatives in three large advertising centers: New York City, Chicago, and Detroit.

In addition to the station representatives maintained outside of Sterling, three local time salespeople are employed. WZYX employs a similar number. WCBA is less aggressive, with the company's president and sales manager comprising the sales staff.

WCOM allows its announcers considerable leeway in program format. Network news is every hour on the hour, except during the so-called prime times of 6:30–9:00 AM and 4:30–6:30 PM. During these two time periods, when automobile audiences are larger, news and weather are broadcast more frequently.

The music pattern during all time periods of the day and night is "rock" of all types. This type of music is prevalent among all Sterling AM stations. Several years ago one of the competing stations dropped rock, but their audience ratings decreased and within six months the decision was made to return to rock music.

At the present time, WCOM and WZYX have approximately the same size audiences. Audience data provided less than a year ago by a syndicated research service revealed the data shown in Table 1.

Table 1 Audience Data for Monday Through Friday—November

Station	Percentage of Sets on at			
	6:30 AM– 9:00 AM	9:00 AM– 4:30 PM	4:30 PM– 6:30 PM	6:30 PM– 10:00 PM
WCOM-AM	31	27	32	22
WZYX-AM	30	30	33	24
WCBA-AM	15	19	14	12
Out of town	20	18	17	32
All FM	4	6	4	10

WCOM had earned a satisfactory return until about two years ago when advertising revenue began to decline. The drop in corporate profitability during that period resulting from advertising sales was 17 percent. However, the decline was most pronounced for the prime times of 6:30–9:00 AM and 4:30–6:30 PM. These two time periods account for nearly 70 percent of all advertising revenue during the Monday through Friday periods.

WCOM's profit picture from 1966 through 1974 is shown in Table 2.

Table 2 Prime Time and Non-Prime Time Profit for WCOM—1966–1974
(In Thousands of Dollars)

	1966	1968	1970	1972	1973	1974
Total profit	93	96	95	100	93	83
Prime time	73	76	73	77	69	61
Non-prime time	20	20	22	23	24	22

The announcers during the two prime times have been with the station for more than five years. The revenue decline has been similar for both time periods. The first six months of the current fiscal period has not shown any evidence that the situation is correcting itself.

The two competing stations in Sterling are apparently not showing a similar decline in advertising revenue. Although financial data for these competing stations are not available, a monitoring of their broadcasts does not reveal any perceptible drop in sales. Neither of the stations has made any great change in their programming.

The management of WCOM is rather socially inclined, often combining entertainment with selling. Probably for this reason their sales efforts are directed more toward the department stores, status jewelry retailers, gift shops, and the like. Thus, the station's advertisers for several years have tended to represent this type of merchant.

The management of WCOM is at a loss to explain its drop in advertising sales. From time to time the company president has discussed the problem with various management people. Finally, a meeting was called to determine what step or steps should be taken to reverse this ominous decline in revenue which, if not corrected, would have serious profit consequences.

In addition to the president, those invited to the meeting were: (1) the executive vice-president (in charge of operations); (2) the sales manager (responsible for all advertising sales); and (3) the programming director (responsible for gathering audience data as well as programming).

QUESTIONS FOR DISCUSSION

1. What is the "problem" that has arisen to confront the WCOM management? Why is it a "problem"?
2. Do you feel that additional information should be obtained in order to aid the WCOM management—information that would be environmental in nature? If so, what would such information reveal?
3. Audience data for Monday through Friday are shown in the case. Are these environmental or actionable data?
4. As they enter the meeting called by the station's president, where are the decision makers in the decision-making process?
5. What is the "basic, unresolved issue"?

WCOM Radio Station, II

After considerable discussion by the WCOM management, it was agreed that the music programming should be reviewed with the possibility of some change in the type of music broadcast. WCOM's programming director was assigned the task of gathering the necessary data aimed at resolving the issue of what type of music would be most effective in generating sales for advertisers among the target market of homemakers with two or more children in families having middle- or upper-income buying power.

Even though the study was local in nature, the programming director thought it advisable to call in an outside research organization for both counsel and data collection. This assignment included the designing of a research study. The station's management did not authorize a stated sum for the conduct of the study. Instead it asked the station's programming director to confer with the WCOM president before proceeding with the actual data collection. It was thought by both the station management and the programming director that this approach to allocation of funds for the study would result in a more efficient use of the money. At the same time the WCOM programming director could participate in the design and gain a better understanding of the price to be submitted by the research organization. Marketing Research Center was the firm selected for the study.

A meeting was held between Paula McArthur, WCOM's programming director, and Jack Hirsch, an account executive of Marketing Research Center. McArthur outlined the need for data, pointing out that the station's management could not agree on the type of music the station should broadcast. They had agreed to try to attract young homemakers, particularly those with two or more children and having middle- to upper-income buying power.

McArthur further emphasized that from a practical point of view a relatively small radio station such as WCOM could not afford large sums of money for marketing research. However, she insisted that they seek reliable information because of the consequences looming as a result of continued declining profits. McArthur suggested to Hirsch that a "radio coincidental" survey of existing listenership might be adequate for their purposes. This type of study, she observed, would be quite inexpensive inasmuch as the data collection could be handled by phone with interviewers asking, "What station or program are you listening to right now?"—after a couple of qualifying questions.

At this point McArthur and Hirsch began discussing other research options available for data collection. The telephone radio coincidental survey mentioned by McArthur was one. Mailing diaries to a sample of families in the listening area was another. The personal in-home interview was still another, wherein the interviewer would ask the respondent to recall the programs listened to on the previous day. (This type of interview would be on a so-called "aided recall" basis where the respondent is shown a list of the programs and the broadcasting stations.)

It was finally agreed that the coincidental listenership study would be conducted and the survey was initiated by Marketing Research Center.

QUESTIONS FOR DISCUSSION

1. What basic error did McArthur and Hirsch make when they initiated their discussion of the proposed survey?
2. McArthur pointed out to Hirsch that WCOM could not afford large sums of money for the contemplated research. Yet she followed this comment with the insistence that they seek "reliable information because of the consequences looming as a result of continued declining profits." Are these two statements compatible, assuming that generally speaking it is more expensive to obtain highly accurate and reliable information?
3. Is the decision that WCOM is about to make on programming an identical-cost or a diverse-cost decision? How can the type of decision affect criteria selection?
4. Should the criterion for the music type decision be monetary or nonmonetary in nature? Why?
5. McArthur's and Hirsch's research decision to obtain radio coincidental information suggests that they have already agreed on some criterion. What would that criterion have been in terms of a complete if-then statement? What are the weaknesses of such a criterion?
6. The WCOM management has already agreed on the target market of young homemakers with two or more children in families having middle- or upper-income buying power. What bearing does this agreement on market segment have on the decision-making process pertaining to music preferences?
7. Prepare the complete criterion statement that you would recommend for WCOM management approval.

WCOM Radio Station, III

The marketing research study completed, the two researchers, Paula McArthur, WCOM programming director, and Jack Hirsch, account executive for Market Research Center, began reviewing the data and attempted to determine its meaning and significance.

It was agreed that the presentation of the data to WCOM management would be made in two forms—an oral, graphic portrayal of the data, and a written report which would be submitted within ten days after the graphic presentation. This sequence was thought desirable in view of the opportunity to obtain management's reaction to the data before submitting a final written report. The two presentations, however, would follow the same content sequence and would use the same tables of data. In this way the tables in the graphic presentation could be reproduced for inclusion in the written report.

Hirsch agreed to prepare the written report and submit it to McArthur for review and possible changes. From the written report would emerge the graphic portrayal, using the essential elements that would lend themselves to discussion.

The data for the WCOM programming report follow. The sample characteristics appear in Table 1. The survey data are shown in Tables 2 and 3.

Table 1 Sample Design

WCOM Market Area	Phones	Population		Sample	
		Number	Percentage	Number	Percentage
Sterling, environs	9,000	44,000	66%	870	87%
University of the Midwest students	—	16,000	24	—	—
Birmingham, Illinois	500	2,000	3	130	13
Other communities	1,200	5,000	7	—	—
		67,000	100%	1,000	100%

Table 2 Percentage of Homemakers Who Listened to Radio

	Income Groups					
		Middle and Upper				
	Lower	1–2	3–4	5 + *	Total	Grand Total
Listened to radio between 6:30–9 AM	40%	38%	46%	59%	51%	47%
Did not listen	60	62	54	41	49	53
Number of interviews	300	120	260	320	700	1,000

*Number of people in family.

Table 3 Preferences of Radio Listeners (6:30–9 AM Time Period)

	Income Groups				
		Middle and Upper			Grand
Music Preferences	Lower	1–2	3–4	5 + *	Total
Rock	51%	52%	24%	11%	28%
Jazz	3	2	3	3	3
Country-Western	11	13	10	9	10
Popular	17	11	30	30	25
Folk	7	6	5	8	7
Semiclassical	5	9	22	30	20
Religious	6	7	6	9	7
Number of homemakers who listen	120	46	120	189	475

*Number of people in family.

QUESTIONS FOR DISCUSSION

1. What is the function of the data in Table 1? In Table 2? In Table 3?
2. On the basis of the study conducted, what programming action would you take?
3. Prepare a written report for the decision makers, based on the data uncovered by the radio coincidental survey.

Wycoff Equipment, Inc.

Wycoff Equipment, Inc., has long been an innovator in the metalworking field. The company, organized in 1958 by Ryan R. Wycoff, has garnered a sizable share of the punch press and related markets. This success has been achieved largely through the inventiveness of Wycoff.

Wycoff is a man in his forties and is recognized for his genius in creating new and improved presses. From a modest beginning he has built a company with annual sales in excess of $88 million. During the company's first few years, the management decisions were made solely by Wycoff, even though he had neither financial nor marketing training or education. In the past several years, with the company now incorporated, the management has grown and the decision-making process has become more complicated.

Wycoff has devoted the great bulk of his time to product design. He also has been making the final decisions on whether to place his several innovations on the market. Until recently his record of successes was phenomenal—each one proving to be profitable. During the past four years, however, with competition more keen and his own management more critical, Wycoff recommended three new machines for commercialization and all three failed to turn a profit.

The company's management contended that the primary reason for these product failures was the company's weakness in its marketing efforts. In the past the company relied heavily on the reputation of Wycoff and his ability to predict what the metalworking market would accept. However, three successive failures suggested to several management people that the company was losing touch with the needs of the metalworking and fabrication firms because of their lack of a marketing staff which could keep in close touch with customers and prospects.

This thinking led to the hiring of a marketing director, a nonexistent position up to that time. Daniel Hammond, the person hired for the job, was a sophisticated marketer and understood the role of marketing within an industrial firm. He brought with him a marketing research director, Maria Fazio, who was well schooled in the latest techniques of the discipline.

Shortly after Hammond and Fazio joined the ranks of the company, Wycoff talked to them about still another machine he had perfected. It was termed a "nondestructive integrated drift press." Wycoff pointed out that there was considerable indecision on the part of management as to the specific attributes and, even more basic, whether to place the new product on the market. Wycoff, now impressed with the backgrounds of his two new marketing people, thought this project would be an excellent one for them to undertake.

Fazio pointed out that there were marketing research techniques available which lent themselves well to predicting the appropriate product attributes as well as forecasting the sales of the optimum product. She referred to one such technique called Product Specification Analysis (PSA). Stressing that although such an approach was no guarantee, it would reduce the risk considerably. Fazio contended that the company's recent failures could have been avoided had this PSA approach been employed.

In explaining the technique to Wycoff, Fazio described the uniqueness of the questioning process and how it worked. To illustrate, she pointed out that consumer judgments concerning the importance of various product attributes are usually ambiguous unless great care is taken in defining the attributes. Odor, for example, may be an important attribute when considering products that differ noticeably in odor, but may be quite unimportant with a different sample of products from the same category if they all happen to smell the same. Safety may be considered an overpoweringly important attribute of airlines when considered in the abstract. Yet, if airlines are not greatly different in their degree of safety, it cannot affect a passenger's choice of airline. Important judgments are therefore not necessarily meaningful unless discussed in a highly specific context.

The identification of "ideal levels" of product attributes is also frequently inadequate. There are many attributes for which ideal levels do differ from consumer to consumer, such as saltiness of pretzels, lightness of beer, or sudsiness of a soap or detergent. But for attributes such as convenience, economy, or levels of performance, it can be safely assumed that every consumer would prefer a product having as high a level of each attribute as possible. What is needed in such cases, continued Fazio, is information about consumer trade-offs, since no manufacturer can afford to sell an infinitely convenient and high performing product for a price of zero. Thus, it becomes relevant to determine how consumers value various levels of each attribute and the extent to which they would forego a high level of one attribute to achieve a higher level of another.

This Product Specification Analysis is based on the premise that each consumer's choice behavior is governed by trade-off values and that, although consumers may be incapable of articulation, their values may be revealed by their choices among product concepts having characteristics that are varied in systematic ways. PSA involves conjoint measurement and requires rank-order data, but it produces measurements that are stronger than rank orders, concluded Fazio.

Wycoff then explained the new product in terms of the possible attributes it could have. The price would fall between $5,000 and $12,000—the range now existing for the three best-selling makes now on the market. The output could range from ten units per hour to two units hourly. A warranty could be of one, two, or four years' duration. Delivery could be made within one, two, or four months of the order. Obviously, Wycoff pointed out, the price would be related to the attributes decided upon. For example, it would cost more to build a machine tlat would have a four-year warranty. Likewise, a machine that could produce ten units an hour would be more expensive to build than one producing only two per hour. The issue, Wycoff stressed, was twofold: what should be the attributes incorporated into the machine, and would this machine garner a sufficient market to justify its production? In brief, where is the balance between maximum unit profitability and maximum market share?

In designing a study aimed at gathering the necessary information, Fazio drew a sample of 150 companies from a total market of 954 firms known to be using metalworking presses. The sample was drawn so that the chance of a company falling into the sample was proportional to the number of machines now being used by the company. In this way the larger the number of presses in use, the greater the chances of being included in the sample. Such a sample made it possible to project the data collected, assuming the data were valid.

The data collection process involved personal interviews with the production managers of the sample companies. These managers were known to be the decision makers on whether new presses would be purchased and which make would be bought. The interview developed a situation whereby the respondent was forced into a trade-off among the four attributes under consideration. This trade-off was achieved through the use of matrices. Two attributes were used to form a matrix.

Figure 1 illustrates how warranty and output are measured. Years of warranty are shown in the columns (four years, two years, and one year) and output per hour in rows (ten, five, and two units per hour). These two attributes, with three levels each, provide nine possible product combinations.

Figure 1   *Measuring the Respondent's Trade-Offs*

In the Wycoff study, the respondent was asked to indicate his or her preferred combination. Logically a production manager would prefer the one cell with the highest output and the greatest warranty. Then the respondent was asked to assume that this combination was not available and to indicate a second preference. The production manager was then forced to trade off between performance and warranty. Was performance so important that the warranty would be cut in half? Or was warranty so important that output would be reduced to half? Once the respondent made this choice, additional decisions had to be made by working through the matrix. If the respondent was a rational buyer, the ninth choice would be one year of warranty and two units per hour.

Figure 2 lists the trade-offs of one hypothetical production manager. This buyer's first choice is ten units per hour and a four-year warranty. The second choice is two years of warranty and ten units per hour, indicating the production manager's greater concern with performance. On making the third choice, however, the respondent is not willing to drop to a one-year warranty. Four years of warranty are preferred and five units per hour to one year of warranty and ten units per hour. From viewing the matrix, it can be concluded that, to this hypothetical production manager, performance is generally more important than warranty.

Rank Order of Preference
Years of Warranty

Output per Hour	4	2	1
10	1	2	5
5	3	4	6
2	7	8	9

Figure 2   One Hypothetical Production Manager's Trade-Offs

From responses in matrices like this, utilities can be calculated expressing the worth the respondent holds for each attribute. Table 1 shows these utilities. There is a 1.0 utility for ten units per hour, a .5 utility for five units per hour, and a .1 utility for two units per hour. Thus, a ten-unit-per-hour product is preferred twice as much as a five-unit-per-hour product (tle 1.0 utility being twice the .5 utility). The preference for a ten-unit-per-hour product is ten times greater than for a two-unit-per-hour product (1.0 is 10 times .1). In terms of warranty, the respondent prefers a four-year warranted product half again more than a two-year warranted product (1.0 is about 50 percent greater than .7). The preference for a four-year warranted product is three times greater than for that of a one-year warranted product (1.0 is 3⅓ times greater than .3).

Table 1 Hypothetical Production Manager's Utilities

Output (Units per Hour)		Warranty (Years)	
Level	Utilities	Level	Utilities
10	1.00	4	1.00
5	.50	2	.70
2	.10	1	.30

The matrix in Figure 3 is similar to the one in Figure 2; that is, it has four-year, two-year and one-year columns, and ten-, five-, and two-unit rows. The numbers in parentheses are the respondent's rank order of preference previously given. The first choice was four years and ten units, the second choice was two years and ten units, and the third choice was four years and five units.

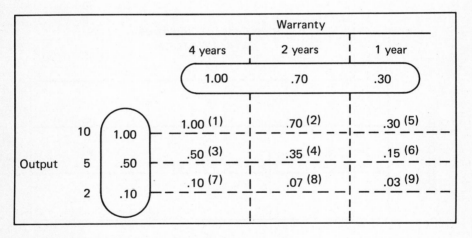

Figure 3 Pairwise Products of the Utilities

The utilities are determined for each level of each attribute using a computer-based program. The products of each pair of utilities must fit in such a way as to match the respondent's rank order of preference.[1] As an example, looking at four years warranty and ten units per hour performance, the utilities (enclosed in the boxes) for each level are 1.00, respectively (1.00 times 1.00 is 1.00). One is the highest number. This combination of levels is also the respondent's first choice.

---

[1] The numerical technique employed most frequently is an iterative procedure that attempts to minimize a measure of "badness of fit" of the utilities to the data. Since the data consist of only rank orders, the measure of fit must indicate the extent to which the pairwise products of utilities have rank orders similar to the data.

In Table 2 one can see that the $5,000 price level carries a 1.0 utility index, $8,000 a .8, and $12,000 a .4. This buyer prefers an $8,000 machine twice as much as a $12,000 machine. The preference for a $5,000 machine is 2.5 times that of a $12,000 product. Output and warranty already have been discussed.

Table 2 Utilities on Four Attributes

Attribute	Utilities
Price	
$ 5,000	1.00
$ 8,000	.80
$12,000	.40
Output	
10 specimens per hour	1.00
5 specimens per hour	.50
2 specimens per hour	.10
Warranty	
4 years	1.00
2 years	.70
1 year	.30
Delivery	
1 month	1.00
2 months	.90
4 months	.80

Looking at the delivery attribute, it becomes apparent that this is not as sensitive an attribute for this hypothetical buyer as the others. This buyer prefers a machine that can be delivered in one month only about 10 percent more than one that is delivered in two months. And the buyer prefers a one-month delivery cycle only about 25 percent more than a four-month delivery cycle. Increasing delivery time, then, is not particularly useful to this buyer. If investment decisions were being made about warehouse and distribution, in terms of this one respondent's utilities, the expenditure should not be great. That is, by shortening the delivery cycle to one month, there would only be a 10 percent greater preference for that particular product over a product delivered in two months.

A value system composed of the utilities for various levels of these attributes has been developed on this hypothetical buyer. The utilization of such a system can be shown through the following example. Suppose the sales department described Machine A, the most preferred product currently in the industry, as follows:

$5,000 price (lowest)
Performance at the level of two specimens per hour (the lowest)
A moderate warranty of two years
A one-month delivery cycle (the shortest)

In comparison, Wycoff feels another product, Machine B, should be manufactured. It would have the following specifications:

$8,000 price (mid-range)
Five specimens per hour (mid-range)
Two-year warranty (mid-range)
Four-month delivery cycle (the longest)

Which of these two machines would this hypothetical buyer prefer? Table 3 indicates the respondent's utilities for each of the relevant attributes. There is a 1.0 utility the respondent placed on a $5,000 price, a .10 utility for a two specimen-per-hour output, a .70 utility for a two-year warranty period, and a 1.0 utility for a one-month delivery.

Table 3 One Respondent's Utilities—Machine A

Attributes	Utilities
Price	
$ 5,000	1.00*
$ 8,000	.80
$12,000	.40
Output	
10 specimens per hour	1.00
5 specimens per hour	.50
2 specimens per hour	.10*
Warranty	
4 years	1.00
2 years	.70*
1 year	.30
Delivery	
1 month	1.00*
2 months	.90
4 months	.80

* Hypothetical production manager's preferences.

In calculating the buyer's preference for Machine A, the utilities are multiplied as in Table 4. With this multiplicative model, the buyer has a .070 relative preference for Machine A.

Table 4 Likelihood of Buying Machine A

Feature	Utilities
$5,000	1.00
2 specimens per hour	.10
2-year warranty	.70
1-month delivery	1.00
Relative Likelihood of Buying:*	
1.00 × .10 × .70 × 1.00 = .070	

* In prior studies persons interviewed have been asked how likely they would be to buy product concepts described in terms of attributes that have been traded off. This makes possible a calibration of the model's estimates of overall utility for a product with stated buying likelihood. The relationship has been quite close in actual experience.

The same procedure in describing Wycoff's contemplated Machine B is shown in Table 5. That is, Machine B carries, for the buyer, a .8 utility for an $8,000 price; a .5 utility for five specimens per hour; a .7 utility for a two-year warranty; and a .8 utility for a four-month delivery.

Table 5 One Respondent's Utilities—Machine B

Attribute	Utilities
Price	
$ 5,000	1.00
$ 8,000	.80*
$12,000	.40
Output	
10 specimens per hour	1.00
5 specimens per hour	.50*
2 specimens per hour	.10
Warranty	
4 years	1.00
2 years	.70*
1 year	.30
Delivery	
1 month	1.00
2 months	.90
4 months	.80*

* Hypothetical production manager's preferences.

The calculation for the relative preference for Machine B is seen in Table 6 (along with a repeat of Machine A's values). Multiplying the utilities, it is seen that the buyer would be three times as likely to choose Machine B (with a score of .224) as Machine A (with a score of .070). If the market were composed solely of this one buyer, the manufacturer would do well to market Machine B.

Table 6 Relative Likelihood of Buying Machine A vs. Machine B

	Feature	Utilities
Machine A	$5,000	1.00
	2 specimens per hour	.10
	2-year warranty	.70
	1-month delivery	1.00
Relative likelihood of buying: $1.00 \times .10 \times .70 \times 1.00 = .070$		
Machine B	$8,000	.80
	5 specimens per hour	.50
	2-year warranty	.70
	4-month delivery	.80
Relative likelihood of buying: $.80 \times .50 \times .70 \times .80 = .224$		

Data gathered earlier by Wycoff and other sources had established that a total of 5,260 machines would be sold annually over the next three or four years. The study conducted then could be projected against this known potential. Two comparative products were included in the survey—Jones Microval and Apex Precision. Both have attributes which fall within the four attributes being considered by Wycoff.

Table 7 shows data for a Wycoff Product X1 projected against Jones and Apex. This Product X1 has the least attractive attributes: highest price, least performance and warranty, and the longest delivery period. This, however, is the product attribute mix which would yield the greatest *unit* gross margin.

Table 7 Predicted Annual Sales—Product X1

Jones Microval	3,030
Apex Precision	2,190
Product X1*	40
Total	5,260 machines

* Product X1 is $12,000, produces two specimens per hour, has a one-year warranty, and has a four-month delivery.

Wycoff's Product X1 then is the minimum product situation. This can be contrasted with a maximum product situation by running a simulation on the basis of the data collected from the sample of machine buyers.[2] This is Product

---

[2] The method used to convert the data into something more nearly approaching market share is described in detail on page 124 of the *Journal of Marketing Research*, Vol. XI (May, 1974).

X2, the least expensive with the most attractive performance, warranty, and delivery. From these data, as shown in Table 8, Product X2 would garner a market share of more than 90 percent. However, Wycoff knew very well that their internal cost figures would show a considerable loss on each unit sold.

Table 8 Predicted Annual Sales—Product X2

Jones Microval	320
Apex Precision	160
Product X2*	4,780
Total	5,260 machines

* Product X2 is $5,000, produces ten specimens per hour, has a four-year warranty, and has a one-month delivery.

In presenting the data to Wycoff's management, Fazio pointed out that the issue has now been narrowed to locating the optimum product, somewhere between the extremes of the minimum and maximum simulations. The goal, she stressed, is to market that product with intermediate market share and unit gross margin that would yield maximum total gross profit.

Several simulations were run through the computer, refining levels of various attributes. Product X27 emerged. It would obtain a market share of approximately 40 percent (2,110 units). Fazio presented Product X27 to Wycoff and Hammond as the optimal product and recommended its being placed on the market.

Table 9 Predicted Annual Sales—Product X27

Jones Microval	2,070
Apex Precision	1,080
Product X27*	2,110
Total	5,260 machines

* Product X27 is $8,000 produces 10 specimens per hour, has a four-year warranty, and has a four-month delivery.

QUESTIONS FOR DISCUSSION

1. What is the basic issue to be resolved by the decision makers?
2. What are the product options available to Wycoff on the nondestructive drift press?
3. Fazio presented Product X27 as the optimal product. Based on the material in the case, in what way did Fazio fail to submit sufficient information when she recommended the marketing of Product X27?
4. Prepare a complete criterion statement.
5. The trade-off model has great value in many situations, especially those involving industrial products. However, the technique is not without its weaknesses. What would be some of the shortcomings?

APPENDIX A

Guidelines for Writing a Business Report

Writing a business report can be a relatively simple task. You simply put in writing that which you wish to communicate to the reader. But there the simplicity ends. The sequence of the presentation, the use of data, and the technical level of the language will vary greatly from one report to another. The purpose of this appendix is to aid the writer in preparing business reports.

FORMAT

Business reports, like term papers, theses, and dissertations, have certain elements in common, especially with regard to the format. Turabian[1] describes the format of a paper as containing three main parts: the front matter or preliminaries, the text, and the references. The *front matter* is comprised of:

1. Title page.
2. Preface.
3. Table of contents.
4. List of illustrations.
5. List of tables.

The title itself should be accurate in describing the nature of the content. Many report titles are overly general, such as "The Marketing of the Automatic Washing Machine." This title is too broad, leaving the reader with only a vague notion of its content. Does it describe the marketing process of washing machines? Or does it relate to whether a particular type of machine should be marketed? It should be more specific, but not so specific that the title reveals the outcome of the study, especially when the report is actionable in nature. Using the above illustration, a poor title would be: "Why the XYZ Company Should Market an Automatic Washer." It tips the hand of the report writer

---

[1] Kate L. Turabian, *A Manual for Writers of Term Papers, Theses, and Dissertations* (4th ed.; Chicago: University of Chicago Press, 1973). All writers of reports should consider owning this manual.

and may fly directly in the face of those who, up to the report's presentation, had resisted marketing the product. The title in Figure 1 is acceptable.

The style of the title page can vary, but in general all title pages should contain the title itself, the person or persons to whom the report is directed, the date of preparation of the report, and the name of the author. These items should be carefully spaced, using a combination of all capital letters, capital and lowercase letters, and underlining in order to create a pleasant appearance for the page. An example of an attractive title page is shown in Figure 1.

FEASIBILITY OF MARKETING AN AUTOMATIC WASHER

BY THE XYZ COMPANY

A Report to the Marketing Committee

of the XYZ Company

Prepared by:

Patricia H. Jones
Director of Marketing Research

November 20, 1978

Figure 1   Title Page of a Business Report

The text of the report normally begins with an introduction which may or may not be labelled as such. The reader is usually more intrigued by a description of an introduction more specific in nature. Here are a few examples:

"Evidence Suggesting a New Washer Should Be Developed."
"Events Leading to the Development of the New Automatic Washer."
"Considerations Leading to the Possibility of Marketing an Automatic Washer."

The main body of the text is often divided into chapters. Each chapter has its own title, is numbered, and begins on a new page. The chapter title is centered and is capitalized. Chapters in turn are often divided into sections and subsections and even into further subsections. The style of heading is dependent upon the number of sections and subsections. Usually, the following plan is acceptable, with each level of subtitle representing a lower level:

1. Centered heading (usually the chapter heading) in all capital letters.
2. Side heading, underlined, flush to left margin, in capital and lowercase letters.
3. Paragraph heading underlined—as the first part of a sentence.
4. Key words at or near the beginning of a paragraph underlined.

In a brief report, when fewer than four levels are needed, any of the above can be employed but always in descending order. It is not necessary to start a new page for each new section.

STYLE

The writer should treat the subject of the report from a factual, practical standpoint. For every point made, the writer should ask: "Will this help the reader follow my thought and aid in understanding what I am attempting to communicate?"

It is, of course, highly desirable to have each page of the report appear neat and inviting to read. The typist should leave sufficient margins. The goal is not to crowd as much as possible on every page, but to present an attractive page with white space not only at the sides but also at the top and bottom.

Most reports are double spaced simply because they are easier to read when typed in that manner. To make the reading even more inviting, triple spacing between paragraphs may be used. Triple spacing also allows the reader to write thoughts and comments between the lines and in the margins, thereby involving the reader in the report.

Single spacing is sometimes appropriate when a paragraph or two is being quoted. In such instances, the quoted material should be indented from both margins.

When a series of items is being presented, indent and list them. Do not include them in the narrative. It is helpful to number or letter the items in some way. "Bullets" (•) are sometimes used in lists to avoid the implication that there is a number one choice or preferential ranking of the items on the list.

Footnotes should be used for reference purposes only, and not employed for discussion. If an idea is not worth stating in the body of the text, it should be omitted. Footnotes should be placed at the bottom of the page on which the material to which they refer appears, and should be numbered consecutively.

Every reference to an *article* should provide specific information in the following order: the author's name, title of the article, name of the publication (not to be abbreviated), volume number, date of publication (in parentheses), both the beginning and ending pages of the article, and (where applicable) specific page references.

> *Example:* F. F. Stephan, "The Art of Inquiry," *Public Opinion Quarterly,* Volume XXIV (Summer, 1965), pp. 268–297.

Reference to a *book* should provide specific information in the following order: the author's complete name; title of the book; place of publication, name of publisher, and year in parentheses; and (where applicable) specific page reference. If there is more than one volume or edition, this information must also be given.

> *Example:* H. W. Boyd, Jr., R. Westfall, and S. F. Stasch, *Marketing Research—Text and Cases* (4th ed.; Homewood, Ill.: Richard D. Irwin, Inc., 1977), pp. 221–253.

Using personal pronouns (I, me, my, we, us, our) should be avoided in report writing. A business report is a logical presentation, supported by data and appropriate information when necessary. It is not a place for personal opinion; it is a rational presentation. This does not mean that an "actionable report" should not persuade; but it should do so through logical argument with informational support.

The writer should get the attention of the reader in the opening sentences and paragraphs. The reader should be told at the outset what the chapter is about. Paragraphs should be made relatively short, especially at the beginning of the report and the beginnings of chapters. Long, involved sentences should not be used. Jargon that does not communicate easily to the readers should also be avoided. The report writer should omit unnecessary details and should constantly ask: "Is this statement really necessary?"

USE OF NUMBERS IN NARRATIVE

Most business reports involve the use of numbers and it is essential that the writer of reports understand their correct handling. In the narrative several rules apply for the treatment of numbers and adherence to them will make the report more readable and more easily understood. The use of figures for numbers over ten and words for smaller numbers is an informal rule generally used for newspapers and other informal writing. A more general rule for report writing (and for magazines and books) is to use figures only for numbers over one hundred, unless such numbers can be written in two words; e.g., 25,000 but two thousand. Words are used for numbers under one hundred.

There are several exceptions to this general rule:

1. When a phrase or sentence has two numbers that normally would call for one numeral and one number spelled out, use numerals for both. For example: the sample was further divided into subsamples of 75 and 125.
2. For percentages, decimals, and exact sums of money, numerals should always be used. However, very large numbers are frequently shown in a combination of figures and words; e. g., $3 billion instead of $3,000,000,000. A numeral should always be used with the word "percent" and percent should always be spelled out in narrative.
3. A sentence should never be started with a numeral, even when there are numerals in the rest of the sentence. Spell out the first number (or better yet, recast the sentence).
4. The time of day should be spelled out except when A.M. or P.M. is used.
5. Ordinals and fractions should be spelled out; e.g., first, second, one third, one fourth.

TABLES

Tables in a report should be as simple as feasible, commensurate with providing the reader with the necessary data. Only those data that contribute to the intent of the table should be included. For example, if a table is to portray consumer attitudes toward a given branded product for the entire United States, there is no reason to clutter the table with a showing of attitudes by geographic region. All data that do not pertain to the central thrust of the table should be omitted.

The discussion of the significance and meaning of the data in a table should precede the table itself. In other words, the table should follow any narrative describing the data in the table. The report writer places a table in the report because it is expected that the data will clarify or document some point being developed. The writer seeks to have the reader accept a particular point and the table is shown more or less to quantify that point. To permit the reader to view a table prior to the completion of the discussion may raise a question in the reader's mind that would not have occurred had the table been shown after the conclusion of the discussion.

Table Number and Caption

The top of a table should include the table number and the title (caption). In the past numbering employed the use of Roman numerals (Table V), but recently the trend is toward using Arabic numbers (Table 5). The title for the entire table should describe the nature of the data, but should not reveal the significance of its content. For example, "PER CAPITA CONSUMPTION OF MALT BEVERAGES SINCE 1964" is preferred over "PER CAPITA CONSUMPTION OF MALT BEVERAGES INCREASES DURING PAST 15 YEARS." The latter reveals a key point that is better covered in the narrative.

The table number and the title should be centered, with a double space between the two. Table 1 is shown as an example.

Table 1

PER CAPITA CONSUMPTION OF MALT BEVERAGES SINCE 1964

Tables should be numbered in the sequence in which they are cited in the text. Tables that are being compared in the text should be assigned different numbers (e.g., Tables 8, 9, and 10 rather than Tables 8a, 8b, and 8c).

Column Headings

Column headings in tables should identify the data in each column and should be as concise as possible. It is permissible to use symbols, such as %, $, and #, for purposes of brevity. Accepted abbreviations may also be used. (Such symbols and abbreviations, however, should not be used in the caption of a table.)

The Stub

The left column of the table is called the stub and it lists the items for which data are provided in the columns of the table. A column heading is used for the stub only if it is necessary to clarify the meaning of the items listed.

The Body

The body of the table consists of all the data in the columns to the right of the stub and under the column headings. The specific handling of the data within the body of the table will, of course, vary greatly from one table to the next. However, one general rule does apply: Data should be presented in a form that can be readily grasped by a reader viewing the table for the first time. To achieve this requires considerable thought and effort. Only those data essential to the central thought to be conveyed by the table should be included. An example of poor handling of data for a business report appears in Table 2.

No central thought emerges from the presentation of data in Table 2. It would take a first-time reader considerable time and effort to decipher the data without substantial help from the narrative. Even then, the data are confusing because the percentages (dollar share) do not "add up to anything."

A simplified handling of the data in Table 2 would aid the reader in readily understanding the meaning of the data in the table. These data have been

Table 2

READY-MIX DOLLAR SALES BY PACKAGE/PRICE COMBINATION

Audit Period	4-for-89¢		3-for-69¢		4-for-79¢		3-for-59¢	
	Dollar Sales	Dollar Share	Dollar Sales	Dollar Share	Dollar Sales	Dollar Share	Dollar Sales	Dollar Share
July 6–July 19	221.3	17.2	144.4	12.5	319.4	19.7	198.6	16.7
July 20–Aug. 2	663.9	28.1	386.1	21.3	525.0	20.5	517.8	19.4
Aug. 3–Aug. 16	557.7	36.0	408.7	32.7	575.8	29.9	461.4	37.2
Aug. 17–Aug. 30	543.8	33.6	415.4	24.7	506.4	29.2	435.4	27.8
Aug. 31–Sept. 13	408.7	29.2	394.9	30.3	380.2	27.5	370.8	25.8
Sept. 14–Sept. 27	341.6	27.2	249.1	27.4	398.2	33.0	284.6	27.8
Sept. 28–Oct. 11	367.4	35.4	262.9	28.7	301.2	29.1	241.8	24.9
Oct. 12–Oct. 25	319.6	28.8	276.7	32.1	253.8	27.5	250.8	22.6
Total for final 12 weeks of test period	2538.8	32.2	2007.7	29.3	2415.6	29.5	2044.8	28.6

restated in Table 3 in which the weekly data (from July 6 to October 25) have been eliminated and the percentages of dollar sales attributed to "other brands" have been added to the data.

Table 3

READY-MIX DOLLAR SHARE BY PACKAGE/PRICE COMBINATION

	4 for 89¢	3 for 69¢	4 for 79¢	3 for 59¢
Ready-Mix share	32.2%	29.3%	29.5%	28.6%
Other brands	67.8	70.7	70.5	71.4
Total dollar sales during test	$2,539	$2,008	$2,416	$2,045

The mass of data shown in Table 2 should appear in the appendix of the business report, where it could be referred to at anytime by the readers of the report, either during or after the presentation of the report. Certainly such data should be included in the report, for other persons may wish to examine the data; e.g., statisticians who may seek to challenge the validity of the generalizations made from the test study.

Table 3 could have been improved further if the percentage figures had been rounded off. To present percentages based on samples used in commercial research carried out to tenths or hundredths suggests a degree of accuracy that has not really been achieved in the data gathering and processing.

All tables employing percentages should show the *base figure*—i.e., that figure on which the percentages are based. This base figure must be fully and accurately described. To say that the percentages are based on "Total Number Interviewed" does not tell the reader much, if anything. The real question still remains: *Who* was interviewed? Many writers of business reports place all base figures in parentheses in order to aid the reader in quickly identifying a "number" and not a "percentage figure." This is especially appropriate when a report includes a large number of tables presenting percentage figures.

Any percentage less than .5 but greater than 0 should be designated by a dash (—) in the percentage column rather than "0." The latter suggests that the frequency of occurrence in the sample was zero, which is not the case.

Use of Space

A simple device that will make a table more readable is the placement of a space or spaces between selected line items where the list of items is long. If there are, for example, 10 or 15 items listed vertically in a table, the eye often has difficulty following a line across the columns in the middle of a list. Placing an extra space between selected items will aid the reader. Compare the ease of reading Tables 4 and 5. A further improvement in Table 5 can be made to aid the reader. Reordering the entries so that they are ranked from high to low in terms of "Percentage of Students Agreeing," would help the reader in comparing the responses.

Table 4

STUDENTS' PERCEPTIONS OF COLLEGE LIFE
AT HARTON UNIVERSITY

	Percentage of Students Agreeing
There are too many general course requirements.	10%
Library facilities are inadequate.	7
Classrooms are overcrowded.	5
Residence facilities are poorly maintained.	12
Semester breaks are too short.	15
Semester breaks are too long.	2
Course selection is inadequate.	18
Campus bookstore offers poor merchandise selection.	14
There are an adequate number of planned social activities.	62
Food service is poor.	43
Career counseling is regularly available.	32
Regular notices are given of financial aid availability.	57
Number of undergraduates interviewed	(843)

Table 5

STUDENTS' PERCEPTIONS OF COLLEGE LIFE
AT HARTON UNIVERSITY

	Percentage of Students Agreeing
There are too many general course requirements.	10%
Library facilities are inadequate.	7
Classrooms are overcrowded.	5
Residence facilities are poorly maintained.	12
Semester breaks are too short.	15
Semester breaks are too long.	2
Course selection is inadequate.	18
Campus bookstore offers poor merchandise selection.	14
There are an adequate number of planned social activities.	62
Food service is poor.	43
Career counseling is regularly available.	32
Regular notices are given of financial aid availability.	57
Number of undergraduates interviewed	(843)

Narrative Style of Table Construction

An alternative way to present tabular data is to modify the heading and stub wording so that a narrative effect is achieved. A table from the Brady-Bushey Ford case is cast in this format below.

Table 6

OPINION OF BRADY-BUSHEY FORD AS RELATED TO MILES DRIVEN

	This % of Those Having Driven		
	Under 10,000 Miles	10,000– 20,000 Miles	Over 20,000 Miles
Held This View of B-B Ford:			
Very favorable	29%	25%	15%
Somewhat favorable	53	48	40
Unfavorable	18	27	45
(Number of Brady-Bushey Owners)	(38)	(66)	(41)

Thus, Table 6 may be read: "A total of 29 percent of those who have driven less than 10,000 miles view Brady-Bushey in a very favorable light. This is in contrast to 25 percent of those having driven 10,000–20,000 miles, and to 15 percent who have driven more than 20,000 miles. . . ." In this example the *number of miles driven* is the independent variable, while the *drivers' attitudes toward Brady-Bushey Ford* is the dependent variable. Or, the *cause* of the differences in attitudes (*effect*) toward Brady-Bushey is related to the *number of miles driven*.

In general, column headings should represent the "*cause*" and the listings down the left-hand side of a table should be the "*effect*." Rephrased, the rule is that the independent variable is the basis for the column headings, with the dependent variable down the side. On a graph, the independent variable is placed on the horizontal axis and the dependent is placed on the vertical axis.

The narrative approach to table construction can be difficult for the novice report writer to carry out. Properly done, narrative-format tables result in high reader appeal and make good "originals" for visual aids. The experienced report writer should give serious consideration to using the narrative approach.

ILLUSTRATIONS

In a report illustrations may consist of a number of different graphical presentations; e.g., charts, graphs, maps, forms, photographs, etc. As is the case with tables, illustrations should be numbered consecutively within a work in the order of citation and should be positioned as close as possible to the narrative in which they are cited.

In presenting illustrative material, both aesthetic and ethical considerations must be recognized. Aesthetic considerations require that charts and graphs be made as pleasing to the eye as possible. Attractive graphics enhance the attention-getting power and communication effectiveness of the display. Ethical considerations require that certain conventions and practices be observed in chart and graph preparation so that the reader is not deceived by what is presented. Clear and complete labelling of axes, captions, data sources, and plotted lines is one such practice. Alerting the reader to a break in the vertical axis is another.

Format of Illustrations

Illustrations should be as clear and as concise as possible. A good illustration is self-contained; the user finds all the information needed to understand it on the figure itself and does not have to seek supplementary information. An illustration should add to the reader's immediate comprehension of the narrative; if it does not do so, it should be placed in an appendix to the report where those who wish to do so may study background information.

An illustration should bear a number and a caption, in addition to any source notes or footnotes that may be needed. A frequently used, general designation for an illustration is "Figure." The caption describing the illustration and the figure number are both generally placed at the bottom of a figure. If the figure requires a source or credit line and notes, they are generally placed above the figure number and caption.

Types of Illustrations

There are many types of illustrations that may be used in a report. The choice of a type of illustration is dependent upon the data the report writer wishes to illustrate and how that data may be presented to the reader most clearly. Two types of illustrations frequently used in reports are the line graph and the bar chart, both of which are described in the following paragraphs.

The Line Graph. This graph is highly useful for showing data on a time series basis. Figure 2 illustrates this type of portrayal in its simplest form, revealing that sales over the 12-month period have increased from 16 to 18 million dollars.

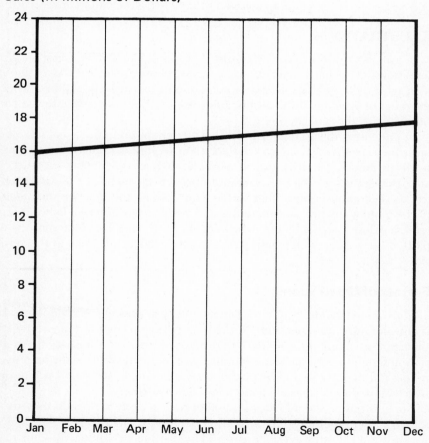

Sales (In Millions of Dollars)

Figure 2   Line Graph Showing Data Presented Fully on Proper Scales

When presenting data in a graphic form, the writer must be careful to avoid gross distortions, such as those caused by changes in scale. If the audience detects that the figures, whether they are in a report or in an oral presentation, are disguising true conditions, the total report will suffer a loss of credibility. For example, assume that the writer of a report wished to save space and decided to use only the middle section of the graph shown in Figure 2. The result is shown in Figure 3. What has happened? The data presented are the same, but an illusion has been created, suggesting that the increase in sales was more dramatic than it really was.

Sales (In Millions of Dollars)

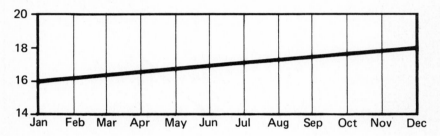

**Figure 3   Line Graph With Portion Deleted, Creating Illusion of
Significant Sales Growth**

The data in Figure 3 are accurate enough, but the chart is misleading. One glance at the graph and the reader could come away with a mistaken notion of the growth in sales. Where space constraints force the use of a portion of a graph, the writer should so alert the reader by using a break in the vertical axis, as shown in Figure 4.

Sales (In Millions of Dollars)

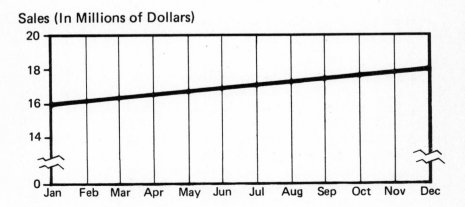

Figure 4   Line Graph With Broken Vertical Axis

Of course, it is possible to increase the misrepresentation in a graph even more. All one has to do is to change the proportion between the ordinate and the abscissa. In Figure 5, once again the data are all there, but the gentle sales increase of 12½ percent shown in Figure 2 now appears to soar dramatically.

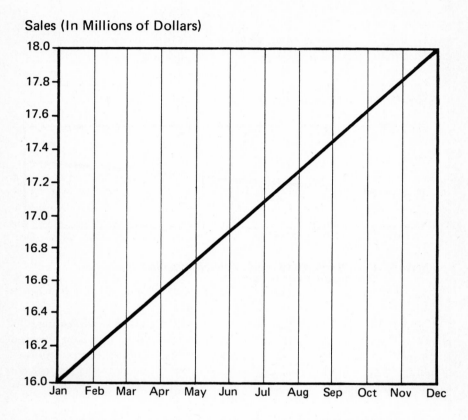

Figure 5 *Line Graph With Proportion Between Ordinate and Abscissa Changed, Creating Illusion of Dramatic Sales Growth*

The Bar Chart. Bar charts are sometimes quite deceptive in the impression they convey, depending on how expertly they are prepared. For example, assume that the management of an advertising medium desires to do a little bragging about their revenue growth over a three-year period. Sales have increased 11 percent over that period and the management is eager to communicate this fact to prospective buyers of their medium.

In Figure 6 the data are presented so as to make the sales gain more dramatic than it really is. Note that the lower portion of each bar has been deleted, creating an illusion that sales have doubled or tripled—or whatever impression it provides the reader unless the chart is examined carefully.

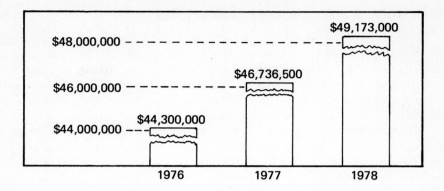

Figure 6   Bar Chart with Center Portion Deleted, Creating Illusion of Dramatic Sales Growth

In a general sense there is no rigid rule for the development of charts and graphs. However, the choice of the proper scales is very important so as to give the correct impression to the reader. Graphics should be tested by showing them to third parties, if possible. If they create erroneous impressions, they should be revised.

STANDARD SIGNS AND ABBREVIATIONS

The following are some signs and abbreviations that are generally accepted in business reports—narrative, tables, and footnotes:

c. or *ca.*	about, used in the context of time
cf.	compare
chap. or *chaps.*	chapter or chapters
e.g.	for example
est.	estimated
et al.	and others, and other people
etc.	and so forth, and other things
f.	and the following page
ff.	and the following pages
ibid.	the same book, chapter, or page
i.e.	that is
loc. cit.	place or passage already cited
n.a.	not available or not applicable
no. or #	number
op. cit.	the work cited or quoted
p. or *pp.*	page or pages
q.v.	which see
rev.	revised
sic	so; thus (often used parenthetically to show that something has been copied or quoted exactly as in the original, including any errors that may have been in it)
vol.	volume

SUMMARIES AND RECOMMENDATIONS

Reports based on environmental data call for summaries or conclusions. *Summaries* are simply brief statements of the chief findings. *Conclusions* additionally make some interpretation of the data, such as estimates of causal factors. Summaries can be located at the beginning of environmental data reports to facilitate rapid communication of findings. Sometimes, when such reports are lengthy, separate Executive Summaries are prepared.

In reports based on actionable data, some *recommended course of action* is called for. Certainly if the report describes data obtained to aid in the making of a decision, the report should identify one or more recommended actions to be taken by the decision makers. Recommendations should be placed in the report *after* the logical build-up of arguments to support them. Recommendations given in advance of their rationale can harden lines of disagreement.

APPENDIX B

Guidelines for Making an Oral Presentation of a Business Report

Fundamental principle: Know your audience, know your material, watch your time.

Much marketing research data and information are conveyed to decision makers through oral presentations. Unlike the written business report which can be digested at the reader's own pace, the oral presentation has a particular time frame which presents a constraint not only on the volume of material that can be delivered but also on the patience of the participants. Listening to a presentation will be but one of many events on the decision maker's daily calendar. Completion of the presentation on time is not only good manners but good business practice as well.

TYPE OF AUDIENCE

As with written reports, the technical level of the audience dictates what details of data gathering, analysis, and the like are covered. A managerially oriented audience wants to hear (and see) what the data and information mean to them as managers of given activities. The technically oriented audience desires greater detail, especially concerning quantitative procedures used in the analysis.

TYPE OF MATERIAL

Again, analogous to what should be done in written business reports, material calling for or supporting a particular course of action (actionable data) should be presented so that a sequential, logical case is built. To borrow advice from the lawyer: don't tip your hand. Instead, progressively disclose the facts and objective evidence so that the jury (audience), no matter how negatively biased at the outset, cannot rationally come to any other conclusion but that to which your case builds. Anticipate questions, especially those from the opposition. Develop your answers in advance.

Environmental data, on the other hand, can be conveyed in summary fashion. Additional layers of detailed findings can be revealed as time permits. Generalizations, where warranted, should be highlighted.

VISUAL AID OPTIONS

Three principal modes of visual presentation are:

- flip-chart displays, usually easel-mounted.
- transparencies projected onto a screen.
- 35 mm. slides, usually employed where color plays an important role.

Each has advantages and disadvantages, but the user's central concerns should be for visibility/legibility and communicability. The visual display should work in concert with the verbal discussion; each should reinforce the other. Here are some specific points relative to each of the three modes of presentation.

Flip-Charts

Flip-charts work best for small groups, say three to six persons. Quadrille-ruled chart pads are available to facilitate the construction of graphs, tables, and lists. "Shirt-cuff notes" can be lightly penciled on a page to aid the presenter's memory and yet be invisible to the audience. Certain lines or figures can be lightly written in for later "spontaneous" writing or drawing in as the presenter develops the argument or conveys facts and conclusions. Through these simple devices the presenter is able to carry out the progressive disclosure of the material. A fully completed figure shown to the audience may sometimes lead to premature conclusions by them before the presenter has had a chance to explain the figure.

Index tabs can be added to the flip-chart pages to permit going back and forth between pages. Such tabs are especially helpful in the question-and-answer period.

Because of their bulk, flip charts are often used for in-house presentations. Transporting them, even in rolled-up form, can present problems. However, carrying cases are available on the market.

Transparencies

Small transparency projectors are very portable, and the clear plastic films of the presenter's material create no portage problem. Very often the transparencies can be made directly from charts and tables in the written report that accompanies the presentation. Use of such materials from the report has the beneficial side effect of facilitating audience recollection of the presentation when they subsequently read the report. A word of caution here, however. Transparencies made directly from report pages may project poorly. Usually typewritten material does not "blow-up" large enough to be visible to the audience. Such charts, graphs, and the like may have to be redrawn to increase legibility. Keeping the diagrams simple, omitting unnecessary data, and rounding numbers will speed the audience's grasp of the points being made.

Progressive disclosure can be implemented with transparencies by using peel-away strips which cover numbers or lines until removal at the appropriate time, and by the use of overlays—additional transparencies containing only the new lines or numbers. Felt-tip pens with water-based inks or grease pencils can be used to write or draw on the transparency being projected. Writing may be cleaned off later using a cloth or tissue.

To make handling of the transparency film easier, cardboard frames are often used. Speaker's notes can be written on these frames.

One of the advantages of the transparency projector is that it is not necessary to dim the room lights to any great extent during the presentation. Of course the lowering of the lighting intensity will depend to some extent on the brightness of existing room light as well as the distance from the projector to the screen. When dimming is necessary, the presenter must be alert to the possible sleep-inducing effect of the lowered lights on the audience (especially if the session is after lunch!).

When the projector is of the "over-the-shoulder" type, the presenter has the advantage of facing the audience at all times. This approach is in contrast to turning one's back on the audience and using a pointer directed at the screen itself. Instead, one can watch the reaction of the audience and use a pointer directly on the transparency itself for emphasis. In fact, with the "over-the-shoulder" type, the presenter should remember that it is never necessary to turn to the screen, even though those in the audience have their eyes glued on the screen. The presenter should not, of course, make audience-distracting movements.

Using the so-called view-graph projector with its transparencies requires considerable practice before a smooth presentation results. The presenter should handle the transparencies alone, rather than engage a second person to assist. An assistant requires considerable cue arrangements and close coordination between the presenter and the projectionist. Rather, the presenter should practice the development of a fluid style, eliminating any clumsiness in transparency placement and focusing that could distract the audience.

Improvements in transparency reproduction (e.g., photographs can be translated into a transparency) are increasing in popularity as a versatile visual aid. Charting and typing and lettering can be accomplished in relatively short time for transparency use. It is a graphic portrayal procedure that is highly flexible and skill in its use is something every business person should acquire.

Slide Presentations

Color photographs, charts, tables, etc., with very high graphic appeal may be included through the use of 35 mm. slides. Their proper preparation costs more in time and money than for view-graph versions. Unlike the transparencies, overlays and writing on images are difficult to accomplish on individual slides; a sequence of slides is required to achieve such effects. Another disadvantage is the dark room setting required. The speaker may even have trouble reading notes. This sleep-inducing condition is somewhat countered by the high visual appeal of most slides. Well done, a slide presentation can be very effective in conveying information and establishing a line of reasoning. Poorly executed, a slide show can alienate an audience.

Summary Advice on Visual Presentations

- Each chart (graph, slide, etc.) should make one point. Keep it simple.
- Use color for emphasis; be consistent in its use.
- Make sure the audience in the rear of the room can read the projected image.
- Document the presentation so that someone else could step in and deliver it without difficulty.
- Make sure the presentation and its companion written report agree.
- Make as many dry runs (practice sessions) as time permits—the more the better.
- Move slowly through the charts; remember that the audience is viewing them for the first time.

Index